W9-CSL-799

Izzy

PETER C. NEWMAN

Izzy

The Passionate Life
and Turbulent Times
of Izzy Asper,
Canada's Media Mogul

HarperCollins*PublishersLtd*

Izzy
© 2008 by Dragonmaster Productions Inc.
All rights reserved.

Published by HarperCollins Publishers Ltd.

First Edition

No part of this book may be used or
reproduced in any manner whatsoever without
the prior written permission of the publisher,
except in the case of brief quotations embodied
in reviews.

All photographs courtesy of Canwest and the
Asper family.

HarperCollins books may be purchased for
educational, business, or sales promotional use
through our Special Markets Department.

HarperCollins Publishers Ltd
2 Bloor Street East, 20th Floor
Toronto, Ontario, Canada
M4W 1A8

www.harpercollins.ca

Library and Archives Canada Cataloguing in
Publication

Newman, Peter C., 1929–
Izzy : the passionate life and turbulent times of
Izzy Asper, Canada's media mogul / Peter C.
Newman. —1st ed.

1. Asper, I. H., 1932–2003.
2. Canwest Global Communications Corp.
–Biography.
3. Mass media–Canada–Biography.
4. Businessmen–Canada–Biography.
5. Lawyers–Canada–Biography.
6. Jews–Canada–Biography.
I. Title.

P92.5.A86N49 2008   070.092
C2008-901924-5

ISBN: 978-1-55468-089-4

HC 9 8 7 6 5 4 3 2 1

Printed and bound in the United States
Text design by Sharon Kish

With love to my granddaughter, Katie-Joe Newman.
May your "magic drawer" always be full.

Contents

Prologue

Reaching for the Stars

"We've never been able to say exactly where we think Canwest
will wind up. If we did, people would put us in a straitjacket."
—Izzy Asper, on his company's future prospects

"It was October 1987, and I'd been selected to go on this Canadian military mission, really a NATO war game," recalled Israel Asper, the tax lawyer, Liberal politician, merchant banker and television wizard. To fill the spare hours he didn't have, he had agreed to serve as an honorary lieutenant colonel in the Canadian Army Reserves.

Now he was in Lahr, West Germany, on the Cold War's front lines, engaged in a realistic Panzer tank exercise. The Americans and Canadians were on the same side, ranked against the Brits and the Germans, while the French were somewhere else. The North American contingent had these guys surrounded and the jaws of the pincer movement were about to close. "We were going to fry those guys and the war would be over," Asper recalled. "It *had* to be over that day. I had important appointments back in Winnipeg.

"It's now five in the morning, a great time for me, and we have to get up because we're going to rendezvous with the Americans in our final movement, our final strategy. Anyway, we pull up and get our Canadian Army breakfast. It is gruel, straight out of *Oliver Twist*. Porridge. Then the Americans pull up and they're three or four hundred yards away. The McDonald's armoured truck is there and the Wendy's armoured car is there and out come these juicy cheeseburgers. It was just brutal.

"Our general is junior to the U.S. commanding officer, so we have to go to him. We arrive at his tent and our guy is all spiffed up, ready for a big battle, while the American has no tie, is unshaven and is stomping around his tent, cursing.

"Our general comes to attention with a loud stomp of his right boot and says, '*Sah! Reporting for duty! Sir!*'

"The American general interrupts him and yells, 'What the fuck are you talking about? This is over. Haven't you heard the news? This war game is over. We are returning to base right *now*.' The Canadian general repeats his parrot-like bleat, '*Sah?*' and continues standing there at stalagmite-like attention, with an uncomprehending look on his face.

"'Don't you know, man?' asks the American warrior, deciding to let loose the ten-ton gorilla into the room. 'THE DOW HAS DROPPED 508 POINTS!' This produces no visible effect. The Canadian general vaguely replies, '*Yes, Sah!*'—still on his flight plan to nowhere.

"At this point, the Yankee warlock softens a bit. 'Don't you know that the crash is on? The Russians are going to attack, and World War III is going to begin. We've got to get back to base. THE DOW IS CRASHING!'

"'Sir,' ventures our befuddled general, 'what's the Dow?'"

It was not Canada's finest hour.

Colonel Asper was meanwhile trying to find a goddamn phone so he could pull two of his stock issues due to hit the market that day. Every communications instrument had been commandeered by American army officers urgently whispering to their brokers. Finally the Yankee general decided to resume the war games, clamped a two-star helmet on his head and barked, "Okay, let's go and get the buggers!"

For Asper, the mundane incident remained a vivid memory because it was so bizarre, so totally outside his daily experience. "You've got to appreciate the absurdities in life," he reminded himself. "Otherwise everything is much too painful."

That thought ought to have been mounted in petit point above his desk, because his professional life was a constant struggle not to allow the preposterous to obliterate the desirable. So many of his impossible dreams remained just that, succumbing to the tight-ass realities of uptight bankers, sleepwalking broadcast regulation commissioners, and the *rigor mortis* Bay Street boys who hadn't taken a risk since they managed to survive puberty. This was the trio of spoilers who were not prepared to grant Izzy the free-range operational code that his outsize ambitions demanded.

Only family members were aware of Izzy's interstellar objectives, but during the 1990s, his aspirations knew no bounds. He bid for the American network CBS; attempted to take over his chief Canadian rival, CTV; nearly won ownership of Scotland's dominant TV operation (the one that Lord Thomson described as being "just like having a licence to print your own money"); came close to acquiring a transcontinental U.S. religious TV network that reached most of urban America; seriously negotiated for the television operations of Bertelsmann, the huge German multimedia conglomerate; and took a shot at owning Air Canada, the sports network TSN and Royal Trust. None of these propositions materialized, but they legitimized the inscription on his official coat of arms—"Reach for the Stars"—and accurately reflected the limits of his ambitions. There were none. When asked how he saw himself as a media baron, he primly replied, "It doesn't bring you any new friends—it only brings you a better class of enemies."

He became a billionaire several times over by doing real deals that turned him into the country's most successful—and most controversial—media mogul. Asper, whose first job was scraping the gum off the bottoms of the seats in his father's theatre in tiny Minnedosa, Manitoba, became a metaphor for power wielded and riches gained. But in the arena that was his highest personal priority—his ability to influence national policies—his influence remained marginal, more the cause of trouble than the source of change.

———————

Back in 1969, having just survived a potentially fatal case of infectious hepatitis, Israel Asper, then thirty-eight, spent many an evening at his cottage on Falcon Lake jotting down his "personal letter of intent." The ambitious future trajectory, for family eyes only, set out his intentions:

- To develop a country (St. Lucia)
- To write a Broadway musical
- To start a bank in Israel and move there
- To write a novel
- To re-study the piano
- To work as a journalist
- To launch a chartered bank in Western Canada

When Asper died at seventy-one in the autumn of 2003, his life tragically ended by a fatal heart attack, the list remained untouched. But during the interval he had far surpassed the scope and magnitude of his stated aspirations. The realities he had achieved were exponentially more impressive, but they led him into unaccustomed notoriety. He inadvertently became a polarizing presence on the national scene: worshipped by his friends and followers, the object of fear and loathing among his critics and disillusioned journalists. He was born to make trouble, and he did. "If you phoned Izzy and talked about the weather," recalled his legal beagle, Yale Lerner, "there was bound to be some Palestinian plot to change Canada's climate. There was always something, and he would always embellish it."

4

Israel Harold Asper led a compelling life.

He was a singular man whose defining brand was his refusal to distinguish the possible from the impossible. Early on, he evolved an impressive trio of characteristics that never varied but grew more intense with age: his single-mindedness, which defied gravity; his brass-plated determination to wrestle obstacles, real and imagined, into oblivion; his inexhaustible fund of self-deprecating humour, which made the other two traits bearable. He was the butt of his own best jokes. One morning in 1998, he phoned me to report that he had just had a pacemaker implanted into his upper chest to tame his runaway heart. When I made the appropriate sympathetic noises, he cut me off. "No, no, it's great," he enthused. "I can now broadcast as a stand-alone transmitter—and besides, the damn thing opens my garage door!"

One of the most charismatic and most combative Canadian tycoons of the past quarter century, he was the quintessential entre-preneur, constantly in flight and flux, each improbable venture feeding on the next. A posthumous survey in *Canadian Entrepreneur* named him as the equal of such titans as K.C. Irving and as Jim Balsillie and Mike Lazaridis, the team that produced the magi-cal BlackBerry. He was voted ahead of such capitalist luminaries as Ted Rogers, Frank Stronach, Paul Desmarais, Joseph-Armand Bombardier, Ron Joyce, Roy Thomson, Galen Weston, Timothy Eaton, Terry Matthews, Frank Sobey, Samuel Bronfman and Conrad Black. Only the McCain brothers, Jimmy Pattison, Ken Thomson, Max Ward and Alexander Graham Bell ranked higher.

Any assessment of Asper's life and career must be set against his mundane formative circumstances. The son of a musically trained local cinema owner in Minnedosa, Manitoba, a postcard settlement two hundred kilometres northwest of Winnipeg that once had been the departure point for the great buffalo hunts, young Israel sim-mered up in a good place to start from. With only two thousand inhabitants and no sustaining economy, the community's limited horizons instilled urgency in its young to get up and leave. If you belonged to one of the only two Jewish families in town, you had twice the motivation.

From that modest toe line, Asper created a media conglomerate that spanned four continents and combined every form of modern communications, including the occasional use of hand and finger gestures. In his frantic life, Izzy, as he was known by anyone who ever shared an elevator with him, created a dizzy momentum. His serial risk taking produced a fever in the blood that no successful streak of accomplishments could relieve. "I'm like the Son of Sam—I can't stop myself from making deals," he confessed to Cameron Millikin, a Calgary-based policy adviser, adopting as his metaphor the dark compulsions of David Berkowitz, the serial killer who terrorized New York City during the late 1970s.

The epic struggle to hammer together a third cross-country television network; his mulish determination to treat Winnipeg as the shimmering centre of the universe; his obsession with fostering Israel as a democratic Utopia in a landscape of cutthroat infidels— these were his root passions. They were virtually interchangeable and none was negotiable.

A significant catalyst in Asper's evolution from being a fringe operator to dominating the media mainstream was his realization, on September 28, 1995, that the capitalization of his television enterprise that he had started on the parking lot of an abandoned Winnipeg supermarket had for the first time exceeded $1 billion in value. That evening, Izzy had dinner with Michael MacMillan, the best of the independent television producers, and wistfully complained, "Nobody mentioned it. I was at work all day and nobody called." He sent out sixty faxes announcing the news, but the congratulations still didn't pour in—too many of his investors had sold out too early. Nevertheless, it was a significant marker because, in his mind, nothing seemed impossible once that magic figure had been attained. Asper wrote his daughter, Gail, that day, "I just wanted to share this market landmark with you and the handful of others who have been part of this unique adventure. After a permitted moment of pleasure, we turn to future challenges and ponder the question, 2 B or not 2 B."

During a quarter century of gruelling effort, Asper gathered an à la carte menu of investments with a market capitalization that at one point reached $4 billion. From a standing start, the Asper domain grew into what was then the mightiest communications company in Canadian history.

Izzy's storybook career was built not on privilege or influential contacts, nor was it motivated by any Pavlovian quest for money or power. The source of his remarkable commercial triumphs was easy to pinpoint: he made his own luck and was armed with the balls of a canal horse. The ordinary rules of doing business didn't apply. "We've never been able to say exactly where we think Canwest will wind up," he once told me, "If we did, people would put us in a straitjacket."

This was not your usual corporate mission statement, but for Izzy it was gospel. Since the future could not be predicted, it had to be invented, and he felt destined to do just that. Casual acquaintances were awed by his show of self-confidence, which appeared to border on a private cult. It was an act. His close friends and associates (you could hardly be one without becoming the other) realized he was far too Jewish and much too Canadian to feel smug about what he had done. If his religion anointed him with guilt, his citizenship sprinkled him with deference. When he boasted about being humble, he recognized no contradiction in that oxymoronic posture. It was an easy gig for a veteran stager the likes of Izzy. Fortunately for him, his choice of fields to conquer—the media world, as quixotic as the man himself—bestowed on him the opportunity to deal in improbable dreams, which is the essence of creating and disseminating mass entertainment.

Asper ignored most Establishment rites, and its paladins returned the favour, doing their uppity best to tolerate him, since they had learned the hard way that he was far too audacious and much too shrewd to be ignored. Canada's fiscal establishment is an uptight universe—"hunting preserve" would be a more suitable description—unilaterally dedicated to perpetuating its members' status quo. "I don't want to be part of it," Izzy maintained. "I'm not a hermit, but I turn down 99 percent of their invitations. I don't dislike the Establishment—I just don't think it's relevant. It was really a kind of gentry; financial power is much more widely diffused today, and I don't want to be a part of it."

He wasn't. No self-respecting ruling class would dare enlist an original mind backed by the enforcer mentality of an Israel Asper. Except for his sons and daughter, plus a loyal crew of perhaps a dozen close associates, he flew solo, and made the power brokers come to him. He lived and worked in a self-generated high-pressure atmosphere close to lethal intensity. In others that would have guaranteed a case of bleeding ulcers. Except that Izzy didn't get ulcers; he gave them. His stream of post-midnight emails to his senior executives ("Do that again and I'll cut your nuts off") were an expression less of his bravura intent than of his macho disposition. But they stung just the same. Izzy's biggest challenge was to catch up with himself—and he never did.

Still, he created the country's most profitable communications empire. His seven networks and dozen major stations reached 94 percent of Canada's TV-viewing public; outside Toronto, his newspapers enjoyed something close to a monopoly for serious readers. While he never stopped considering himself an outsider, in terms of his personal clout and public image, he was regarded as the ultimate insider, more feared than loved for besting his peers at their paper games. "There's method in whatever madness Izzy seems to be embracing," Fil Fraser, president of VisionTV and a friendly Asper observer, assured the doubters.

Izzy belonged to no power cabals and remained comfortably ensconced in the Manitoba capital, far removed from Canada's fiscal and psychic mainstream. The members of Toronto's financial wolf pack, who made fun of Asper's perverse loyalty to Winnipeg, were inadvertently playing into his hands. Had he succumbed to the siren calls of Bay Street's flashy *machers*—doing deals their way instead of his—he would not have accomplished nearly as much. It was precisely because he never stopped thinking of himself as the skeptical country bumpkin from Minnedosa that he remained ahead of his competitors.

Canwest's growth and profits were limited by the daring of its investors, the faith of its directors and the patience of its shareholders—but never by the disposable energy of its CEO. Asper was the prototype Energizer Bunny, working fifteen- to seventeen-hour days, fuelled by martinis, cigarettes and defiance of the ordinary. He resolved the inevitable tension between cold-blooded analysis and hot-blooded passion by granting each equal time. He was truly an entrepreneur without borders.

From a modest beginning—running a mom-and-pop TV station out of the parking lot of an abandoned Winnipeg Safeway supermarket back in 1975—Canwest's national and international networks eventually generated annual revenues of $3 billion. Bay Street's assessment of the company's worth grew exponentially. His company's stock reached a high of $42.85 on April 19, 1996, before the three-for-one share split some months later. If you had given Asper $1,000 in 1977 as an investment, it would have been worth $303,000 by 2001. At its peak, the Asper chain of television networks and newspapers spread over four continents and reached a total of 30 million readers and viewers—*daily*. The Asper family's control position was—and continues to be—held through their lock (94 percent) on the company's unlisted 76 million multiple voting shares. "Izzy is brilliantly successful in this country," wrote communications analyst Murray Grossner of CIBC Wood Gundy. "He's got 16 percent of the viewing audience but more than 30 percent of the profits."

Izzy Asper became something of a public punching bag as a result of the controversies that followed his acquisition of the Southam newspaper chain from Conrad Black in 2000. That was unusual since Izzy spent most of his working life outside the eye of the publicity hurricane. "I just get immersed to the exclusion of everything else, whether I'm playing jazz or doing business," he told me in one of our frequent conversations. "I've never had much sense of balance. But I make no bones about being tough on management and tough on my kids. Life is tough. It's tough on me, too. When I do something wrong, you don't have to give me hell, because I've already given myself more hell than anybody else could possibly give me."

During his Jamaican-bobsled career, Asper not so much challenged the status quo as ignored it. Instead of trying to alter existing realities, he was able, thanks to his legal training, to use the courts almost as branch offices that enforced his edicts. "Izzy regarded opposing litigants as unfortunates who were about to give up their skins in order to save their bones," one observer remarked. He seldom set off the original conflagrations, but once engaged, his commando tactics against pesky competitors and even peskier partners became legendary. If acquiring CKVU from its former owners took nine years of trials by fire that cost nearly as much as the Vancouver television station was then worth, so be it. If taking over ultimate control of Global TV from his former compadres, who had attempted to freeze him out, took five years of legal mayhem and the payment of enough lawyers' fees to finance their children and grandchildren through university in perpetuity, that was the going price, and Izzy was willing to pay it. Don Johnston, the Liberal cabinet minister who became an Asper confidant, had a simple answer to the eternal question, What made Izzy run? "Sheer enjoyment," was Johnston's assessment. "He got his kicks out of winning and was extremely tenacious. I am convinced that he enjoyed all those lawsuits."*

---

*Nothing seemed to be too minor to command Izzy's concern, providing it contained a competitive element. "If Trivial Pursuit had been invented in Winnipeg,"

He was very different from his fellow media princes. A sworn enemy of the elitist sense of entitlement that characterized Canada's high and mighty, he could be one tough mother. During a visit to Manhattan in the mid-1980s, when he was in his fifties, he stayed in the Waldorf-Astoria, and as he went to pick up his car in the hotel parking lot, four thugs jumped him, bent on stealing his wallet. He fought back valiantly against impossible odds and was beaten up so badly he had to be hospitalized. One assailant even jumped into a car and tried to run him down. New York mayor Ed Koch heard about the incident, apologized on behalf of the city and sent him a new wallet.

Izzy's daily bungee-jump agendas kept him off balance so that he was constantly reaching for creative escape routes from financial bear traps set by his protagonists. He eluded most of their snares by reinventing himself for each occasion. How he managed that sequence of daredevil stratagems provides the narrative arc of this volume. "I get enough exercise, just pushing my luck," Asper maintained. He beat the odds by moving beyond Herbert Spencer's oft-quoted admonition about "survival of the fittest." During most of his life, Izzy was about as fit as your average lounge lizard—and the lounge was his favourite habitat, especially when they allowed him near a piano keyboard. Instead of pretending to number himself among Darwin's muscular devotees, Izzy opted for a variation of Charles Darwin's more realistic claim: that the future of the species belonged to those who were "the most adaptable." Now, here was a maxim Izzy could live by. That the nimble always prevailed was at the core of his belief system.

He navigated by sheer nerve, swinging on a star. Late in life, long after he had become an overnight success, journalists laboured hard to divine his motivations, usually concluding that he did it "for

---

wrote Michael Hanlon in a *Toronto Star* profile, "the name Israel Asper would be found among the answers in just about every category. There might even be a special Izzy edition, and one of its questions could be, Who stayed up all night memorizing the answers, so he could beat his visitors at Trivial Pursuit the next day?"

the love of the game." They ignored the fact he was the walking per-
sonification of an overwrought case of Jewish chutzpah, seizing each
moment to indulge in the courage of the early morning. (In his case
that meant 3 a.m., not breakfast time.)

Izzy was more at home in showbiz than in MBA territory, and
loved to leave the impression that most of his moves were plotted
in scrawled notes on the back of his cigarette packages. It wasn't
true. His wife, the former Ruth Bernstein, known to everyone as
Babs, who was also his best friend and occasional conscience, set
the record straight: "Izzy moved by recognizing opportunities and
being prepared to capitalize on them," she told me. "His sweat equity
took the form of massive homework and grinding preparation. He
would spend weeks, months, studying the figures and legal implications of situations and opportunities that seemed to come out of
nowhere. When he won a deal he wanted, it was because he was the
best prepared."

In so many ways, Asper led a charmed existence. He became
the ruling monarch of Canada's most-read publications and most
popular (if imported) television programs. Yet, despite every out-
ward sign that he had met and exceeded his impossibly high expectations, there remained a sense of poignancy about the man, an
engaging vulnerability that lurked just below the surface and came
out in unusual ways. "He was super bright and had the charisma,
the personality, the charm," said Lerner. "But when people asked
me if I envied Izzy, I told them that I would never have traded my
life for the torment that he went through. He suffered from what I
call 'the Devils,' and while he didn't need my sympathy, I always felt
sorry for him." Asper's protective camouflage was that business was
just another gig, and that he really didn't care which deals flew and
which didn't. In fact, he cared too much.

There was a tough carpet-trader side to the man that brooked
no opposition. He was the most loyal of allies and the most toxic of
enemies. He took everything personally, even weather reports, and
defended his turf with the single-mindedness of a cornered Bengal

tiger. His friends and loyalists could do no wrong, and he often kept them on his payroll past their effective shelf life. His critics and enemies were allocated no quarter or consideration.

Asper enjoyed the fringe benefits of his success but he felt much more comfortable being underestimated. "He wanted to be the person who people under-weighed, the guy who didn't stand a chance—and then he would surprise them with his intellect, his moves and his brilliance," speculated Jim Sward, one of his most senior lieutenants." He didn't want to portray his successes. He wanted to argue the underdog position."

Asper's combativeness was difficult to reconcile with his casual demeanour. But anyone he considered to be hostile—that is, anyone brave enough to deliberately challenge his personal beliefs and priorities—became the object of his fury. (An anonymous wit dubbed him "perfectly balanced—a chip on each shoulder.") When he took over the newspaper chain, its staff included publishers, editors and columnists unable or unwilling to share his convictions. That he could not tolerate. As owner of the publications, he recognized no reason why they shouldn't reflect his points of view. That simplistic notion, harshly applied, made more trouble for him than any of his daredevil schemes or ideas. Ray Heard, the distinguished former foreign editor of the London *Observer* and managing editor of the *Montreal Star* who headed Global's news operation, summed him up best: "Izzy was brilliant, mercurial, and inspired. He was good to his friends and brutal to his enemies—and he had plenty of both. He had shrewd business instincts and could shave the beaver off a nickel."

In private, Asper was a *mensch*—what Jews call those individuals who are not only possessed by generous instincts, but act on them. His personal and public philanthropies had few equals. Only his family occupied higher ground than his business deals, but alongside the comforting pleasures of home life he exercised killer instincts at work. Both were essential sides of him.

In the end, Izzy Asper was addicted as much to the game as to the prize, as much to the chase as to its rewards. What made him so special was that he could create and share warm electric moments in his life that became glowing embers of his legacy. He left behind not only a corporate behemoth and a worthy foundation but a treasure chest of stories, told and retold, that will perpetuate his memory. His was an immense footprint on the country's popular culture, its partisan politics and Winnipeg's dormant psyche.

It is the reconstruction of Izzy Asper's stints as a lawyer, politician, merchant banker, television executive, backstage power broker and newspaper publisher—the detailed anatomy and analysis of his reign as Canada's most cussed and discussed media mogul, that is the subject of the pages that follow.

I

The Big Noise from "Flyover" Country

*Winnipeggers alone among the globe's
inhabitants pray for global warming.*

F uture generations will no doubt pick the Canadian Museum
for Human Rights—a legacy in large part of Izzy Asper and
his daughter, Gail—as Winnipeg's signature landmark. But at the
moment, the city lacks such a distinctive structure—there is no
local equivalent of Toronto's CN Tower, Montreal's Notre Dame
Cathedral or Vancouver's Canada Place. The Forks, where the Red
and Assiniboine rivers meet, is a handy waypoint for history-minded
tourists since that's where Winnipeg was founded, but there is little
there now to gawk at or talk about.

In my hunt for a more representational marker, I settled on the
intersection of Portage Avenue and Main Street, because it is after
all, Canada's most famous corner. But trying to walk across this
landmark—the junction of Winnipeg's major downtown shopping
streets, smack dab in the middle of the city—proved to be impossible. Great effort has been spent to make this hub impassable. The

sidewalks have been power-drilled into extinction; every corner and one-time pedestrian access route is blocked by waist-high cement barriers, placed so you can't leap over or walk around them. Instead of the elegant urban square that Winnipeg deserves, the intersection has been turned into a bleak depository of concrete abutments. Not since Checkpoint Charlie, the choke point between East and West Berlin during the Cold War, have major city arteries been turned into tank traps that also obstruct human traffic.

Gail Asper, who should know, commented, "What I've learned in talking to everybody who's trying to do things is that everything takes a lot of work. It takes just as much work to get a crosswalk built on Portage Avenue as it does to build a museum. I mean that seriously, because it would take forty-two committees to do research for forty years on whether crosswalks should go here or there or whatever."

What's so jarring about this architectural insult to public access is its rude symbolism. Built to protect pedestrians from Winnipeg's bitter winter winds by directing them into an underground mall, the bizarre obstacle course is the cry of an uptight metropolis, proclaiming that it doesn't trust its own citizens to learn the art of crossing its defining intersection. (At anything below hurricane strength, you walk backwards into the prevailing wind.) Rick Waugh, a Winnipeg native who was Izzy's friend and who left to rise eventually to be president and CEO of Scotiabank, agrees with the critics. "They tried to put Portage and Main, which was one of the country's great corners, underground and took away its whole ambiance. You can't get across as a pedestrian, but even driving through it doesn't look good, with the physical interface of all those cement barriers."*

---

*The city planners who sanctified this monstrosity were more weak than irresponsible. Property owners on the corner of Portage and Main, particularly Trizec, declared that they would not build their new office complexes unless the municipal government forced all passers-by underground into their shops. Desperate for the office space, the City agreed, but never considered charging admission to local Cold War enthusiasts, who might have wanted to experience this North American version of Checkpoint Charlie.

As I contemplated this civic faux pas, I recalled how much real time I had spent in Winnipeg over the past decades. My longest sojourn was during the 1980s, when I was writing a four-volume history of the Hudson's Bay Company, whose sixty-eight tons of corporate archives, housed in the company's own building in Winnipeg's downtown core, spread across more than 1,800 metres of shelf space and documented the Company of Adventurers' history back to 1670. I returned to the Manitoba capital to research my series on the anatomy of the Canadian Establishment and wrote three sequential chapters about the evolution of its Winnipeg branch. Since Sam Bronfman's bootleg liquor empire had its shady beginnings here, I was also a frequent visitor while writing the *Bronfman Dynasty: The Rothschilds of the New World*. These were all interesting projects, but Winnipeg was only the incidental backdrop for the events they portrayed.

This biography of Israel Harold Asper, which has occupied me for most of the past three years, is different. To an astonishing degree, the Asper saga is the history of modern Winnipeg, and vice versa. The story of how the man and the city intersected are at the root of the Winnipeg experience—its glorious past, fall from grace and current semi-revival. And that story, in turn, flows from my past published observations.

Winnipeg is an inviting and forgiving place, proudly holding down the territory between East and West, impatient for its return to the national spotlight. The city occupies what hardcore Toronto literati are pleased to call "flyover country," demonstrating their usual sensitivity for that "booooring" cultural desert between whatever watering hole happens to be Toronto's "in" nosher of the moment and Calgary or, more likely, the Polo Lounge at the Beverly Hills Hotel, the signature Hollywood hangout that at one time, it was claimed, would seat neither blacks nor brunettes.

The Canadian "West" (no such land mass exists, of course—only four provinces with more than their share of flat earth, mouthy politicians, mountain ranges and lousy winters) isn't caught up in the self-indulgences that mesmerize those in the chi-chi East. To understand the Winnipeg syndrome, it helps to sympathize with—or better still, to *feel*—the emptiness and sense of exclusion that dominate the plains reality. The Western American novelist Joan Didion best evoked that mood in her description of the Midwest's wind-blown terrain, as she followed the trail of those "human voices that fade out, trail off, like skywriting." She caught the marrow of the plains experience—that gnawing pain of missing something—the frustration of the incompleteness that comes with exclusion. That had little to do with contemporary Winnipeg, but it caught the city's residual feelings of snub and isolation. "People here [in the Midwest]," she wrote, "sense that their hold on their place in the larger scheme of things remains precarious at very best . . . The women do not on the whole believe that events can be influenced. A kind of desolate wind seems to blow through their lives." Winnipeg isn't like that—not now, if it ever was—but that sense of exclusion from the larger scheme of things abides.

To the loving eyes of its inhabitants, the city's attractions are the best-kept secret in Canada, and they prefer it that way. Their feelings regularly get tested in bitter contests with two of nature's most potent terminators: frost and floods. (Not to mention the annual plague of mosquitoes that appear to be the size of and whirr like flying snowmobiles.) The deep-freeze winter chill is a chronic condition, which explains why Winnipeggers alone among the globe's inhabitants pray for global warming.

The decennial floods are no joke. The city is built on the bottom of the ancient, glacial-age Lake Agassiz, which every once in a while reclaims its original shoreline and turns the Red River Valley into a raging quagmire. "In a strange way, Winnipeggers need the Red River floods," mused journalist and former Winnipegger Tom Ford at the time of the last big one, in the spring of 1997. "The swirling waters pull together people with many different ethnic backgrounds into a common cause—the saving of their city and homes. The floods have made Winnipeg, which is a good city, into a great city. The flooding of the Nile nourishes Egypt's crops; the Red River floods nourish Winnipeg's soul."

Maybe, but no other municipal jurisdiction in Canada has so much history to live down. No matter how brightly Winnipeg boosters view the present and extrapolate the future, they can't match the past. Winnipeg is the Vienna of Canada, a city-state that lost its empire. What might have been—indeed, *should* have been—was caught by the *Chicago Record-Herald*'s William E. Curtis, who visited the city in September 1911: "All roads lead to Winnipeg. It is the focal point of the three transcontinental lines of Canada, and nobody, neither manufacturer, capitalist, farmer, mechanic, lawyer, doctor, merchant, priest, nor labourer, can pass from one part of Canada to another without going through Winnipeg. No city, in America at least, has such absolute and complete command over the wholesale trade of so vast an area. It is destined to become one of the greatest distributing commercial centers of the continent as well as a manufacturing community of great importance." What the visiting journalist failed to report was that the city's most active commerce was prostitution, with one hundred brothels going at full tilt. According to a contemporary observer,

The Winnipeg girls were quite frisky,
putting cocaine in their whisky.

In fact, Winnipeg was known as one of the most evil places in Canada.

That was also a time when Winnipeg could boast (and did) of having more millionaires per downtown block than any other Canadian city. The Winnipeg *Telegram* proudly reported in 1910 that the city had nineteen millionaires but that "the list could be extended to twenty-five without stretching the truth," then pointedly added, "The *Telegram*'s Toronto correspondent put his city's list at twenty-one."

It was a boom time for the grain trade. The first lake shipment from Port Arthur was dispatched east by James Richardson & Sons in 1883, and the business spawned its own Grain Exchange four years later. It was here, in the raucous bidding of the trading pit, that Winnipeg's original fortunes were made. By 1911, Winnipeg had grown into the country's third-largest city, with twenty-four rail lines servicing its 200 wholesale warehousing operations that sold goods across Western Canada, and a burgeoning population of 200,000. The banks and other financial institutions moved their elaborate regional headquarters here. These magnificent Edwardian structures—numbering well over a hundred, spread over twenty blocks mostly on and off Main Street—combined Romanesque Revival architecture with exuberant overlapping mixtures of Tudor, Italian and French or German Gothic. They were designed to impress borrowers and depositors alike, and it was from these money palaces that the original development of Canada's West was financed. They stand mostly silent and empty now, their portals boarded up, remnants of Winnipeg's Gilded Age, mute monuments to the city's heyday. The banks cannot afford to reopen their founding regional branches because there isn't enough business to pay for upkeep or for heating their magnificent, cavernous interiors. "Winnipeg made the West," wrote Robert Collison about his home town in *Saturday Night* magazine, "created it in its own image to serve its own needs and appease its own appetites. It carved a civilization, and an agrarian business empire out of the unwelcoming prairie flatlands."

The Winnipeg grain merchants made inordinate profits, though they stoutly maintained that their commissions added only a quarter of a cent to the price of a bushel of grain. When one Saskatchewan farm leader came to town, James Richardson drove him around Wellington Crescent and the avenues that run off it, pointing out the grain dealers' impressive mansions. The puzzled visitor's only recorded comment was, "All this on a quarter of a cent?" There is no record of Richardson's reply.

"At its apogee during the 1920s and 1930s, when the action in the trading pits was hectic, the Winnipeg Grain Exchange epitomized the capitalist spirit that had built the city," wrote historian

Allan Levine in *The Exchange*. "This was free enterprise's finest hour as millions of bushels of wheat were traded daily. Then, exchange seats went for nearly $30,000. The Exchange put Winnipeg on the international map. As a leading North American commodity market, it linked the city with the other great world grain and financial centres of New York, Chicago and London." Those glory days ended in 1935, with nationalization of the grain trade through Ottawa's establishment of the Canadian Wheat Board, and earlier, with the building of the Panama Canal, which allowed Pacific-bound cargo to bypass the city.

Winnipeg's great grain families buckled under the pressure, and except for the Richardson dynasty—today ably managed by Hartley, the eighth Richardson to head the firm—they nearly all disappeared as if they had never existed, though lively remnants remain of the Patersons, Parrishes and Heimbeckers. Few of their progeny had the foresight to look farther west and grab a stake in the booming oil and gas fields of Alberta or the rich forests and fisheries of the Pacific coast. Winnipeg's fortunes were quickly dissipated by the sons and daughters of the city's founding families as the grain clans scattered. Some joined the international jet set; others retired to Caribbean tax havens; others still sat out their lives in the mansions on Wellington Crescent and clipped coupons. They disappeared without a trace, leaving no museums, monuments, endowments or even, one assumes, memories. It was as if they had never existed. The final blow was dealt in August 2007 when the historic Winnipeg Grain Exchange company vanished as a Canadian icon and became a local way station for its new owners, a multinational operating out of Atlanta, Georgia, that renamed it ICE Futures Canada.

"They're all gone, the whole bunch of them," lamented William Palk, the vintage trader who is the former head of the local Eaton's store (which covered an entire downtown block and has also disappeared). "Much of the second generation partied, drank and drove fast cars, but they didn't carry on the family fortunes. It's a very conservative place. People tend to advance through dead men's shoes."

The runaways carried with them Winnipeg's chance to perpetuate its glory-filled past. The once-proud city became little more than a reminder of the daring risk takers who had established Western Canada's economic foundations. Much of the Winnipeg business community is peopled by ghosts. The most successful of its major enterprises, Great-West Life and Investors Syndicate, were taken over and are now run out of Montreal by Paul Desmarais. Even most of the surviving entrepreneurs and CEOs who have solid local reputations are not well enough plugged into the future to live down Manitoba historian W.L. Morton's stinging indictment that private business in Winnipeg was "dominated by adherence to routine and precedent."

A significant cut-off point that tested the clout of the city's business establishment was its inability in 1996 to raise the necessary cash or exert the required political clout to retain the NHL's Winnipeg Jets in the city. The incident spread far beyond the team's fans because it dramatically defined the limits of the Winnipeg business community's entrepreneurial instincts. A good case can be made not so much for why the Jets left as for why they didn't stay. They fled to Phoenix because that city built a brand-new arena by imposing a special tax. Other teams stayed in Tampa, where the municipal government provided matching funds and a sweetheart lease. Nashville, Columbus and Los Angeles made similar arrangements and recruited generous sponsors. Winnipeg tax money was harder to come by and there were no sugar daddies, especially when the Jets had no salary cap, so that some players were demanding US$6 million a year at a time when the American dollar was at $1.35 Canadian.

Sports matter in Winnipeg—the Jets almost as much as the Blue Bombers—yet more than a decade ago, the team was forced to fly south and ignominiously turn itself into the Phoenix Coyotes. "The fate of the Jets is an instance in microcosm of the plight of Winnipeg," wrote Jim Silver in *Thin Ice*, a book about the incident. "The same powerful market forces that marginalized the Jets in a changing NHL are marginalizing Winnipeg in an increasingly

continentalized economy. The failure to save the Jets is a symptom
of Winnipeg's economic decline and provides further evidence of
the perilous state of the city's corporate business class." As Alan
Sweatman, the chairman of Spirit (the volunteer business group
formed to save the team) put it, "being identified with failure per-
meates the institutional people here—and this defines the problem:
Winnipeg has become an economically marginalized and declining
city with a weak, fragmented and fearful business class—a class lack-
ing in leadership or a coherent vision."

Others saw the crisis more in bottom-line terms. "If the Winnipeg establishment had been more powerful, the Jets would still be
here," maintained John Fraser, chairman of Air Canada and one of
the local Establishment's charter activists.

Izzy Asper found himself involved in the salvation effort and at
one point raised pledges of $63 million from the private sector to
help save the team, but, as he put it, "then the circus started. Radio
stations got involved, promoting public rallies. One night there were
50,000 people at the Forks, contributing a dollar apiece, while everybody was emptying out their piggy banks all over the province and the
media was hyping it to the sky. This was supposed to be a very quiet,
private effort, but one by one the pieces fell apart. First of all, the
Jets backed out of the sale because they got a better offer. A bunch of
jocks got into it and wanted to turn the Jets back from a community-
owned team into a profit-making thing. Other guys started getting
cute with wanting tax benefits, and it just fell apart. And I walked
away. You needed an army to be able to pull it together, all the egos
and the jocks. It got down to who's going to be on the board of the
Jets and who would have access to the team's locker room."

The Winnipeg Arena, where the Jets once played, was demol-
ished and replaced by the $134 million MTS Centre (named for
Manitoba Telecom Services), an indoor arena on Portage Avenue
on the former Eaton's site. Resistance to the idea was championed
by loyal Eaton's shoppers, who organized "a group hug for the Big
Store." Exactly eighteen mourners showed up.

The modern facility can seat 15,015 for hockey and 16,333 for concerts. The home of the AHL's Manitoba Moose hockey team, it has hosted the 2005 Juno Awards and an NBA exhibition game between the Toronto Raptors and the Portland Trail Blazers, as well as a pre-season match between the Coyotes and the Toronto Maple Leafs. The hunger for better sports facilities continues and a new $65 million stadium (and retail complex) is planned by David Asper, who also intends to buy the Blue Bombers to play in it. The final word on the great Jets controversy belongs to Glen Murray, the outspoken onetime Winnipeg mayor: "The Jets' departure was a good turning point because it forced the city to get rid of a second-rate hockey team that was subsidized with over $20 million a year and ironically Winnipeg now has the best entertainment complex in Canada—the MTS Centre."

The Canadian West is a land of long memories. During the Great Depression of the thirties, the Prairies suffered the worst drop in living standards anywhere in the civilized world. The money that wasn't lost during that fearful decade stayed frightened for a very long time. In Winnipeg, a quarter of the houses were owned by the City for back taxes right up until 1941. That devastating interlude triggered the search for scapegoats, a blame-shifting habit best caught by the apocryphal story, told without place names, of the Western farmer who returned home one afternoon to find that a hailstorm had ruined his crops, his house had been struck by lightning and set on fire, and his wife had run away with the hired man. He inspected the damage, ran out to a high point of land, shook his fist at heaven and screamed, "Goddamn the CPR!"

The habit of blaming powerful, Eastern-based institutions and politicians for every disaster, whether it's drought, plagues of locusts, runaway wives or yet another nation-saving constitutional accord, is based more on instinct than on considered thought. But it is no less powerful for that. Winnipeggers never feel sure whether they are in the centre of the country or in the middle of nowhere. The level of frustration on the part of the proud inhabitants of the Prairies has always been fuelled by their certain knowledge that Torontonians can't comprehend why the hole in the doughnut between their Empire City and the metropolitan areas of the West Coast can't be more like Mississauga—on the unruffled margin of things, quietly making Jolly Jumpers and barbecue gloves or whatever it is they do out there—and not bother anyone about anything important.

The roots of Prairie discontent stretch back to the turn of the twentieth century, when the Western territories struck the questionable bargains that brought them into Confederation. The prime issues were tariffs and freight rates, but more significant was the feeling that the industrialized East was using political means to subjugate the rural West and turn it into an exploitable hinterland. The original settlers had been at the forefront of Canadian civilization, with Winnipeg leading the way. They had arm-wrestled the country from the wilderness, dug up and removed the stumps and rocks by hand and plough, and turned forests and wild pastures into farms, villages and towns. As the wartime and postwar industrialization of the Canadian economy took hold, they felt abandoned: their way of life lost, control of the lives they had invented out of hope, twine and back-breaking labour given over to the navel-gazers and midnight philosophers from the big Eastern cities, who had never served their harsh apprenticeships.

Winnipeg always stood slightly apart from both Prairie discontents and Eastern metropolitan ambitions, historically acting more as an emporium than as an independent power base. The city was the great halfway house of the Canadian mosaic, the distribution hub for most of Western Canada. But Winnipeg lost that mandate in 1920 when the Panama Canal was completed and most of the traffic that had once moved overland through its gateways was permanently diverted. Another reason for the decline was the historic Crow Rate, a federally sponsored system of transportation subsidies that made it cheaper for raw products grown on the prairies to be refined at their destinations rather than their places of origin. That killed processing in Winnipeg: the indigenous commodities went straight to the port cities, mostly Vancouver and Montreal, where the value-added benefits shifted.

With some notable exceptions—none more assertively so than the rambunctious Asper clan—there still pervades a sense among the city's elite of being urban outcasts in an increasingly metropolitan society. Winnipeg hosts two great universities and Western Canada's best private secondary school. Significant authors abound, cultivating Carol Shields's magnificent legacy, and culturally Winnipeg easily trumps any Canadian city its size. The local talent pool overflowed, with Burton Cummings and Randy Bachman, Len Cariou, Tracy Dahl, Margaret Laurence, Gabrielle Roy, Guy Maddin (Canada's most original documentary maker), animators Richard Condie and Cordell Barker, Fred Penner, Leo Mol, the Crash Test Dummies, Bif Naked, Lenny Breau, Nia Vardalos (of *My Big Fat Greek Wedding* fame), and the Group of Seven's Francis Hans Johnston and LeMoine Fitzgerald. The Royal Winnipeg Ballet leads its art form, having been granted a royal charter three years before London's Royal Ballet.

But it has become a truism of the twenty-first century that only those city states that possess the critical economic and demographic critical mass to maximize the applications of contemporary technology can triumph—and Winnipeg isn't one of them. The city's prevailing ethic still testifies to living on a human scale that takes the time to practise all the homely virtues, doing a little business so you can socialize instead of socializing to do business. That laissez-faire attitude (or *lasso-faire*, as Ralph Klein used to say) encouraged a mood of relaxed fatalism—a feeling that whatever happened here didn't really matter much, because no one would stay mad or happy very long.

The defining comment on the puzzling reality that the country seemed to be filled with impressively successful ex-Winnipeggers was in reply to ex-Winnipegger Michael Decter's comment to ex-Winnipegger Ian Delaney, who created a major Cuban-based mining conglomerate.

"Did you notice that Winnipeggers who move to Toronto do pretty well?" asked Delaney.

"Yeah, I've noticed that," replied Decter, who had achieved impressive prominence in health care circles across the country.

"Do you know why?"

Decter began to spin a complicated theory about immigrants making good and Manitobans being the beneficiaries of a superior education system, but Delaney cut him off.

"Because if you don't do well—you have to go back."

———————

This was the dormant context into which Israel Asper injected himself: first, with his successful national tax law practice; then, in politics, as the dynamic (but failed) leader of the provincial Liberal Party; then, in a lucrative stint, as a merchant banker; and, finally, as the innovative, if controversial, builder of the communications empire that made him a billionaire. He did all this from Winnipeg, which made it both easier—because the talent and determination of his home team were chronically underestimated and because, in any case, he carried most of his support system in his briefcase—and more difficult, since the senior Asper had trouble separating reality from his impossible dreams. The man's gregarious personality helped disarm rivals, and the sting of his legal challenges held them in check, but being a loner from a part of Canada that was its heartland only geographically made his success incalculably more complicated—and that much more remarkable.

Israel Asper's civic loyalty required no grand rationalizations; he preferred self-evident truths: "This is where my successors are, my family. This is where we started from. I practised law here, yet nearly everything I did involved Toronto, Montreal, New York, Chicago or Vancouver. Inevitably, the first words I would hear from the big city lawyers were, 'Hey, that's a terrific idea. Wow, you really ought to move here, you could make it in Toronto [or wherever he was].' My back just went up, and reinforced my stubbornness to stay in Winnipeg. There is a political and a constitutional structure in this country aimed, either by intent, design or happenstance, at protecting and preserving the dominance of the Toronto-Montreal-Ottawa triangle—what we call Eastern Canada and what they call Central Canada. The country's longitudinal centre, by the way, is nine miles east of my Winnipeg office. We keep rubbing everybody's nose in that." Asper's one-time partner Gerry Schwartz caught the spirit of Izzy's home-grown patriotism: "He simply was committed to Winnipeg, when almost anybody in his position would have moved to Toronto. He had a wonderful, enchanted feeling about the city and was determined he wouldn't switch."

"I'm a pathological Canadian and love Manitoba, I really do. I live here by choice," Asper readily confessed. "I like smaller centres, a simpler society—life is complicated enough. This is a kind of haven. Life here is just what you see: there's no stratification, there's no social classifications—just nice people. It's a love of land, it's strong pioneering roots of breaking that land and making a living out of it. And because we're not large, and because we're a long distance from other major centres, there is a tremendous esprit de corps in Winnipeg. Where else would you get 50,000 volunteers out fighting a flood? Where else would you get 22,000 volunteers putting on the Pan Am Games? It was said that you couldn't build a national television network out of Winnipeg, that you couldn't run a national anything out of Winnipeg. I wasn't angry. I took it as a challenge."

Asper consistently refused any position that would mean leaving Winnipeg, although he was offered prestigious slots as chairman of major Canadian companies, ambassadorships and even the federal ministry of finance.* Instead, Izzy stayed home and made the world come to him. For Asper, remaining in Winnipeg was gospel:

---

*This informal offer was made by Pierre Trudeau when John Turner notified him he wanted out of the finance portfolio. When Trudeau sounded Asper out, Izzy asked the PM, "Have you read my columns in the *Globe and Mail*? Have you read anything I've written?" The prime minister confessed that he hadn't. Asper replied, "You wouldn't enjoy my being around here if I were the minister of finance," and told him what he had in mind. Trudeau quickly agreed with Izzy's assessment.

"One night, about two in the morning, I called up Sam Walton, the founder of Wal-Mart, who lived and worked in Bentonville, Arkansas. He was sick with the cancer that eventually killed him, but he took my call. And I asked him why he ran what was then the most profitable U.S. company out of a place that was away from everywhere and not even big enough to have its own Wal-Mart store. We talked for quite a while. He was very forthcoming, telling me, for example, that rent at his rural head-office building was $3.17 per square foot, compared to $55 in New York.* Talking to Sam, I realized how important decentralization in a country can be. Sure, we could all pack up and move to Toronto, which would become as big as New York. But what would that do for nation building? If the objective is to have a country, why isn't the Bank of Nova Scotia's head office in Halifax? The Bank of Montreal's in Montreal? And the Royal Bank's in Winnipeg? We've got to keep the country together the hard way, because it's no fun doing it the easy way."

Asper's municipal jingoism hit close to home. In November 1983, when he suffered a serious heart attack at age fifty, Asper never considered the desirable alternative of immediate attention at the legendary, relatively close and, to him, affordable Mayo Clinic and insisted on being treated locally, even though that meant waiting in line for six weeks while his doctors warned him that he could die at any moment. His decision wasn't based entirely on municipal patriotism: Izzy had heart surgery at St. Boniface because it had one or two of the best heart surgeons on the continent, who had been trained at the Mayo.**

---

*Asper's business heroes were Sam Walton and Warren Buffett, because both men forged their remarkable successes without moving to New York or Los Angeles, instead remaining in the small towns where they had grown up. He figured that if they could do it, so could he.

**Asper recalled peeking in his medical file, which included this report from a cardiologist to his GP: "This is the most stoic patient I've ever met. Nothing bothers him. Nothing fazes him. He accepts with equanimity everything I tell him. There are no recriminations."

The main exception to his grim life plan was his time at Asper Lodge, his unpretentious summer place on Falcon Lake. The Aspers' cottage caper began in the spring of 1963 when Izzy, who had never heard of group excursions, cottages, holidays, spare time and the like, told Babs, "All right, if you want a cottage, go out and rent one for a month." She found one on the south shore of Falcon Lake for $50 a week, which was what they could afford at the time. It had a rainwater barrel under the sink, and a wood stove. "So we were going to give it a try, and he came out with his briefcases," she recalled. "I was worried that we wouldn't have enough water. It rained the whole month. The rain barrel was full. I had to get into one of the kids' rubber boots to visit the outhouse and thought, 'Oh my God, this is going to be a disaster. I'll never get him out here again.' He would arrive on weekends, plunk down his briefcases and lie down on the sofa. Late at night he would get up from the sofa and go to bed. In the morning he would get up from bed and go to the sofa and he kept saying, 'This is fabulous. We should buy a cottage.' He didn't give a hoot about the weather and never went near the lake or even looked at it. I couldn't believe my ears, but we bought the cottage that we still have for $9,000, completely winterized with concrete steps, a boathouse and a basement workshop.

"I really sweated whether we could afford the $9,000 at that point, but he said, 'Okay, let's go for it.' So we did, and we came out for our first New Year's with Dee and Harold Buchwald and it was a disaster. We had no idea how the cottage worked or anything. It had a coal furnace in the basement. We brought lots of wine but forgot the milk so it became, what kind of wine do we have with our cereal? And we couldn't get the cottage warm enough. We started the furnace, but it was so cold because the heat wasn't coming through. If you put a glass down on the counter, it froze to the surface instantly. We found out afterwards that we hadn't opened the vents, so there was this blazing fire in the basement but nothing was coming up. So we went to sleep in our snowsuits and all of a sudden the heat started to work and we woke up in the middle of the night sweating, but we thought it was really hilarious."

The Aspers came out every New Year's and eventually added decks and reconfigured the bedrooms. The cottage was also the site of Izzy's seventieth birthday party in 2002, during which the second and third generations organized an "Izzy Medley" that included this verse, sung to the tune of Gershwin's "Summertime":

> Summertime, at the cottage with Izzy
> Fish are jumpin', and he couldn't care less.
> Phone calls, dictation, catchin' up on his email,
> Awaiting the package coming by Fedex.
> Not one of these mornings will he be risin' up early.
> Gonna eat some wings, read a book and unwind.
> Though mosquitoes bite, there ain't a nothin' can harm him.
> 'Cause Izzy's never been outside.

He spent nearly every three-day summer weekend driving to the cottage and sitting on an L-shaped sofa in a screened-off porch, until the furniture had to be replaced because of cigarette burns. He did eventually venture into the water—well, not *into* it exactly, but on top of it, slouched in a floating plastic easy chair that had two deep holes cut into its arms: one for his ashtray, the other for his martini glass. "Dad told us about lake living and how to coexist with Mother Nature," Izzy's son David recalled. "As Dad got smarter, he taught us the ultimate hazard avoidance system: stay indoors. We watched man land on the moon from the lake. Unfortunately, Dad took with him to the grave his secret recipe for moon juice."

"The thing about Izzy is that he was always introducing things that would be out of this world or a concept you hadn't thought of before," recalled Richard Kroft, one of his best friends, who had the cottage next door. "Izzy was a night person. We had neighbouring verandas and he would play his music into the night, accompanied

31

only by his dogs Tuffy, a miniature Lhasa Apso, and later Bernie the Attorney, of the same breed. He was incredibly attached to his little pets, mainly because they alone would stay up with him until three or four in the morning and seemed to like the same music. Almost anything could come out of those evenings—except a swim."

"His idea of having a good time was to drive to the cottage and talk business in his shorts," recalled Peter Viner, who held just about every executive office in the company, including CEO. "I'd say, 'Let's go down on the dock,' and he'd answer, 'Why would we do that? The beer's right here.'"

His loyalty to Winnipeg and Asper's physical absence from the national mainstream became an essential yet paradoxically favourable element in his success. "I have contempt for arrogance wherever I find it," he insisted, referring to the "not invented here" syndrome prevalent among the big players of Bay and Wall streets. "I don't resent it philosophically. I smile and laugh at it. But to the extent of deciding where I'm trying to go and getting there, yeah, I battle it, and I battle it openly."

While he was deaf to the many friends or associates who harped on the notion of how much more practical it would have been to move his operational headquarters out of Winnipeg, Izzy didn't suffer substantially from his stubbornness. By the time his conglomerate required serious financing or other legitimizing gestures, he had spent several decades establishing his networks in the East, especially in Toronto and New York, networks that he expanded during his numerous expeditions away from the Manitoba capital.

"Izzy told me that one reason he loved Winnipeg," admits his jazz buddy, fellow Winnipegger Ross Porter, "was that he could enjoy a life outside the city as well." Izzy agreed that it was a good place to come back to as long as he was able to do other things and have different stimuli in his life. For Izzy, being out of town at the local level meant staying at his cottage on Falcon Lake, on the edge of the

Canadian Shield, near the city. Farther afield he could be caught roughing it at his cozy Toronto *pied-à-terre* in Yorkville, or luxuriating in his condo overlooking New York's Central Park reservoir, so that it was almost like being at Falcon Lake but with the world's best jazz clubs at his feet.

If Asper's presence enriched Winnipeg, his absence, when he died in 2003, was felt even more keenly. "He really did make this town believe in itself," recalled Lloyd Axworthy, who returned home from a successful career in federal politics to run the University of Winnipeg. "Izzy was made for this town. It took a couple of years after he died to realize how much impact he had—not just for business and specific accomplishments, but he set a tone, a kind of can-do attitude that Winnipeg's a place where you can get things done. And that's his legacy." Senator Sharon Carstairs emphasized that exact point when she declared, "The most important mark he made in Manitoba was not leaving. Izzy thought that was his role, and that was an incredible statement and influence on other entrepreneurs."

"Winnipeg was built in a very cold place with lots of mosquitoes, and it was created by sheer determination and nearly went bankrupt building the rail lines so that the railroad didn't cross the river in Selkirk," maintained Glen Murray, the city's most imaginative mayor. "In that sense, Izzy was of Winnipeg and Winnipeg was of Izzy. It was just this stubborn determination to make it work. Winnipeg was a city of questionable location by temperature and climate and geography, harshness, isolation and floods. The only way it existed was through absolute stubborn determination, and when the Panama Canal opened and trade policies changed, it went through very hard times. It's been abandoned by so many of its business risk takers. Winnipeg and Izzy are both inexplicable successes. They had a passion for each other—that city, which doesn't give back a lot to many people, gave a lot back to him. It was kind of extraordinary, but that city does extraordinary things. It's the best place I've ever lived in the world and it's also the hardest place I've ever lived in the world."

Winnipeg was Asper's Magic Kingdom, always on his mind. Yale Lerner, who guided him through many a defining business deal, was convinced that "Izzy dreamed Winnipeg would one day become the capital of Canada. He had that kind of vision. I thought he was nuts."

2

Formative Stirrings

Gail Asper maintains, flat out, that "the relationship with his father was the key issue in Izzy's life."

Israel Harold Asper was descended from the Great Russian nobleman Baron Ausereper—distantly related to Prince Monyi—who was thought to have been killed in the Russian Revolution but who had somehow managed to flee. Captured and imprisoned by the Germans during the First World War, he escaped from prison camp to perform miraculous and daring exploits of sabotage against the invading Huns. He was apprehended in Bessarabia, Romania, by the liberating Communist forces only to be betrayed by his treacherous Fifth Columnist daughter, Golda, and left to rot in a Russian gulag in northern Siberia after the conclusion of the war.

He wrote extensively from his prison cell, but died of food poisoning planted by his Stalinist mistress, who was really a Maid Mer—top half fish, bottom half female. His grandsons, Dov and Lanya, having been recently freed from Communist imprisonment, redeemed his fortune in gold from the Swiss banks in which he had wisely stored his money during the Bolshevik Revolution. The original deposit, only $1,000 in 1914, thanks to the magic and miracle of compounding, is now thought to be worth several billion dollars, which Dov and Lanya are determined to invest wisely in Canadian real estate.

The crafty and evil Golda's granddaughter, Golda Asper III, had a rapprochement with her second cousins and joined them in expanding the family's billion-dollar empire.

Dov, Lanya and Golda have never permitted their pictures to be taken and have refused all press interviews as they scour Canada for real estate opportunities.

———————

That comic-book Gothic version of his family history was contained in a letter Asper sent his children on October 24, 1996, in reply to David's suggestion that a new real estate venture be called Ausereper Property Inc. Izzy admired his elder son's idea, since Ausereper had been the original family name before it was anglicized to Asper. But, as jazz-driven cats always do, Izzy spun the idea into an appropriate tale of dark deeds and intrigue of the ill-met-by-moonlight variety that he suggested ought to be included in the corporate prospectus.

That was the fun side of living with Izzy. It also provides a rare glimpse into his romantic nature and the dissatisfaction he felt about his plebeian roots. In fact, his parents had fled Moscow's murderous anti-Jewish pogroms and had their own harrowing stories to tell.

Israel Harold Asper was born prematurely ("in a hurry, as usual," remarked his wife, Babs) on August 11, 1932, in Minnedosa, a puppy settlement perched on what was once wild buffalo country, a couple of hundred kilometres northwest of Winnipeg. During the 1880s it had been a regional supply, livestock and trading centre, but it was supplanted by nearby Neepawa. Among the immigrants who settled in Minnedosa were Asper's parents. His mother, Cecilia, was the daughter of Rabbi Ben Zion Zwet, who had immigrated to

Winnipeg in 1913 and who later circumcised Izzy ("He threw away the wrong end").

Izzy's parents were classically trained musicians in Odessa, where they had been childhood sweethearts. Leon had studied the violin and conducting at the conservatory under Leopold Auer (the virtuoso violinist Jascha Heifetz was in his class); Cecilia specialized in classical piano. She snuck past Russian border guards and immigrated to Canada in 1919. When Leon escaped, first to Belgium, he had to leave behind six sisters. Then he had to wait an extra five years for his documentation—years he spent conducting the orchestra of the Belgian State Opera in Brussels. He finally left for Winnipeg in 1924. Once in Canada, he married Cecilia and both played in the city's Orchestral Society, which later became the first Winnipeg Symphony Orchestra. After its demise, they moved to Calgary, where Leon rode herd over the Palliser Hotel house band before conducting the Palace Theatre Orchestra (Cecilia played piano), featured at the largest local movie house, accompanying silent films. That was an amazing production. Asper's twenty-nine-piece orchestra accompanied the movie, simulating its moods and dramatic cadences. Each performance's success depended on the choice of music to match the action, on tight scheduling and on the musicians' ability to switch scores in a flash. For a Hollywood potboiler titled *3 Bad Men,* for example, Asper chose sixty-two musical scores while watching the preview, then picked as little as four bars from each as background sound for the action on the screen. Because he was conducting in the dark, Leon had set up small lights on each musician's stand, which he controlled by foot pedal, so that he could bring the musicians in together at the start of each selection with a press of his foot. When talkies arrived in the late 1920s and early 1930s, these musical aggregations vanished and the family went into the small-town movie-house business. They took over the bankrupt Lyric Opera House in Minnedosa, and later the Roxy in Neepawa and the Boyne in Carman.

At the time, downtown Minnedosa consisted of the Lyric, the Tremont Hotel (which served elegant roast beef dinners on Sunday evenings) and an ice cream parlour run by Tubby Anderson, whose stomach was so huge that, according to local legend, he exploded when he died—or died when he exploded. The town also featured a dry goods outlet, two law offices and Henson's photo store. Local farmers with their good, wind-reddened faces spent hours allowing countless cups of bitter coffee to grow cold between them at the Patricia Café, trading those shattering small quips that burn away the scrub of a hidebound life. Outside, the wind howled, moving up from the great plains of North Dakota, making little jib sails out of the vents in the men's jackets. Their wives, dressed up in small crowns of afternoon hats, sat impatiently in the pickup trucks, waiting for their husbands to finish their man-talk so they could go shopping in Neepawa, twenty-nine kilometres west.

The Asper children—Aubrey, born in 1929; Hettie, 1930; and Israel, 1932—earned top marks at the local grade school. Their house had a huge lawn but no electricity, telephone or indoor plumbing. Whenever a member of the family was using the outhouse, they were said to have "gone north," because the one-holer was situated on that compass point from the house. His father insisted that Izzy practise the piano classics daily from 3 to 5 p.m., as well as take lessons with Mrs. Henson or Cecilia, who took turns as his frustrated teachers. Izzy loved the piano but hated the music.

The youthful Izzy found a counterweight to the strict parental regime by stirring up more than his share of mischief. In the early evenings, while his parents were busy in the theatre, he would secretly peer into the windows of the local headquarters of the Girl Guides, located next door. He also enjoyed setting traps for Mr. Tippet, their handyman. On one occasion, he dug a hole on the garden path, filled it with water and covered it with shingles and earth, then watched as Mr. Tippet and his rake went flying into the puddle. (Half a century later, Izzy still laughed hysterically at the memory.) The property had stables, and Izzy would lure girls into the barn by promising to show them the family pony. He felt so confined at home that one spring morning he ran away with one of the Rykiss girls.* They got as far as Franklin on their bicycles before they were spotted by a bus driver, who turned them back. Izzy was brought up in an old-fashioned European framework of iron discipline. He was not allowed to see movies unless they had been pre-screened by his father. He felt most relaxed playing road hockey for the Minnedosa Midgets, using frozen horse turds as pucks. Larry Zolf suggests that Izzy's "constant, easy contacts with small-town people and farmers provided him with a bit of a populist streak early in life," and—in spite of the pre-screening—growing up in Minnedosa "also kindled Izzy's love of mass entertainment as both a suitable and profitable way of life."

The Aspers exempted Hettie, the family's middle child, from most duties. Hettie could do no wrong. She was exalted—no tricks on her. "My father had no expectations of Hettie, except that she get educated," said Izzy. "He was a typical immigrant. The things he didn't have, he wanted for his children. Hettie rarely had to help out in the family business, certainly not to the extent Aubrey and I did." The brothers resented having to work in the theatres because it left little time to enjoy the natural pursuits of their teen years. "The requirement to work negated fun, and the pay was terrible. We got $15 a week less than friends earned at similar jobs," Izzy complained. By the time he was seventeen, he was manager of the Boyne theatre in Carman and had to take the bus after classes to Neepawa, where he acted as MC of the popular photo nights. "Aubrey and I worked sometimes at two jobs. And it wasn't negotiable. It was a way to pay for our room and board. I was always being fired and thrown out, arguing with my dad. He would get mad if I forgot to put up signs of what movie was playing. I was a bit irresponsible, which made

---

*William Rykiss, the family patriarch, was one of hundreds of Jews who manned general stores across the Prairies and the grandfather of Paula Abdul, now of *American Idol* fame.

him furious. At least once a year or more I was permanently dismissed then promptly rehired but had to pay penance." Promotions came hard. Izzy was moved up from having to scrape the hard-dried chewing gum off the undersides of the theatre seats with his pocket knife to tearing tickets at the door and being an usher. Significantly, he never became cashier, presumably because his father detected a trait that most of his unindicted conspirators noticed later in his son's meteoric career: Izzy refused to sweat the small stuff, and while his ability to negotiate mega-deals was unequalled, his hold on the basics of arithmetic was tenuous at best.

A serious problem about living in a place like Minnedosa was that the Aspers were one of only two Jewish families; the other was the Rykiss clan, who ran the dry goods store. The boys were targets of frequent anti-Semitic taunts but only the occasional beating. The Asper children had to take their bar mitzvah training in Brandon, which wasn't all that close. They left on Friday evenings by bus, stayed at the YMCA and returned Saturday nights. For high holidays (Rosh Hashanah) they went to Winnipeg, where prayers were led by Izzy's grandfather, the Ukrainian rabbi. The Passover seders were lengthy, and never finished before eleven. He found the singing in seventeen-part harmony particularly memorable.

During the week, Leon brought kosher meat out from Winnipeg in unrefrigerated vans, and it tasted awful. Despite their faith, the family exchanged Yuletide presents around a Christmas tree, and Izzy claimed that it broke his heart to discover there was no real Santa Claus. His was a highly unusual household for an Orthodox Jewish family.

Everything changed in the fall of 1946 when the family, after a five-year sojourn in Neepawa, moved to Winnipeg. Leon purchased a couple of downtown theatres, and Izzy found himself immersed in a freshly minted and invigorating urban atmosphere. "It was a very tough transition to a big-city school at age fourteen," he recalled. "I was a country hick, or at least felt like one—the clothes we wore. We moved because my older brother, Aubrey, needed to go to university. I joined the Jewish community and very quickly became a Zionist by joining left-wing organizations such as Habonim. The girls were more sexually generous on the left side of things, enjoying a much more bohemian social life. The prudes were nearly all Young Judaea Zionists."

The family lived at 65 Cambridge Street in a house that boasted two indoor toilets. Izzy attended Kelvin High School, but it took a couple of years for him to lose the feeling that he was socially awkward. He surrounded himself with kids who one day would be old friends, including Rick Stillwater and Robert Kopstein, and gradually, like a ripening chrysalid, metamorphosed into his gregarious self. He made the school football team and founded the school paper, the *Kelvin Gazette*. When he wrote a story about a Grade 12 party in which reference was made to labels on whiskey bottles, such as Three Roses—references that, according to Izzy's account, were really people's nicknames—the principal assumed it was to the alcohol consumed, suspended him from school for a week and closed the paper. The entry in Izzy's Grade 11 yearbook was uncannily prophetic: "Has 'A' complex—who needs Einstein or Lincoln, when Izzy's around? He'll do the thinking." As well as working in the cinemas, during his high school summers he attended the B'nai Brith camp at Sandy Hook, where one of his counsellors was Nathan "Tuzzy" Divinsky (who later married future prime minister Kim Campbell). Divinsky was an avid disciple of Ayn Rand and preached that reactionary gospel to the impressionable Asper. A fellow camper was gadabout CBC broadcaster-to-be Larry Zolf, who vividly recalled that Asper, two years older, had saved him from drowning. Izzy claimed not to remember the incident but also refused to confirm that he considered throwing him back.

As well as meeting his continuing obligation to help operate the family's movie houses, Izzy somehow made time to take on extra summer jobs that included laying dynamite for construction of the

TransCanada pipeline through the Rockies and crawling through Winnipeg sewers to turn off the water whenever a main burst. At one point he also took a part-time job at Aronovitch & Leipsic, a local real estate firm, to learn the business. One of his co-workers was John Hirsch, the European-born theatre director and founder of the Manitoba Theatre Centre, who lived with the distinguished writer Sybil Shack, his adopted stepsister. Izzy began to climb, socially, personally and even professionally—although the city's narrow-minded burghers knew only too well how to douse with cold showers the overt ambitions of pushy youngsters.

His youth was softened by his relationships with a series of remarkable young women. Izzy's first main girlfriend was Dorothy Fainstein from his Grade 8 class, who was attractive, compatible and loving. They dated pretty exclusively for five years and even stayed in touch when one of them went out of town. In the summer of 1950, when Dorothy visited a friend in Chicago, she wrote,

> Dear Izzy,
>
> I'm very sorry I happened to miss writing to you two days ago. Darling, please forgive me, it's because I just didn't get a chance to. Ask Marlene how nervous and lonesome I felt after she took me for a walk, and I couldn't think of anything or anyone but you. I couldn't hold it in and started to cry and said that all I wanted was Izzy. But I guess that was asking too much. Sometimes I wonder if God meant us to have each other. I never seem to have you at the times we can really enjoy ourselves, Xmas, holidays, Easter and summer time. Izzy, believe me I get so lonesome, I can't see straight. I kept thinking of New Year's Eve. Izzy, I don't think I'll ever get over last New Year's. It was just like a dream and you were wonderful . . . I realize you are only human and you are probably glad to get rid of me for a while so you can brush up on your hustling. Izzy honestly, I guess I did feel funny when Ketz [her friend] received 12-page letters and I didn't

but that wasn't your fault and I'm not blaming you. I mean, I don't know but Izzy I love you so much and all I want for you is to be happy. Darling, you'll never know how much I love you and miss you. Absence makes the heart grow fonder, but also gives me heart aches.

I love you darling,
Dorothy

P.S. I showed my aunt your picture and she thought you were cute. It was a lousy picture, but I love you anyway.

A very different letter arrived that same summer, when Izzy was tending the family cinema at Carman, from his school pals Richard Stillwater and Robert Kopstein, who were pretending that they were writing a dispatch "from somewhere in Korea," stationed with the Canadian troops then serving there:

Commander Lance Corporal Ikey Asper
Fuck Q Company
Division 2C Company at your house,
somewhere in southern Manitoba

Dear General Titsqueezer:
As you know, our forces are outnumbered 100 to 100. We are urgently in need of equipment and safes. My commander corporal Robert Lionel Train Kopstein orders you to round up all the ammunition there is in Carman and send it up to the front lines with the 1,000,000 prostitutes who are urgently needed by our brave fighting men.

That was the message from two seventeen-year-old virgins with gobs of hormones rushing through their veins.

Izzy's original girlfriend, Dorothy, became a nurse. Her family put enormous pressure on her to marry and she eventually wed a doctor. "I wanted to go to law school," Izzy recalled. "We broke up at the end of my arts degree and she later married a doctor. It was difficult, but she remained the cornerstone of my other relationships." (According to family folklore—as told by Dorothy's niece—Dorothy's father made her break up with the young Asper because, he predicted, "Izzy would never amount to anything." (Five decades later, members of the Fainstein family still emit half-hearted guffaws over that premature assessment.)

Izzy escaped his Manitoba movie-house routine only once. In 1952, he left home with his two friends and spent a season working for the forestry service in British Columbia—"The most incredible five months of my life," he remembered. "I was in trouble financially because I had broken with my dad. I was with Rick Stillwater and Bob Kopstein, and we took a bus to the coast. On the way, we visited the Pig and Whistle in Jasper, which was full of beer and hookers. We went west, literally, to count trees as timber cruisers doing a government-sponsored inventory. We arrived in Wadhams, BC, on May 4 when it started to rain and didn't stop for two months. We were never dry. I stuck it out even though I didn't enjoy it. But I wouldn't give my father the satisfaction of quitting. In a town called Namu, we said we were inspectors and went into a fish cannery to inspect the women's bums."

While Izzy was doing his penance counting trees in British Columbia, Cecilia lived up to her Jewish-mother stereotype. "I'm keeping a prayer in my heart for you, that you may come back a healthier and wiser boy," she wrote. "Please for your sake, try to save all the money you can, it's very important. Also look after your health. Hard work may be good for you, but cleanliness both in body and mind is very important. I wonder if you manage to wash yourself everyday or do you live like the Eskimos and accumulate dirt to keep you warm?"

Izzy didn't reply and Cecilia quickly turned inconsolable. "I'm absolutely going frantic from not hearing a word from you. Tomorrow will be two weeks since I received your letter dated May 25th. I don't sleep nights worrying, I just can't help that, so while you know this why don't you write?" In contrast, another one of Izzy's pals had some cheerful news: "Saw Babs Bernstein today . . . what a doll!!"

He had first met the beautiful and lively Ruth Miriam Bernstein when her family moved from the North End and settled in River Heights, a couple of streets over from the Aspers. Izzy and Babs wound up at the same school and she remembered him as "the new boy around, not terribly interesting. But he was short, and I think he asked me out because I was shorter than he was. We had one disastrous New Year's blind date, and never really saw each other again for years and years. We were in the same school but didn't move in the same group at all. We were geeky kids at that time. So there was nothing, no real friendship. No sparks flew. I had lots of friends but our lives ran on separate tracks through high school and early university."

She graduated in English and philosophy at the University of Manitoba but didn't date Izzy there. "I had a boyfriend, he had a girlfriend. And then, towards the end of university, before he went into law school, I broke up with my boyfriend, who was in medical school, and, much to my mother's dismay, Izzy started showing up on the scene. It was a rather tenuous situation. It was nuts. All of a sudden, mutual friends kept insisting that we should get together. And maybe over a period of a year or so, it never happened. But Izzy used to direct the annual student variety shows, where all the groups put on skits. I was active in Hillel, which was the Jewish student organization, and we performed a show that he directed. So it sort of developed a little bit from there, in his last year of arts before he headed to law school. He was so busy that the only times we saw each other was late at night. My parents started calling Izzy 'Coffee,' because at eleven o'clock, I'd say, 'I'm going for coffee,' and head out. You'd think I would have learned from that."

Back in Winnipeg they courted, partly by mail because Izzy kept moving around to service his father's theatres. Babs to Izzy, in Neepawa at the King Edward Hotel, Room 3, July 24, 1954:

Hi Love,

Golly I missed you—it would've been a perfect weekend if you had been here . . . You won't even recognize me when you see me—I've changed colour. I'm now a bright glaring red and I hurt! You'll have to be awfully gentle!

Love you madly,
Me

Babs to Izzy, August 17, 1954:

Guess what day it is today! Oh I know it's August 17, but it's something else too. It's a day closer than it was yesterday to the time when I'll see you again and that's pretty important, you know. You must think I'm awful silly—but gee I miss you Izzy . . . I can't get over this honestly. Little me—who never missed anybody in my whole life—and all of a sudden I miss you, need you and want you—aside from being in love with you. So what happens? You go off to Neepawa. I think I was born to suffer. And I'll bet you don't even miss me—you're probably having such a good time there. Tell me, have they set you up with any girls yet? Oooh, I'll kill you—honestly I will. Boy, it's a good thing I trust you (I keep telling myself) or else I'd go insane before you got back.

Babs to Izzy, August 18, 1954:

You know when I used to hear of people writing to each other every day (not that we're writing to *each other*) I used to wonder how in the world they could do it. What could they possibly say and what a nuisance it would be writing every day. Now, I can hardly wait for night-time so I can write you, even though I have nothing particular to tell you. When I write you I sort of pretend that you're here and I'm talking to you and then I'm not quite so lonesome. It would help though, if you made with the conversation sometimes too. I expect at least a postcard while you're away (just to have some record of our affair in future years).

Babs to Izzy, August 25, 1954:

Dear Sir:

The strangest thing happened to me today—I still haven't gotten over it. I got a letter from you, of all things! . . . My mother will be cross, though, you sealed the letter so well that she didn't have a chance of opening it without my knowing . . . I'm awfully lonely for you too, dear . . . I never felt lonely before I met you but always felt alone. Oh, it's not that I felt no one cared, but no one really mattered to me (except my family, that's different). Everyone was quite expendable until you, love. And you're very indispensable and irreplaceable. And I don't feel a bit alone anymore.

Babs

Babs to Izzy, who was visiting New York, December 19, 1954:

Well, I guess you finally got there, by hook or by crook. I hope so anyway. Instead of taking the Constellation flight you took the consolation flight (that's a joke, son) but aren't you glad you went? I don't know why I'm talking like this. I don't even know if you're there, and what with all these crashes, I can tell you I've been worried sick. When they broke into the opera broadcast this afternoon with the news flash that a plane crashed in New York, I was almost hysterical till someone pointed out that it was an Italian plane . . . Dad gave me an idea. He said you should have phoned here when you got there, and asked for Mr. Asper. Naturally, we wouldn't accept the call, but I would know that you were there and it wouldn't cost anything . . .

> Golly, I miss you,
> Babs

A card from Babs to Izzy, December 22, 1954:

Dear Izzy,
This is just a little note to say . . . [reader opens the card]
I HATE YOU!!!

> Yours very truly (little do you know),
> Ruth Bernstein

(The least you could have done is write one letter.)

Babs to Izzy, December 23, 1954:

Dear Izz,
Golly, I'm sorry darling. I don't really hate you—I love you, but when there was nothing from you in this morning's mail—I was really disappointed and then I got boiling mad. Then your letter came this afternoon, I really felt ashamed of myself. But I was mad too—because you had upset my plans. Once I was mad, I was determined to stay mad, and I was getting more steamed up every minute. Why I didn't care if you NEVER came home or NEVER wrote a letter (I kept telling myself) and by George I was ready to do something drastic, like accepting the next boy who asked me out (they have been calling much to my surprise). But your letter made me all un-mad and I can hardly wait now for you to come home and I think I'll stick strictly to Rick & Sheppy for escorts. Jeepers, it sounds as though you're having an exciting time.

One of the seminal influences on Asper as he was formulating his ideas were the teachings of Ayn Rand, the novelist and Objectivist philosopher who had a sizable following in his home town. Rand's second-in-command was Leonard Peikoff, a Winnipegger who eventually inherited her estate and who still carries on her movement. "Izzy was intellectually courageous," said Peikoff. "He took positions that were highly contentious and stuck to them. We spent some time in New York together. I encouraged him to write a musical for Broadway, about the only dream he never fulfilled. We agreed about most things—business and capitalism. But not about Israel. We corresponded after that. And I received the last letter from him on the day he died."

"Leonard and Izzy were good friends," recalled Babs, "but a lot of people's lives were ruined because of the rigidity of Ayn Rand's doctrine. It's incompatible with real living, but there was a huge Winnipeg involvement. Rand was a very compelling person in real life, with piercing eyes. I could see how people could be drawn into her philosophy."

Peikoff travelled from Winnipeg to New York every six months to visit Rand and, in 1953, he transferred to New York University, where he took a doctorate in philosophy. During this period, his friendship with Rand—and with Izzy—deepened. Like several other bright young men who were part of Rand's inner circle (among them Alan Greenspan, later chairman of the Federal Reserve Board), Peikoff and Izzy were attracted to Objectivism because of its view of man as a heroic being, with personal happiness as the moral purpose of life, and productive achievement as the noblest activity. Objectivism rejected religion and transparency while worshipping self-righteousness.

"I met Izzy at the University of Manitoba when I was a freshman and he was a sophomore," Peikoff recalled. "He was very intelligent but not an intellectual—very fast and decisive—funny, ironic and sarcastic in a positive way. He was talented in just about everything. A marvellous pianist, and I don't think he took any lessons. Once, my mother, who was a band teacher, taught me how to play something and Izzy said, no, that's not how it's done, and proceeded to play it perfectly. He called a spade a spade. No hidden agendas. He could be the life of the party or he would sit in a corner and be withdrawn and moody."

––––––––––

The big event of the law-school years was the marriage of Babs and Izzy after his third year, undertaken with a measure of mutual reluctance. "I started going out with Babs in first-year law school but didn't want to get married," Izzy recalled. "I asked her out to a faculty freshmen's ball because I needed a date desperately. We had a great time. She signed a document that we would never marry or have children. Her mother lobbied against such an agreement. We then started going out more. Here was this good-looking girl, who liked the right kind of jazz and didn't want to get married. You can build on that! But then we started talking about getting married. I said no, but Sarah Bernstein [Babs's mother] and my father said yes. He was a big fan of Babs's. I liked her father, Maurice, my kind of scientist. I spent a lot of time at her place. At the end of first-year law, I realized how poor I was. Babs had a job [as office manager] at Phillips Paint [partly owned by her father], so I thought I'd be better off married. More important, she owned the first long-playing record I'd ever seen. That got me. Here was a girl who understood my music and loved it—and had the record [Dave Brubeck's *Time Out*, played in 5/4 time with the blind and magical Joe Morello featured on drums]. The Brubeck quartet was playing at the Black Hawk in San Francisco and you couldn't travel with a girl if you were single. So we got married (on May 27, 1956) and went to see Brubeck in San Francisco. Imagine!" (Izzy privately described Babs as "the only broad who was gorgeous, sexy, intellectually liberated and had a 12" Brubeck LP.")

"I originally went to university to participate in the extracurricular activities," Izzy confessed, and there wasn't a professor to contradict him. "Classes were a necessary evil." First- and second-year arts were then on Broadway, third and fourth years at the Fort Garry campus. The law school was downtown. Izzy gave serious thought to going into medicine because many of his friends did, but he really wanted to be a lawyer. He enjoyed the clash of ideas, which he expressed endlessly to anyone who would listen—in fact he won the Western Canadian debating championship. As a "big man on campus," he created a personal following for the leading roles he played putting on Varsity Varieties, the annual satirical pageant. He wrote catchy and ribald lyrics to a wide range of songs and acted as the MC along with his friend Ron Meyers. "He played Dean Martin, and I did my Jerry Lewis shtick," recalled Meyers, who later became a Manitoba judge. "The campus and its five thousand students was a beehive of activity—and putting on the annual entertainment was a great cohesive experience," he fondly remembered. "It was the making of me."

Prior to becoming involved with Babs, Izzy was editor of the Brown and Gold yearbook, as well as Freshie Chairman. That was when he fell in love with a girl named Brenlee, who would later marry an eye doctor, Nate Werner. He helped organize the striking co-ed's election as the year's Freshie Queen. "He had a sparkling personality and always had something to say that was clever and funny," she recalled. "I remember one particular event, when we were dancing, he said something which I thought was very original at the time and didn't really know that anyone had said it before him. 'You realize,' he whispered as we were dancing, 'that this is the vertical fulfillment of a horizontal desire.' And of course I thought, 'Oh boy, this is smart, this is wonderful.'" Izzy had a way of promoting himself that outpaced his ego, such as his slogans for various campus elections: "IZZY CLEVER? IZZY EVER! IZZY ASPER." Or, worse, "ARTS GOT A HEADACHE? GET Asper-IN."

"I only knew of and occasionally observed the Israel Harold Asper who wheeled across the academic firmament of the University of Manitoba in the 1950s, but his trajectory was highly visible," Ted Allan reported in the *Winnipeg Free Press* on his university time with Izzy. "One soon learned to recognize the rites of passage and to learn who had juice and who didn't. Izzy Asper had it. In an ill-focused and fading photo in a back issue of *The Manitoban,* the now-familiar hooded eyes and half-smiling, failing, mocking mouth are arranged in an expression of such consuming confidence that it could serve as an incarnation of manifest destiny."

Asper was suspended only once, when he attended a Communist-sponsored conference to help students from Czechoslovakia (then behind the Iron Curtain) visit Canada. He became news editor of the student newspaper, *The Manitoban,* after being fired as a proofreader when he deliberately missed a typo. ("The sports coach wouldn't give the paper an interview, so the headline on the story that was supposed to be 'Why the Shrinking Violet?' came out as 'Why the Shtinking Violet?'") His friend Guy Kroft coined the term "half-Asper" when Izzy played halfback for the Arts football team. Izzy's biggest journalistic thrill was writing a music column that allowed him to interview Duke Ellington, George Shearing and many other jazz greats who played Winnipeg's Rancho Don Carlos nightclub. He also started to broaden his knowledge of jazz and its practitioners with regular visits to New York.

During his first two years of law school, there was precious little evidence of the youthful Izzy's thirst for legal knowledge. While he pretended to study, his attendance didn't even rank as sporadic. "Law school was death warmed over—you had to have 80 percent attendance," Asper recalled with no hint of chagrin. "I was thrown out in my first year because I barely managed to be there 12 percent of the time, and had to plead before the Manitoba Court of Appeal to get back in. Later on I quit but was really chucked out. In law classes they didn't want to debate or discuss. I couldn't take it. I remember putting my hand up and giving my version of the law and the prof saying, 'What's your name?'

"'Asper.'

"'Oh right, we know about you.'"

Izzy was firmly admonished that he was there not to advocate what laws ought to be, but to study what they were. "It was only when

I visualized spending the rest of my life tearing theatre tickets in Neepawa that I went back to law school," he recalled. At the time, students went to lectures in the mornings and articled in the afternoons, right from their first year. That was tough because only Jewish firms took in Jewish students and only Jewish clients used Jewish firms, so they were not particularly prosperous and could afford few junior openings. Izzy wormed his way into a slot at Harold Buchwald's office at Matlin Kushner Buchwald and stayed there four years. "An articling student in those days," he recalled, "was the guy who took the urine samples from clients to the insurance company, which was then required, and that was essentially what I did."

Not quite. He and his partners—first Roy Baker, then Gordon Pollock—made money by flipping real estate. "We paid one hundred dollars down for a lot and sold it by noon, before we had to pay for it. Or we'd build a house on it and then flip. This was a way to make some quick cash to buy cigarettes. The lot would cost $2,000 but only required $200 down. You'd get a carpenter, have him put up a house on money borrowed from the bank, sell it and make a profit of $500 or so. Babs always called her engagement ring '215 Beliveau Road' because that's where the money came from to buy it. When we were in law school, Gordon Pollock and I went into more serious business. The City of Winnipeg auctioned off lots of vacant land. We'd buy five or six building sites in River Heights and hang out at the YMHA [Young Men's Hebrew Association] dining area, where the Jewish lawyers ate lunch. We'd go around the room and sell the lots and make $500 to $1,000 per sale. That was how I afforded the tuition and going out on dates." It was also when Asper learned one of his most valuable lessons: the easiest way to make money was to use other people's funds.*

His marriage to the perky Babs materially and spiritually improved his life as well as his attitude. He still had to work nearly

---

*Asper was also part of a teenage gang of twelve strong boys who, as a prank, would sneak into people's garages, lift their cars and set them down sideways so they couldn't be driven out.

each evening at one of his father's theatres (the nighthawk in training), but instead of sleeping until noon the next morning and missing lectures, as he had in his bachelor days, he had a built-in alarm
clock. "Babs used to throw a pail of water on me and then run,"
he recalled. The happy, if dripping, groom got to school on time
and his grades improved dramatically. In 1957 Asper was awarded a
prize of $150 from the Law Society for achieving the second-highest
standing in his final year.

When called to the bar, Asper joined the office of Sam Drache,
a florid veteran litigator who dressed in garish suits with a daily
fresh bloom in his button hole and a wide-rimmed fedora, and who
gained a reputation for challenging Sam Bronfman's ascendancy
in the Canadian Jewish Congress. "I became his indentured slave,"
Izzy recalled. "He was a brilliant lawyer—nothing in the world he
couldn't do. If not for anti-Semitism, he would have been far more
successful. But he was a bit of a madman. I slowly built up a practice with all of the construction guys I had worked with. One of my
clients was Irwin Spletzer, who had been a private in the Wermacht
during the war. Drache made me give my clients to his partners; I
got 20 percent of the business. I was eventually paid $250 a month
to shadow Sam Drache, eighteen hours a day for two years. The
day I got called to the bar, on July 4, 1957, instead of celebrating I
went straight to the Court of Appeal and argued a case against W.B.
Scarth and W.P. Fillmore, among the top counsels in town. There
was a whole bank of judges and at one point Judge Moncrief gave me
a tongue-lashing about arguing. I was humiliated, went for a walk by
the river reviewing my life, figuring that my career was over. Three
months later I found out that I had won the case. The main thing I
learned from Drache was that nothing was too outrageous to consider. It was mind-boggling watching his thought process. The first
thing he taught me was that the way to solve a problem was not to
work from the edge to the centre but to find the nub of it and figure
out how to work your way back to the starting point."

By the time his contract expired in 1959, Izzy had lost confidence in his mentor's fairness and decided to go out on his own. Drache was very upset. "He couldn't believe it," Izzy reminisced. "'No one leaves Sam Drache!' he kept shouting as he marched around the office. He pulled me over to the window and pointed to an old man on the corner selling newspapers, 'That's what you'll end up doing one day!'" That was more prophetic than insulting, but on the August long weekend of that year, Izzy packed up two boxes of his files and left. Drache denied the fact of his departure for the next twenty-four months, telling people who phoned for him that Asper was away on sabbatical.

"Babs was pregnant with David at the time and I no longer had a job," Izzy remembered, with no nostalgia. "We only had $843 in the bank. I was walking down the street one Saturday afternoon and realized I'd have to tell Babs. We were living at an apartment on Smith Street, paying $85 a month. I had a 1957 Bel Air convertible, bought for $1,500, second-hand. There's a photo of David peeing on it. We were married two years before we had a car and used to walk home together in 30-below weather."

When he ran into Bert Nitikman, a local chartered accountant he knew, and told him what had happened, his friend introduced him to his own contacts at the Bank of Nova Scotia, who installed Izzy in a tiny office on a pay-when-you-can basis. The office had a desk, supplied by Harold Buchwald, and a counter built by a friend. Nitikman sent over a typewriter.

Then began the long siege.

The office was right on top of the bank's vault, so the joke among Izzy's friends was, "Don't worry about Izzy, he's sitting on top of a million dollars." But while most of his fellow graduates were doing real estate deals, wills and divorces, Izzy refused to take the easy way out—not even when his $843 had dwindled to zero. "I didn't want to get my desk cluttered," was his only explanation. Most of the time he just sat in his empty, soundless office reading old cases. He went eight months without a client. "You have to own yourself," he mysteriously informed his friends.

The first case came in over Izzy's transom after having been turned down by three other firms. It concerned a young man named Ben Greenfeld who had worked for a car dealership and was fantastically successful. One night he dropped dead. Succession duties were very high in those days, and he had done no estate planning. Ottawa's tax department was going to take 74 percent of his estate. His wife had nothing. "She had gone to the major firms and then came to me on the recommendation of an accountant named Gerry Kalef, who told her that I was a nut but a genius in taxes. I got it together and won the case, which left the widow and her children with a lot more money. My fee, which she opposed, was $1,500. But I won. That unlocked floodgates of assignments. In the following year I went from an income of $2,000 to $50,000."

He ended up working twenty-four hours a day for a time and realized he had to expand the firm. He enlisted Martin Freedman, one of his former sidekicks from the Varsity Varieties, as his partner, and added eight other notable colleagues over the next decade.

———————

Throughout their teenage years, the two Asper boys felt that they had been robbed of what ought to have been a carefree youth by their father's Slavic notion of the father as the family's commander-in-chief and by his demands that they help run the family business. "I had a little kid's perspective of my father as being the czar. He demanded excellence. He lectured us about ethics, honesty, making contributions. He was very public-spirited, did concerts for the army in Minnedosa during the war, and was later recognized by the Legion with an honorary membership. He also formed the Canadian Legion Symphony (not to be confused with the Minnedosa Symphony), consisting of about fifteen people who came to our house on Sundays and rehearsed in the theatre on off nights. Later, when we moved to Neepawa, he started an orchestra there as well."

Leon Asper became a good citizen, but his fathering was rooted in a different culture. It was the most grievous regret of Izzy's life that his father did not live long enough to witness the dramatic turnaround in his son's law firm and the glories that followed.

The Asper family was close so that they could protect one another from the sea of WASPs that surrounded them, but there were corrosive internal tensions that surfaced all too often. The familial love that flowed between Izzy and his father was seriously diluted by profound generational differences—between the traditions of the old Europe and the aspirations of the new America, by the very different kinds of music they played and listened to, but mostly by the disappointment of the elder Asper in his son's choice of career, which at the time amounted to being the sole partner in a walk-up law office with few clients and fewer prospects. Leon had great contempt for lawyers, who in his home country had been paid by local farmer-clients in eggs and cabbages, and was heartbroken that neither of his sons wanted to go into business.*

Gail Asper maintained, flat out, that "the relationship with his father was the key issue in Izzy's life." Her brother, Leonard, shared that view: "Dad didn't mention his father that much to me except to say that he clearly didn't like him. He might have loved his father, but he didn't *like* his father and just saw him as an authoritarian figure, and obviously they had vigorous and chasmic disagreements about jazz—the music he listened to—and the fact that he was going to be a lawyer. So the two things he cared about the most his father never approved of. I don't know if he was trying to prove himself to his father, but he had demons that were inserted into him by his father, is the way I would put it. He was upset that his father wasn't there to see how wrong he had been. He was always like, 'Fuck you, I showed you and I was right and you were wrong and you're not here to see it.' That was there for sure."

---

*Izzy's older brother, Aubrey, experienced his own set of paternal problems. He was banned from the Asper family home for a year because he insisted on becoming a teacher. According to the senior Asper, the only worse thing than being a teacher was being a lawyer.

It took Izzy a good half a century to allay his father's spirit and prove to himself that he was a real *macher*. "Father was tough," Izzy recalled. "I resented his sternness. My father was the czar. I lived in fear of him. My mother protected me. She was the intermediary between my father and me. She negotiated the rapprochements. I used to think my father was mean to her, but I was wrong. She didn't think so. Mother had faith that God dictated life's ups and downs. That was how she persevered. I had a kid's perspective of my father as being a boss. He demanded excellence in everything I did."

He remembered his father whipping him only once, when the people who ran the general store in Neepawa put out a box of medals to commemorate a British royal occasion. Izzy took the medals, not realizing, he claimed, that it was theft. The store owner told his mother, who demanded he give them back. He had hidden the loot in the garage of their next-door neighbour, from which a local character known as Jimmy the Albino took them so they couldn't be found. His father beat him, "shrieking as he gave me the licking with his open hand."

The disillusioned Leon, who had hoped—and probably prayed—that his youngest son would go into business, considered Izzy to have become mentally defective for having become a lawyer, and said so. He kept asking Israel, rather pointlessly, "Who the hell do you think you are?" Leon smoked a dozen cigars a day and had been losing serious money at his Winnipeg theatres. He died in 1961, when Izzy was twenty-nine and monumentally unsuccessful. It was much too soon to validate his chosen profession. The time gap created an aching, open wound in Israel's psyche from which he never recovered. That sense of irreplaceable loss, of being robbed of the opportunity to prove his father wrong, haunted Asper the rest of his life.

And that's what made Izzy run.

3

Serving the Law:
The Remarkable Mr. Asper

*No Canadian tycoon has ever advanced so steadily
along a trail of legal firefights than the Winnipeg
legalist Israel Asper by name and occupation.*

In the ongoing controversy about when life begins, it is a dubious but persistent belief among Jewish mothers that a fetus becomes viable only when it graduates from medical school. It is also rumoured that Mona Lisa's mother, had she been Jewish, would have complained, "This you call a smile, after all the money your father and I spent on braces?" Christopher Columbus's mom, on the other hand, might have lamented, "I don't care what you discovered, you still should have *written!*" The remarkable thing about my own *maminka* was that for thirty years she served us leftovers. I don't remember ever seeing or tasting the original meal.

The mother stories are perpetually silly but very much part of Jewish culture. So, why are there no Jewish *father* jokes? For a very good reason, I discovered when I was writing a profile of Gerry Schwartz, who was the only direct partner that Izzy Asper ever had. On and off for fifteen years they enjoyed an intense camaraderie, each allowing the other to invade his space—so much so that when they had adjoining offices, their connecting door was always open.

When I noticed Schwartz's name on the list of Canada's highest-paid executives, back in 1997, I felt a momentary sympathy for the man. True, his compensation of $19 million was up 124 percent from the previous year—and he did manage to pay himself three times as much as, say, Conrad Black, of Conrad Black infamy, even though the (then) Hollinger chief had more than doubled his income. In fact, Schwartz earned considerably more than Jean Monty, who at the time headed Canada's largest corporation, BCE Inc., and just about everybody else, including the Queen of England.

Still, no matter how impressive the size of Gerry's compensation that year, he did place *second*, behind Robert Gratton, CEO of Montreal's Power Financial Corp., who had stuffed a tidy $27 million into his jeans—and I could visualize the poor guy trying to explain to his father why he wasn't first. The previous year, when Gerry's conglomerate, Onex Corp., which he had founded from a standing start, had jumped to fourteenth on the *Financial Post* list of Canada's top 500 companies, the usual taciturn Schwartz had allowed himself to feel happy—*excited* even. After all, in FP's listings, Onex was now just behind Imperial Oil, the biggest of the energy majors, and just ahead of Canadian Pacific, the country's defining corporation. If he hadn't been in his Bay Street office forty-nine floors above ground that morning, he might have a done a little cake-walkin' in the spring sunshine, so exhilarated did he feel.

He couldn't resist calling his father in Winnipeg to share the thrill. When Andy Schwartz came on the line and his son announced the great news, the phone went silent for a split second or three. Then his father issued rather subdued congratulations, and they went on to talk of family matters. The younger Schwartz knew only too well what that hesitation meant. He had, after all, come in fourteenth, and fourteenth wasn't first, which is what every Jewish father expects of his son.

Now, only one year later, he had come in second in his pay packet, stuck at a lousy $18 mil. "There's an apocryphal story of the kid who comes home after he gets 98 in his exams," Schwartz recalled. "Of course his Jewish father says, 'Why didn't you bother to think about the area where you could get those two extra marks? Why didn't you study that? At least for the next exam prepare yourself.' The kid goes back, studies like crazy, comes home after the next exam and says, 'Pop, I got 100.' The father replies, 'So don't rest on your laurels.'"

"The morning when that FP list came out was a very defining moment for me," Schwartz vividly recalled. His father's "sort of luke-warm" voice on the phone caused all the other lukewarm moments to well up in his memory, like the time when he was going to Manitoba law school. "I stood first for a while, and then in the final year I was fifth because I was engrossed in a couple of business deals. My father didn't come to my graduation or talk to me for a couple of months. He kept saying, 'You could have been first, all you had to do was work hard enough, you knew how to do it, you already proved you were smarter than the others.'"

And that's why there aren't any Jewish father jokes.* Izzy confessed that his kids accused him of reacting the same way. "They'd bring home an exam paper of 99 percent. I'd say, 'What did you get wrong? What did you do wrong?' I don't know if I ever did that or not. I can't believe I did but they claim I did. So who knows. I think it's ingrained."

Schwartz deserves his own book (as does the dynamic Heather Reisman, who single-handedly keeps Canada's publishing industry afloat), but he warrants much more than casual mention in this volume because of his lengthy, intimate and pivotal association both

---

*Schwartz may have disappointed his father on those occasions, but what a good son he was to have backstopped his career with a surefire fallback position before it even started! He enrolled in university only after completing a vocational course at a Winnipeg high school, and is a certified auto mechanic.

with Asper's legal career and, later, as an equal partner in the merchant bank that earned them both their first serious money.

They had watched each other growing up half a block apart on Winnipeg's Oxford Street. Young Izzy walked to school with Gerry's older sister, and Andy, Gerry's father, had been an Asper tax client. The two graduated from the same courses at university and Izzy became Gerry's role model. "From Izzy I learned persistence, hard work—which included sleeping over at the office—and to look at problems as opportunities," Schwartz recalled. "Izzy set high standards, ones I've spent a lifetime trying to live up to."

Both men can be described as unique; there are no comparables. "There is a buffed Schwartzian veneer that envelops the small tight figure within it," wrote Jennifer Wells in a Schwartz profile published by the *Globe*'s *Report on Business*. "It must be kept intact, and so an orchestration of the corporate and personal tableaux must be conducted."* Gerry, in short, was the perfect partner for his buddy Izzy, another theatrical construct, except that no creative enterprise, be it a law firm or an orchestra, can have two conductors. In one way, they were too close for comfort: both suffered from having a Presbyterian conscience, which, *oy vey,* is a heavy burden to bear for any Jewish boy.

The seeds of the partnership were force-fed by Schwartz. Almost every day in the early 1960s, Gerry, then a youthful law student articling elsewhere, would barge his way into Asper's law office and demand to be taken on staff. "We kept throwing him out and he kept insisting he wanted to work for us," Asper recalled. "I would come to work on a Saturday afternoon and Gerry would be waiting at my car. We did finally take him on. We had no air conditioning, so we kept the window open. Gerry had this big case, *Clydesdale versus the City of Winnipeg*—it was a land dispute with the city. The entire

---

*Wells was one of the few journalists who took the trouble to study her subject. The several profiles she wrote of Izzy Asper caught the man's contradictions and aspirations, while acknowledging his faults. "Izzy once sent me a set of martini coasters," she recalled. "They were . . . well, ugly, and stamped with a rather unattractive Canwest logo. But there was a nice note attached that said, 'Spill one for me.'"

case was in files on the bookshelf near the window. When Schwartz went out for a cheeseburger, a gust of wind blew all the documents out the window. We were on the ninth floor. I got a call from the police that the papers were on the lanes of Winnipeg and spent hours fishing the papers. But we won the case."

The most remarkable aspect of Asper's legal career was that while his public reputation was almost entirely based on his tax work, the source of his greatest triumphs was in exploiting the laws of contract and defamation more lethally than his opponents. No Canadian tycoon has ever advanced so steadily along a trail of legal firefights than the Winnipeg legalist Israel Asper by name and occupation. As anyone who has been involved in the agonizing rumpus of defending one's good name (including the author of this heavily lawyered tome), whatever the outcome, the legal process drains the spirit and empties the pocketbook faster and to less good purpose than any other human activity—except perhaps spending a karaoke evening at the neighbourhood pub. Both rank among civilization's most wasteful pastimes. Not so for Izzy. "He loved it, he absolutely loved it," emphasized Greg Gilhooly, one of his executives, and he wasn't referring to Japanese singsongs. "His attraction to court actions speaks to what I perceived as being his motivation: the idea that if you were king, and if you believed that you were on the right side of the facts, you had to accept challenges. It was a sport, it was fun to try and prove yourself right." Ironically, while Izzy pursued the court cases with every weapon short of a siege cannon, he did not originate most of his legal vendettas. As his son, Leonard, has pointed out, "When people wrote that he was litigious, they didn't look beyond the fact that he was involved in lawsuits, all of which vindicated him, none of which he started and all of which were issues of him enforcing rights that he had by contract."

Because there was not enough big money in Winnipeg paying tax, Izzy's practice had to be in Toronto. Every Wednesday he flew there, and he came back Friday evenings. He was being paid Winnipeg not Toronto rates. Word of mouth spread and that Izzy did good work and he got more clients, immeasurably helped by his *Globe and Mail* tax column, syndicated in ten other papers.

———————

"It was an unbelievable law firm," reminisced Jack London, who was an early Asper partner and later became dean of the law school at the University of Manitoba. "It was one of his two or three unfulfilled dreams—to build the largest and most powerful Jewish law firm in Western Canada. He had the nucleus which would have allowed him to do that, because we had rising stars like Gerry Schwartz, Martin Freedman, Michael Nozick and Richard Shead. The office operated as a kind of legal think tank filled with intellectual sharks. This was a group of people who were so bright, so absolutely creative, that no matter what statement was made, what issue arose, what proceeding was taking place, it was immediately jumped upon, dissected and deconstructed—before deconstruction became a technique of interpretation—put back together again, tested and challenged.

"Izzy himself was of course the main source of business that was being done in the firm, his most important talent being that he was the ultimate delegator. Once he decided that you were capable, he gave you full head without any hesitation that you didn't have the experience that was required. He trusted that we would do it, and to a person, that's exactly what happened. Everyone fulfilled his notion—I would call it his fantasy—of what we were capable of doing. The other significant dynamic in the firm was Izzy himself, easily the most creative man I ever met—bar none. He was absolutely magical in the way he could put together a vision and the structures that were required to manifest that vision. You can't teach that kind of intellectual and artistic magic to someone else. But if you had a spark of it, and most of the people in the office did, you learned to think several steps ahead, not in a linear fashion, but in a holistic sort of fashion. And it was infectious—a fabulous way to start out as a young lawyer."

Like everyone else in that dynamic partnership, London wondered what made Izzy so different, such a child of some distant destiny only he could define. "The most prevalent of the theories was that he worked all of his young life and later, in order to demonstrate to his father that he had the stuff. I personally didn't think that he was out to prove anything to anybody but that what drove him was sheer genius. His creativity produced in him an energy that drove him to exercise his mental capacity to its full extent. There was no second gear. Also, Izzy was a bit of a charming rogue. I had nothing but affection for him, but like so many successful people, he was prepared to bend and stretch all and any rules to allow him to accomplish what he wanted. And he did it, as I say, in a charming way. He wasn't a con man, he just had the characteristics of one.

"If I were kind of lying on my back, trying to visualize the two images of Izzy," London mused, "the first would be of him, metaphorically, sitting at his desk in the law office on the telephone with the minister of finance of Canada, of Manitoba or of Uganda, having a conversation while twiddling a straw—he always held something in his hand, a toothpick or a straw, and he would put it in and out of his mouth as he talked. No matter what the subject was, no matter how scant had been the time that he'd had to review the material, he was able to engage in a conversation on economics, on politics, on law or on policy in a way that you could only marvel at because he actually knew what he was talking about. He had the creative skill to instantly fashion policy, and the people on the other end of the line who might have thousands of bureaucrats advising them were listening and heeding the advice of 'Izzy from Winnipeg.'

"The second image, which would most aptly demonstrate his dichotomous character, would be of Izzy in the middle of a wedding reception of, say, four hundred people at a hotel ballroom or at the synagogue, in a place where there are no-smoking signs all the way around the hall. He lights up in the middle of the room and he's the only one smoking that cigarette defiantly, absolutely defiantly. No one was going to tell him, a libertarian of the absolute first order, that he couldn't smoke, and the notion that somehow he was infringing on someone else's rights or liberties was absolutely unimportant to him because he was only concerned, at that moment, with his own liberty to do as he would. He just didn't see second-hand smoking as hitting someone. But that's a metaphor for Izzy, it's a metaphor for his life. That's what he did, he smoked in the middle of the room when he wasn't supposed to, and he got away with it. Nobody challenged him because he was so all-powerful and satisfied his needs, as and whenever he wanted."

Even though he was already netting $200,000 a year, Asper decided to try his own hand at business. Challenged by Walter Weir, Izzy said he could build something from scratch and create jobs, and decided to prove it. Canada's most successful company at the time was Seagram's, so Izzy naturally threw out a challenge to the Bronfmans by building a distillery—where else but in Minnedosa. "The town fathers came to me and said that Minnedosa was dying, needed new industry, and that they had this fab-quality water, which could be turned into great booze," he recalled. "Don Gordon and I got a bunch of guys together and we spent a summer reading up on how to make liquor. This was not going to be just another whiskey plant; this was planned as a world-class operation—another Seagram's, but bigger. We drew up a thirty-three-year business plan, so elaborate that its outline [was] written on large sheets of paper that covered every inch of the walls of my recreation room." It was vintage Asper and, surprisingly, the scheme worked. The little company, known as Canada's Manitoba Distillery, produced liquor entirely for export, which meant that it didn't have to carry inventory. The operation was profitable in its first month.

"What a schmuck I was," Asper lamented. "At the start my partners told me, 'Yeah, yeah, this is great, let's go, let's go.' But nobody really believed me that it could actually be done. When it began to happen, they weren't willing to stay the course."

His partners insisted on selling out when Melchers of Montreal made an attractive offer only eight months after the distillery went on tap. "I learned a sobering lesson," Izzy grieved. "No matter what your partners agree to do when they go into a transaction, ultimately they forget what they had for breakfast when it comes time for lunch. I learned the hard way that amnesia is the curse of the business world."

Since he couldn't save his company, Asper decided instead to save Canada, or at least Manitoba. That was just as Prime Minister Pierre Trudeau, one of Izzy's favourite sparring partners, was beginning to tinker with the Constitution in a way that the Winnipegger found distasteful. Asper believed that he could influence national affairs in an enlightened direction only by becoming Manitoba's premier, and he quickly—too quickly—found himself running for the leadership of the province's defunct Liberal Party. From the outset, the contest amounted to drawing straws—with the loser taking the job. Izzy was set up to get the short straw.

Asper's abrupt departure from his legal career was typically impulsive. By 1970, he had been actively practising law for over a dozen frantic years as well as writing a nationally syndicated newspaper column on taxes, which spawned his only published book. Titled *The Benson Iceberg: A Critical Analysis of the White Paper on Tax Reform in Canada,* his 130,000-word manifesto wasn't exactly a bodice-ripper, but it became a bestseller. In his view, Liberal finance minister Edgar Benson's sweeping reforms not only introduced a capital gains tax but had hidden implications that Asper felt would dangerously tilt the tax system toward statism. Is the government entitled to take nearly half of all the money earned in Canada? was his subtext, echoing the laissez-faire gospels of Joseph Schumpeter and Ayn Rand. Winnipeg broadcaster and social critic Larry Zolf dismissed the book as a guide "to showing the rich how they could destroy the welfare state and get even richer—and all on tax reform." A quarter century later, the volume seems hardly relevant except that it displays the author's profound familiarity with the country's tax regulations, and that it widened his already high reputation among his legal peers.

Naturally, he interpreted such an endorsement as a resounding sign that it was time to move on. "I had been quite successful and had done a couple of business deals and had some money, but I was out of gas as a practising lawyer, so in May 1970 I got off a plane, phoned my great pal Harold Buchwald and said, 'You know we've been negotiating a merger for four years. If you want to do this deal, meet me at my house in twenty minutes, and if we haven't got a deal by dinner'—this was three o'clock in the afternoon—'we'll never talk about it again.' Well, within an hour we had a deal. They had offered me a lot of money the year before to merge. I said, no, I don't want money. I want out. So the big condition was we would merge the firms and I would be sprung, I would be free."*

One of his few distinct memories of that time was a lobster dinner in Halifax while attending a bar convention with Nova Scotia premier Gerald Regan, federal justice minister John Turner and Winnipeg political brokers Lloyd Axworthy and Charlie Huband. "We sat around and talked about who the next leader of the Manitoba Liberal Party should be: someone with rural roots who now lived in an urban area, his ethnic background and so on. The hated NDP was in office, and I emerged as the consensus candidate. It was not a sought-after job, but I was persuaded that I could change things," he recalled with a touch of bitterness. "It turned out that I had been wrongly persuaded, badly persuaded, but they put on a lot of pressure and I agreed to do it. I became leader five months later, and if anyone had told me that this was what I would do when I walked out of the law firm, I'd have laughed."

But for Izzy Asper, venturing into Manitoba politics turned out to be no laughing matter.

---

*The Buchwald Asper firm evolved into Pitblado Buchwald, after Izzy negotiated his name off the letterhead around the time of the merger with Pitblado & Hoskin. It remains one of Winnipeg's largest law firms.

4

The Day "Landslide Asper" Fell to Earth

"If Louis Riel were alive today, I would
be in the trenches with him."
—Manitoba Liberal leader Israel Asper

Politics in these northern latitudes is a drawn-out process, the strong, slow boring of boards. Success requires patience, dedication and an overdose of masochism. This was particularly true in the fiercely partisan world of Manitoba politics during the 1970s. No one, no matter how statesmanlike, had a chance of attaining power without swearing allegiance to one of the polarized extremes: the Rigid (socialist) Left or the Rigid (Conservative) Right. Between these extremes existed, in uncertain twilight, the Mushy (Liberal) Middle. It housed those rare individuals who didn't crumble when the daily grind became too bizarre or too base for whatever talent and grace they had to offer. They faced little choice except to put on a brave front and run as burnt offerings. None did so with more panache than Israel Asper, professional politician, 1970 to 1975.

Izzy entered the political arena at an awkward moment. The
defining figure of modern Manitoba politics had been Duff Roblin,
who was premier from 1958 to 1967. The province's version of Peter
Lougheed—the best head of government Alberta ever had—Roblin
was a superbly capable operator who combined conservative principles with a hyperactive social conscience. But neither premier
provided for his succession. Roblin was followed by Walter Weir, a
reactionary undertaker who buried the Tories by alienating urban
and centre-left voters. The Liberals, missing the opportunity to fill
the vacuum, chose Robert Bend, a folksy populist who campaigned
from the back of his chuckwagon on a rodeo theme. Instead of
being merely powerless, the party was turned into a laughing stock.
By contrast, NDP leader Ed Schreyer was an attractive centrist who
ran an effective if overly pragmatic administration and was still in
his honeymoon period when Asper appeared on the scene.

It was a measure of Izzy's determination that at one point in
his ambitious 1973 election campaign he went on record with a
non sequitur that rang through the ages: "If Louis Riel were alive
today, I would be in the trenches with him." It was an empty boast,
of course, and yet in a peculiar way it rang true, since the Métis
rebel's most telling characteristic was also the reason he was put to
death: he refused to hide behind a justified insanity plea that could
have saved his life—an attitude that would have qualified him as a
Manitoba-style Liberal leader any time.*

The ever-optimistic Asper believed that his party was only in
remission and that he was the Moses who could lead its entrails out

---

*Izzy's relationship with the Métis provided one of the great comic scenes of
Canadian politics. Asper had been invited by the Manitoba Metis Federation to
meet their delegation in Minnedosa. Izzy thought, "Well, I'm not going to wear my
three-piece suit to the city because they don't have a lot of money and I don't want
to make them feel uncomfortable," so he and Babs put on blue jeans and T-shirts.
Of course, the Metis Federation folk thought, "Asper's coming. He's this big tax
lawyer," so they all went out and got three-piece suits. As they were walking down
Main Street toward each other, both sides realized what had happened and figured
that they'd have a great meeting—if they could ever stop laughing.

of the political wilderness, which the Manitoba Grits had occupied since 1922 and then only as part of a coalition. On Halloween of 1970, when he joined the political wars, Izzy typically figured that he would start at the top, which he did, even if by then Liberals were protected mainly by the province's hunting laws. Facing the effective rule of NDP premier Ed Schreyer, the Liberals had been forced to abandon their traditionally sedate populism, which might have allowed them to strike a marketable balance between elitism and egalitarianism. Instead they were left to defend a nebulous make-believe mandate that connected with almost no one on Planet Manitoba.

From the start, Asper cultivated a Kennedyesque speaking manner, then very much in style, that didn't quite come off. He began his leadership acceptance speech on October 31, 1970, with the bold declaration, "Let the word go out from this convention hall." That didn't ring the same bells as JFK's stirring inaugural declaration, "Let us go forth to lead the land we love." Still, there was never any doubt that the youthful Asper was deadly serious in convincing himself he could and would champion the ideal public policy mix for Manitobans: "The main thrust of any government I lead," he declared right off the mark, "will be to guarantee each citizen equality of opportunity in all things, social, cultural, and economic, leaving, as a Liberal must, each individual to exercise free choice as to how he wishes to pursue life's options." That endowed voters with more slack than they might have wished, but the new leader mercifully assured them that on his watch, the Liberal Party of Manitoba "would be nourished by an insatiable desire to improve the human condition." Well, all right then.

"The election of Liberal leader Izzy Asper in 1972 brought new excitement to the legislature," noted Herb Schultz (the premier's brother-in-law) in *A View from the Ledge*, his lively chronicle of the Schreyer years. "Intellectually agile and swift of tongue, he delighted in keeping the government off balance with oblique assertions disguised as questions: a niggling point here, an implied accusation there; a scholastic argumentation on an obscure issue, sometimes farcical but enough to embarrass the government." One day Asper revealed, with appropriate fanfare, that the Americans were buying up Canada—although this conquest had been proceeding at a prodigious rate since 1947 and, by the time the freshly minted Liberal leader took note of the phenomenon, nearly two-thirds of the country's manufacturing capacity was owned by Uncle Sam's vulture capitalists. Schultz accurately described Asper as "a slim, ambitious, peripatetic, nattily-dressed chain smoker with permanent dark bags under his hooded eyes from lack of sleep, a keen mind, and a coiled-spring body that appeared congenitally unable to relax. He seemed out of his element in the cloying confines of the legislature. An unreconstructed capitalist, even his most liberal interpretations of problems seemed to lead to conservative solutions."

While Asper genuinely believed in social justice (such as exempting seniors from having to pay health care premiums), many of his priorities were aimed at a libertarian wing of his party that didn't exist. He championed the heretical notions that people on welfare should work, proposed the abolition of capital gains taxes for the rich and advocated "elimination of the welfare state." Such Ayn Randish remedies didn't play well in Red River Valley country. This was a hangover from Asper's earlier years as a Rand disciple, when he had come under her hypnotic spell and had become an advocate of Objectivism, an evangelical philosophy that embraced reason, individualism and free markets.

Izzy's political belief system was both exploratory and reactive, in the sense that he would always land on the side of conservatism but was open to considerable tweaking. Most politicians regard their craft as making the inevitable seem planned; for Izzy it was the other way around: he had no shortage of plans for Manitoba's future, but there was nothing inevitable about his Liberal rump except extinction. His political sojourn fed his vanity but starved his self-respect. He had expected that political leadership at the top would flow from philosophical concepts that were somewhat more profound than the "Don't Feed the Monkeys" signs at zoos. Instead he discovered that, unlike the Bible, Canada's political operational code contained only one commandment: Thou shalt remain firmly ambiguous. That advice Israel Asper was not capable of following.

At the same time, Asper managed to anger the federal Liberals by supporting Conservative leader Robert Stanfield's proposed tax reforms. Typical of the national coverage Izzy received was that of *Toronto Star* columnist Peter Desbarats, who compared him to Quebec's separatist leader René Lévesque—"both nervous, constant smokers who complain that the citizens of their provinces are treated as second-class citizens and give the impression of living constantly on the edge of enthusiasm and the edge of exhaustion. Though it was only 9 a.m. when we met, his hair was sticking out in all directions and his ideas were tumbling from his thin lips in smoky, staccato bursts as if his brain were puffing nervously on a long ideological cigarette."

Asper's lack of national clout didn't stop him from thinking big. Without a moment's hesitation, he dedicated his barely existent party to "the renegotiation of Confederation, regional development, decentralization of social and economic opportunity, political and constitutional reform, the protection of civil liberties through a permanent bill of rights, reform of the education system, tax reform, northern development, economic growth to combat our brain drain, programs to make our major cities models of the best in urban living, dismantling the massive and often obsolete bureaucracies that intimidate people, to bring the sympathy and assistance of our entire province to the problems of the poor and our Native peoples, to bring economic justice to the silent but suffering rural communities and to restore government to its proper role as servant and not as master of the people." And that was only the first sentence of his party's manifesto. "Everybody wanted to talk about paving Main Street while I wanted to discuss great political mountain ranges," he complained.

During his tenure there was constant pressure on Asper and on Manitoba Progressive Conservative leader Sidney Spivak to unite their parties and join an anti-NDP citizens' coalition that had been established by Winnipeg businessmen who called their movement the Group for Good Government. Dedicated to permanently exporting socialism to Saskatchewan, they wanted Asper to throw his lot in with Spivak's Tories. Spivak had earned his master of law degree from Harvard, and daily managed the enviable trick of surviving simultaneous attacks from his caucus for being "too far left" and "too far right." Against the intuitions of his lively wife, Mira, who came from a poor but socialistically inclined family, Spivak became a successful politician, a man of substance but without Izzy's flash and style. "Sidney and Izzy had a mutual best friend, Bert Nitikman, and they both vacationed at cottages on Falcon Lake where we would visit," recalled Mira Spivak, who was later appointed a senator. "Sidney and Izzy used to play Ping-Pong downstairs in Izzy's cottage for hours. It got, like, fierce. Sidney was a good Ping-Pong player, but so was Izzy."

Though they were friends, their conversations occasionally become so combative that Asper finally made up a list of taboo subjects—mainly anything having to do with the Group for Good Government. "One day Bert took the two of them out in the middle of the lake on his boat, reminded them that there was a by-election coming up in Minnedosa and said that he wouldn't row them back to shore until they agreed to merge or cooperate," recalled Mira. "So of course they didn't agree, but they agreed to disagree and the boat came back to shore.

"At that time, there were no phones in the cottages and Sidney was driving back to our place at West Hawk when he saw Izzy talking animatedly in the local phone booth, and immediately knew what he was doing. Izzy was phoning his candidate, the mayor of Minnedosa, to tell him the Conservatives had agreed to support them. Sidney came home, took his son Harold with him and drove straight to Minnedosa. It didn't take him long to persuade Dave Blake, a banker, to run for the Conservatives, which wasn't what Izzy had promised his local candidate-mayor. Although John Diefenbaker, the PCs' former federal leader, seldom interfered in provincial elections, he had a birthday coming up, and we invited him to Minnedosa for a celebratory picnic to which five thousand people came—and the Tories won that by-election."

Even if he realized that he wasn't going to move the political Earth, Asper became intensely loyal to his Liberal followers, and vice versa. His most vicious battles were fought behind the scenes to prevent the formation of the intended coalition that might have beaten the NDP but that would have extinguished the embers of a Liberal renaissance in Manitoba, probably forever. "It was the worst thing that ever happened to me politically—it's not that it happened but that somebody thought they could set me up like that—to play patsy in the election and allow the Conservatives to win," Asper later reminisced.

"That was to be the big payoff politically," he said. "You'd get enough money to campaign respectfully, go home and be taken care of. It just demonstrated how far removed from reality those people were, if they thought this was a representative cause. Involved were Bill Palk, the local executive head of Eaton's; Jim Burns, president of the Great-West Life; Dick Malone, commanding officer of the *Free Press* and Ron Williams of the *Tribune;* Harold Thompson from Monarch Life, Bob Jones from Investors, some of the grain people, the regional bank vice-presidents, a few agents of Eastern Light, and those operations, the Bay and that kind of thing. And of course we had no money; we were ostracized financially by the business community.* They were nearly all behind the Good Government Group to stop the Mongol hordes from coming over the hills and taking their cookies away. They'd have put their money on Adolf Hitler if they thought he could win. They were a charming group. They created a difficult ball game because if you didn't have people

---

*At one point Leonard Asper beat senators, judges and cabinet ministers at Ping-Pong, for $5 a game, in the Asper family basement. He won $100, but Izzy made him give it all back, explaining something about the party needing money.

from that community in public life, who could we lean on? So they blackmailed us by saying, we won't give you any money. We found some funds in other places, but their power was very pervasive. The *Winnipeg Tribune* even ran an editorial four days before the election, saying it was regrettable that the Liberal Party couldn't see its patriotic duty clearly enough and had the temerity to run candidates. In other words, that it had become unpatriotic to vote Liberal."

———

The trouble with the Liberals under Izzy Asper's leadership was that he became the party, and yet, including himself, the Grits never elected more than five members; during his best campaign, in 1973, he won his own riding by only four votes, earning for himself the sarcastic title "Landslide Asper." Caught between the grasping Tories and the grasping Socialists, Izzy's was a voice of reason, except that his own reason quickly lost touch with why he had become a politician in the first place. "It was pretty soul-destroying," he recalled, blaming his political sojourn on "a fit of idealism."

In the half decade he spent as a wandering political minstrel on the highways and byways of Manitoba, he came to realize that he could grasp political victory only if it came on his own terms. It took him most of five unhappy years, but in the end he reluctantly concluded that being true to himself was the only endgame worth winning, and that professional politics, as played in Manitoba at that time, was not a viable venue for his platform or his presence, no matter how inspired his intentions.

Unhappily, even the issue of anti-Semitism got into the act when NDP Premier Schreyer referred to Asper as "a disgusting little shyster" and labelled his platform as "crap." "The press got that wrong," the former governor general later claimed. "I was speaking about lawyers generically. I'm not the only one who takes the occasional swing at lawyers, especially lawyers in politics. Lawyers who practise their profession is something, but lawyers seem to dominate politics. I don't think they should have a leg up on every other occupation in the democratic art of politics. I have never thought that the word 'shyster' connoted anything other than someone who was a slick legal practitioner, a slick operative. To me it has never had the slightest Jewish connotation." The anti-Jewish depiction was strengthened by the NDP leader's characterization of Spivak and Asper, two rich Jewish lawyers, as "The Gold Dust Twins from River Heights."

Lloyd Axworthy, later a federal Liberal cabinet minister of considerable note, campaigned with Izzy in 1973, mobilizing the public transportation system to garner votes: "It was dazzling in a way, but I do recall the standard campaigning format. I would show up at seven in the morning, climb on a bus, and I'd be fairly low key because I always figured some people had their second cup of coffee and you shouldn't jolt them too much. So we would chat away. Then Izzy would blow in because he was the leader of the party, and would literally grasp people to his bosom and say, pointing at me, 'You're going to vote for this guy,' and if they didn't answer, he'd ride down with them all the way to the Hudson's Bay store, lecture them, then race back. I was exhausted. He really was a kind of whirlwind." At one point during the campaign, he even won a perogy-eating contest, in Dauphin.

During his political career, Asper painted himself as reigning champion of the West against the entrenched interests of the East. There was nothing artificial about his bias, neither from its Winnipeg perspective nor in its authentic resentment, especially of Toronto's power elite, who seemed to believe that Canada began and ended on Bay Street.* Asper's imaginative stance brought him to national attention, which he exploited and relished. In a private memo to his research director, Cam Osler, when he was preparing to meet Pierre Trudeau for the first time as provincial Liberal leader, Asper wrote, "The main purpose of my meeting with the PM is to

---

*Their outlook was widened somewhat in 1976, after completion of the CN Tower. Their view of Canada then took in the panorama they could see from the top of that cement needle on a clear day—or for that matter, on a cloudy day.

obtain his sympathy for the western economic position, and more specifically, for the Manitoba claim that Confederation is not working as it ought to be. I want to pepper him with economic facts and specific data which support the policies I believe we require. The Caucus must be in a position to put forward a compromise plan which will serve the public well, and at the same time, preserve the jobs associated with private industry, and not violate the free enterprise concept any more than is required—if that is possible."

Asper didn't woo just the standard clusters of voters. For example, he supported groups of young people in their efforts to delete a section of proposed Municipal Act changes that discriminated against rock concerts by refusing to grant permission for any event described as "an entertainment or a recreational activity at which more than 1,000 persons attend or are expected to attend any single day." He won that skirmish, no doubt wishing it could have been on behalf of jazz festivals instead.

In one of her early comments on Asper, Frances Russell, the most astute analyst of Western thought since the legendary *Free Press* editor John Wesley Dafoe, dubbed him "a visionary in Manitoba politics." No doubt she meant it as a compliment, but it was the ultimate irony of Asper's candidacy that he was less successful as a thoughtful populist than he might have been as a Liberal hack. "He is in many ways a strange bird in politics—and has made much of the fact that he isn't wedded to any party labels," Russell wrote. "It isn't a pose, nor is it a sign that he hasn't principles and ideals. He says he's in public life to accomplish certain things. The label you apply to them doesn't really matter to him." How Izzy saw his political career was best summed up in the tagline he used for most of his political speeches: "If I win, I don't want to win for the wrong reasons, and if I lose, I want to lose for the right reasons."

A rare voice of reason in his own household was Izzy's wife, Babs, who supported his efforts but realized all too well that his quest made about as much sense as Don Quixote challenging windmills to a duel. "People were not ready for him," she maintained, "and it became quite a bone of contention between Izzy and me because he didn't like me criticizing him. He would tell me what he planned to announce, and I'd object, 'You can't say that. I'm Mrs. Average. You want to know anything, don't run a poll—ask me.' He just had all these ideas in his head, and I'd ask him, 'Who's going to believe you?' I mean he came out of the blue from a corporate environment where you snap your fingers and something gets done. He had to deal with volunteers. He had to understand where the electorate was coming from. He had a work-for-welfare program. Well, that's fine today, but in those days people thought the Huns were coming when you talked about work-for-welfare, especially with them having elected a New Democratic premier. Even some of the jokes he wanted to tell—he had no sense of what kind of anecdotes you could tell and what kind you can't. But once he got out to meet people, they liked him. On a one-to-one basis they loved him, but there just wasn't enough time."

To save scarce campaign funds, the Aspers would tape TV sound bites in their sunroom, with Izzy making a speech or sound clip and the family providing the loudly cheering audience in the background—pretending to bestow a third-party blessing. "He came full circle because from the outside you would have thought that he'd have to be in politics to accomplish what he wanted to do for the province—but once he actually got there, he realized that it really couldn't be done and maintain his life plan," Babs quickly concluded. "He had five years for this and five years for that. He had a timetable, and this was really messing up his schedule."

Asper finally resigned as leader in February 1975. "It became apparent that you needed a discipline I didn't have," he publicly confessed. "If you wanted the public to hear you once, you had to say what you were saying five or ten times. I didn't have the patience for that. It's just like jazz. If someone plays 'Body and Soul' one way, they can't play it the same way again. You reconstruct it, re-harmonize it. You can't do that in politics."

His letter of resignation to party president Stan Roberts stated, "I have made my decision to stand aside and relinquish the Liberal

Leadership in favour of someone who I think will be able to take the Party further down the path toward forming a government. While I have decided to leave the Leadership, I have agreed to remain closely involved in Party affairs and, in effect, I am only changing the role that I will be playing. I really think it is for the best, all things considered."

The phrase "baptism of fire" comes to mind in summing up Izzy's political caper. His motto might have been, "I'm a Liberal but I disagree with most of the things they do"—which wasn't a great start. On top of that, the two trajectories—the Mach 2 speed of his brain and the drawn-out political process—were terminally incompatible. "These political five years were painful in a lot of ways," Asper reminisced. "You have to be in Swan River one day and Thompson the next and attend national conferences. I lost those five years and I was deeply sorry about it. By the time I got back home, I didn't recognize my family. That's why we moved from 970 Wellington Crescent to 1063: we wanted to live in a bungalow so I wouldn't be in the basement and my family on the third floor. I hated the political side of it—people would bother you everywhere. No privacy whatsoever. Everyone wanted to talk politics, hassling you. Some people, it rolls off. Trudeau had the discipline not to let his political life intrude on his privacy. But I didn't. I found that I had made Manitobans an offer that they could easily refuse, although we had an explosion of support—increased our standing in the legislature by 80 percent, going from three to five seats."

Did his political experience humble Izzy, who up to then had succeeded at every one of his endeavours? "Humble—Izzy? No, that would be an oxymoron," Babs shot back with a smile. "'Humble' wouldn't be the word. But it did crush him. He was very, very low after he resigned and realized that he wasn't getting there, or certainly not getting there as fast as he thought he would. He felt very badly after he quit politics. He thought that nobody wanted him, didn't want to go back to law but kept asking himself, 'Who's going to want me?' I looked at him and said, 'Izzy, you've still got the same brain. Everybody would be dying to have you back. They're sorry they lost you.'"

"I'm glad I did it," Izzy pretended. "I learned how the real world works, and that served me well in my next career." That career never took him very far from participating in the political feuds of his time, and he was certainly more influential outside the system than in it. Gordon Pitts summed it up best, in the *Globe and Mail*, when he wrote, "If the voters had been kinder, Izzy Asper might have ended up as a premier of the province—and ultimately faded into retirement as a jazz-loving elder statesman of the Liberal Party. Instead, he built one of Canada's major communications companies, ignited a firestorm of controversy over media diversity and left a long string of fierce friends and bitter foes in his considerable wake."

What attracted Asper back into active politics was the 1987 debate over Brian Mulroney's constitutional accord, named after the Gatineau lake on whose shores it had been negotiated. Izzy regarded the Meech Lake Accord as his political Waterloo, in the sense that he felt its defeat was essential because it granted Quebec special powers and ignored the West's demands for a Senate that was equal, elected and effective. "I was in John Turner's office as his communications director on the day he and NDP leader Ed Broadbent crossed the floor of the Commons to shake Mulroney's hand in public support of Meech," Ray Heard, Global's vice-president of news, recalled. "That same evening Izzy called Turner and warned that the deal would end in disaster, and that he would help undo it. And he did."

Asper's chief ally in the struggle that followed was Don Johnston, a senior Liberal cabinet minister who shared his cause and his hobby. Both lively speakers (and serious piano players), they toured much of the country enumerating Meech's shortcomings, sharing their concern that the accord was a major stepping stone to separation because everything would be interpreted in light of Quebec's becoming a distinct society. The federal Liberal Party's most effective contrarian, Don Johnston stepped into the political wilderness by voting to support free trade and to topple the Meech Accord, both decisions going directly against the gospel according to Liberal leader John Turner. But he became an effective and amiable ally of Asper's.

Izzy was a major influence in organizing the Manitoba strategy to join Newfoundland and sink the accord. At one point Johnston and Asper visited Pierre Trudeau at his fancy digs in Montreal. The former PM had come out of retirement to lead the charge against Meech. "We went up to see him at his house on Pine Avenue and had a great time," Johnston recalled. "Izzy very much liked his martinis, and he's the only person I know, quite frankly, who could drink martinis after dinner instead of, for instance, having a brandy or something else. But anyway, we arrived at Trudeau's and he had nothing for us to drink. He scrounged around and finally came up with a bottle of gin in his kitchen. Izzy eyed it up and down and asked, 'Do you have vermouth?' Trudeau replied that he didn't. 'That's okay,' Izzy replied, pouring himself a generous splash of raw gin. 'We call these 'Prairie martinis'—you know, 'Beefeater on the rocks.'"

Asper earned some of the credit for helping Manitoba sabotage the Meech Lake agreement. "How," he wrote in a private letter to Deborah Coyne, one of the accord's chief critics, "did 5,000 people get organized to sign on to speak at the public hearings that would have delayed Meech's passage; who created the Elijah Harper obstruction; and what, as I discussed with you on the phone at that time, was our back-up plan to talk out the clock if Elijah crashed, and we had to knock off the June 23 deadline? The performance of a lot of people and a lot of institutions, not to mention the terrorists of the Canadian business Establishment, needs to be reviewed in this affair."

There was one more political disillusionment in store for Asper, and since it was not witnessed by any journalist, it never surfaced in the public prints, but it must have been devastating all the same. He had supported Jean Chrétien, publicly and privately, before and after

Chrétien won the Liberal crown, and he usually hosted the annual Winnipeg prime ministers' dinners, which were really regional Liberal fundraisers but which became important social occasions.

At one of the last of these involving the Shawinigan politician, Asper was anxious to pin down the PM about the details of the tax treatment on donations to private foundations, and used the pre-dinner reception to corner Chrétien and make his case. It was a semi-public venue, in that most of the guests were lining up for their private turns with the guest of honour. "I vividly remember Mr. Asper cornering Chrétien as he was circulating around the room and trying to bend his ear for the thirty seconds that he had with him," recalled a Canwest executive who overheard their exchange. "I thought that Mr. Asper could have had Chrétien's time for as long as he wanted, but for whatever reason he wasn't willing to do that, and Mr. Asper stumbled across Chrétien as they were going in to dinner. After he had made his case, the prime minister looked at him very coldly, not even making eye contact, put a hand on his arm and said in a flat, bullying tone, 'Izzy, you have enough money'— and just walked away from him. Mr. Asper acted composed, and as he looked at those of us standing around him, he winked. But you knew then and there that a line had been crossed and that things were going to be different going forward. This hadn't happened in private, and it was an affront—it was as big an affront as Chrétien could have delivered to Mr. Asper at the time."

As he drifted away from the Liberals, Asper explored some of the wilder shores of Canadian politics. On July 21, 1993, he met with Preston Manning and was impressed enough to donate $5,000 to the Reform Party and write part of its platform. "I don't think he ever helped Stephen Harper financially, but he tried to help him intellectually," his friend Don Johnston recalled. "Izzy pulled out all the stops on that one. He was prepared to invest his personal time and capital for the cause. He was quite a guy." Perhaps his true political label was earned only during his Global TV phase, when he became a confirmed CRTC Liberal.

Having already abandoned the practice of law, and now having turned away from politics, Izzy Asper faced a mid-life crisis. "It was my second turning point," he lamented. "Having spent all the profit I made from the distillery on living and election expenses, I was, yet again, out of work and out of money." It was time to get serious.

5

The Merchant Bank Caper

"I have been betrayed by everyone—Gerry, the board. The relationship is finished. They have taken the crown jewel. So I told them let's wind it up and sell everything. It was the most stressful time of my life."
—Izzy Asper, after the forced sale of Monarch Life

Somebody was always lecturing Israel Asper, patiently trying to explain why he couldn't do something that he had just finished doing.

Izzy would sit there, trying to stay awake, going along with the gag, never bothering to remind his well-intentioned mentor that in his book, the arcane rules by which Canada's business elite played didn't apply. "We're nowhere near where we want to go," he boasted about Canwest Capital, the Winnipeg-based merchant bank he launched in 1977 with Gerry Schwartz as his full partner.

It was the chairman of one of the Big Five Canadian Banks who took Israel aside one day to explain how things worked—to interpret for him how the circles of corporate power in Canada limit access and spread privilege. In a series of carefully drawn tableaux, he pointed out that Asper belonged to Dick Thomson's coterie because it was his bank, the Toronto-Dominion, that financed his first several ventures, and that he had made similar arrangements with the federally sponsored Canada Development Corporation that signified certain things. It meant that he should shy away from Conrad Black's then princely financial retinue (which dealt only in large sums and big words) and refrain from cozying up to Power Corporation, the regal Montreal conglomerate which fell into Paul Desmarais' rarefied and sophisticated sphere of influence.

Presenting his august profile, fit for a Roman coin, the chairman explained the subtle differences between wealth and power, between influence and control, between a country's monetary climate and its fiscal meteorology. There had to be an order of precedence, rules to follow, seniority to be observed—as in any other exclusive hierarchy.

Izzy just sat there with the besieged air of innocence of a pilgrim at Lourdes, not bothering to point out to the bank chairman that Jim Burns, then president of Great-West Life, had been the first to support his Canwest venture and had purchased a goodly slice on behalf of his corporate parent, Power Corporation. Burns, who prided himself as being an unreconstructed Tory, guffawed as he signed up. "Sure, we'll take 10 percent of your company, Izzy—it's worth a $2 million investment to see whether a Liberal like you knows how to make money, because you Liberals sure know how to squander it!"

At the same time, Conrad Black had already sold Asper one of the gems of his Argus empire, Crown Trust, and was actively helping to expand its roster of clients. The dissertation rolled on, with the bank chairman explaining to Izzy how to fit in with the country's *machers* should he be fortunate enough to catch their attention, perhaps even attract a sliver of investments out of whatever backwoods reserve fund they maintained for the occasional flyer on some guy—any guy in a presentable suit—from Winnipeg.

The big pooh-bah from Bay Street ended his sermon by asking what right Asper and his partners had to call their Red River Rocket a "merchant bank," pointing out that this was a distinguished trademark of London's privately owned prime financial institutions, nestled along Threadneedle Street, where discreet money was courted behind daffodils in window boxes and whispered about aboard biscuit-coloured Bentleys driven up from Kent and Surrey. Those were *real merchant banks.*

Izzy just shrugged, broke into a beatific smile and replied, "We called ourselves a merchant bank because it was a pretty name and nobody knew what the hell it meant."

At times like that, Izzy's mind slipped back to a certain day in August of 1978 when he was resting in his room at Vancouver's Four Seasons Hotel, immobilized by a migraine headache. He happened to glance at a two-day-old *Globe and Mail* to read that Conrad Riley's bid for control of Monarch Life, a seventy-two-year-old insurance company that was Winnipeg's last remaining locally controlled financial head office, was about to be topped by several out-of-town offers. Asper telephoned Riley, a Prairie patriot who by chance was Conrad Black's uncle and who was also a Monarch director and its chairman, and discovered he had no plans to raise his price against any outside bidders. He then called Brigadier General Richard Sankey Malone, OBE, ED, chairman of FP Publications, which had a 20 percent interest in the life insurance company, to register his strong emotions about not "seeing all our decent stuff get bought up," and inquired whether FP's block was committed. Malone, a pusser military type and a confidant of Sir Winston Churchill's who had beaten Hemingway into Paris on Liberation Day in August 1944, clicked his heels and agreed not to back other bidders.

Asper sat there, temples pounding, while a fragment of dialogue from *Anatomy of a Murder* flashed through his mind. In the movie, James Stewart, who played the defence attorney, blames his client's "irresistible impulse" for compelling him to commit the crime. Izzy felt precisely that way about Monarch Life: it was no crime, but he damn well had to keep Winnipeg's last major corporate entity out of the hands of some blowhard vulture capitalist from foreign parts.

That was a Thursday. He flew home and spent Friday studying the company's financial details, then drove out to his cottage at Falcon Lake. Harold Thompson, Monarch's president, had a summer place nearby, so Asper went over to find out exactly where the bidding stood. Thompson explained that a voting trust agreement that had kept the company from becoming a takeover target was about to expire, and that in addition to the $55-a-share offer from Riley, the Toronto-based Eaton Bay Financial group would be coming in with a $57.50 bid, while Sam Belzberg, the bold and brawny investor from Vancouver, was floating an even higher price. The deadline was 1 p.m. Monday.

Izzy rushed back to his cottage, telephoned around to contact members of his board and tried to find a lawyer who could draw up a binding bid. He couldn't raise anybody. His house was beginning to fill with guests who had been invited for the weekend. His partner, Gerry Schwartz, was in Marion, Ohio, on business but agreed to fly back immediately. The two stayed up most of Sunday night, working in the basement of Asper's cottage while a party tinkled on upstairs without them. By 4 a.m. they had decided to enter the bidding contest for Monarch at $61 a share and had drafted an impressive-looking offer. On Monday morning they drove back to town. Izzy contacted as many Canwest directors as he could find, then went to meet the Monarch board. Schwartz, meanwhile, called on Great-West's Jim Burns, then one of the country's shrewdest insurance executives. Before their bid could be accepted, it had to be approved by the superintendent of insurance in Ottawa. It took until noon for Burns and Schwartz to clear that obstacle. By 12:10 Schwartz was able to telephone Asper that it was a "go," so that he could present their bid to Monarch's executives. The offer was accepted on the spot even though Sam Belzberg's entry (at $63 a share) was due to arrive at any moment.

At this point, Izzy and Gerry had managed to obtain control of Monarch and its $350 million in hard assets for a bargain basement price of $33 million. But one small problem remained: they had neither the cash nor the credit to pay for it. All they had was an expression of "warm feelings" about the deal from the TD Bank, whose CEO, Dick Thomson, had attended Kelvin High School in the 1940s with Izzy and Babs. The TD chairman authorized a modest Canwest loan. In the following five days, Gerry Schwartz put a financial package in place that allowed the firm to sew up the deal for an astonishingly low $2 million cash down payment. That set the pattern for future negotiations: Izzy would be the animator and noisy front man; Schwartz, the backstage negotiator who made the deals possible.

"What the Monarch purchase did for us," Asper declared, "was to send out the message that we were serious. It gave credence to me, to our board and to our company. Before that it was still an open-ended question whether the money boys would support us or would say that it was okay for us to buy hot-dog stands but not life insurance companies."

Ever the gentleman, Conrad Riley stayed on the Monarch board for another two years, retiring in 1981, when he felt that the policyholders had been properly protected and the shareholders were in good hands. But the bold Asper-Schwartz takeover of a company that Izzy described as "the pristine bastion of the WASP Establishment of Winnipeg" sent shockwaves through the city's upper crust. Power was being transferred to an exotic new strain of bravura entrepreneurs who had bulled their way into contention while the slumbering stalwarts at the Manitoba Club never noticed. "Izzy's quite a fellow," Riley commented after leaving the Monarch board. "He's just like spilled mercury—got a million ideas."

The arrival in the big time of Messrs. Asper and Schwartz signalled the birth of a bold Prairie-oriented elite that mutated to fit the times. The Monarch acquisition marked a significant turning point in Asper's career and in his relationship with Schwartz. At the first Monarch directors' meeting that they were invited to attend as dominant shareholders, Izzy and Gerry playfully announced that they intended to raise the firm's morale by having employees start the day by singing the new Monarch hymn. They picked "Oyfn Pripitchik," a Yiddish folk song from Eastern Poland that weaved in and out of the epic *Schindler's List* soundtrack.

———————

Asper's direct partner, the only one he ever had and who quickly became his alter ego, was not the same Gerry Schwartz who had joined his law firm as a neophyte articling student back in 1963. He had left the firm and Winnipeg in 1968 to take an MBA at the Harvard Business School and, later, to work on some of Wall Street's most sophisticated trading floors.

While studying at Harvard, Schwartz operated a chain of carpet stores in Winnipeg, Calgary and Edmonton and used to fly up on weekends to take care of business. Peter Herrndorf, the CBC guru and National Arts Centre godfather, who attended Harvard at the same time, remembered bumping into him at the business school library. While everyone else was studying case histories, Gerry was tweaking his companies' current cash flow statements.

One of the advantages Schwartz enjoyed at Harvard was running the business school's Speakers Club. That gave him the chance to meet Bernie Cornfeld, the Turkish-born former social worker in New York who had become the high-flying head of Investors Overseas Services, which, before its spectacular collapse in 1971, operated the world's largest group of mutual funds (worth more than US$2.5 billion), with 85,000 sales people on its payroll. The youthful Gerry made such a strong impression that Cornfeld offered him a summer job in Geneva. "Bernie looked like a little rabbi from Philadelphia," Schwartz recalled. "He knew nothing about business, knew nothing about finance, but he knew everything about what motivates individuals and what they most fear. He was Rasputin-like and could transfix you with his eyes, as if he was looking right into you. It was an eye-opener to see how a lot of these big shots humbled themselves to Cornfeld. I shared his office, and accompanied him on every trip he took—every place he went, he took me with him. It was fun, and the people I met were unbelievable."

Like the time Schwartz was sent to Rome aboard the IOS jet so he could meet with a cardinal in one of the hallowed reception chambers at the Vatican to dispense financial advice to the Holy See. Or another time, when the most coveted of smuggled goods appeared in Geneva. "I remember going out to the airport to meet Charles Bluhdorn, chairman of Gulf and Western. When we arrived back at the IOS mansion, Bluhdorn put his briefcase out on his knees, and Cornfeld said, 'Well, Charlie, did you bring it?' Bluhdorn grinned and brought out not one but two giant salamis from a New York deli. Bernie hugged him and danced a little jig of joy."

Schwartz was grateful to his mentor, but not to the point of emulation. "I was the young dauphin," Schwartz recalled. "I had the run of the place. What became increasingly clear was that Cornfeld took a blithely reckless approach to the funds in his care. IOS wasn't a scam, but it was unbelievably badly managed. There were no budgets, no controls, no anything, because so much money was coming in that they were always ahead of the game. We used to have dinner at the beautiful chateau that Napoleon had originally built for Josephine on Lake Geneva, and Bernie always had four or five girls living in the house who were available to anybody.

"There were usually three or four business people in town who we entertained in a constant round of big dinners, a party every night. The scene could get sickening," Schwartz complained. "One night, I was sitting there and had my feet up, just watching the goings-on, and thought to myself, 'This is really stupid.' I stood up and walked out the back door and headed to the office, because I had left my car there. A light misty rain was falling, and I'm walking on the gravel at the side of the road when I hear this crunch, crunch behind me. I turn around and there's Bernie. He puts his arm on my shoulder, walks me back to the office and says, 'I know you hate this.'

"Everybody asked," Schwartz later recalled, "didn't I regret being in that den of thieves? I didn't regret a minute of it. I had a great time, met some fabulous people and learned a lot. I guess what I realized most was that the big-time stuff takes place the same as everything else, and that nobody is better than anyone else."

After graduating from Harvard, Schwartz moved to New York, where he eventually became vice-president of corporate finance for Bear, Stearns & Co. (when it was still a Wall Street heavyweight), which meant practising the fine Italian art of leveraged buyouts. Leveraged buyouts have been characterized as trading the short-term expectations of your stockholders for the short-term expectations of your bankers. Technically, they involve the purchase of an undervalued company by a small group of investors financed largely—even 90 percent—by debt, the cost of which is borne by the acquired company, either from its treasury or by selling off its assets. Properly executed, LBOs are as close as you can legally get to a perpetual money machine, because you grow by using somebody else's money. In other words, they are the corporate equivalent of that country-and-western ditty about becoming "your own grandpa."

At this point Israel Asper was spending much of his spare time in New York searching for the ultimate jazz sounds, under the pretext of hunting for business opportunities. He and Gerry would enjoy those pleasurable musical outings, which occasionally turned stressful because of the two men's widely divergent musical preferences. Schwartz's tastes were eclectic, ranging from Vivaldi 'n' Haydn to country 'n' western. "One of the banes of my existence," he complained at the time, "was Izzy dragging me from jazz joint to jazz joint. I was always trying to corral him into the Lone Star Cafe to hear some country music, but it was quite a battle. During one trip to Manhattan with Izzy and Babs, we ran into Martin Freedman and his wife, Roxy, who loved country music as much as I did. So we split up—we went to the Lone Star and Izzy went off to some jazz dive. At five in the morning we picked him up and he was the only guy left in the place, completely mesmerized by some zonked-out piano player.

We drove back to the hotel and were completely exhausted. But Izzy started in on the cab driver, insisting that there's gotta be some place left open. So we got out and Izzy disappeared, off to Greenwich Village to see if there was *one* more jazz spot that he hadn't closed."

They also talked shop, searching for something entrepreneurial to engage their talents. Asper only had one precondition—that whatever he did would not involve his having to move away from Winnipeg. They hit upon the idea of launching a Western-based "merchant bank," a description that, like the term "postmodern," sounded good but meant nothing or everything, depending on the disposition and refinement of the beholder. "I remember when we were planning to create Canwest, we went down to Scottsdale, Arizona, to the tennis range, and were supposed to take tennis lessons every day," Schwartz recalled. "Instead, we sat around the pool and dreamed up what we were going to do and what we were going to become. We used to have a code name for how big and grand we would be. 'CP' was what we would whisper to each other. CP stood for Canadian Pacific, which at that time was a really great company that we intended to take over. The only time we played tennis was at the end of the day. In my opinion, we were both hopeless tennis players. Fortunately, neither of us was much more hopeless than the other, so we would stage these epic battles that would go on until finally the sun would go down and we couldn't keep playing."

In tennis as in business, Schwartz is a paradoxical combination of ruthless energy and inner calm. His favourite literary quotation is from Blaise Pascal, the seventeenth-century philosopher: "It has struck me that all men's misfortunes spring from the single cause that they're unable to stay quietly in one room." He may be more flamboyant than that, but he advises business associates—at Canwest and later at his own outfit—not to jump at buying companies, lecturing them against the notion that "just because we've got money to spend doesn't mean we've got to find something to buy." The maxim he coolly preaches is that you're usually sorrier for the mistakes you make than you are happy for the great deals you conclude.

During their New York sojourn the two men became close friends. "Besides being great business partners and liking each other, we had wonderful times together. We'd go to New York on business and go down to the Village and listen to some music and then go somewhere else to drink, and before you knew it, it was four in the morning and we were making our way home and agreed, 'We're not leaving tomorrow.' So we'd cancel everything we had planned for the next day and go walking in Central Park instead. Those are just things you do with a friend, not with people who are simply business." Izzy felt the same way.

On January 17, 1977, Asper and Schwartz received a federal charter to set up Canwest Capital Corporation. Its structure reflected an intriguing marriage between institutional financiers and freelance entrepreneurs, with the former putting in most of the money but the latter making most of the decisions. Investors pledged themselves to stay in for ten years without taking out dividends, though results were monitored annually. By 1987, if they had done spectacularly well, Asper and Schwartz would be rewarded with 20 percent of the stock. What gave the concept momentum was George Richardson's decision to lend his personal and corporate prestige to the new venture by putting forward his company as Canwest's fiscal agent and unofficial sponsor. Both partners were constantly shopping around for more acquisitions, hunting down companies with an established present and a promising future. "If you don't keep moving," said Asper, "you get passed by. You have to run to stay still." At times, twenty potential deals a day would arrive at their offices, but very few made the cut.

As in several of Izzy's ventures the main burden of the initial fundraising rested with Arni Thorsteinson, a Winnipeg self-starter with the best financial connections in Western Canada. (He and his wife, Susan Glass, who was a driving force behind the Royal

Winnipeg Ballet, relaxed by spinning toward the flat horizon of Prairie evenings aboard their Heritage Softail Harleys.)*

"In his myriad pursuits, public and private, Israel Harold Asper has always maintained the precipitous incline of a man tuned to the faint footfall of destiny," wrote Ted Allan, the Red River Valley's talented Tom Wolfe, at the time. "Triumphant and trampled—and he's been both—he holds to the absolute belief of his divine right to graze the common of conventional success. His lamentable years as leader of Manitoba's moribund Liberal party firmly buried in the detritus of his curriculum vitae, Izzy Asper, having burned through another half-dozen careers like a scalded dog, seems finally to have settled on his calling. At 45, with the same hard, obsidian determination and cheerful *chutzpah* that characterized his previous passages, he's put a million dollars of his own money where his mouth has always been and become a Prairie expansionist."

Guided by Asper's dynamism and fuelled by Schwartz's negotiating and money-raising skills, by the summer of 1981 the young firm had corralled assets that exceeded $2 billion, with sales revenues of $700 million. The financial division came under the direct supervision of Donald Payne, a former executive vice-president of finance and administration at the Bank of Montreal, but nearly all the major policy decisions were made by

---

*The founding investors in the $20 million fund (soon raised to $50 million), other than Asper, Schwartz and Thorsteinson, were the Canada Development Corp. (35 percent), the Toronto-Dominion Bank (10 percent) and Great-West Life (10 percent), with the balance divided among Paul Morton, whose family owned the Odeon movie-house chain in Winnipeg; Sydney Kahanoff, founder of Voyager Petroleum; Aaron Shtabsky, an Edmonton lawyer who was Izzy's cousin; Ted Riback, an Alberta energy investor; and Jack Wigen of Wynndel Lumber Sales, representing a group of BC investors (Wigen was later replaced by Harold Zlotnik). There were actually at least fifty financial sources contacted by Izzy and Gerry, who treated them to a full briefing, before they found any takers. It was a real test of what makes a successful entrepreneur, like not taking no for an answer.

Schwartz and Asper—well, actually, Asper and Schwartz. In addition to Monarch Life, Canwest's acquisitions included Crown Trust; Canreit Advisory Corp.; the 526-store Macleod-Stedman chain, purchased in partnership with Dick Bonnycastle; Na-Churs International (liquid fertilizers); and Aristar Inc., a Miami-based financial services company whose holdings consisted of Blazer Financial Services and John Alden Life Insurance, representing combined assets of $750 million.

Schwartz put to good use his training as a leveraged buyout specialist and Olympic-class deal maker. He negotiated the purchase of 51 percent of Aristar (worth $103 million) for a down payment of only $5.1 million. Similarly, he structured the $24 million Na-Churs buyout for an initial layout of less than $3 million. He and Izzy kept referring to Canwest as a merchant bank, but what they were really running was a holding company with hands-on operational responsibilities (*their* hands). "In terms of each of our subsidiaries," Schwartz explained, "Canwest runs the company and management runs the business. Maybe that's a bit of a distinction without a difference, but it makes the point that we don't just monitor our investments the way most holding companies do and that we participate in decision making at a board level and not at an operating level." The two partners formed a near-perfect team, though their high-octane enthusiasm made it impossible to tell which one was holding the other back. "We spent eighteen hours a day in each other's company and did everything except sleep together," Schwartz reminisced. "We had adjoining offices and would shout at each other all day." (Shouting was their speciality. "You don't yell at your enemies, you yell at your friends," Izzy explained.)

Their most intriguing takeover was Crown Trust because it introduced them to its then proprietor, Conrad Black, who a quarter century later would sell his Canadian newspapers to Asper in what was the country's largest and most controversial media transaction. Bud McDougald, who was Conrad Black's predecessor, had run most of his deals through Crown, a captive trust company over which he exercised voting control from 1941 until his death in 1978.*

Black inherited Crown as part of his takeover of the McDougald estate, but he was never interested in running it. When he began shopping around for a buyer, his prime prospect was Reuben Cohen, the elegant financier from Moncton, New Brunswick, who had missed out in a previous deal with the McMartin estate and who by then owned 32 percent of the trust company's stock. Cohen and his partner, Leonard Ellen of Montreal, had visited Black in Palm Beach in January 1979, where the Argus chairman assured them that although he was not actively planning to auction off Crown, he would accept the highest offer. The Maritimer's suggestion of $41.50 a share struck Black as eminently fair, and he promised to warn Cohen if a more generous bid was received. David Radler, who was Black's partner, had become Crown's chairman and recognized its unrealized potential. He began to sound out Western investors— including Izzy Asper. During a cookout on June 23, 1979, at the Harbour Square condominium of Igor Kaplan, then Conrad's lawyer, everyone got giggly from an overdose of chicken teriyaki and

---

*Crown had assets of $1.33 billion and an interesting history. Bud's uncle, John McMartin, who was one of the original backers of the Hollinger gold mine in Timmins (which later donated its name to become Black's main holding instruments), left an estate so large that a separate trust company was established to handle its administration. McMartin's son Jack and his nephews Allen and Duncan showed little interest in business, so McDougald gradually took over the firm and in 1946 amalgamated it with Crown Trust. In addition to his own considerable holdings, McDougald voted the 26 percent of Crown still held by the McMartins, who eventually moved to Bermuda. The family became known for its off-centre characters. John McMartin's niece Melba once bought a sixty-four-carat diamond the size of a man's thumb joint but only wore its paste imitation. Her cousin Jack used to march into Montreal bars with his walking stick and calmly proceed to smash every bottle behind the counter. Weary bartenders let him enjoy himself because they knew they could charge him a flat $1,000 fee per performance. When Melba's brother Duncan was an RCAF instructor near Calgary during the Second World War, one Friday the pay packet failed to arrive, so he wrote a cheque to cover the station's payroll.

sake. In mid-party, Asper and Black reached a tentative agreement for Canwest to buy Crown Trust at $44 a share. Just before the $17.7 million sale (for 53.7 percent of the company) was finalized at a later meeting between the two of them, Kaplan excused himself, murmuring, "I have to call Monte"—implying that he required Conrad's elder brother's permission. Instead, this was a pre-arranged signal to send a last-minute message to Cohen, tipping him off to the higher offer. Cohen didn't believe Crown was worth that much and stuck with his $41.50 bid. Crown went to Canwest, and Black realized a profit of $4 million simply by holding the trust company for an extra year. But Canwest gained a financial and physical presence on Toronto's Bay Street, which it intended to exploit.

When they moved in to jointly occupy the chairman's office of Crown Trust, which up to then had been the stuffiest firm in a moribund industry, the partners had Mickey Mouse telephones installed.

Visitor to Schwartz: "What's the significance of the Mickey Mouse telephone?"

Schwartz to Visitor: "I do Mickey Mouse deals."

Izzy and Schwartz could have grabbed the opportunity to run with their first Bay Street acquisition; instead an unsolicited offer arrived from Leonard Rosenberg of Greymac Trust. Izzy was against accepting it, but the price was right. Rosenberg had simply told him to name his bottom line, which was $62 a share, for a total of $26 million—a profit of $8 million for the three-year hold. Suspicious of his buyer's generosity, Asper checked with the Ontario Securities Commission, but they had no adverse reaction to the deal. Shortly afterwards, Rosenberg began to fraudulently value the real estate he was flipping. He was eventually charged with seventy-eight counts of fraud and sent to jail.

At about this time, Gerry began spending an increasing portion of his time in Toronto instead of Winnipeg, courting the love of his life. His Winnipeg marriage was on the rocks, and on a visit to Montreal, in the office of Claude Frenette, a former president of the Quebec Liberal Party and a Global director, he met one of Frenette's senior associates, the glamorous Heather Reisman. A hundred days after that encounter they knew they would be married, and a thousand days later, they were. They decided to live in Toronto, but neither had family there at the time, so Izzy Asper offered to plan and pay for their wedding ($8,957.26), held on May 15, 1982.

It turned out to be an event to remember—or forget, if you happened to be one of the principals. Held in the top, panorama floor of the Four Seasons Hotel in two reception rooms large enough to accommodate the hundred guests, Asper had made arrangements with the comedy club Yuk Yuk's that while Gerry was introducing his bride from the back of the room, an actress who looked like a very, very pregnant peasant with rubber boots, babushka and horn-rimmed glasses would interrupt him, screaming in a thick accent, "Geraldo, Geraldo, look whatta you do to me. You promise we getta married." Standing at the front, right in the middle of the room, she spun around and gave a kick at the podium. Heather was not amused. Knowing Izzy, Gerry realized he was being had, but he took it well, and just laughed as his disillusioned "Transylvanian" bride was being escorted out, still loudly protesting his unfaithfulness.

Guests who hoped that this was the entertainment for the evening were disappointed. Dinner was next, and one of the menu options was veal. Just as dessert was being served, an ambulance pulled up to the hotel, and off the elevator came a gurney, on which languished a groaning victim tended to by concerned-looking paramedics accompanied by two distraught nurses. They pushed their patient right through the dining room, as one of the medics repeated an urgent plea, "Anyone else eat the veal? Who had the veal!" People dropped their cutlery and panic set in until the saner wedding guests realized this was more of Izzy's boisterous humour.

At the conclusion of the dinner, Asper invited everybody to take their drinks back to the reception area to watch Global's evening news, which of course turned out to be a satirical history of the betrothed couple. It ended with a fake news story about the Schwartz/Reisman reception at the Four Seasons and host Peter

Trueman saying something like, "There's a story, I think, that is happening right now at the Four Seasons Hotel. Gerry Schwartz, president of Canwest Capital Corporation, just got married, and now I take you directly to the Four Seasons." There followed a take-off on Quasimodo, the hunchback of Notre Dame, with hordes of people storming the gates of Paris, and an Izzy-like figure hitting them with rakes and shovels, shouting, "Take that you pushy, upstart shareholders!" He was next seen pouring boiling oil on the rioters. Trueman then reported that the marriage had been consummated. A rocket was seen taking off and a train puffed into a tunnel. At the conclusion there were pictures of the couple's summer home in the woods—a rusted, rotted old barn—which blew up. Gerry pronounced the coda: "Oh, that was a wonderful night, dear. How was it for you?" The guests, who by now felt comfortable in the groove of the event's outrages, went home feeling relaxed and happy that Izzy hadn't been involved in planning *their* nuptials.

Meanwhile, the recession and its 22 percent interest rates were seriously hurting Canwest's prospects, and by late 1983 the founding shareholders (who had done well, earning annual net returns of 27 percent) were being pressed for cash. At the same time, the Asper-Schwartz partnership was showing signs of serious strain. At the start of their venture, Schwartz had continued to play the role of Izzy s protégé, deferential and not quite equal in reputation or managerial heft. But as the financial deals and acquisitions became more complex and more lucrative, Schwartz came into his own, though he saw the world differently than his former mentor. Asper became obsessed with investing millions in a risky (dangerously so, as it turned out) pay-TV scheme in the United States—an idea too far ahead of its time. The venture seriously dented Canwest Capital's bottom line and placed at risk the cozy relations between the two managing partners.

Some of their private exchanges now echoed with white-hot

anger. After one especially vivid blow-up, Schwartz sent Asper a four-page handwritten note that concluded, "The other 'surrounding' issue that I want to deal with is the pressure on you. You and I can take unreasonable amounts of pressure better than almost anybody I know. In fact, we both tend to perform better in a crisis than otherwise. However, that ability shouldn't obscure what can be a real problem. I believe there has been a relationship between, on the one hand, your rages, disappointment with Canwest, anger with me, need to 'feel' your supremacy as 'boss,' frustration with Paul [Morton] and Seymour [Epstein] . . . and on the other hand, the time to time bleakness and possibility of failure in US-TV. Last night I reviewed in my own mind what I understand to be the problems of USTV. I think they are staggering and immediate; while Boston looks great and the STV concept looks good as ever, our entry into the field is beset with such real difficulties that everything is threatened. I presume that you have some realization plus the frustration of having to live with it. I think there is a relationship between these problems and your tearing into me. I care about it because of how it affects me, but frankly I care about it more, right now, because of how it affects you—not as a partner but as a friend. There are other things than just our ability to work harmoniously that suffer. If you want to, let's talk about them."

Similarly, their divergent attitude to public relations caused a rupture. In a note dated August 18, 1981, after Gerry had given an unusually frank interview to *Pacific Western,* Izzy basically muzzled his partner, forbidding him to make any more public statements about Canwest's affairs: "Rod Zimmer happened to have a copy of the interview you gave Pacific Western and gave it to me for my comments," Asper wrote Schwartz. "I tried to reach you but you were on your trip. I have never been more amazed. It probably is the worst piece of PR I have ever seen on Canwest, or for that matter, on any other company, and if it is published, as written, it does more damage than any piece of good PR we have, ever had. It ranges from insulting to arrogance. I would love to have killed the entire article, but that was impossible, but I have asked Rod Zimmer to see if he can take out the most offensive aspects in an effort to protect reputations. Even if the most offensive material comes out, there will still be enough damaging material to set back our program of trying to create a refined image. The article and its tenor feeds exactly the image that we are seeking to avoid—glib, slick, smart-alecky and egotistic.

"It is clear to me that dealing with the media is simply not your bag, and therefore I must insist that you give no more statements to the media about Canwest's affairs. I have no objection to anything you want to do on a personal basis, but I do not want anything said which characterizes, describes or reflects on Canwest." His tough love was getting tougher.

Canwest's problems were all too easy to personalize as an accelerating feud between its principals, but the underlying cause was more profound and less fixable. Izzy's ambition had turned to television and to making a difference in the U.S. market. He thought he could accomplish both by jumping headlong into pay television's nascent American grazing grounds. The first step up from having rabbit ears mounted on their TVs, the existing technology would allow viewers to subscribe to a limited number of channels, as long as they were in line of sight from the transmitter. The matrix for a functioning pay-TV system wasn't in place—or had even been invented. Izzy had good people on the ground, mainly Harry Ethans and Yale Lerner, but they experienced serious trouble recruiting an American management team. It was too new a technology, launched at a time when insiders knew that cable TV distribution that would wipe out the primitive pay-TV system was in the works. Canwest's franchisers would install a box in a house in Boston, for example, at a cost of $250. In those days you couldn't turn it off. Once the person had possession of the box, they kept receiving the signal as long as they wanted. People would pay for two months then stop, but it cost too much to go out and get the boxes back. The vision for a new medium was there but the technology was not.

Izzy's first warning about the viability of his pioneering enterprise ought to have been some of the recruits to his crusade. Certainly there were some winners who came aboard, including Gerald Levin, who later became CEO of AOL Time Warner, but several others fit into the same category as "Mad Dog" Spiegleman.

When Izzy suggested that in order to secure Canwest's investments, the franchisees would have to place insurance on their lives made out in his favour, they flipped out, interpreting the move as Asper taking out a contract to have them rubbed out. A partner in the Boston franchise named Don Spiegleman was so upset that when he met with Harry Ethans to discuss the issue, "he hit the floor of this room we were in, started to froth at the mouth and actually began chewing the carpet. His senior partner and keeper, Byron Lasky, looked down and gently advised, 'Easy, Mad Dog, easy.'"

"Whether it was for theatrical effect or what have you, it was surreal," Ethans reminisced. "This guy was growling and grunting. I used to walk into the office when we were negotiating a deal and try to move things along. Spiegleman was already there. Each morning I'd say, 'Good morning, Don.' And he'd reply, 'Go fuck your hat'— every single day. That was the opening comment. Not 'How was your night's sleep?' or 'Have a coffee,' but 'Go fuck your hat.' So one day I walk in and I say, 'Good morning, Don,' and he says, 'Good morning, Harry,' and I said, 'What? You don't love me anymore?' His answer? 'Go fuck your hat.' It's a true story. He was a crazy guy but wildly intelligent. It was fun."

Eventually Mad Dog loosened up a bit and explained that his wife had to co-sign the personal guarantees because their house and everything else was in her name. Spiegleman told Ethans that he had bribed her with a $10,000 diamond bracelet. "'I've always had a sneaking hunch that my wife practises a subtle form of anti-Semitism,' Mad Dog speculated. 'She's broken every Heb she's ever been married to.' I thought Izzy was going to lose it he was laughing so hard. I didn't know how to react."

Izzy's contrarian stubbornness in not backing away from his TV dreams created animosities on Canwest's board and a showdown with Schwartz, his partner, who calculated that the pay-television caper had lost the company $40 million, and had to stop. At the same time, high interest rates and the downturn in energy prices triggered fierce cash demands among investors and board members. The only obvious solution was to sell off assets.

In that context, the firm's most saleable property was Monarch Life Insurance, and in 1983 the board voted to spin off Monarch to the U.S.-owned North American Life for $68 million, which yielded a profit of $36 million to Canwest's shareholders.

Asper, who alone cast a vote against the sale, was crushed. "The shareholders had all signed up for what was to have been a ten-year ride. They were supposed to leave us alone for ten years, and this was only year seven. We had told them, 'Give us the money you are prepared to lose and don't ask any questions. Come to board meetings, we certainly are responsive, we will listen to you, but we get a ten-year run. It was a no-cut contract, and we laid out exactly what we were going to do."

He philosophized, after he had calmed down a bit (though not much), "To be able to sell a good business is a piece of cake. But to replace it is dynamite. I just don't have the same level of confidence that I can redeploy capital as profitably, as effectively as my colleagues did. They wanted to take their profits out of Canwest. All through this period, I just sat there shaking my head at people who wanted to realize their profit. They would have the pleasure of paying a huge capital gains tax and then having to find something comparable."

Schwartz told it differently. "The sale of Monarch wasn't a loose event," he emphasized. "The TD Bank was pushing us very hard to pay back the loans in the holding company for the investment we'd made in the U.S. pay-television business, which was disastrous. It's true that Izzy and I didn't agree, but it was more a matter of what we each wanted to do with our lives than how we wanted to run the business. The board had kind of lost faith in management's ability to run the company because those TV losses were just mounting every week. Once we made the decision to sell Monarch, which Izzy opposed and I supported, that was the end. But the actual sale of Monarch was simply a *result* of all those other things; it wasn't the triggering event."

Gerry regarded the sale of Monarch strictly as a profitable business decision, and even if his relationship with Izzy was seriously strained, he saw no reason or purpose in allowing it to wreck their friendship. "I knew him better and I loved him more," Schwartz maintained. "Our business affairs were highly intertwined in a complex way, and undoing that is never easy. It was a difficult time and we had to work that through. People just assumed that because we parted company we had to have bad blood. I know that for my part there was never a time I didn't love Izzy. And I will stand on my grave to tell you that I believe there was never a time Izzy didn't love me. He was bigger than life."

One insurmountable obstacle was built into the partnership from its inception. Izzy was clearly the senior partner in the mix, having hired Schwartz as a student and having spent an extra decade building his national reputation as a tax lawyer and *Globe* columnist. That ought not to have ranked Schwartz as a junior appendage—yet he often felt that he was being treated as such.

In a memo dated November 12, 1976, when Asper had set out the brief that he was the leader and that there could only be one, Schwartz replied, "I agree with your conclusion that the most important thing for us to discuss is the modus operandi. This is as critical to me as it is to you. I am concerned not only with how we will run our deals, the level of our personal involvement and other such business aspects, but also with our relationship with each other in executing our plans. As you know, our relationship started out as equal partners. We agreed on some financial differences and on your right to make the final decision on certain matters in order to take into account your present earnings level and track record, which is more mature and significant than mine. On the other hand, I felt, and still do, that our relationship was to be marked as that of equal partners. I am perfectly happy to make the accommodations with you that have been agreed upon in order to reflect our differing status, but I want to make sure that you see our present relationship as I do; that is to say, that we are equally and together setting forth on this venture and will be constantly and consistently working for the betterment of our mutual position rather than each fending on our own. I don't doubt for a moment that you bring many things to the formation of our new venture which can be viewed as being of more importance than my contributions. These are, hopefully, accommodated by our differing financial arrangement and your casting vote. The fact is, however, that I don't think the situation is quite as one-sided as you outlined."*

The situation presented an insoluble dilemma because, on the one hand, at that point Canwest and its investors felt justified in demanding their money back; on the other hand, they had pledged not to cash in their chips prematurely and keeping Monarch Life was clearly in the company's long-term interest. "There were a lot of similarities between Gerry and Izzy," pointed out Scotiabank chairman Rick Waugh, who was involved in the situation. "So when they didn't agree, they tended to have a degree of inflexibility—not that either one of them was necessarily wrong, but they were convinced that their way was the chance to achieve what they were going to do. Asper had once said, 'Your horse is the strategy' and kept going at it,

---

*Canwest's Management Fee Income schedule for the two equal partners (in terms of their equity holdings) was almost comically complicated, so that it was difficult to determine who was receiving the larger payout: "On the first $200,000 of Management income, $125,000 goes to Asper and $75,000 to Schwartz; on the next $75,000 of Management income $50,000 goes to Asper, and $25,000 to Schwartz; the next $25,000 beyond that of Management income goes directly to Schwartz; and thereafter any additional Management fees are split on the basis of 40% to Asper and 60% to Schwartz, until the effect of that formula is to give them equal income. Thereafter, everything is split on a 50/50 basis."

and Gerry felt somewhat along those same lines. Two great successes and they were both right. There's no loser in that. They had their personal breakup, which was unfortunate, but in terms of where they wanted to go they were both right."

Izzy maintained a harsher view of their split: "The dichotomy in business objectives had become overwhelming, at a given point compelling a breakup. Two guys wanted to go in different directions. There was no point arguing with each other. That's what divorces are for."

Asper was as angry as he ever became in a business setting. Canwest Capital's shareholders were given the choice of taking out their winnings and investing them in Schwartz's new enterprise or leaving the company, along with Asper. "Monarch to me was a jewel, and it could have been developed into another Great-West," Izzy lamented. "I had been betrayed by everyone—Gerry, the board. The relationship was finished. They had taken the crown jewel. So I told them, let's wind it up and sell everything, except the television, because I had brought that in separately. I was terribly burned by the Monarch issue; it was the most stressful time of my life." But when North American Life bid for Monarch at a price that gave the partnership a cash gain of $36 million on a $2 million investment four years earlier, Izzy was voted down by his own board, 9 to 1.

For Gerry too, the post-Canwest period had its sad moments, but he also knew that he needed to be on his own in order to come into his own. He invested $2 million of his Monarch winnings into establishing Onex Corporation, a new-style conglomerate that was really a private but publicly listed equity firm and that eventually became the largest on the continent. He recruited a high-octane staff who revered him for the Zen calm at his core as he pulled off some of Canada's most lucrative deals. "There's no question that Gerry has a very, very soft centre, wrapped in lots of layers of insulation that create a legitimate interface between the essence of his emotions and what he's experiencing—the barrier between feelings and knowing," commented his wife, Heather, the proprietor of the mega-bookstore chain, Indigo, that saved Canadian publishing. "From a business point of view, the value of that interface is that while he's always processing at an intellectual level, he never seems bogged down by an emotional reaction to something which could in any way deter his intelligent judgment in strategic situations. His outward lack of emotion prevents outsiders from sharing his vulnerabilities, so that he comes off as being much more cerebral than he really is." If that seems an oddly analytical way for one soulmate to describe another, consider the source. At first glance, Heather Reisman seems soft and shy. She is not. She is whip smart, fiercely ambitious, and constantly testing herself. She profoundly loves her "Gerr" but is very much her own woman. She is quick and proud to say of her husband, "When he's doing business, his emotions never get in the way."

That was the essential difference. Unlike his partner, Izzy took the Monarch dispersal personally, as a rejection not only of his dream, but of him. "I've never been so wounded, despondent, almost suicidal in my life," he recalled nearly a quarter century later. "That was my big break with Gerry. I couldn't believe it. When he threw his vote in to sell, that was the rupture of our relationship, because to me it was a violation of what we had agreed to do. The only thing that makes me mad at anybody is when he or she wastes my time, because it's all I've got. And here I'd spent seven years building this thing, only to see it unravel." He was equally heartbroken by Arni Thorsteinson's defection, and kept muttering, "*Et tu,* Arni . . . Why did you do it?" His veteran supporter explained, "You were going to lose anyway, so there was no point in dividing the board . . . Even in hindsight it was probably the right decision—I shouldn't say the right decision—it was a reasoned decision." (In the end, Arni cast his vote against his old friend but divided his investment evenly in the ventures of the two former partners—as did Duncan Jessiman and Ray Williams.) All of the investors received a 27 percent cumulative annual return on their money—a killing by any definition.

Izzy never got over it. He had been firmly convinced that Monarch could have become as large and powerful as Great-West Life, and could have elevated him—and Winnipeg—into Establishment contention. Instead, the new owners not only turned a great Canadian financial institution into a feckless branch plant but later sold the building to the Workers Compensation Board of Manitoba. Izzy was again inconsolable: "I had already bought two city blocks from Broadway right back to the next two streets because I envisioned a monumental head office. That was fifteen years ago, and those blocks in the heart of Winnipeg are parking lots. I was planning the design, a spectacular atrium that would have made the Trump Towers look like slums."

The wound was psychic but its effects were physical. Asper's heart—and this was very much a matter of the heart—which had been in bearable shape despite all the martinis and Craven A's, suffered the consequences. He was visiting Gerry in 1983 when it hit. "Izzy and I were in Toronto and I don't recall what we were doing there, but I remember we were walking from place to place and Izzy was getting more and more and more out of breath," Schwartz recalled. "I just literally and physically almost had to carry him with one arm under his shoulder and around his back and lugged him back to the hotel. I didn't think he was going to make it. He flew home that night and the next day he was in the hospital." Within hours of returning to Winnipeg, Israel Asper suffered a massive heart attack that required a quadruple bypass.

While he was recovering but still in pain, he flew to Sarasota in Florida along with his friends and executives Harry Ethans and Yale Lerner. They vividly recalled the pledge Izzy made to himself, as he pronounced Canwest Capital's epitaph. "I will never," Asper declared through clenched teeth, "ever, place myself in the position again where someone can outvote me. From now on, I will stay strictly independent."

6

To Hell and Back: Building the Television Networks

"If you are tenacious enough, you can do whatever you set
out to do. Because all you need is more determination
than the guys who are trying to stop you."
—Izzy Asper, 1997

Since the advent of the Internet and especially of eBay, auctions have become a way of life. Bidders are mesmerized by bargains and opportunities, enthralled by the thrill of the game, which becomes as compelling as the prize. But the auction that took place in the boardroom of the Richardson Building on the square formed by the juncture of Portage and Main streets in Winnipeg on Friday, December 14, 1989, made history. Two small anterooms accommodated the bidders and their advisers. At stake was ownership of Global Television, an invaluable property breach-birthed in bankruptcy, the object of a drawn-out, deadly vendetta between its hot-headed owners and of a court case that lasted almost as long and was almost as vicious—all leading to this day at this place that would decide a winner and a loser. There would be no Mr. In-Between.

"My life was on the line," Israel Asper, who was one of the contenders, later admitted. "And incidentally, Paul Morton and Seymour Epstein, the duo who had been running Global and were now determined to own it, also placed their lives on the table. Their future identities and investments were as intimately joined to the future of Global as mine."

This auction was about to decide whether Asper would become a benchwarmer or a serious player. At the time he had virtually nothing, and was risking everything. "When I joined Izzy in 1986, we were just unbuckling ourselves from the past," Tom Strike, his VP of finance, recalled. "If I had known better, I would have gone elsewhere, because we were technically bankrupt. If I had been a bit more sophisticated and had done my homework, I never would have come here, which would have been my undoing. In 1986, we had a piece of Global, a piece of CKVU, both of which we were fighting over, and CKND, which we were also fighting over."

It was showtime.

―――――――――

While a blizzard spread Arctic fury across downtown Winnipeg, both sides in the Great Auction arrived for their final showdown. The proceedings were supervised by a master of the court (Marilyn Goldberg), who stated the rules and directed the traffic. The auction started at 9:21 a.m. and was scheduled to go on until 11 p.m.— no meal breaks—and to proceed on the same timetable until the following Monday. Every thirty minutes the contenders would raise their signed bids, which would begin at $125,000,000, by a minimum of $2 million. This was high-stakes poker with Himalayan risks.

The toss of a coin would determine who went first. But none of these big-money types had any change. Finally, somebody liberated a loonie from the coffee-tray collection plate. "I see you have a loonie," Izzy Asper said to Seymour Epstein. "It is very symbolic of this process." Epstein replied, without a smile, that while one side of the coin had a clear impression of Elizabeth II's head, the obverse was the carving of a water bird that had both a head and a tail. Operating within the dark cloud of suspicion that had shrouded nearly every Global transaction for the past decade and had forced its directors to tape-record their board meetings so they wouldn't contradict one another about what they had been saying (actually, *shouting*), Seymour was hinting that Asper might deliberately misinterpret the coin toss. Izzy didn't even recognize the damn animal on the coin, which he described as "the Queen's pet swan." It was, of course, a loon—as in *loonie*. So much for Canada's national bird.

The bidding leaped directly from its $125 million debut by the Morton/Epstein duo to $205 million from Izzy's corner, an astounding $80 million gambit. There followed three big bumps of $24 million each plus several smaller notches that took the total to $328 million.*

"We've just passed one of my plateaus," Izzy announced to his inner circle. "Now, who the hell in their right mind would walk away from a straight and clear two hundred million dollars in cash?" The ensuing silence indicated that there were no walkers in the room. Stephen Gross, then Izzy's right-hand man, alone spoke out. "Not me," he said.

What the Epstein/Morton side never knew was that Izzy felt so confident about winning that he whiled away most of the intervals between bids by signing Christmas cards—not the usual diversion for a proud Jew. His daughter, Gail, was the runner, delivering

---

*The raw figures are deceptive because, with 62 percent ownership of Global already in his pocket, Asper had to buy only the balance of 38 percent, while Morton and Epstein, who owned 38 percent, had to purchase the balance of 62 percent.

her father's offers to the court and bringing back the counter-bids. Three more bids moved the total to $336 million, and that turned out to be the moment of decision. Exactly one hour, one minute and twenty-six seconds after the auction had started, it was all over. Having exhausted their bank loans, the Global operators had reached their mezzanine level of financing, which represented a considerably more expensive debt assumption. That was why Seymour Epstein and Paul Morton chose this moment to take the money and run. They caved and signed their acceptances of Izzy's bid, then swaggered out of the building with a cool $150 million in their jeans.

Asper said nothing but took a little solitary walk, and the cadence of his gait told the story. He was prancing like a proud young buck cakewalking in the sun. At last the air was clear and he could begin to exploit Global his way. He had won because he couldn't lose, and he couldn't lose because he had been strategizing his tactics for four years, while his adversaries may not have probed deeply enough into the psychology of their obsessive opponent. It added injury to insult when the judge who had presided over the trial ordered Morton and Epstein to cover Asper's legal costs, which amounted to $1.37 million.

In the next fourteen years, Asper would build on this moment and create the country's third national TV network, though he could not, at this point in his journey, realize that doing so would be the equivalent of a harrowing pilgrimage to hell and back.

The auction itself had been a flash event—like the shootout at the O.K. Corral in the aptly named Tombstone, Arizona, which had actually lasted only thirty seconds. But history had been made here. The Asper people left the building with the same exuberant feelings as described by the American historian Garry Wills, who has immortalized the audience's reaction to President Abraham Lincoln's historic address at Gettysburg, on November 19, 1863. "They walked off," was his evocative line, "from those curving graves on the hillside, under a changed sky, into a new America." Izzy felt equally exuberant.*

Now that the auction was sealed, Asper began to reminisce about the past decade and a half—how he had morphed into television from politics, what had driven him to help save Global in the first place—and reliving the details of the toxic feuds that followed.

———————

Back in 1974, Israel Asper was in the process of extracting himself from Manitoba politics and the Liberal leadership—an experience not unlike the subsequent Global fiasco—and when Peter Liba, his executive assistant, saw a CRTC ad in the *Winnipeg Tribune* calling for submissions to open a third TV station in the city, Izzy decided to apply. His political sojourn had convinced him that the centre of the action was in the media, because they set the tone and climate in which everything happened, while their proprietors prospered. Since there was a scarcity of investment opportunities in the field, he created an off-beat but ingenious entry point into the business. He conceived the idea of buying on the cheap a U.S. border television station: KCND Channel 12 in Pembina, North Dakota, specifically set up to pirate Winnipeg TV commercial revenues, which were about to dry up. Frustrated with this tax dodge by American broadcasters who were circumventing Canadian regulations, the federal government was about to pass Bill C-58, which disallowed advertisers on these border-hugging stations from claiming tax credits, a move specifically aimed to drive the pirates six fathoms deep.

Asper decided to purchase the North Dakota operation and move it to Winnipeg, since it was going out of business anyway, but

———————

*The auction's combatants were not done with one another. The two groups were also joint shareholders in a company called Canwest Broadcasting Ltd., which owned CKND in Winnipeg and CKVU in Vancouver, as well as stations in Regina and Saskatoon. Morton and Epstein, who held 27 per cent, are still suing the Aspers for a payout on these and other Western Canadian operations. The feud continues.

first he had to convince its mega-wealthy owner, a Texan named Gordon McLendon, to sell. That was a tough assignment because McLendon was an evangelical free-enterprise fanatic, so right wing that he didn't believe governments had the right to print currencies, and would deal only in gold. He had all the assets (and gold) he needed, owned sixty radio stations and as many movie theatres, and was not impressed by the visiting Canadian. When Izzy went down to the Texan's several-thousand-acre ranch, he was invited to stay for dinner, which turned out to be a bonfire roasting an entire cow. The negotiations were not easy, but he persuaded his host that Ottawa's Bill C-58 would shut him down, and if that wasn't enough of a deterrent, Asper threatened that should McLendon persevere, Izzy would launch a competing Winnipeg station with identical programming and put him out of business anyway. Asper ended up paying $750,000 for the rig, but the Federal Communications Commission in Washington demanded that although the station was being moved, its transmitter must never shut down. The Asper people bought a used rattle-trap transmission tower in London, Ontario, gathered up what equipment they required in Pembina and made it to air in Winnipeg without a break. Crammed into an abandoned Safeway supermarket on St. Mary's Road, it was the cheapest Canadian TV station that ever became operational. With its call letters changed to CKND, it soon turned a profit.

Stan Thomas, who was Asper's chief lieutenant in getting the station launched, recalled a 1977 licence renewal hearing: "When a short, thin-faced CRTC staff bureaucrat mounted a large chart behind the CKND table, just prior to our opening remarks, our guys' heads kept craning around to see what the hell he was doing. It was a chart showing what promises had been made when our licence was awarded and what had been achieved in the interval. It was pretty devastating, and the roasting began. The result was a very short licence renewal and the determination not to get caught in that trap again."

This led to CKND's doing thirty-three hours of local programming a week. "Looking back on it," Thomas contended, "our credibility experienced a major shift forward when we won the contract to telecast Winnipeg's [NHL] Jets hockey games, converted CKND into Canada's first twenty-four-hour TV station mainly filled by running classic movies, and seriously extended original local programming. At the same time, we struggled to get the best U.S. shows and hit the jackpot with reruns of *M*A*S*H*." The popular American comedy that satirized the Korean War cost the fledgling station only $235 per episode, and at its peak CKND was selling thirty-second ads for $1,000, which created a $12,000 return for each thirty-minute show. Now, this was a business Izzy could believe in. CKND's greatest boast was that it knocked out the CBC's six-o'clock news as Winnipeg's most-watched program—by counter-scheduling *The Gong Show*, which was nothing more than institutionalized idiocy.

"I can recall a very good friend of mine who was a pretty wealthy guy, and we were chatting one day and he was saying, 'Oh gosh, Izzy's got the crazy idea of buying this TV station and it's down in North Dakota,'" recalled Lloyd Axworthy, a friend of Asper's and later president of the University of Winnipeg. "'He's offered me shares but I wouldn't touch it with a ten-foot pole.' It was known as 'Izzy's folly.' Later, there were a lot of people walking around this town checking their bank accounts, saying, 'I would be in a very different place if I'd listened to him.'"

Asper's move into television brought him into closer contact with Seymour Epstein, an electronics genius then trying to rescue the Global Television network from the deep financial trouble that had overwhelmed its troubled inception. Epstein had been plugging away since he was thirteen years old, when his father died soon after young Seymour's bar mitzvah. He began working in a Montreal haberdashery on weekends, storing away the insights he gained as a tie salesman while playing with electronic equipment in his spare time. He did so well in ties that he was able to collect spiffs, the bonuses given to hucksters who could sell difficult-todispose-of merchandise. "This is an unusual tie," he would say, "but you're an unusual person." Sold. He learned so well that by the time he reached Grade 11, he was managing the store. After graduating from McGill as an electrical engineer, and briefly working for RCA, he joined the CRTC in Ottawa, where he helped draft the regulations under which a third TV network was eventually mandated. Now he found himself floundering in Global's fall from grace, still owed $300,000 for his efforts in getting the station to air. He helped persuade Asper's Winnipeg group to join the Ivey-family-led IWC Communications conglomerate, headed by wealthy veteran radio producer Allan Slaight, to participate in its salvation. Epstein earned a 10 percent foothold in the package through sweat equity and became a pivotal figure in the $6 million Global resuscitation.

"My introduction to Global was a phone call from Israel Asper late in the spring of 1974, saying, 'Can you have an income debenture ready for me by next Tuesday?'" recalled Yale Lerner, who was just joining Izzy as his corporate legal counsel. "I didn't want to sound stupid so I said, 'Uh-huh.'

"'If you can't, don't worry about it,' he replied. 'I'll get Trevor Eyton to do it.'

"Because Trevor was acting for the other side I said, 'Oh no, Izzy, I'll get you a debenture.' I didn't know what it was, had never heard of such a thing. I got on the phone, called guys, and nobody was quite sure either. Finally I turned out about 120 pages of boilerplate contracts to have something to put in front of Izzy, because I didn't know him well at that time. But I knew that when he said Tuesday, it meant Tuesday. I thought he'd take the time to read it, but he never did. Anyway, the next thing I knew I was involved in the whole Global thing with him, creating the Winnipeg syndicate that structured its turnaround.

"I wouldn't say that Izzy planned for litigation when we did a deal, but it was certainly in the background that something might go wrong whenever you have a partner," Lerner mused. "So that was all structured into the Global deal. I like the old expression 'The devil's in the details,' though I prefer Ludwig Mies van der Rohe's version, 'God is in the details.' Detail bailed us out a number of times. We never failed to build in protections, and that's really, I guess, why I was as good as I was, because I'm no Asper, but I could think his way. I'm a very soft, mild guy. But when I acted for Izzy, I put on my mask. I became Zorro, somebody that nobody could recognize."

Global's new television operation was housed in a fancy building in a Toronto suburb, equipped with modern technology and deep-pile carpets. Founded by broadcasting entrepreneur Al Bruner, Global had been launched with great fanfare on January 6, 1974. By the ides of March it was bankrupt, its bank credits of $21 million exhausted. Describing the series of errors involved, Ed Greenspon, later editor-in-chief of the *Globe,* rightly called it "the biggest embarrassment in Canadian broadcasting history." As an inaugural incentive the CRTC had awarded Bruner the most generous licence in its history: the range of Global's repeaters covered most of Ontario (an audience of 7.5 million) instead of the city-wide permits usually granted. Bruner failed to recruit an adequate advertising sales staff (and had, in any event, missed being included in the year's ad budgets) and was so hopelessly disorganized that he was soon losing $50,000 a day—despite having several junior employees constantly touring the building to turn out lights and lower thermostats. His revenue budget was unrealistic; his expenditures side, unwarranted.

"I worked out of Toronto, spending the better part of the summer fighting with Eyton, to buy Global out of bankruptcy," Lerner recalled. "Richard Ivey of London, Ontario, whose family had founded Empire Brass, got the winning bid, but Izzy had somehow convinced the CRTC that it needed Western representation, and so they mandated that there be two owners. The London people didn't really need our money, which was just as well since we didn't have any.

Izzy put the deal together with Paul Morton, whose family owned the Winnipeg franchise for the fifteen-unit Odeon theatre chain. Paul had good contacts as president of the Winnipeg Blue Bombers. They pledged to raise $1 million locally, but when I was ready to make the deal in Toronto, we only had cash of $100,000 each from Izzy and Paul, so the rest of the million had yet to be raised, which Arni Thorsteinson took care of later. But I had a cheque for $1 million drawn on my trust account which still needed my signature, that I could flash around Toronto. This was the first time I had ever seen a million dollars. When I got to the Winnipeg airport, I was so nervous that I handed the lady at the counter the cheque instead of my ticket. We worked through the deal, but they hated us. They didn't want partners. Trevor never liked me, or Izzy. But I remember his law office, which was done up in British Admiralty chic, with hand-carved chairs, ancient charts and a telescope so that he could see across Toronto Harbour to the Royal Canadian Yacht Club, where his daughter was taking sailing lessons."

When Global got into serious trouble, Epstein persuaded the team of Asper and Morton, plus Allan Slaight, who headed the Iveys' IWC, to reorganize the company's assets and try to reverse its balance sheets. In this undertaking, it was just as well that Slaight, a veteran broadcaster who had once commanded Radio Caroline, the fleet of pirate radio stations transmitting into the United Kingdom, was also an amateur magician of international repute. Magic was exactly what Global needed.*

Under Slaight's management, costs were cut, controls were set in place and gradually the company turned around, though it was a close call. For example, Slaight told Bill Cunningham, his news dir-

---

*Unlike most magicians, Slaight disliked performing at private parties merely as a trickster; he preferred serious venues. At a party hosted by Anna and Julian Porter at their elegant Rosedale residence, Julian kept asking him to give the guests a sample of his magical skills, but Slaight steadfastly refused. Finally he asked the host if he had any scissors, which Julian promptly produced. Allan, just as promptly, cut off his tie, announcing to the gathered guests, "That's my trick for tonight."

ector, that he was about to cut his departmental budget in half but expected double the weekly output of news. "And the bugger did it for me," Slaight later conceded, with some surprise. The operation first broke even only forty-nine days before it ran out of money. But that didn't make it a happy ship; by mid-1976 the Asper/Slaight relationship had deteriorated. Two activists couldn't be in charge: the one who was in Winnipeg kept bugging the one who was in Toronto with suggestions and criticisms that would trigger objections and leave them both resentful. In mid-November, at a time when they were reassessing their future, Asper, Morton and Epstein were having a late-night strategy session at the Global offices when a janitor who was cleaning up spilled a garbage can full of discarded documents.

"Being the nice people we were, we got down on our hands and knees and helped the caretaker reload his bag of garbage," Asper mischievously told the tale. "I fixed my eyes on a piece of paper which was a memorandum from Trevor Eyton, Slaight's lawyer, to the IWC guys: 'I say, chaps, speaking of the Global Ventures buy-sell, I have a devilishly clever idea. We all know that Asper goes to Falcon Lake for Christmas, Morton goes to Florida and Epstein goes some-place else. The buy-sell is 30 days, so if we serve them with the notice on December 22 they will all be gone and won't be able to respond until January 5. Therefore, they won't have the time to go out and raise sufficient capital.'" (Under the shotgun, either party could pull the trigger by stating a sales price, and the other guys then had the option to buy or sell at that price.)

Suddenly aware of Slaight's plans, Asper rushed to his TD bankers the following morning and arranged to extend his group's line of credit to cover the shotgun probability. In late December, the four partners dined at Winston's, then Toronto's in-crowd restaurant, to celebrate the end of a CRTC hearing. "I am at this stage notorious for martini-drinking," Asper remembered all too well. "Allan Slaight loved martinis too, and I liked Allan, but he shouldn't have kept us in the dark. My bad fortune turned out to be the greatest thing that ever happened—it was one of a string of misfortunes. I didn't want to have to buy him out; we were still mortgaged up to our eyeballs on the original purchase, and I was getting deeper and deeper into this thing and had no way of ever coming out. But we decide the tensions had to end and Allan was going to spring the shotgun on us anyway, so we'd better do it first.

"So Paul Morton and I take him out for dinner and I go to the bartender and tell him, now look, I'll be ordering martinis, but whatever I say, just put water in the glass instead. I got him to understand that. The evening begins and I'm drinking water while everybody's getting drunker and drunker, and I'm provoking Allan: 'You haven't got the guts to pull the buy-sell shotgun, you fucking son of a bitch, you don't dare.' Stuff like that. He finally leaps across the table, grabs me by the throat and storms out. Next day the buy-sell is sprung. But that's an abbreviated version. It was quite a night, with the martinis and the provocative debate. Slaight could see that we were coming on strong—that we were going to add more logs to the fire. It was the usual Toronto arrogance, keeping at bay the clowns from the country.

"The bottom line was that he was egged on, and I'm told he went roaring out and called Trevor and said, give them the buy-sell. And sure enough, they lowballed it, with seven million bucks. Now, we knew that we were buying but didn't want them to realize that we intended to savour the moment, and couldn't agree on who was going to walk into Slaight's office with the document. So Morton and I play a hundred games of tennis—hard, hard matches—and the first to win fifty-one games gets to drop the thing. We are very competitive players. We go ninety-six games and he wins, so he gets to pull the shotgun but generously agrees that I can walk in behind him and watch Allan's jaw drop. He was in his glass office—it was all glass—and Morton does the deed, and I'm in the back watching, and sure enough, his jaw literally drops, the sound heard around the world. Allan was a hot-tempered guy, and he was stunned. He just picked up his stuff, made some gesture like throwing his keys on the desk and stormed out."

And that's why the Asper saga will never make it as a case history in the curriculum of MBA students. Everybody knows that real business deals are never conducted in such an outrageous fashion. Everybody except Izzy.*

––––––––––––

At this point, Paul Morton and Seymour Epstein moved to Toronto, where they took over Global's daily operations. Asper now held 62 percent of Global but exercised only a 50–50 vote; that was the arrangement he had volunteered since his Toronto partners felt claustrophobic with him having a majority. It didn't work. "They had no dreams, no vision," Asper complained. "I started to get uneasy because I had been asking to have my own office at Global since I didn't like standing out in the hall when I came to Toronto, always waiting outside other people's doors. Every time I asked for space there was some new excuse, such as 'We need more room ourselves,' 'You're never here,' and eventually the excuses started to wear thin." By contrast, Asper felt that Epstein encouraged Canwest's involvement and ideas.

Although he was willing to buy peace by selling his own shares to the resident operators, Asper's gut told him to question the figures that Morton was giving him as the basis of the negotiations to merge. "We were into draft 78 and it was now sixty-some pages and we still couldn't reach agreement as to values and what our respective roles were going to be," Izzy recalled. "We broke off the talks and they sued us, claiming that we had reached an agreement and had welshed on it. They sued in the most spectacular way possible—in Winnipeg, a fatal mistake, because it was they who were living in the hotel rooms, not me. And they sued for $50 million, a foolish and astronomical

––––––––––––

*It was a lucky day for Slaight as well. He invested the Global proceeds and other funds in the purchase of Standard Broadcasting, which owned fifty-two radio stations (later sold to Astral Media), then became founding shareholder of the Toronto Raptors NBA franchise, which turned him into a billionaire. He is currently resident in Florida, writing books about magic—and enjoying life.

sum, in order to embarrass me in my home town. I was still sensitive about the bruising of the Canwest Capital breakup, and so their expectation was that since I didn't die in surgery during my bypass, this embarrassing lawsuit would bring me crashing down. It was then that I decided I had turned the other cheek for the last time. Stephen Gross, my closest associate, had warned me that if I didn't take care of these guys once and for all, my estate would be pilloried."

"Look, these people are not your friends," he told Izzy. "They were praying that you would die during the heart operation, and are going to fry your children, so you'd better face this problem on behalf of your family, *now*." Asper decided to sue for fraud and misrepresentation as well as corporate misconduct, and everything else that had been boiling up in his craw for the past five years. One of his major complaints was that the Morton duo refused to distribute dividends and there was $15 million in Global's coffers that Asper couldn't access, though he had big plans for extending the company into Europe.

The court case that followed featured searing testimony during which the two sides couldn't agree whether Tuesday followed Monday. It was accusatory on both sides, but the judge stated that "whenever there is a difference in the testimony, I choose to believe Mr. Asper." A key factor was that when Izzy had reached the stage of being fed up with all the harassment and offered to sell his shares to Morton and Epstein, he asked for a corporate valuation statement, so that he could establish a selling price. During the trial the former Global comptroller appeared one day on the courthouse steps and gave the Asper people the last existing copy of the authentic 1985 projection of Global's earnings, which established the station's value. The earnings came in at $16.7 million, as opposed to the low evaluation of $5 million that had been presented to Asper by Morton. Along with the true worth, the document contained a stern notation that all its copies "must be destroyed." But pride of authorship was too strong for the whistle-blower, who kept one sample of his projections hidden and decided to make them public at this crucial moment. That revelation, on top of other evidence about Morton's abusing the contra system for fringe benefits, swung the trial into a decisive victory for Asper, though it dragged on through 63 days and 10,000 pages of testimony. "Tom Heintzman, my definition of a lawyer who cared about his clients, nursed me through four very difficult, brutal years," Asper gratefully recalled.

Judge Peter Morse decided that the two sides were "hopelessly and irretrievably deadlocked" and that the company ought to be dissolved. It was Asper who suggested that the way out was an open auction to decide the winner, once and for all. "Morton and Epstein would have appealed the verdict and that would have taken another two or three years," he explained, "so I opted for a remedy that was equitable. I said, 'You want to buy it? You buy it. Let's have a real auction—whoever wants it the most will get it.'" And it worked. The auction short-circuited the whole process and set Asper free. "I couldn't borrow against my assets because they claimed they owned them," he complained. "Since I couldn't deal with my assets, I couldn't do anything. And at that time I was still choked with the debt I'd incurred buying out the shareholders at Canwest Capital."

The Global auction was coming up, and Izzy had to somehow obtain the funds required to propel his bids. At the time Asper was not, as usual, rationing his cash and being nervous about having to plead for yet another loan from the Toronto-Dominion Bank, which had backed his other ventures. This time it wasn't a case of being hard up for money; there quite simply wasn't any.

The TD may have been the Asper bank, but it offered only exorbitantly priced bridge financing with exploding interest rates, which started off at prime and jumped to prime plus 18. Stephen Gross, who was president of Izzy's holding company, put the case bluntly. Not certain whether he should laugh or cry, he decided to attack. "This is usurious—you're breaking the law, asking for this kind of money," he bargained with the bankers. They came back with a revised proposal, which was a barely improved loan package that went up to prime plus 12 but had to be paid off within a year, when Asper would have had to refinance the deal. At that point Asper counted the TD out of the running. The Royal Bank, where he had also applied, never did send him a proposal but just kept asking for more information, stringing him along, hoping he would go away.

Izzy's next port of call, the third and last on his list, was the Bank of Nova Scotia, whose head office was then located across King Street from the TD. Back in 1959, when Izzy had been temporarily unemployed and was down to $843 in his bank account, the Scotia's Winnipeg branch had given him free space to start a new law office. "There wasn't a president of the Bank of Nova Scotia who wasn't sentenced to be the manager in Winnipeg for a few years, so I got to know them all," Izzy recalled. That included his current hosts, CEO Ced Ritchie and Peter Godsoe, vice-chairman and head of corporate banking. They had done their homework.

When Asper and his retinue arrived to make their urgent plea, they hadn't even sat down before Izzy launched his pitch. His hands subliminally bent in a supplicant's pose, he kept looking around the room to see if he could detect where they stored the loot. Godsoe, who was the main target of his presentation, had in his time raised a lot of dollars and almost as many eyebrows. He was not your average banker. Growing up three blocks from Toronto's Upper Canada College, he had tried the private school for a week then switched to a less prestigious but much more academically advanced alternative. He had a sterling reputation among banking insiders as being highly intelligent and equally intuitive but not really one of them. He was possessed by too subtle a sense of humour and too acute a sense of occasion.

He now called on both these traits, and quietly interrupted Izzy's harangue. "You've got the money," he informed Asper, trying not to wink.

That wasn't enough to stop or even slow down the Winnipeg Winnebago from continuing his spiel—*allegro fortissimo*. Finally, trying to haul him back to Planet Earth, Godsoe exclaimed, "Stop, Izzy. Stop!"

"What!?" Asper blurted out. Were these Bay Street marionettes playing games with him? Did they think he had just arrived on the turnip truck from Minnedosa?

"You've got the money," Godsoe repeated, his eyebrows arched over a toothy smile.

"But I haven't asked you for the money . . . yet."

"Don't worry. It's what you want. We'll give you $240 million."

What followed ought to have been commemorated by a hootenanny in a big blue barn with Grande Prairie line dancers gracing the proceedings, or by a troupe of slap-happy beavers smacking the surface of some distant northern pond in unison, beating out "You Are the Sunshine of My Life." For the very first and probably last time in his adult existence, Israel Harold Asper was speechless.

"Well" was all he could muster after a long pause. "Well, we haven't discussed the terms yet."

"Don't worry about the terms—you'll like them."

As they were leaving, Ritchie said to Asper, "You may think that you've just got a great deal because you got everything you wanted—plus. You did get a good deal, but so did we. This loan makes us the largest communications industry lender in Canada, and I'm gonna call Dick Thomson at the TD, the previous champion, to tell him that."

Despite that explanation, Izzy still felt there had to be a trick. It was too good to be true. He had come ready to do a little strip mining in the Big Hochelaga. Instead they had handed him the keys to the kingdom. And these guys were supposed to be the national economy's fiscal father confessors, the guardians at the gates. They didn't behave at all like the tight-ass bankers he had expected them to be, creatures of habit who discharged their duties with the self-conscious virtue of representative elders at a Presbyterian synod—or something equally absurd. Yet here was this Santa Claus in a three-piece suit from a serious bank offering him serious money.

Asper's thoughts wandered. He had always admired the Yankee stock trader Michael Milken, not because he had invented junk bonds but because he was an executive who left so little to chance— just like Izzy imagined himself to be. Milken had gained Asper's admiration for his perfectionism, which expressed itself even in how he dealt with being bald. Milken had purchased thirty wigs, each with slightly longer strands of hair, so that he could simulate its daily growth until he pretended to get his monthly haircut—and started all over again with the first, short-hair toupee. Now, that was the way to take care of business. But these Bay Street bankers and their fiscal sorcery made Asper feel more discombobulated than comfortable. For once, his paranoia had been unjustified. The $240 million line of credit was good for two years at prime, which is the best of corporate rates, with a renewal option and accompanied by negotiable and easily acceptable covenants. This bank, obviously headquartered in the Land of Oz where troubles melt like lemon drops, enjoys a strong relationship with the Aspers, even financing the purchase of Conrad Black's newspaper chain in 2000, mainly via a phone call.

The Great Auction was the biggest corporate shootout in the history of Manitoba. Every Winnipeg business person wanted to attend, and Izzy was even talking about charging admission at $2,000 a seat to establish a scholarship fund. "I had financing for $240 million but sure as hell didn't want to go that high, though I certainly expected they were going to fight hard for it," Izzy recalled. "Because of the different percentages of ownership, we ultimately paid Morton and Epstein the equivalent of $75 million each, but I would have paid them a total of $200 million before I started to think seriously whether to continue. What was on the table for us was much more than Global," he conceded. "At the end of the day, if we had been sellers, we would have had to liquidate our company because there was no point in going on. So really what was at stake was our raison d'être. But it broke my heart to think of how long it had taken to finally control my destiny. And I knew I wouldn't see it through, I wouldn't see the end of it."

For those who had followed the Great Auction, the thought of Izzy not knowing what to say or do next was one to savour. Peter Godsoe had literally ripped the carpet from under his feet. His fifth and final career—the one that would make Asper a multi-billionaire and take him into the jaws of national controversy—was now well and truly launched. The past was prologue.

———————

In the years that followed the Great Auction, Global Television became Asper's life and times. It was better known as a gold mine that broadcast American hit shows at huge profits than as a creative enterprise, but it did feature at least one memorable dramatic offering. That was *Traders,* a sleek, emotionally charged portrait of Canadian capitalism's sharks, doubling as stockbrokers with attitude. The superb production, first aired in January 1996, never exceeded its relatively modest $800,000 budget per episode (Global invested $3.5 million), but the whole was greater than its parts. *Traders* aired the voices and transmitted the visuals of a Canada shedding its Puritan roots and opting for a subarctic money culture of its own. Bay Street, just like Wall Street in the movie of the same name, was portrayed less as a place than as a metaphor. Its players decided the price of money, picked the stock market's winners and losers, and to a disturbing degree set the country's ethical standards—or lack of them—disseminating a way of looking at the world that equated self-worth with net worth.

The secret of *Traders'* success was that it cut so close to the bone that the teleplay came perilously close to being a documentary—and it was this sense of the authentic which attracted a loyal audience of a million-plus every week. The grainy portrayal of Bay Street's

Darwinian realities held viewers in its grip. Compassion was for losers; money was the new sex of the 1990s.

Produced for Global by Toronto-based Atlantis Communications, the show's writers—mainly Alyson Feltes—managed to suspend disbelief without becoming preachy. (The original outline was written by Jim Sward.) Bay Street was filmed as a battle zone lit by the eerie green glow of computer terminals as brokers frantically dialled for dollars. The shouting never stopped. The camera became a predator, probing each character's vulnerabilities with cool indifference. The show's star was Marty Stephens (played by Patrick McKenna), a charming rat fink who not only propelled the action but drew out the cast's killer instincts. And, yes, there too was Izzy Asper, doing his star turn as an all-too-lifelike cocktail-lounge pianist, demanding union scale and an ashtray.

Along with *Traders,* Atlantis and its successor companies produced twenty-eight TV series and documentaries for Global, including TV adaptations of books by Kurt Vonnegut, Ray Bradbury and Dennis Lee. "They were our biggest customers," recalled Michael MacMillan, who ran the specialty channels and production houses involved.

The creative architect who gave Global TV its original voice, both good and bad, was David Mintz, a former morning DJ at WKBW, a Buffalo rock radio station, who later ran the CBS affiliate in Bellingham, Washington, which fed off Vancouver advertising revenues. When Global was still in dire straits, Seymour Epstein suggested they hire Mintz and appoint him as CEO of Global. Within months, Mintz rapidly turned the operation around with his optimism, his sales skills—and cheap American shows. "Mintz was Global's real operator," Schwartz recalled. "Dave was very well respected in Hollywood because even in his time in Bellingham, before we hired him, he had done an extraordinarily good job of being part of the fabric of Hollywood."

Mintz's key skill, which turned out to be Global's salvation, was his ability to mobilize mass audiences that attracted premium

PETER C. NEWMAN

advertisers. He was well connected in Los Angeles, but unlike his competitors, he didn't arrive at LAX only for the annual buying week: he carefully cultivated his professional relationships between auctions, even living in Los Angeles for a time. Most important of all, he courted not only the top producers—which is what everybody else did, because they hosted the sexiest receptions—he also got to know the actual directors, script writers and actors who kept careful tabs on which shows were creating a buzz and would produce a following that would tempt advertisers. The Hollywood in-crowd called him first, whenever they had something big coming along.

Mintz knew exactly what minute of what day other network contracts were due to run out and would be there with a pen and draft contract just before dawn, knocking on the doors of Aaron Spelling, for example, the producer of *The Love Boat*—one of the many shows he stole away from his competitors. Mintz was gregarious and a health nut; he swam a lot, ate properly and was a good bit older than he looked. A hard-nosed hombre, not particularly interested in Canadian content, he turned Global into the Love Boat Network by not only broadcasting new weekly episodes but putting that vapid series on the air daily—five half-hours in prime time and five-half hours every afternoon. It filled the available time slots, and since its contract didn't limit the number of showings, the reruns were almost free. His nose for what turned ordinary citizens into couch potatoes was tuned strictly to the commercial aspects of the medium, and that in turn depended on airing the hit shows bought from the U.S. television networks. Some years—1996, for example—Mintz managed to sign up a dozen of the fifteen top-rated U.S. programs, including *Seinfeld, NYPD Blue, Cheers* (which he stole from under CTV while in a bar), *The X Files* and *60 Minutes*. He was an unsentimental entrepreneur in a field of dreams and loved making deals, yet hated meetings. He just liked to get things done, and if he ever took the time to read a book, it would be a TV ratings guide.

130

Asper regarded the perpetual controversy over Global's lack of prime-time Canadian content as being a media invention based less on fact than fiction. He felt that he succeeded despite of, not because of, the CRTC's rulings that allowed the rebroadcast of low-rent American fare, laced with Canadian advertising. "We do not broadcast one minute more American programming than CTV does, and we spend more money, proportionate to audience, on quality Canadian programming than CTV," Izzy insisted, though he admitted that he would have much preferred to invade the American market and to have bought one of its networks. "I've argued for twenty-five years now, maybe longer, that we will only have world-class Canadian programming that Canadians will want to watch when we make it relevant to their lives," he preached. "And we can only do that with big budgets because that's the only way you get international distribution. That's why American programming works. So, if Canadians were allowed to own NBC or CBS, or at least half of one, you would see a great deal of quality Canadian programming."

"The fact is that we have lived up to every one of our commitments," emphasized Peter Viner, one of Global's most senior executives. "There is a community out there that frankly can never be satisfied in terms of our commitments and who have a vested interest in the independent production community. We did some very innovative things, and as I say, we never were reprimanded for being below our commitments.*

"The frustrating thing is that people confuse lack of success with lack of desire in television sometimes, particularly in the production community. To create Canadian hits beyond news and sports is very, very difficult. So Izzy was quite pragmatic about how we divided the budget between foreign and Canadian content. We couldn't outdo the CBC, so people felt that we never did enough."

---

*In 1992 the CRTC renewed Global's broadcast licence for only four years, instead of the usual seven, demanding that the network live up to the spirit of its Canadian content requirements.

Although Izzy's network won an impressive shelf of awards (in 1997 alone claiming eleven Geminis), Canadian production was not Global's priority or its preoccupation. Asper turned many of the country's cultural mavens against him when he reasserted his boast, originally issued in New Zealand, that "television is not a complicated business; TV stations are gigantic advertising machines there to be filled with product." (Not a description to make you jump up and down waving the maple leaf, but it was a step up from a declaration by Washington's Federal Communications Commission chairman Mark Fowler, who described television as "a toaster with pictures.")

The critics homed in on Asper's telecasting schedules, which to a bruising degree treated domestic programming as an afterthought, in much the same way as the country's bookshops had once stocked indigenous books in back-of-the-store "Canadiana" sections. Most Canadian productions—except news, public affairs and the occasional showpiece series—ran between revenue-producing American blockbusters, except during prime time, when they must have been shown in Izzy's cellar. Still, Global did manage to field some impressive TV dramas, notably the adaptation of W.O. Mitchell's *Jake and the Kid, Diamonds, Destiny Ridge, Madison,* and *The Outer Limits,* but definitely not including such industrial domestic outtakes as *Top Cops* and *Super Dave.*

When he was president of Global Television, Jim Sward argued before the CRTC against further investment in Canadian programming. "Frankly," he told the regulators, "I don't think it's the commission's business to be in the private sector. We all got where we are on our own. God bless private enterprise. That's the juice. And if we decide to stomp on it, then it will lose its liveliness." Commissioner Andrée Wylie nearly fell on Sward, lecturing him that Global owed its profits not to free markets but to regulatory protection. None of the several post-Morton operating heads of Global could match Sward's record. The station achieved an operating profit of 32 percent and in the 1998–99 season, the ten most successful American TV shows were shown on Global.

Matthew Fraser, then a professor of communications at Ryerson Polytechnic University, accused Asper of turning Global into "an idea-free zone" and of practising "strict separation between profits and patriotism." That sentiment was perpetuated by filmmaker Robert Lantos, who charged Asper with being part of the private broadcasters' cabal, "whose greed is surpassed only by their hypocrisy." (These up-yours observations were rewarded with opposite reactions: Asper appointed Fraser as editor-in-chief of the *National Post,* his most prestigious newspaper, and slapped Lantos with a $7 million defamation suit.)

One legitimate claim to original and significant Canadian programming was Global's news operation. Even during fallow periods it was budgeted at $12 million a year. "This country has got to develop a new pride and respect for itself," Asper emphasized, "and the best way we can do that is with more public affairs and documentary programming." The station's lively news operation was founded by Bill Cunningham, a pioneer of CBC's television news who was credited with the idea of the CBC's epic news series *The Journal.* His tenure was key in gaining Global News editorial legitimacy. Cunningham was succeeded by Ray Heard, former Washington correspondent for the London *Observer* and bureau chief (later managing editor) of the *Montreal Star,* who was a scholarship graduate from Harvard. Apart from his "nose for news and way with words," as the cliché of the time had it, he possessed something of the quality of an exploding Mexican flag, its colours and emotions bursting in periodic detonations. He never hesitated to exploit his communicable passions to the fullest and was the only North American television news director in captivity who attended social occasions dressed in the black pyjamas favoured by Viet Cong snipers. "I used to put on the casual battle dress of the Viet Cong at social events where Global entertained people, usually at the Toronto Racquet Club," Heard recalled. "The pyjamas signified that we thought of ourselves as guerrilla fighters winning the news wars against the Pentagon, which we regarded as the equivalent of the CBC, with too much expensive equipment but a lack of nerve."

There were many reasons why Global did so well, none more important than its informality and use of offbeat talent. Heard harnessed the abilities of some of the best and brightest, including Bruce Garvey, Tom Gould, Claude Adams, Nigel Gibson, Jeffrey Kofman, Christina Pochmursky and Percy Saltzman, the chalk-throwing weatherman whom Heard had brought out of retirement. They referred to their leader as the Tasmanian Devil, or just Taz. It was a rare non-union shop, which allowed Heard the freedom to raise salaries, even by as much as 30 percent, for his most junior people—including for Kevin Newman (unfortunately, no relation), the youngest of his production assistants.

Heard constantly watched all the competing news shows, on eight television sets in his office ("Morton hated me for it") to check on what his roving crew had missed. If they hadn't covered an important event, he would take it out, loudly and colourfully, on the senior people who were getting the big salaries. Heard was a journalist who created his own mandates, which in his mind became revolutionary instruments that required original thought and decisive action. From his stories it seemed that he had covered almost every war since the Boers had revolted in his homeland of South Africa, and he remains a singularly acute observer, an essential power link between Toronto's big hitters. He modelled his news operation on his reading of Izzy Asper's combative character: it was an explosive, creative place, constantly in pre-revolutionary mode. The turmoil produced an uneven but mesmerizing product, fuelled by the Global News team, later impressively augmented by the grown-up Kevin Newman.

There wasn't any trio equivalent to Izzy Asper, Dave Mintz and Ray Heard anywhere else in broadcast purgatory, and they turned a mediocre seat-of-the-pants television station into the country's most profitable television network.*

*No conflict of interest exists, but for five years during the 1980s I hosted a weekly Global series, *Everybody's Business,* which was the first documentary program to bring most of the country's CEOs before TV cameras, where they had to deal with

This was happening at a time when nearly all the television news programs were hosted by local Ken and Barbie combinations: handsome youngsters, one of each predominant sex, toilet-trained to never ask embarrassing questions or raise controversial issues. They were characterized mainly by their hair. The boy toy would sport a wavy hairline just above the eyelashes that gave him a touch of gravitas. His female partner would boast a perfectly coiffed face-framing helmet of hair that she would toss about for emphasis, as if trying to dislodge a nesting bird—especially when reporting the latest outrage of some badly dressed Latin American rebels seizing the official government radio or television station. This made for routine, if repetitive, viewing, but only as long as their teleprompter kept turning. Whenever it broke down, they had little ability to generate small talk and usually sat there gasping at the camera like two drowning guppies. Not on Global.

Global's defining anchor was former print journalist Peter Trueman. An Andrew Wyeth country boy with Gary Cooper dignity, Trueman was one of those rare TV personalities who exuded authority just by showing up. He hosted Global News for fourteen years—only five years short of Walter Cronkite's eternal hitch on CBS. His sign-off, "That's not news but that too is reality," was perfect because it followed his brief but biting commentary, and yet no one (including himself) was sure exactly what it meant.

Heard's problem was to find a compatible female on-air partner for the redoubtable Trueman. Among the candidates was Suzanne

---

my probes into their corporate psyches—with occasionally toxic results. I wore my Greek fisherman's cap, but the Heard guerrilla-fighter comparison held, with respect to uneven odds and facilities, if not to costume. Our business show had a part-time staff of four: a cameraman who doubled as sound recorder; Raoul Engel, a wild man who commented on stock swings (whenever he appeared in the Toronto Stock Exchange's press gallery, the traders on the floor would greet him with a round of applause); a staff announcer; and me. The CBC's equivalent business feature had a full-time complement of eighteen, including a guy who did nothing but clap those black-and-white striped sound boards to mark the start of their recording machines.

Perry, then press secretary to Pierre Trudeau (and mother of *Friends* star Matthew Perry). Her rag-doll natural beauty and killer smile didn't translate into great television, or, as Heard delicately reported about her demo tape, "She was as nervous as a Prairie jackrabbit in a thunderstorm."

"I was at my farm in Vermont and looking for a female to match Trueman, when I watched Jan Tennant, who was then a substitute newsreader on the CBC, and realized that there she was, the answer to my search," he recalled. "Jan was then about forty years old and looked great, read well, had credibility and authority. I saw her as a role model for younger women, and phoned her when I got back to Toronto, and went up to see her, accompanied by Trueman. I knocked on her door and said, 'I'm Ray Heard. I don't think we've met.'

"'Oh yes, we have,' she replied. 'I was the girlfriend of the Man from Glad when you and he got drunk one night, flew up from Washington and broke down my front door.'" So that was how the recruitment of Jan Tennant started. Heard told her, "I want to hire you to read the news with Peter Trueman." Heard confirmed the offer the next day and she became the perfect foil for Trueman, while ratings soared.*

In its early days, Global's chief mission was survival, which in turn meant cost-cutting, which occasionally took on some weird forms. At one point, Seymour Epstein called Heard to announce that he had asked a Global producer named Michael Spivak, who was also a composer, to write an original piece of Canadian music. It was titled something like *Global Nocturne* and would be played on the air as background on all news and public affairs programs, which then totalled three and a half hours daily.

When Heard asked him what this was all about, Seymour, sound-

---

*As part of her natural look, Tennant allowed her hair to turn grey on camera while her tenure grew longer, and when asked about it, she produced her only catty remark on record: "I used to say at *The National,* when I was reading the news with Knowlton Nash and George McLean, that I was the only one who didn't colour their hair."

ing mysterious, pointed out that there was no official definition of "music," and admitted that it would actually be the taped sound of the office Telex-type machine.

"Why are you doing this, Seymour?" Heard asked.

"Because under the CRTC regulations, any time you play an original Canadian musical composition on TV, money is paid out at 1 percent of the gross profit to this fund that we can access—so Global will receive a substantial payback just for playing the ticker tape."

Trueman called Heard during his first commercial break after the system was installed because he could hear this strange sound under the newscast, and asked, "What's going on here? Why do they have this noise on while I'm doing the show?"

"Well, actually, Peter, that's an original composition. It's Canadian music."

Trueman, who never swore, lost it. "Those fuckers upstairs will stop at nothing," he barked and continued to read the news of the day over the clickety-clacking of the *Global Nocturne*.

Global was being upgraded into what turned out to be its ultimate role as the flagship for the third television network Asper hoped to put together. That dream enterprise, which in its way was as improbable as anything actually shown on the tube, involved waging several battles, many feuds and later even hand-to-hand combat with opponents perceived to be anti-Semitic. Its first element—CKVU-TV in Vancouver—provided a fair sampling of the obstructions involved.

The station's founders were Norman Klenman (who had written the scripts for the original *Mission Impossible* series) and, more important, Daryl Duke, a headstrong but immensely talented television and film director. They fulfilled the dream of every creative soul by establishing their own production facility, an independent Vancouver television station. Duke had pioneered the best of the early CBC-TV programs, such as *This Hour Has Seven Days*, after working his way through university with a variety of odd jobs, including parking cars at a Vancouver racetrack. Bad tippers had to walk an extra 150 metres to retrieve their vehicles. Such attention to annoying details characterized the man as much as did his streak of successful films, including his 1983 hit, the 10-hour TV serial *The Thorn Birds*, which played to 140 million viewers around the globe and won him an Emmy nomination. Three years later, his golden touch faltered with *Tai-Pan*, a $23 million adaptation of the book by James Clavell, the first Western feature film shot in China. It didn't help that Duke had to work through 25 translators and to direct a cast of a thousand extras. He described the experienced as being "akin to running a water-logged marathon."

Ten years earlier, he and his partner had established a small but influential television operation dedicated to public access, largely through their nightly two-hour, free-form *Vancouver Show*. Duke made no concessions to political or commercial realities and found himself playing to a tiny (if dedicated) audience, and turning no discernable profit. In 1979, at a meeting Duke convened with Asper in the first-class lounge of the Toronto airport, the Winnipeg broadcaster had agreed to help Daryl and his partner ward off Dr. Charles Allard, an Alberta surgeon/entrepreneur and owner of an Edmonton television station, who was attempting a hostile takeover. Asper himself was interested in securing a stake in the BC station, but not quite yet. He promised Duke that Canwest would guarantee him a $4 million line of credit at the TD Bank—all on a handshake. The loan was later raised to $12 million, but at that point Canwest received an option to acquire the station if its investments seemed to be at risk. When that trigger was pulled in 1984, Klenman and Duke went berserk and there ensued what the *Globe and Mail* described as "one of the most bizarre and drawn out sagas in Canadian broadcast history." That turned out to be understatement. Asper had put much of his net worth on the line to try to save the station—for its operators or for himself—because at the time Morton and Epstein had frozen his dividends from Global, and he had little available cash. During the CRTC hearings in July 1986, Duke and Klenman tried to sabotage Canwest's application, declaring that if they were allowed to keep the station, they would produce higher-quality programming. But they had had ten years to do just that, and their case was dismissed. Asper was confirmed as the station's new owner. And that was when the in-fighting really started. During drawn-out negotiations on the handover, Duke banned smoking in CKVU's boardroom, where the serious showdowns were staged. Asper pretended to find it all very funny. "What was even more comical was when he banned smoking from the building entirely," he recalled. "And as far as I was concerned, I owned the damn station." A lengthy trial ensued, during which the court ruled that Duke's mandate had expired, that any Allard claims were without merit and that Canwest's ownership should be left intact. It took another four years of mutual harassment and name-calling before Asper actually took over the station he renamed U.TV.

Typical of the struggle's final moments was this exchange of correspondence between Asper and Duke, about the station's sponsorship of the Vancouver Arts Awards:

December 9, 1987
Re: 1988 Vancouver Awards Show

Dear Daryl,
In case you don't understand what I have been saying to you for the last several months, I will try once again to put our position:

1. We are not campaigning against this television show—I am opposed to your abuse of your authority and the squandering of substantial corporate funds in this production and many others. I am advised that the show could be produced for a fraction of what you are attempting to spend.

2. As to your claim to have proprietary rights in this and other programming, you know perfectly well that we take the position that these contracts were self-dealing, oppressive to the other shareholders of Western Approaches Limited, are not enforceable, and have never been properly authorized.

3. There is no point in your attempting to make the argument that this show is required by the CRTC commitment. You were asked to consult with our representative to management, Donald Brinton, in order to try to work out a *modus operandi* until you are paid out. You have failed to do this and continue to operate as though you own the company personally and will always continue to own it, notwithstanding that it is our money, not yours, that you are spending.

At the appropriate time you will be held accountable for everything you have done in violation of the law & our agreement.

I. H. Asper

December 9, 1987
TO: Israel H. Asper
FROM: Daryl Duke
RE: "The 1988 Vancouver Awards Show"

You would think by this point in your career you would have developed some kind of early warning system between the impulses of your brain and the output of your Dictaphone. Surely you as a master of finance and broadcaster to the nation have better things to do?

Such does not appear to be the case as evidenced by your continued campaign against this one television show. A show, by the way, which is an important feature in the more than twelve hundred hours of local production which taken together on a weekly, monthly and yearly basis forms the CRTC Promise of Performance of CKVU.

One television show, Izzy.

You waste your time and ours.

Daryl Duke

The reason Daryl's dukedom was so essential to Izzy that he would wage a decade-long fight for its ownership was that at the time he saw it as a key element of the third television network he intended to establish across the country. There were many other waypoints along that journey. None came easily.

In September 1985, Canwest was granted licences for its two Saskatchewan stations by the CRTC, but local competitors fought the decision and, through their political connections, appealed directly to the federal cabinet of Conservative prime minister Brian Mulroney. In an unprecedented act, the cabinet overturned the CRTC's decision and ordered another hearing. "I don't think it had ever been done before, the actual reversing of an application," recalled Don Brinton, then in charge of the Saskatchewan operation. "But they forced us to another hearing, based on the fact that, as Ray Hnatyshyn (later governor general) put it, 'Nobody in Saskatchewan opposed the idea of having us opposed.'" The CRTC reaffirmed its choice; the Regina and Saskatoon stations went on air in 1987.

In 1993–94, Jim Sward, then president of Global, masterminded Canwest's expansion into the Maritimes with the acquisition of two money-losing stations owned by the Irving family: CIHF-TV-1 in Dartmouth/Halifax, Nova Scotia, and CIHF-TV-2 in Saint John, New Brunswick, and Prince Edward Island, collectively known as MITV. Cost-cutting quickly made them profitable. Two years later, with Montreal's Télé-Métropole as a partner, Canwest took control of CKMI-TV, the small English-language CBC affiliate in Quebec City. An infusion of $25 million for modern transmitters and new studios as well as a re-staffed newsroom created an audience of 900,000 English-speaking Quebecers and upward of a million of the province's bilingual francophones. At the CRTC hearings in December 1996, Asper insisted that this latest venture was purely patriotic. "I'm doing it," he declared, "for the country. Our success in Quebec may make the difference in the next referendum, if 10,000 people get a good feeling about the rest of the country. That's how razor-thin the margin was last time."

The missing building block was Alberta. The first CRTC round, in 1994, had summarily rejected Canwest's applications for stations in Calgary and Edmonton in favour of the spunky but tiny Craig Broadcast Systems out of Brandon, Manitoba. The regulators suggested that Canwest's bid "failed to offer anything by way of program quality or distinctiveness to offset the negative impact on the existing three licensees." Izzy and his commandos were astonished and not at all sporting. They had clearly bought their way into Alberta, and were convinced that they deserved to win. After all, Canwest had been responsible for more than $40 million worth of productions in a province where they had no outlets, with two series—*Destiny Ridge* and *Jake and the Kid*—having subsequently been broadcast across Canada and sold overseas. "It was a stunning loss," declared Jim Sward, in charge of the Global network. "It was beyond comprehension to me that in the 1990s five people from the CRTC would think that what we needed in Canada is more television boutiques. For the CRTC, Global is a bit too aggressive. It's successful, it's big. It's exactly the kind of player Canada needs as we go to more of a single North American market. But when you put Global in the middle of Alberta, we made a difference. The Craig application was like dropping a pebble in the water in Alberta. They won't bother the existing broadcasters, as we would have."

The second attempt began about a year later, in November 1995, when Leonard Asper, then Canwest's vice-president, corporate development, led the launch of a $636 million takeover of WIC. Controlled by the Griffiths family of Vancouver, WIC was a significant media conglomerate that owned, among other investments, eight television stations, including outlets in Calgary, Edmonton, Red Deer and Lethbridge that particularly appealed to the Aspers. Canwest's best hope of entering Alberta was to purchase WIC from Frank and Emily Griffiths, who were selling—but not to them.

It would be Izzy's last great television purchase, partly because he had by then decided to phase himself out of the line of direct corporate fire, but mostly because there was nothing left undone. He would set his vaunted third network in place, convinced, like a boy playing with trains, that it was a historic event, a piece of nation building. It was indeed a bold move, but history would not be on Izzy's side. Here was this giant of analogue technology realizing his dream of building the very last national Canadian television network at a time when networks had moved far from the leading edge of technology. Izzy's personal motto was "Reach for the Stars," but there, right beside that twinkling little bugger up there in the dark firmament, was a fleet of tiny aluminum birds, circling the earth in geostationary orbit, beaming down digital signals that had once required an old bunny-ear antenna sitting on a TV set. And, of course, the Internet was about to explode the very concept of television viewing.

When Asper tried to interest Frank and Emily Griffiths in talking about their future and his, to see if there might be some meeting of minds and corporations, there was no reply, except for the flash of a meaningful glance between the two WASP owners. Like a guard dog arching its tail in the presence of a familiar scent of danger, Izzy could sense something disturbing in his viscera. Then he put a name to what he felt it was. He felt suddenly as if he were back in Minnedosa, being taunted for being Jewish. He spoke about it only to a friend, not to be repeated. "It's not only there, but everywhere," he said, describing what he saw as anti-Semitism in his industry. "I lectured my family very carefully, very thoroughly on anti-Semitism because nothing's changed. Before we became involved in broadcasting, no Jew had owned anything in network television. It wasn't done. It was an exclusive WASP domain. In Montreal, the Bronfmans tried it briefly but never held a licence. They were not made to feel welcome and left the industry. And we were not made to feel welcome [by the Griffiths]. I felt frustrated over all those years of discussions, going nowhere. Why? Because we were considered to be nothing. We had Winnipeg and a piece of Global. Frank couldn't bring himself to treat us as peers—or as his equivalent. He was a very urbane guy, very West Coast, which is a very distinct personality—a different personality you develop out there. So we despaired of ever doing a deal. We began discussions on Alberta. We tried and tried and tried. We also tried with Allard, but nobody would sell to us. So we had all these meetings with the Griffiths, every year, or two or three. We drove up for Expo '86, for example. Frank, his wife, Emily, and his CEO, Ray Peters, as well as Babs, went up and down the coast in Frank's yacht. I tried to work out a deal. I said, 'Look, Frank. You're the senior man. You'll be the CEO for five years, then you'll move to chairman, as long as you want.' But nothing ever caught his attention. We could never come to terms about who was going to run what because he wanted to keep running everything. We would make them a proposal, and Frank would say, 'Make me another proposal.' I'd do that and he would turn it down. Finally it got insulting."

The only element they ever agreed on was to allow Global programming onto WIC stations. "We weren't trying to make money," Izzy recalled. "We just told them, your audience represents 11 percent of English Canadian viewers, so pay us 11 percent of our programming costs. They paid whatever they felt like and insisted on cherry picking. For example, they didn't pick *Jake and the Kid*, one of Global's biggest successes, which was never seen in Alberta, the location of its story. We offered them *Traders* at $2,000 per episode, which cost us $200,000 to make, and they still turned it down. So in the end, I said, 'Fuck you, we'll keep applying for our own stations, and if we don't get them, we'll build someplace else.' Milwaukee or Minneapolis started to look pretty good to me."

Izzy's daughter, Gail, was on the same wavelength. She not only felt she knew what was really going on, but saw a way around it. "We should have had better human relations, better understanding, better intelligence and better inside information—we would have been able to get to Emily—because it always comes down to more than just the money. And of course that's what the Shaws [who eventually bought the Griffiths' company] did, obviously. They just felt more comfortable. I do believe that familiarity breeds affection, so you must always get the right people. You don't bring in the Jews, you bring in somebody who's not Jewish, to assuage any concerns. So we ought to have brought in Pete Viner or whoever. I also believe that as you circulate, you eliminate the fear of the unknown—the 'who are these people?' feeling—these Jews. My dad would have been very charming, but I don't think he really ever sat down with Emily. And you'd have to assume that his enemies were telling her bad things about him. That's why it's always good to just get there and try to get in front of people instead of having it be diluted three or four times."

In the opinion of one quoted insider about the ultimate sale of WIC, it didn't matter to the Griffiths who they sold to; it was simply a question of the best commercial terms. But another observer of the negotiations, Greg Gilhooly, then a Canwest executive, had a very different gut reaction. "I think what happened with WIC is a bit darker than what others are willing to admit," he contended. "I truly, truly believe that there was no way that [they] were ever going to sell to the Aspers. They just weren't, and it wasn't because of anything that happened in terms of trying to carve a better deal, it wasn't anything that had anything to do with anything other than—I don't even know how to put words to it. They were not going to sell to the Aspers. Look, as an Irish Catholic I can tell you that my sense from the get-go was that they were never going to sell to the Aspers."

It was time to let the digital universe take over—and all the technological offshoots that were beyond Izzy's concern and comprehension. It had taken him only six months to master the art of sending an email, but that was as far as he wanted to venture. Having made himself a moving target for the past quarter century, Izzy let his chosen heir, Leonard, do much of the fighting on the WIC applications, though he remained in charge of the strategy, which consisted mainly of knocking himself out by hitting his head against a stone wall named Frank and Emily Griffiths. Erecting a television network—or anything—across this country requires more patience than any entrepreneur can possibly muster. Jack Larkin, a character in the TV series *Traders*, defined the problem exactly. "This isn't poker," he said. "This is chess. It's not about the bluff. It's about knowing where you're going to be ten moves in advance."

It was Leonard's energy that led the final assault, and, yes, his sense of humour, which got a workout at one of the last CRTC hearings. Madame Françoise Bertrand, one of the commissioners, had made some mildly disparaging remark about how long this process had gone on, which was now being measured in decades instead of years. Leonard took her up on it. "Listen," he said, "please don't complain. If you think this deal is taking a long time for you, think of me. I've had three kids since I started this project!"

When Frank Griffiths died in April 1994, control of WIC fell into the hands of his wife, Emily, and son Frank Jr., leaving WIC vulnerable. Within six months, his widow sold, for $6 million, a 26 percent interest in WIC's voting stock to the Allard family of Edmonton, in order to thwart a possible takeover from Winnipeg. She also gave the Allards two directors' seats. It was at this point that Canwest, which revealed that it had secretly acquired 9.7 percent of the Class B shares, publicly entered the fray. The Griffiths and the Allards, who held all of the voting shares but less than 10 percent of WIC's equity, made it very clear they wanted no part of a deal with the

Aspers. Canwest then tried to force the issue in the BC courts, but in January 1996 a judge ruled against them.

There followed another Canwest application for new stations in Calgary, Edmonton, Lethbridge and Red Deer, as well as Victoria. Throughout the summer of 1996, both Izzy and David Asper spent time in Alberta drumming up support. Asper Senior promised that, if successful, Canwest would contribute $190 million to the Alberta economy over seven years and create at least three hundred new jobs. But again, the existing stations expressed stormy reservations about the loss of advertising revenue, and the CRTC sided with them. The following year, the CRTC also rejected Canwest's Victoria application—even after receiving a petition with the names of 65,000 Vancouver Island supporters.

During the early part of 1997, Canwest continued to purchase WIC's Class B non-voting shares so that by December, Asper held 30 percent of all of WIC's class B non-voting shares. Canwest formally asked for seats on the WIC board of directors, but was summarily rebuffed. Emily Griffiths was now seventy-five years old, and she had had enough. Her sons, Frank Jr. (whom she had pushed out of the company in 1996) and Arthur, the one-time owner of the NHL's Vancouver Canucks and the NBA's Vancouver Grizzlies, were no longer involved. Emily got ready to sell her 62 percent controlling interest in WIC's small number of Class A voting shares. Unknown to the Aspers, lengthy negotiations were taking place in Vancouver as platoons of lawyers representing the Griffiths, Shaws and Allards brokered an agreement. "From Canwest's view, I guess we came out of the dark," says Jim Shaw, the president and CEO of Calgary-based Shaw Communications. "They were not expecting it. The fact was we had had a long relationship with the Allards and they were the ones who convinced us to have a closer look at WIC." On March 14, 1998, Emily Griffiths announced that, pending CRTC approval, the Allards now held 49.99 percent of WIC's Class A voting shares, but only 14 percent (or 3.44 million) of the equity B shares; the

Shaws had walked away from the table with 49.96 per cent of the A shares and 10.6 per cent (or 2.65 million) of the B shares. Since neither party held more than 50 percent of the voting power, lawyers argued that the "coattail" provision triggering a share conversion (which would have put Canwest in control) did not apply. The entire deal required an outlay of $91 million, not all that much for control of half a billion-dollar broadcasting empire. Canwest was left with .04 percent of the voting A shares, but held a commanding 35 percent (or 8.8 million) of the non-voting stock, and had thus been bested yet again.

The Aspers called the Shaws to arrange a meeting. At the end of March, both families were in Toronto for the Business Hall of Fame dinner and induction ceremonies. Asper had been honoured a year earlier, and now it was the turn of J.R. Shaw, who was accompanied by his son Jim. Following the dinner, Izzy and Leonard Asper suggested to the Shaws that they have a private meeting to discuss the WIC predicament. "Nobody wins these wars, except the shareholders, who just keep getting more money," Asper complained. "A year from now, we'll be sitting in this same hotel room, doing exactly the deal I'm proposing to you." Izzy had suggested carving up WIC, with Canwest taking all the television assets (including cable channels), thereby at last obtaining the Alberta link for his third network, while Shaw would get WIC's radio properties and other assets it wanted. The Shaws turned down Asper's proposal, because, as J.R. Shaw explained, they wanted "to go a few rounds, just to see whether Izzy was right." Jim Shaw later added in a statement to the *Edmonton Journal* that they had "shaken Izzy's peaches." Nobody defined "peaches."

On March 23, Canwest launched a takeover bid at $39—$2 more than the stock's trading price—for all of WIC's Class A and Class B shares, worth $650 million. In response, WIC's board of directors initiated a 120-day "poison pill," threatening to flood the market with heavily discounted Class B shares if Canwest was able to acquire only 1 percent more equity than it already held, making a Canwest takeover even more expensive and less likely. Izzy dismissed the move as "the act of arrogant people who must be desperate." Canwest immediately asked the Ontario Securities Commission to convene a hearing and revoke the "poison pill." And at hearings conducted in Toronto in early April, OSC officials agreed with Canwest's arguments and ordered WIC to throw out the deterrent.

In response, WIC's board then negotiated a deal with Shaw in which the Alberta company offered $43.50 for all remaining Class B shares; the offer was in cash and stock, while Canwest's all-cash offer was immediately raised to the same level. Tom Strike traversed the country pitching WIC shareholders to accept the company's offer. There matters stood until a court ruling that, contrary to Canwest's arguments, the WIC-Shaw pre-acquisition agreement was legitimate, so that Shaw ended up controlling 52 percent of Class B shares while Canwest had acquired approximately 46 percent—hardly enough to control WIC outright, but enough to block Shaw's future moves. Meanwhile the Allards were still holding 50 percent of the voting stock, but only 3 percent of the equity. It was as dumb an impasse as could be—or more likely, couldn't be—imagined. Who was on first base? Who knew?

Finally, in June 1998, Jim Shaw sat down with Leonard Asper, and the two men, who had grown to respect one another, exchanged their "wish lists," which turned to be to almost totally complementary: the Shaws walked away with WIC's radio, cable and satellite assets, while the Aspers (at a price of $860 million) became the relieved owners of WIC's nine former TV stations, including their Alberta operations. Jim Shaw credited Leonard for cutting through the "bad blood" and negotiating an acceptable deal for both companies.

But it still wasn't totally clear who owned what, and which company—or rather, which family—was in charge. What had become clear was that the next generation of Griffiths and Allards weren't strong or capable enough to carry on, which was why it was that ultimately the young Shaws and the young Aspers made the only deal that really mattered. In mid-February 2000, Leonard Asper unveiled Canwest's plan for a change-of-control application to the CRTC that set out his intention of keeping WIC's independent station in Hamilton, CHCH, and other assets within his company. As part of its commitment, Asper promised $84.3 million (20 percent more than was prescribed by the CRTC) for local-programming independent productions, a Global national newscast based in Vancouver and a current affairs show from Calgary. That mother of all hearings opened on April 25, 2000, at Vancouver's Plaza 500 Hotel—probably the most significant discussions the CRTC had ever convened. "The question," Leonard posed, "is, should Canwest be allowed to grow?" He demanded that the commissioners "give a vote to entrepreneurship" and bless Canwest's plans for owning and operating all of the former WIC stations, which was exactly what the CRTC commissioners did. Suddenly Global had achieved the impossible: equivalency with CTV. Izzy's crusade had finally ended.

"It's not often one man, one family, one company creates a national network in their own lifetime," Peter Godsoe, now Scotiabank's CEO, wrote to Izzy. "To put this into perspective, it took the banks approximately 100 years to cross the nation—but we're slightly slower than you." In reply Izzy declared, "And the beautiful part is that we've only just begun. Countries are united by national bonds. Sometimes those bonds are made of steel, like railways or pipelines; sometimes they consist of common affection to a person or symbol, like the Queen, or whoever. But in Canada, a new coast-to-coast broadcasting system is the most significant device for achieving a greater sense of citizenship. We badly need a new national window. And that window should be Global, Canada's third network. We've been in training for this moment for twenty years." Well, it had really been twenty-five, but it was good to see Izzy exaggerating downward for a change.

Certainly the railway imagery was not lost on David Asper, the family's eldest son. On July 7, 2000, when the CRTC finally officially approved Canwest's purchase of WIC's television assets, he trumpeted, "This day is the equivalent of the celebration at Craigellachie, when CPR financier Donald Alexander Smith hammered in the final spike. Getting WIC is much like the Last Spike—marking its completion. I can remember us sitting around the dinner table in 1974 and 1975 and seeing my father's eyes light up as he'd describe a vision that has actually come to pass. He saw the day in Technicolor when a third broadcast system would coalesce and create a new national force in Canadian television. And now it has."

At a restaurant in Vancouver, Leonard gave the most meaningful benediction: "The reasonable man adapts to the world around him; the unreasonable man causes the world to adapt to him. Therefore, all progress depends on the unreasonable man. Hail to the most unreasonable man I know, Izzy Asper."

7

Global Goes Global

*Izzy would never have conceded that it might be a bit crazy
for someone from Winnipeg, of all places, to start buying up
TV networks across the world—and be successful at it.*

After taking over control of the Global Television operation on
January 1, 1990, Izzy Asper realized that the world was shrinking faster than his company was growing. "The idea of developing
a national system in a single country, Canada, was no longer good
enough to influence one's destiny within the television industry,"
he later mused. "The Berlin Wall had fallen, and with it, an explosion of new television networks was taking place around the world.
Government privatizations and technological advances in satellite-
delivered programming were upon us. Canwest had to have a con-
stituency beyond just Canada." Within a year, Global completed an
initial public offering substantial enough to recapitalize itself for
future international growth.

Asper had been channelling his energy into establishing Canada's
third television network, a dream that would elude him for nearly a

decade. As his children entered the business, he was determined to make his company more diversified, so they would stick it out for the long term—and that meant expanding into foreign markets. In his overseas ventures, Asper eventually connected three national broadcast systems on as many continents to reach an impressive daily total of 30 million television viewers. His one-trick pony had grown into a global circus, representing a quantum leap from its initial audience of 600,000 Winnipeggers, fifteen years earlier. In the process, Izzy joined the posse of corporate paladins who exploited the digital revolution and moved out to operate international media empires. They were fast on both feet, swift to capitalize on new opportunities, mercenary in their methods but not afraid to challenge foreign corporate cultures, no matter how eccentric. The Minnedosa Kid had become a soldier of fortune in the march of globalization, the dominant economic force of the twenty-first century.

Izzy's overseas adventures included several failed attempts to buy TV networks and operate them. "We tried Chile and withdrew; we tried Romania and withdrew; we tried Czechoslovakia and withdrew; we tried the UK and were withdrawn," he lamented. "We owe a great deal to our Catholic executives for teaching us the perfection of the withdrawal method."

On the other side of the ledger, Canwest's forays into Australia, New Zealand and Ireland were phenomenally successful. "Our experiment worked," Asper boasted. "We found that Canadian management techniques travelled well, and so, following the takeover of a bankrupt television network, TV3, in New Zealand, we moved to expand our South Pacific presence by entering Australia. By January 1993, its Network TEN, only a year out of receivership, had joined our family."

Neither move was that simple. Not nearly. In keeping with the tradition that nothing ever came easily to Canwest, the Australian takeover, in particular, did not disappoint. The Aussie caper was significant in its positive impact on Canwest's balance sheets and played perfectly to Izzy's predilection for attempting the impossible.

His intended purchase of Network TEN (which owned stations in Sydney, Melbourne and Brisbane) marked him from the start as an unwanted intruder bent on an illegal act. The country's draconian laws against foreign ownership were significantly more restrictive than the equivalent Canadian regulations. "Don't even try it, mate!" was the Aussies' war cry. There seemed no visible route for a Canadian to buy his way into an Aussie TV channel and grab control. Interlopers were limited to 15 percent of voting common stock in domestic media companies. To Asper, that sounded like an irresistible invitation to a tea party he didn't want to miss.

As a diehard Prairie boy who had spent a decade battling Toronto smugness and American domination of the airwaves, Izzy was sympathetic to foreign restriction laws whose sole purpose was to protect a country's national and cultural identity—but only up to a point. He believed that being Canadian was an advantage, because those who claim that ill-defined nationality are overly sensitive to cultural domination—and are citizens of the least imperialistic power on earth. That was a useful and valid exemption to claim when applying for broadcast licences in foreign parts. "The Americans think that every place in the world is Milwaukee, but we don't try to impose Canadian culture," Asper pledged, pretending he knew what that was. He envisioned the television universe of the future as belonging to "huge families with international relationships." Interestingly, the only cultural promise he made in his regulatory applications was to highlight the Maori culture of New Zealand and the aboriginal presence in Australia—just as Canwest had pioneered First Nations programming in Canada.

Utilizing generous gobs of chutzpah that tested even Izzy's considerable capacity for that priceless commodity, plus a few obscure legalisms mixed with a dash of accounting alchemy—along with the exquisitely timed issue of non-voting convertible debentures that kept his ownership of voting shares below the 15 percent limit— Asper was able to spin his effective control of Network TEN into a commanding 57.5 percent. To his competitors' dismay and in spite of their repeated attempts to have him and his scheme declared a travesty of existing laws, the arrangement eventually won the unqualified approval of the government and its broadcasting regulators. Moses had parted the Red Sea.*

Australia and Asper were made for each other. The island continent's hard-ass business class operated on rock-ribbed conservatism mixed with shootout opportunism. That placed its titans at a tipping point in the corporate food chain, which was precisely where Izzy loved to roam and lure competitors into his lair.

Izzy found himself dealing with such Orangutans of Capitalism as Kerry Packer, a much younger and tougher Rupert Murdoch, and a supporting cast of adventure capitalists. They tended to have closely cropped hair that left their ears exposed, a combination that endowed them with a deceptive air of amiable candour. That Izzy was able to best them on their own turf said a great deal about his determination (those who witnessed its implacable character compared it to the surge of an incoming tide) and his muscular style of capitalism. In short, even among the Darwin-defying entrepreneurs who were convinced they had a solid case against his incursion into their cozy corporate playpens, his presence could not be denied.

If that sounds extreme, consider the case of Conrad Black, whose similar adventures Down Under involved, in his words, "the

---

*Late in 2007, Leonard Asper used a gambit roughly based on the reverse of the Australian formula to win CRTC approval for his complicated purchase of some premium specialty channels. Earlier in the year, he had partnered with Goldman Sachs in the $2.3 billion acquisition of Alliance Atlantis Communications, Canada's most active film and TV-series provider, as well as co-producer of the hit crime series *CSI*. Although the New York merchant bank had put up the majority of the cash, by naming a Canadian board with real programming powers Leonard was able to persuade the CRTC that the American investors, who were in the majority, would not dictate editorial content. "We are satisfied that this transaction meets the requirements for Canadian control, both in law and fact," ruled CRTC chairman Konrad von Finckenstein.

roughest takeover battle" of his career, as he faced many of the same players—but without equivalent success. Black was never able to corral more than 25 percent of the Fairfax newspaper group, and finally abandoned his quest. He once described his erstwhile partner Kerry Packer (who later threw his lot in with Izzy) as being "a bully, brilliant though dyslexic, domineering but convivial, completely without pretense but a lonely man, fiercely possessive, ferocious and vindictive in dispute, yet strangely gentle and protective at times." Except for "dyslexic," that description was eerily close to characterizing his subarctic clone from where the Red River meets the Assiniboine, now pawing the same ground.

The tales of doing business Down Under enthrall. I've personally known only one very minor Aussie titan, Michael Gore, by name, yet my brief acquaintance with him exposed me to the barnyard mentality faced by Asper in his impossible quest. I met Gore in Vancouver during the 1990s, when he arrived there to forge a new career, the Australian economy having, as he so elegantly put it, "turned to shit in a hand basin." He was an outsized character who recognized no limits of speech, dress or behaviour. A former racing driver (the kind who rattles his competitors by ripping off their door handles), he had worked as an extreme-case process server and was once taken to court for selling "Holy Dirt from Lourdes." Gore's dress code dated back to the jungle films of the mid-1950s—safari-guide khakis with an open shirt, topped by a bronzed face and a Cheshire-cat grin. "I don't perm my chest hair and don't wear gold dicks around my neck," he told me, redundantly adding, "I'm not with the Establishments of this world. I'm not frightened of sticking my arm down the shithouse to unplug it. I believe that's what has always carried me. Some of those public-company types are as slick as snot on a doorknob. But you turn them over and they're not worth the price of Paddle-Poop."

I found his authentic Australian gibberish endearing, especially when he got on the subject of music. There was an orchestra known as the Daly-Wilson Big Band touring the coastal cities and the outback in those days, blowing jazz-funk and raising hell. But times and tastes were changing. During an all-night post-concert booze-up, co-bandleaders Warren Daly and Ed Wilson decided that in order to bring back an audience, they had to let the fans *see* the band, not just hear it. According to their impeccable Gilbey's-fuelled Australian logic, that meant play naked. They did just that. For a time, nineteen nude musicians toured the Gold Coast, blowing their horns and having the time of their lives.

Gore actually hired the Daly-Wilson Band for the opening ceremonies of the luxury $340-million subdivision he built in Queensland. The main attraction at that extravaganza was Frank Sinatra (fully clothed), who didn't want to hold a press conference, being hounded mercilessly by paparazzi at the time. Gore persuaded him to do so by promising there would be no rude questions about Frank's sex life, his toupee or any other embarrassing topic. And there weren't. What Sinatra didn't know was that Gore had gathered the media twenty minutes before the press was due to meet the nervous crooner and told them, "Now, fellows, any talk about prostitutes, molls, illicit affairs of Mr. Sinatra's, whether he's bald, whether he reads cue cards—anything untoward and I'll stop this fucking conference. Do you understand me? And the reason I'm going to stop it is because the power lead that feeds every single camera you've got here, and all those fucking lights, is between my feet. I will simply reach down and pull the thing apart and that will be the end of you. Okay?" It all went as smoothly as Gore's description of that doorknob above, which I won't repeat.

My irrelevant encounter with the irreverent Michael Gore hardly characterizes Australian businessmen, though his ilk represented a new kind of competitor for Izzy. Izzy was much more used to dealing with the stolid head honchos of Bay Street's money pits, also known as chartered banks, whose chairmen had been weaned on porridge and toilet-trained to behave obligingly when negotiating with the wild-eyed supplicant from Winnipeg. Now, all by himself, far away in a strange land and demanding exemptions, Mr. Asper might have been expected to parade his most deferential countenance, but when asked about his impressions of the Australian business community by the local press, he shot right back that "most of its members don't grow on trees, they swing from them."

On another occasion, speaking in front of a wary Sydney audience, Asper wryly observed that the key to success in Australia was to carefully avoid the criminal element: "You will walk along the wharf, the harbour, and somebody will come and put a gun at your head and say, 'Give me your money or I'll blow your brains out.' [Network TEN investor] John Singleton advised me to tell them to go ahead, because you can get along down here without your brains, but not without your money."* Facing such navigational hazards, Izzy decided to operate not only outside the box but outside the box factory. It would never have occurred to him for a nanosecond to concede that it might be, well, crazy for someone from Winnipeg to buy up TV networks on the far side of the globe—and be successful at it. Who had ever done such a thing? His friends rightly warned that he was stretching himself too thin with all that intercontinental travel (especially after the airlines enforced their no-smoking regulations) while having to pick his way through a lethal business culture.

"The people here are all cowboys and frontiersmen, just like the

---

*Although he gave the impression of delivering impromptu speeches that required little planning, Izzy was in fact extremely fussy and unforgiving whenever one of his speech writers let him down. In August 1996, he was addressing the Australia-Israel Chamber of Commerce in Sydney, about how the Australian broadcasting rules ought to be reformed. He had given the assignment to Peter Liba, then Canwest's executive VP, three months earlier, but Liba left the assignment to the last minute. Asper considered Liba's text, faxed to Australia, to be inadequate and poorly promoted, and told Liba so in blunt language: "I can't imagine a more outrageous dropping of the ball than Corp managed on the Australian speech. This thing was decided upon five months ago as being the most prestigious venue for us to make our first major public address in Australia on media reform and Canwest's position, in the hope of influencing the press and business czars. Quite apart from the screw-up in getting the speech together and distributing it in time in Australia, from what I understand, you did nothing to get it publicity in Canada and more unfortunately, in the U.S. international trades."

American Wild West," Izzy explained in the winter of 2002 to Leonard Peikoff, an old friend from Winnipeg and the eccentric genius who had founded the Ayn Rand Institute, to which Asper subscribed. "They're charming, fun-loving and great party people. Unfortunately, however, that Wild West mentality of lawlessness spills over into their ethical behaviour. Doing business in Australia gave me a Ph.D. in Primitive Opportunism. However, once you understand their ethics, or lack thereof, in North American terms, it is very easy to conduct transactions. By the way, that comment on ethics applies not only at the day-to-day street level but right up to the highest possible levels of business, government, lawyers and regulators. I may be judging them too harshly, but I come from an environment where a letter of intent is sacred, a handshake is inviolable, and lying, cheating, dishonesty and deceptiveness are not tolerated."

None of that fazed Izzy. Canwest captured its prey by being the toughest negotiator, investing pots of time and effort, seizing live assets not for the largest amounts of cash up front but by promising unlimited future prospects and delivering on its pledges. Asper purchased effective control, through a syndicate formed for the purpose, for about $51 million, an investment that was multiplied many times over. Still, from the moment he made his play for Australia's Network TEN, he was forced into the black-hat role of the big, bad outsider trying to take over a homegrown icon. Asper's advantage was that he understood the industry and moved into the underdeveloped Australian television market just when its three private networks— Seven, Nine and TEN—were all in deep financial doo-doo. The various tycoons involved in the commercially volatile ventures to own and disown, salvage and scuttle these operations—sometimes simultaneously—represented the who's who of the Australian business hall of fame: Kerry Packer, Rupert Murdoch, Alan Bond, Christopher Skase, Frank Lowy, Steve Cosser and Charles Curran, to name a few. The only obvious bounder in the bunch was Alan Bond, whose hobby was winning blue-water sailing races, including the 1983 America's Cup. Four years after that race he bought the Nine Network from Kerry

Packer for $1 billion but ran it so carelessly that three years later he was forced to sell it back to him for only $250 million. At the time Packer quipped, "An Alan Bond happens to you only once." Bond was eventually convicted of the largest fraud in Australian history and spent three years in jail, though he has since reincarnated as an undercover African diamond-mine operator.*

Asper's eye was on the least viable of the available television operations, the beleaguered Network TEN. From its inception in the late 1970s, it had been passed around like a slippery football from media mogul Rupert Murdoch, to real estate magnate Frank Lowy of the Westfield Group, to financier Charles Curran, and finally to journalist Steve Cosser of Broadcom Australia, a television production company.**

None kept it long enough to make the operation work. In October 1990, TEN's main creditor, the Westpac Bank, closed Cosser down and placed the network into receivership. The station was losing A$2 million a week at the time, though Westpac had injected A$245 million into its rescue effort. By the spring of 1992, Westpac was searching for a buyer with a proven track record. Asper had been mentioned as a candidate, but Westpac executives felt he wasn't

---

*When he moved to London with his bounty-wife Barbara Amiel, Conrad Black purchased Alan Bond's mansion at 14 Cottesmore Gardens, a terraced nineteenth-century townhouse in the best part of Kensington, for $8 million. He then bought the adjoining mansion for another $8 million and hired David Mlinaric, London's most expensive interior decorator, to oversee the year-long conversion into a palace, complete with an echoing marble entrance hall, ten bedrooms (they lived alone) and six magnificently gilded reception areas, plus an "environmental chamber" where Lady Black could transport herself into the climate and ambiance of her choice.

**Apart from Rupert Murdoch, it was Frank Lowy, king of Australia's shopping centres, who was the most interesting of the bunch. He arrived as a teenage Holocaust survivor from Czechoslovakia in the late 1940s. Together with local businessman John Saunders, he eventually built Westfield into a multi-billion-dollar real estate player. Lowy's most famous holding was the ninety-nine-year lease (obtained for US$127 million) his firm held on the retail space under the World Trade Center in New York City. After the terrorist attack on September 11, 2001, Westfield filed a US$3 billion insurance claim that has yet to be settled.

ready for the big leagues. Asper persisted and finally, Frank Conroy, the bank's CEO, said he'd meet with him in Sydney. Asper arrived, accompanied by Babs and Gail, waited for several days for Conroy to set a time for their discussion, but nothing happened. Frustrated, he booked his flight back to Canada. Fifteen minutes before he and his family were set to depart for the airport, a Westpac flunky called to tell Asper that the bank did indeed want to hear him out and had appointed as its agent a merchant banker by the name of Malcolm Turnbull to determine whether he was a serious contender. The same character had been involved in advising Conrad Black on his abortive attempt to takeover the Fairfax newspaper chain; in his memoirs, Black left a memorable description that could fit no other merchant banker in the commercial history of the planet: "Malcolm Turnbull is mercurial and volcanic. He had immense agility at composing scenarios whose common feature was the happy ending of his ruling the world or whatever part of it was currently under consideration. Malcolm's fugues were notorious . . . He became uncommonly belligerent and histrionic, threatening vengeance on people, including occasionally himself."

"Malcolm turned out to be an unbelievable case," Asper agreed. "He was representing Westpac but saying to me how he wanted to be part of the buying group too. In Australia they have a great problem separating conflict of interest. They have these illusory Chinese walls where one partner doesn't talk to the other. It's quite a remarkable place to do business, quite remarkable."*

---

*Turnbull was indeed a controversial character, even for Australia. He had handled a number of highly publicized litigations as a trial lawyer—including the defence of Peter Wright, the former British spy and author of the sensational tell-all memoir *Spycatcher*, which the British government unsuccessfully tried to ban. He also led the campaign to transform Australia into a republic. Once that crusade collapsed in 2000, he ran for a seat in Australia's House of Representatives and was named minister of environment and water resources in the John Howard government. Among his many controversies, Turnbull was ridiculed by the media for accepting a government allowance of $175 a night and paying it to his wife as rent in the townhouse in Canberra, registered under her name, where they lived.

Once Turnbull had confirmed that Asper was for real, he arranged for him to obtain more financial material on his target TV station. Asper returned to Winnipeg, lugged a few cartons of material out to his cottage at Falcon Lake and studied the matter further. When he was satisfied, he and Stephen Gross, as well as Canwest executives Peter Viner and Gerry Noble, returned to Sydney for more intense negotiations.

Westpac refused to budge on its A$236 million asking price. Asper told Turnbull he could handle it but required time to gather a consortium, given that by law Canwest was allowed to formally own only 15 percent of the pot. Secrecy and security were paramount, but the details of Asper's negotiations were nonetheless available in most local papers on the morning after each session. "Even though our meetings with Westpac were conducted in complete confidence, with voice scramblers from every window in the room to prevent transmission to electronic listeners, the next day's *Sydney Morning Herald* had the complete details of the negotiations on page one," Asper complained. "The people at Westpac were utterly paranoid about the leaks, and we took to writing each other notes in the same meeting room on some of the more sensitive subjects."

Asper's letter of intent called for Canwest to be allowed six weeks of unrestricted due diligence and to obtain the approval of the Australian Broadcast Authority (ABA). The deal was structured so that Canwest had to put up about A$52 million of its own money while Westpac agreed to loan the yet-to-be-created consortium A$145 million. That meant Asper and his team had a little over a month to raise the balance in a country where he was virtually unknown to investors.

While Asper realized he had to abide by the 15 percent foreign investment rule, he was clearly interested in reaping a greater percentage of the profit margin. He and his cadre of accountants and lawyers on two continents came up with a highly ingenious scheme, never used before, to stay within the letter of the regulatory laws yet maximize his potential to reap a huge payoff. While Canwest ended up with only 15 percent of the votes, it also owned 57.5 percent of the non-voting equity and could rightly claim (as it did over the next six years) that it did not control Network TEN. Control lay in the hands of the network's board of directors, of which the majority were Australians and independent of Canwest (which had only two representatives on the eleven-member board). This clever play later became known in Australian business circles as "to Canwest"—to get around the rules in a way that was legally unchallengeable.

The due diligence team was headed by David Asper, who had just joined Canwest on a full-time basis, along with Canwest CFO Tom Strike, Gerry Noble (commuting from Auckland), Peter Viner, and Doug Bonar from Global in Toronto. They turned TEN upside down and inside out. Meanwhile, Izzy was working around the clock with Peter Viner and Stephen Gross, combing the Aussie under-brush for potential investors. Given that all three of the television networks were in dire straits, it was a tough gig. "I was like a one-armed paper hanger running from one conference to the next," remembered Asper. "Every two hours there was another meeting. We went through dozens and dozens of potential investors and eventually got it together—barely. But we weren't sure if anybody was actually going to show up for the closing. It was wild. Guys would be in, the next day they'd be out, and we'd start over again."

Asper and Viner's routine was the best show in the country. Like Dean Martin and Jerry Lewis, they played off each other. "I would make the presentation to operations and sales," Viner recalled, "but Izzy would be afraid that if the potential share buyers didn't jump out of their chairs shouting, 'Hallelujah!' somehow I hadn't conveyed the message. I'd say, 'Well, I think we can get it to a 20 percent margin within two years,' and Izzy would quickly correct me—'Well, Peter's always very conservative. In fact what we really think is that it'll be 30 percent, but we just don't want to say it in a written presentation.' And I'd think, 'Where the hell did that come from?' He'd pull off things like that and say, 'Well, this is ultra-conservative,' and of course I was sweating bullets thinking that I'd have to get struck by lightning to make this. As it turned out, it was Izzy who was ultra-conservative. I always thought when I'd see Izzy in a room full of lawyers or accountants or MBA guys, chances were that he was the second smartest accountant, the smartest lawyer, the second smartest MBA guy—he just had the ability to absorb all that stuff and spin it."

Asper also had a bit of help from his old Liberal friends back in Canada. The Honourable Ed Lumley from Cornwall, who served with distinction in the Trudeau government, had returned the year earlier to the private sector as vice-chairman of BMO Nesbitt Burns. In fact, Lumley had assisted in taking Canwest public in 1991. He had an old friend from high school named Jack Cowin, a one-time professional football player who had played five games for the Winnipeg Blue Bombers as a two-hundred-pound lineman but who left Canada in 1969 to settle in Australia. There Cowin became the successful operator of ten Kentucky Fried Chicken franchises and of Hungry Jack's, a fast-food hamburger chain that ranked second only to McDonald's. In the fall of 1992, he received a phone call from Lumley telling him that "this Canadian in the television business" was in Sydney trying to interest investors in Australian television. Cowin found Asper's sales spiel persuasive but told him that he knew nothing about the TV business. "Most people who want to get into the business think it's about Hollywood, champagne and starlets," Asper replied. "That's not what it's about. The business is about selling television commercials and the secret is to spend the minimum amount of money to get the maximum amount of people watching the TV commercials."

That made sense to Cowin because it wasn't that different from slinging fast food. He in turn convinced one of his mates, Jack Singleton, an advertising wizard who had actually bid on Network TEN but had been rebuffed by Westpac. The two of them agreed to invest $A4.5 million each for a 20 percent share. To seal the deal, Cowin recalled, "Izzy promised that we would get to choose the weather girls." (That fringe benefit never came true, though the investment turned out to be one of the smartest Cowin ever

made. Five years later he had parlayed his A$4.5 million invest-
ment into A$68 million.)

Despite the poor economic climate in Australia and their complete lack of knowledge of the local marketplace, Asper and his men
pulled off a miracle. By the end of December, they had formed a
syndicate that met the bank's conditions. Within a year, Peter Viner
had resigned from Canwest and had been appointed the new CEO
of TEN. He earned his title as "master cost-cutter of all time" as he
introduced the Canwest management style to the station. Within
nine years, Canwest's initial investment was worth A$1.5 billion.

But Asper had other Australian headaches. Although the
ABA had approved TEN's change of ownership and had accepted
Canwest's unique position, the arrangement had left a bad aftertaste
in the regulators' mouths. The bureaucrats felt as if they had been
hoodwinked. Rumours and innuendo launched by competitors and
at least one disgruntled employee, plus the connection between
Viner and Asper, convinced the ABA that Canwest was actually running TEN and was in violation of broadcasting regulations.

"Canwest did not control TEN," asserted John Studdy, the network's independent chairman from 1993 to 2002. "Besides me and
the two Canwest people on the board, there were eight other individual entrepreneurs. They had their own businesses and were not used
to working around a board table. Some of them didn't even know
each other. So to say that Canwest was controlling TEN was a joke
because none of these people wanted to be controlled by anyone."
The ABA had different ideas, and three separate investigations of
Canwest's role were convened over the next five years. The legal fees
were huge and the demand for letters, emails, faxes, telephone logs
and all other relevant documents the ABA wanted was infuriating.
As Asper put it, they wanted "every communication made between
all of our executives [from 1992 to 1994] whether they related to
Network TEN or the terms of our office lease in Winnipeg."

ABA chairman Brian Johns (who from 1995 to 2000 had been
managing director of the state-owned Australian Broadcasting

Corporation) was unmoved by Asper's appeals, and the third investigation proceeded. Finally, after the ABA had amassed 950 pages of testimony and 15,000 pages of subpoenaed documents, and had examined 18 witnesses under oath, it concluded a full year later, at the end of November 1995, that "Canwest is not, and has not been in a position to exercise control of TEN." The 208-page report also noted that former Canwest executive Peter Viner, TEN's CEO, "exercised independent judgment," even though he considered the advice of Canwest as well as others. "Nobody would suggest," declared then ABA chairman Peter Webb, "that Canwest shouldn't have their say at the board table, shouldn't be able to have their directors, and shouldn't be allowed to convince their colleagues that a certain course of action is the best one to take—that is influence, but it is not control.

"When we were in Australia during the heavy litigation, we had all these QCs acting for us, and Izzy would come over every now and again to check with them," recalled Yale Lerner, Asper's legal adviser. "They knew he was a QC [Queen's Counsel], which Down Under is only awarded to the top court lawyers, so they figured he must know something. One time, I remember sitting around in the boardroom, and I couldn't stop laughing. I couldn't believe what was going on. I don't know if Izzy really believed what he was saying, but he wanted the Aussie legal team to draft an equitable remedy called a 'writ of mandamus,' to order the government to take a different course of action.

"'With all respect, Mr. Asper, we can't do that—you just won't get this order,' one of them replied. So Izzy started telling them about all his mandamus cases—though I don't know if he ever had any. He gave them bizarre sets of facts. These guys are hanging on every word because he's a QC and he's rich. It was all a bunch of crap, but these guys sat there for over an hour, and I'm listening to this stuff and I know it ain't true and they were just soaking it up. Izzy could do that and make the facts sound convincing. These guys either thought he was the greatest lawyer who ever lived or that the courts in Canada were insane. I don't know what they thought. But they sat and hung on every word. And Izzy would do stuff like that. He wanted to get them to at least give it a shot, even though that one made no sense because it wasn't appropriate."

Canwest's structure in Australia was not illegal; it was potentially illegal, or allegedly illegal, but not illegal, as all the unsuccessful government challenges proved. A section in the Broadcast Act stated that a foreigner could not be "in a position to control a licensee." The several government inquiries were around how the Aspers were acting, not about the corporate structure itself, which was never successfully challenged and was upheld by the High Court of Australia in 1997–98. What bothered the local business community was that they hadn't thought of it.

Behind the scenes, Tom Strike, who was flying monthly from Winnipeg to Sydney, and Lerner, who had relocated his home base from the island of St. Maarten to Australia to untangle this complex financial and legal quagmire, were in negotiations with another TEN shareholder, Telecasters North Queensland (TNQ). The plan was for TNQ, a publicly listed company with a 40 percent voting equity interest (20 percent economic interest) in TEN, to transform itself into a new holding company and in the process acquire the Selli and Donholken stake, and indirectly offer their TEN shares to the Australian public. While this sounded simple enough, the intricacies of that arrangement occupied Strike and Lerner full-time for the next twenty months. As Strike recalled, "when you have a gun at your head to sell, it becomes quite complicated to construct the proper deal." Asper later estimated that this fiasco cost Canwest more than $5 million in legal fees, including dealing with one unnamed lawyer who had made page one of the *Sydney Morning Herald* when he was caught running around the street in front of his home wearing no clothes.

In 1997, Canwest's head office in Winnipeg still didn't have access to email. Each day Strike received from Australia more than 400 pages by fax, detailing an assortment of legal, financial and tax implications of the planned transaction. The faxes even followed him home. "It would be midnight, my family would be sleeping and I'd be on the phone with lawyers from Australia trying to solve a never-ending number of issues," he recalled. "Then the fax machine started running. The first page came through with a notation that it was the first of 450 pages. I'd call back and tell them to send it to the office. I didn't have that much paper in the house. At the office it was the same story. Each morning, the red light would be on indicating the memory was full and there was a paper jam. This would happen seven days a week. That was one of the reasons why we got email. The fax charges alone were costing thousands of dollars a day. I'd get the documents, read them, make comments and fax them all back. It was nuts."

Meanwhile, in Sydney, Asper was in Federal Court, appearing before Justice Graham Hill, arguing his case against the Australian government. The special eight-day hearing was held to determine whether or not Canwest was now in control of TEN and had thereby violated foreign ownership rules, and whether Peter Costello, treasurer of Australia, had denied Canwest and the other two companies a fair hearing by ordering them to divest their shares in TEN regardless of price. One day as the proceedings dragged on, Justice Hill, noticing that Asper was growing uncomfortable, adjourned for a short break so that he could have a cigarette. "You really know you're a media mogul when the Federal Court stops so you can have a weed," Asper quipped. Later he calculated that the fifteen-minute break probably cost the parties involved about A\$14,000 in legal fees as the multitude of lawyers in the room waited for him to butt out his cigarette.

The Federal Court judge ruled that, contrary to what Costello had announced, Canwest did not have to sell its stake by the end of September "irrespective of price." But at the same time, the judge agreed with the ABA that Canwest had to cut its economic interest in TEN back to the original 57.5 percent.

The Australian investment was probably Asper's most frustrating—and most profitable—venture. All the investigations by government regulators concluded, over and over again, that they had no case against him. Canwest's original $51 million investment delivered a dividend bonanza of more than $1 billion, leaving an asset that was still worth at least $1.2 billion. By 2007, Network TEN was throwing off annual dividends of $100 million.

Laurence Freedman, who sold most of his Network TEN stake in 2003 for more than A$40 million, from an original stake of A$4.5 million, spoke for most of his fellow investors when he told the *Sydney Morning Herald,* "I love the Canadians. I stand up whenever a Canadian walks into the room."

Much earlier, when he was starting out on his foreign adventures, Izzy needed a compass to guide him, and in the spring of 1991 his compass needle pointed due southwest toward Auckland, New Zealand, about as far as you could get from Winnipeg and still remain on terra firma. In one of those bizarre confluences of events more common than not when the worlds of business and politics collide, Izzy Asper owed his initial foray overseas—long before his much more significant entry into the Australian market—to a left-wing middle-aged accountant from Auckland named Roger Douglas. Between 1984 and 1990, as the island country's finance minister, Douglas caused a minor revolution by turning his back on his Labour Party principles to institute his own version of Reaganomics. In Auckland, the media dubbed it "Rogernomics." Though accused by his fellow Labourites of heresy, Douglas rescued a depressed economy by implementing a series of practical polices that created a welcoming environment for foreign investment. That included becoming one of the first countries in the Western world to permit 100 percent foreign ownership of its media.

The country's remoteness and rugged landscape turned contemporary New Zealanders into individualists little different from the first European settlers of the mid-eighteenth century. These pioneers and those who followed the British explorer Captain James Cook's arrival in 1769 had to not only confront the vagaries of nature, but also deal with hostile Maori tribesmen. From that time onward, adaptation and resourcefulness became the hallmark of New Zealanders. Such inventions as frozen meat, electric fences, stamp-vending machines, electric gas pumps, disposable syringes, wide-toothed shearing combs (for all of those sheep) and bungee jumping all are owed to Kiwi ingenuity.

When Asper arrived on the scene, Westpac Bank had lost C$69 million on its investment in TV3, New Zealand's only privately owned television station, which had gone on the air in 1989. Undercapitalized and overhyped, bragging that it would capture 45 percent of New Zealand's television advertising, the station was lucky to obtain 13 percent. Left hanging, TV3 started hemorrhaging and within eighteen months had been placed in receivership by its main creditor, Westpac, which set about finding a more experienced partner. At the time, Canwest executives Peter Viner and Stephen Gross were in Los Angeles shopping for new shows and met a Westpac representative, there on the same mission. Over drinks, some figures were tossed around. It turned out that for C$8 million, Canwest could acquire 20 percent of TV3, with a possibility of increasing its share in the future. Back in Winnipeg, Asper was intrigued, particularly by the lack of foreign ownership restrictions. Don Brinton, who was then running CKVU in Vancouver, and Gerry Noble, a young Toronto accountant who, at age twenty-six, had joined Global as comptroller in 1985, were dispatched to investigate. They discovered a potentially attractive franchise being almost deliberately run into the ground. They were greeted by a staff jubilant from having broadcast New Zealand's international rugby match for the first time. The match had attracted a huge audience, but they had never thought of selling advertising to go with the event. The broadcast had cost NZ$500,000 and produced no revenues, a signal that they needed to recommend that Asper purchase the operation; the profit potential was obvious. Within five years under new management, TV3 grew into such a bonanza that Canwest grabbed the balance of the equity for NZ$120 million. Noble moved to New Zealand and Peter Viner quarterbacked the station's remake of TV3 from Vancouver.

Beyond the usual Global brush cut of programming costs, Asper personally shifted the station's collective psyche in a dramatic confrontation with the staff. Early in the game, when TV3's fate was still uncertain, Izzy stopped in on his way to Australia and asked the assembled executives and heads of department to describe their jobs. "Each dutifully responded," he later recalled, "that their job was to create great dramas for posterity, or, in other cases, they extolled the virtue of shooting programming using six or seven cameras, when three would do. Every person who spoke only referred to items that cost money, but none that made money. I decided that this group needed a cold shower, and, because it wasn't the custom in New Zealand to be as blunt as is necessary in a bankruptcy situation, I launched into a lecture on the fundamentals and basic principles of commercial television."

"You've all described what you think your jobs are, but none of you have put your finger on what this is all about," he chided them. "That's why you're in bankruptcy. I'll tell you what your job is: it's to sell soap; it's to sell pantyhose; it's to sell cars. And the way that you do that is to put on programming that everybody wants to watch and that our advertisers will pay to be part of, in order to sell their soap, pantyhose and cars, and give us the money to provide the wonderful programs that will attract the audiences!"

Izzy's daughter, Gail, who had accompanied him on the trip, cringed against the wall in a back corner as the stunned group almost visibly shivered under that cold shower. "You have to understand, this was our first trip to New Zealand to meet the team that we were going to be working with, and they initially greeted us with a very warm reception," Gail later commented. "We were right in the newsroom, meeting the characters. I think that Dad had a feeling these people all wanted to make things work. But they were on the verge of bankruptcy. They were in serious straits, dire straits. So he thought they needed to hear some practical aspects of the broadcast business. His message was basically this: 'You either recognize that we're here to sell, or there won't be anything at all *to* sell, and you'll all be out of work.' As opposed to having the luxury of having a lot of money, coming in and saying, 'Okay, how are we going to improve the world, and make money at the same time?' So it had to be a pretty hard-hitting statement. At the same time, there were all sorts of other things said at that meeting that went unreported: Dad's commitment to human rights; his commitment to women in the workforce; and that he took all of these things really seriously, that he really was hoping to make this a very successful venture. It was a very positive thing. But you can imagine somebody being shocked by his lecture and then leaking it to the local press. Journalists, who are sometimes cynical, were not listening to the rest of it: that we want to make this work, and here's how we can make it work. And, of course, his talk was over the top—exaggerated—and [was] intended to be. Sometimes when people are doing things, and being sarcastic, or ironic, but trying to be on the same page as someone, it doesn't come out like that. I really think the reaction in the room was still positive. I mean, it's not that Dad created the world that we're in, the broadcasting world. The way that you make money is by selling advertising. That's the reality."

Of the thousands of words spoken by Asper, none were quoted against him more often than his off-the-cuff "soap speech." To this day, competitors and critics of Canwest trot out his words and portray him, as he once put it, "as a callous, soulless and purely profit-oriented media operator." He had, he later admitted, "offended the sensitive nature of people who believed their programs are an art form with inherent value, whether the audience wants to watch them or not." Still, the Auckland staff adapted to the new realities and salvaged most of their jobs. During Canwest's first full year in control, the station produced an operating profit of $465,000. The numbers kept multiplying after that, as did the station's viewing audience. By June 1996, TV3 had posted an impressive annual operating profit of $20 million. That led Asper to acquire the rights for the country's fourth private TV station,* which specialized in an audience between the ages of fifteen and thirty-nine. At about the same time, Canwest spent NZ$23 million to buy a half-dozen FM radio stations, including a transmitter at Christchurch, on New Zealand's South Island at the base of the Banks Peninsula. This purchase delighted Asper, who wrote to a friend, "Just think about it: 'Israel Asper is broadcasting in Christchurch.' No other Jew could make that statement since Jesus Christ himself!"

———

If the planet was shrinking as fast as Asper claimed, he figured that he at least had to attempt entry into the lucrative U.S. market. From Palm Beach, Asper tried to acquire Paxson Communications Corp., an American public television network headquartered there because that was where its controlling shareholder resided. He also made an attempt to buy Larry Tisch's position in CBS in the early 1990s. To pave the way for regulatory approval, Asper flew to Washington and met with Senator John McCain, then chairman of the U.S. Senate Commerce Committee (and later the Republican candidate for the U.S. presidency), which controlled broadcast law, and lobbied for Global's exemption from American foreign ownership rules. Cliff Stearns, another Republican congressman, later took up the issue and introduced a bill in Congress that would have allowed Canadian companies to own up to 40 percent of American stations, providing there was reciprocity. Izzy hired a full-time Capitol Hill lobbyist on a five-year contract to push the idea. But nothing happened.

Izzy's next leap into the unknown was the Hispanic television market, with its 500 million viewers and underdeveloped management techniques. It seemed like a smart idea, but Canwest's

---

*TV4 was a brilliant discovery made by Gerry Noble and his chief engineer. They found a patchwork of unused frequencies around New Zealand, snapped them up, and out of the blue, launched a whole new network.

incursion into the Latino market turned out to be "as unsatisfying as a warm margarita on a hot summer's day." Asper later explained away the missed opportunity as "a learning experience," which was double-talk for "a waste of time." To spearhead his drive into South America, he hired Charlie Weber, a Los Angeles film executive who had worked for George Lucas, marketing such mega-hits as *Raiders of the Lost Ark* and *The Empire Strikes Back*, and who ran Canwest International out of L.A. for half a decade. Weber scoured the globe for TV opportunities, on occasion, Asper later thought, spending a bit too much money in the process. One possibility was La Red, a struggling television station in Chile that had gone on the air in 1991 and that now ranked fifth in a six-station market. Asper paid US$8 million for a half-share in La Red and hired Victor Rodriguez, a forty-four-year-old Spanish-speaking executive with Toronto's CityTV as the station's new CEO. Costs were cut, staff reduced and the operation restructured. The trouble was that there really was no such animal as a "Hispanic market." Every major Spanish-speaking country spoke a different dialect and there were enough cultural variations that the Asper formula of importing American shows with translated dialogue simply didn't attract audiences. The experiment ended after two years in a break-even position but with no long-term prospects. *Hasta la vista*, baby.

During the period that Canwest International was active, from 1994 to 1998, Izzy travelled along with his two sons back and forth to Prague, Budapest, Warsaw and other Eastern European locales, and even investigated possibilities in China and Kazakhstan. At one point Canwest had a signed agreement to buy a TV station in Romania, but the government in Bucharest, which had taken over from President Nicolae Ceausescu in 1989, was too bureaucratic to surrender programming control. When Weber, the Aspers' agent on the potential deal, continued to submit high expense accounts, Asper got fed up. "I don't question what your Romanian expenses were for, I simply ask what they were so I can see what this adventure has cost us," Asper faxed Weber at the InterContinental Hotel in Bucharest in mid-May 1993. "You seem to be missing my point completely. From this moment on, there are *No* Romanian expenses. As of today, unless previously terminated as I instructed earlier this week. You simply don't seem to understand that we have lost all patience with a situation which has been running out of control and which is going nowhere, and in which our people have been taken hostage by the asylum inmates. We are utterly tired of hearing 'We made great progress this week,' week after week, without ever being told what that progress is. And when we're told, we realize the project has gone absolutely nowhere because of a strategy of never confronting the Romanians with what our irreducible minimum position is."

England seemed a more likely prospect, and it was here that the Asper clan, led by eldest son David, who was moving up in the company, made a brave stand. Then thirty-six and director of special projects, David was commuting from Regina (where he was running STV) to London, planning Canwest's run at Channel 5, the private channel that was up for bids. Fully aware that this was as much a cultural as a commercial issue, his primary task was to round up credible domestic partners. This he accomplished, bringing together a consortium that included the Scandinavian Broadcasting System (SBS) of London, headed by Harry Evans Sloan; Allan McKeown of SelecTV (and actress Tracy Ullman's husband); prominent independent television producers; and Canwest associate Australia's Network TEN. The Aspers' total share in UKTV, as the new network was to be called, was 30 percent, with Network TEN at 19.9 percent.

But for David the assignment inevitably led to conflicts with his father. In late November 1994, Izzy wrote a memo critical of David that was distributed to senior executives. It contained several patronizing comments that caused his eldest son great offence. How, David fumed, could the young Aspers do their jobs in such a humiliating context? David was equally infuriated with an interview his father had with Raymond Snoddy, a high-profile British freelance media journalist. Izzy, his son felt, had thrown away a carefully sought opportunity to build Canwest's media presence in the UK, by bragging at length to an uninterested audience about his successes in Australia. David sharply castigated his father on both counts.

A month later, Izzy replied with a classic Asper-style father–son lecture—tough and uncompromising. "I'm returning pages 1, 2, 6, 7, 8, 9, 10, 11, 13 and 21 of your December 22 draft marked up for change," faxed Asper at the end of December 1994 from Palm Beach. "I've warned you previously that: (a) your lawyer is incompetent and thus dangerous; this is the 4th or 5th amateur draft, with glaring and costly errors. He is a menace, get rid of him; (b) my time is far too expensive to spend correcting papers—I'm not your lawyer. You are supposed to be concerned with the quality of the agreement, not me. And most disturbing, (c) you aren't thinking! Look at clause 4.1 that would cost us maybe 100K–200K; look at the absence in 3.5, that would cost us about 400K; the lack of 5.1.4 would have prohibited expulsion . . . the non-competition clause was too weak . . . I want you to sit down and calmly reflect on the above and ask yourself why you missed two key commercial points. This agreement has been through several drafts, and every time I pick it up, I find more flaws that you have missed due to what I fear is a tendency to be superficial and unfocused. David, you cannot occupy senior executive positions or responsibility if your colleagues can't rely on documents you have approved; nor can I act as your 'minder' on your deals and documents. You will lose the respect and confidence of your colleagues if they don't believe you're sharp, crisp, watchful and focused . . . There's no point in being defensive. If you think I'm picking on you, please take the first draft, my handwritten comments, and the Nov. 3, 4 and Dec 22 drafts with these and my previous comments to TCS [Tom Strike] or any other deal-making executive in our shop, and see if they don't conclude that there is sloppiness and a superficiality tendency that has to be overcome. My advice: read everything slowly and carefully and think about the what-if's as you examine things microscopically and syllable by syllable."

"David was very tough," recalled Daniel Sandelson, who acted as Canwest's senior UK lawyer* and remains a good friend of the family. "In fact, in all my dealings with Canwest as a company, they've always been, not difficult, but they've always taken quite tough positions in negotiating with the other side, because they've had success in the past. There was certainly a job to be done because the European style then wasn't a very North American confrontational style, and Canwest knew what they wanted; they were effectively bankrolling this consortium anyway, and they were going to get what they wanted. So I think it was a question of trying to get what they wanted in a sort of European style as opposed to the kind of 'beating your head against a wall' style. It didn't take David very long at all to pick up on that . . . At that time Canwest as a North American company was the subject of a foreign ownership restriction so it couldn't control this business. So we had to go through all sorts of agonizing contortions to come up with a structure that gave Canwest control but didn't, and that, of course, was something that they had done in Australia. So they were quite familiar with that. The more complicated the structure we came up with, the happier Izzy was, and when we had added on a layer on top, his eyes would glow and he'd say, 'Yeah, that looks really good—can you make it more complicated?' David did not have any time for pomposity at all. He just wanted a very straight assessment of what was going on. He knew immediately if you were bullshitting, absolutely, in a nanosecond."

---

*Sandelson, a partner in the law firm of Clifford Chance, which occupies a mammoth tower in the Canary Wharf development, noted how Izzy, who was in London for a fair bit of time in 1995, loved being a lawyer. "I think he took a kind of playful enjoyment in trying to trip up all the other lawyers who were involved, including me," Sandelson recalled. "He read up on obscure aspects of English law, which were nothing to do with the UKTV transaction at all, but decided that he'd have a bit of fun with us. So he looked up some ancient right on grazing your pigs on somebody else's land, and asked me what it was. As it happened I knew just by sheer luck. From my perspective that certainly added a sharper edge to all the work that I was doing because normally I'm the lawyer on the deal and everybody else are business people, and having someone who was a very senior lawyer, and had done endless transactions before, was quite an interesting environment."

The harsh fact was that Izzy inadvertently sabotaged the British application. Every one of the front-rank potential UK partners David approached rejected the Asper approach outright. The deal that Izzy had so cleverly perfected in his own mind refused to acknowledge the fact that the more perfect it became for Canwest, the more odious it was for any potential partners. Still, David was hailed in the British press as the "can-do guy for Channel 5." This attention was not lost on the father, who ended up praising his efforts.

"David was the point man on England," Izzy conceded. "He practically lived there for a year and came of age in that process." Daniel Sandelson agreed. "David didn't come across as being young," he suggested. "He was very tough. He realized that you couldn't bludgeon your consortium partners into agreeing with things and I think he handled the negotiations very skilfully."

As the May 2, 1995, deadline approached, David was joined by Izzy; Richard Leipsic, Canwest's corporate legal counsel; another company lawyer, Greg Gilhooly; and Tom Strike. "Izzy threw himself into the project with more energy than the rest of us," recalled Gilhooly. "He took over the top-floor suite of the luxurious but quaint 22 Jermyn Street hotel, located in a narrow lane a stone's throw from Piccadilly Circus. He made it into his bunker. You could imagine the smoking and the drawn curtains and the dark carpeting—everything quintessentially British, with Mr. Asper up there working in his pyjamas around the clock. Whenever he wasn't in our offices over in Covent Garden, he would be working there, chain smoking on the phone or using his fax machine. He single-handedly took this hotel into twentieth century in terms of having them upgrade the telephones and their faxes. The hotel loved him, although he was their only guest—ever—who got T.G.I. Friday's, a restaurant in Covent Garden, to deliver cheeseburgers and fries to his room."

Assembling the players had its moments. One evening around eleven o'clock, lawyer Tony Ghee, an SBS director and Sloan's London lawyer, received a frantic call ordering him to report immediately to UKTV's offices in Covent Garden. Ghee, who lives in a suburb of Barnes, a fair distance from the city centre, told his caller, who had not even bothered to introduce himself, that he wasn't going any where at this time of the night. "I put the phone down," says Ghee, "and got out of bed, and my wife said, 'What was that about?' I said, 'Some crazy bloke wants me to go to Covent Garden, but it's not going to happen.'" The crazy bloke was Izzy.

Five minutes later Ghee's phone rang again and this time it was Harry Sloan on the line. "You have just spoken to Izzy Asper?" he asked. "Yeah, I suppose I have," replied Ghee. "He rings me up and orders me to do something to which I responded that I didn't think I wanted to." And Sloan said, "Well, you have to, because the final agreement for the consortium has to be settled right away." So Ghee got dressed and an hour later was standing in David Asper's temporary offices in Covent Garden. "I was given all these documents to read and negotiate immediately," Ghee recalled. "Tom Strike, David Asper and Allan McKeown were there, but not Izzy. He came later. The meeting went on through the night and about 5:00 a.m. I said, 'I've done enough. I don't know what I've done but I've done enough.'"

David Asper remained confident, knowing the quality of his partners and the seriousness of his presentation. The informal understanding was that the highest bidder would win. To maintain secrecy, even internally, Tom Strike had calculated ten scenarios with different amounts, only one of which was real. The major players were up for three straight days and nights, and by the third evening no one except the four Canwest people knew the winning numbers. (Strike even erased everyone's computer hard drives and grabbed the backup tapes so that there was no risk of tampering.) Late on May 1, from a restaurant where he was dining, David telephoned Greg Gilhooly in another part of the city, and told him, "My steak was delicious." That was the prearranged code to confirm a bid of £36.3 million ($79.6 million). The moment he hung up, Gilhooly gave the order to Canwest's London printers to proceed with production of the voluminous application. Two days later, when the bids were published, the Asper partnership came in first with the highest tender and an application that included 880 hours of original British programming in its first year, featuring Sir Richard Attenborough's epic series on Winston Churchill.

Izzy was ecstatic. "We had gone out to lunch and then came back to the office," remembered Gilhooly, "and Mr. Asper arrived with this white T-shirt that he had bought. He had got markers—red, white and blue and black—and had hand-drawn a Union Jack and text on his shirt that was the battle pride for us and about the Canadians who came over and won, and he was walking into the room where all the media were. [The text read, "BRITAIN MAY RULE THE WAVES BUT CANWEST RULES THE AIR WAVES."] He was so proud of the deal that he wanted to just come in and celebrate with the group, and so he had this handmade T-shirt on. I vividly remember Kip Meek, one of our consultants, physically grabbing Izzy as he was about to walk in, taking him out in the anteroom and making him change because in the UK, refined business people would never do anything of the sort."

Then reality set in. Concerns about quality programming and business planning were certainly a consideration, but so was domestic politics. The foreign-dominated group was up against two diehard British television groups, and one of them, the Pearson-MAI consortium, which published *The Economist* and owned Thames TV, was eventually awarded the prize, with the commissioners claiming that the Aspers' UKTV would not be able "to secure sufficient programming of high quality." (As Greg Gilhooly later commented, "If you've ever been to the UK and watched Channel 5, you will find it galling that anyone could have thrown out our bid on a quality threshold.")

Having spent eighteen months and $4 million of Canwest's money on the project, David was angry and understandably disappointed. "We should have won this," he said. "No, we *did* win it. We did the most. We had the best application. We had this thing reviewed by a lot of very credible British television broadcasting people . . . Except that what Izzy said was, you need in your life to lose really badly because only if you've lost and plummeted the depths of being a loser can you begin to appreciate even small success. In my view the reason we won and then lost was purely political. Virgin and we pursued a judicial review of the ITC decision and discovered that the professional staff of the ITC had accepted our programming plans. In short, after six months of intensive review, our application was recommended by the staff to the ITC commissioners as being the winner. Nevertheless, in just a few hours of discussion, the ITC rejected their staff recommendation and, incredibly, tossed out Virgin and us in order to award the licence to Pearson, who I believe were their favourites. In the end, I fear that it did not matter what anyone else did because the Pearson group had been anointed, though its bid was $30 million lower. The notion that our programming was not up to acceptable standards is pure nonsense and was a pretext only."

More than a decade later, Daniel Sandelson had a slightly different take on the ITC's decision. "Canwest was an unknown quantity in Europe, even though they had a very good reputation in North America," he recalled. "I don't think a British regulator effectively having control over British assets, mainly the airwaves, was likely to give it to a non-British bid. However, as good as the bid was, and it stacked up as well as any other bid, in respect of every section except one area, the news, which is where they disqualified us. This to me was odd. Because if you look at the news on Channel 5 today, it's a quick ten minutes at about nine o'clock and it's not the main part of the channel. It was even more surprising because we had a contract for the news to be supplied by Reuters. So to fail the bid on the basis of the quality of the news was actually a bit of a joke, but we knew they were looking desperately for some reason to fail us and that was the one that they found. Izzy and Tom and David and everybody else were furious, and rightly so. Izzy, I think, was pretty disappointed because he believed in open markets and he believed that if you have an equal chance to do something you should be given an equal chance."

The Aspers contemplated a legal challenge, but followed their lawyers' advice that a judicial review would be a waste of time and money. That was not the end of it, though. Behind the scenes, Asper had already started preliminary talks about possible Canwest involvement in an Irish broadcasting network.

A story in *The Times* caught Izzy's eye when he was in London in the spring of 1990. It detailed the bureaucratic difficulties experienced by an Irishman named James Morris, who was attempting to establish the Emerald Isle's first private television station. Morris had run up against a barrier of regulatory obstacles and ineptitude that only someone like Asper could truly appreciate. "I phoned him," Asper later related, "and told him that I had been down the same road. I encouraged him to keep on fighting and not to let anyone push him around. And he replied, 'Gosh, you're the first guy who even gave a damn about it.'"

There was more than a little of Izzy Asper in James Morris. Morris had set up his own editing company in 1976 and two years later moved the postproduction business to Windmill Lane in Dublin's Docklands, where he set up Windmill Lane Recording Studios.* Morris was determined to own Ireland's first commercial television station and put together a consortium that included business executive John Kelleher, Paul McGuinness (manager of the pop band U2), and Osmond (Ossie) Kilkenny, a chartered accountant and financial adviser to U2. By 1995, having exhausted other options, Morris contacted Izzy, who handed the Irish file to his son Leonard, then only thirty-two and Canwest's vice-president for corporate development.

---

*The Windmill Lane studios, half a block from the Grand Canal, are the famous sound stages where U2 recorded *The Joshua Tree*, among other hit albums. Today, the wooden fence around the property is covered with spraypainted graffiti messages for Bono and the rest of the band.

Together with Gerry Noble, back in Winnipeg from New Zealand, Leonard flew to Dublin and met Morris at about four o'clock one afternoon. That was followed by dinner, and by eleven o'clock that evening they had the makings of a deal.

From their hotel room at the Dublin Hilton, they ran it by Izzy. "By six in the morning," Leonard proudly recalled, "we had everything scratched out in Gerry's handwriting." They left Dublin with the TV3 deal all but sewn up—or so they thought. Another meeting in New York with Ossie Kilkenny followed, and it took twelve more hours of tough negotiations to get the letter of intent drawn up. At one point Leonard was in Kilkenny's hotel room writing while the accountant changed into a tuxedo for a dinner that evening; he picked up Kilkenny after his function had ended. Kilkenny read the letter in the taxi on the drive to the airport, but he was still hedging. Leonard told him that he couldn't return to Winnipeg without a signed document. Reluctantly, Kilkenny signed the letter and flew back to Ireland. But by the next morning, he had faxed Leonard a letter rescinding the agreement.

Rounds of negotiations followed, until finally in February 1997 all of the details had been ironed out. At the end of April, Canwest announced that it had purchased a 45 percent stake in TV3. James Morris was appointed chairman, while Canwest had a call option on another 35 percent held by ACT, a venture capital group.

David Asper, a member of the TV3 board of directors, was travelling back and forth from Winnipeg to Dublin as the launch date neared. When the day's business was completed, there was time for a bit of fun. "Paul McGuinness is a huge celebrity in Dublin. I mean, he's the manager for U2. And we were out one night," David recalled. "One place we arrived at had a long lineup. We pull up with McGuinness. We're the TV guys and he's the U2 guy and the line parts like the Red Sea. We walk into this bar and there was an area with a thick velvet curtain. You couldn't see what was behind it. The curtain gets pulled back, and there was an area that resembled a living room. In the middle of the room, there was the bar, with

PETER C. NEWMAN

ice buckets and champagne. We were treated like celebrities the entire evening."

Drinking pints of warm, thick and medicinal-tasting Guinness ale with loud music blaring was one thing; the intricacies of starting up a television station, another. In the light of day, Ossie Kilkenny attempted to assert the Irish partners' control over everything from capital expenditures to the appointment of the advertising agency that the consortium should be using. "I was copied on a particularly unappealing letter from Gerry Noble on [the advertising agency] issue which James [Morris] advised me that he was going to respond to," wrote Kilkenny to Leonard in early August 1997 from Venice. "While we do not hold out any real hope of curbing the excesses of your approach in general there are some areas where we will have to go to battle."

Considering that Canwest was putting up all of the money to launch the station, Leonard was not amused. "Ossie, Your provocative faxes today containing gratuitous insults unfortunately overshadowed the substantive points you raised, and for reasons I am sure you will understand I have decided to wait until the end of the day to respond," replied Leonard. "At first glance, it appears that you are trying to improve your position relative to our letter of agreement, which is a non-starter . . . While I am sure you genuinely feel the transaction between Canwest and the Consortium is one sided in favour of Canwest, I am sure you will understand that the feeling exists from Canwest's point of view that this is the most lucrative arrangement that has ever been offered to someone in your position . . . What really disappoints me, however, is that you have resorted to name-calling and innuendo once again. I thought that was behind us and it comes at an inopportune time, in that Gilhooly is already in Ireland, and I was planning to arrive next week as you know, hoping that we would find ourselves in an atmosphere of mutual co-operation."

The storm passed and the Aspers solidified Canwest's position in Ireland, taking matters one step further. At the end of October

1997, the company bought 7.4 percent (2.45 million shares) of Ulster Television (UTV) in Northern Ireland. By mid-1998, its stake had risen to a healthy 29.9 percent, the maximum allowed a foreign investor under British broadcasting rules. The operation became doubly lucrative when Tom Strike and Rick Hetherington were able to negotiate a shift by the mega-popular *Coronation Street* to their TV3 channel.

––––––––––

Prickly bureaucratic regulations and surly politicians did not diminish Canwest's presence on the world stage. But the Irish and New Zealand operations were sold off, partly to reduce the debt from the Hollinger newspaper purchase and partly because Leonard Asper's strategy called for the elimination of foreign stand-alone conventional properties. Australia's Network TEN was also placed on the market. Leonard insisted on a selling price fourteen or fifteen times TEN's earnings, or more than $3.10 a share, but prospective buyers such as Blackstone and the Carlyle Group offered only eleven times earnings, and Canwest would not budge. Instead Leonard took advantage of Australia's reformed media regulations on foreign ownership to convert its debentures into equity, so that Canwest's voting share in the network went up to 56 percent.

The Network TEN purchase in Australia had been one of Izzy Asper's toughest and nastiest negotiations. He narrowly beat out News Corp.'s Rupert Murdoch, who had the advantage of being a hometown boy able to either rent or buy platoons of Australian politicians to support his cause.

To celebrate the signing of their new acquisition, Asper and Canwest executive Peter Viner found an out-of-the-way restaurant and were enjoying their martinis and dinner when a stranger approached them.

"Mr. Asper," said the man, "I know you've just done a deal with Westpac Bank to buy Network TEN and I'm going to give you the offer of a lifetime. You see, Mr. Rupert Murdoch wants the network very badly, and he'll give you $10 million to turn the deal over to him and walk away."

Viner and Asper looked at each other in disbelief. "We don't know you," Izzy told the stranger, "and don't even know if you're authorized to make such a proposal."

The man assured them that he was legitimate. "All right, I've heard you're a tough dealmaker," he purred, "so I'll put my best offer on the table. We'll pay you $20 million in any currency you like, payable to any bank account you direct, if you just walk away and tell your people that you were simply outbid."

Asper told him, "Take a walk."

Izzy never discovered if the offer was authentic or whether Murdoch was really involved. Asper later reflected that it was the first time he had ever been offered a bribe. When Viner asked Izzy why he hadn't accepted it or at least bargained, Asper replied with a smile, "If I had taken the bribe, I would have had to share it with you . . . Anyway, I'll make more than that amount through my Canwest Global stock, once we own Network TEN."

And that was precisely what happened.

8

How Jazz Created Izzy's Groove

The fact that jazz is invented spontaneously meshed perfectly
with Asper's way of doing business. Both were performance art.

The narrative arc of Israel Asper's life was music, specifically modern jazz. Its high-octane energy and existential currents provided the life force from which everything flowed. I was the first to link his bizarre work habits with jazz music, since improvisation is the root and essence of both disciplines. Asper was swift to realize that to put the most creative spin on his business strategy required the same spontaneous creativity that fuelled his variety of hip sounds. Albert Goldman, the New York music critic, isolated the qualities of quintessential jazz artists as "emotional depth, technical assurance and the vast experience of a man with a million miles on his meter."

That was Izzy.

During his first quarter century in business, whenever journalists tried to divine Asper's complex motivations and unique business methods, they usually speculated that he did it not for the money or for fame, or for "the love of the game." What they missed was that while unbridled chutzpah defined Izzy's style, in his work and play, he followed his private voice—the finger-snapping cadences of the jukebox in his head that never stopped playing. "My greatest love in life is music," he freely admitted. "And that means jazz."

The fundamental intent of jazz music is only tangentially to entertain, but more vitally to recharge the spirit with sensory awareness. No music depends so much on the inventiveness of its players. The best of them become non-repetitive poets, spilling their psyches through their instruments. The legendary saxophonist Sonny Rollins touched the essence of the art of improvisation when he told J.D. Considine, jazz critic for the *Globe and Mail,* "You can't think and play at the same time. When I go on the stand, the music is just happening. It plays me."

Izzy assessed his jazz idols by how convincingly they fit this category and how creatively they could broaden the chord structures and harmonies of a composer's or arranger's intentions. They included Dave Brubeck, Oscar Peterson, George Shearing, David Frishberg, Marian McPartland, Don Shirley, Dave Young, Peter Appleyard and Michael Feinstein.* (Pianist Bill Evans, once a member of that august company, "became too cerebral, he wasn't coherent, he lost his rationality.")

Izzy could have followed his parents and gone the classical route, but as early as thirteen he recognized jazz as his entry point into the New World's culture and adopted its revolutionary beat and heretical formats. It all started when his elder brother, Aubrey, gave him, as a bar mitzvah present, twelve-inch 78 r.p.m. recordings of George

---

*"Feinstein was a Gershwin purist for a number of years," Leonard recalled, "but one day Izzy took us to see his Christmas special and he had gone completely 'pop,' playing almost no Gershwin and bringing in second-rate talent, including some soap opera stars trying to sing. Izzy was despondent, so much so that he wrote a ten-page, single-spaced letter to Feinstein accusing him of selling out, going commercial and, despite his promising years of greatness, ultimately being a hoax. None of us could fathom why Izzy had become so upset over this turn of events."

Gershwin's *Rhapsody in Blue* and three of his preludes, played by the American virtuoso Oscar Levant. From that moment on, Asper became a Gershwin groupie. It started with his admiration for the composer as the agent provocateur who took jazz out of smoke-filled bars into concert halls ("He took a streetwalker and made a lady out of her").

The Asper house on Winnipeg's fashionable Wellington Crescent was gradually turned into a shrine to his idol. As well as countless scores and photographs of the composer, Izzy snagged some truly valuable memorabilia, such as his original tune books, rhyming dictionary and the seventeen pages of brown wrapping paper on which was sketched the original libretto to *Porgy and Bess*. The centrepieces of his collection were three huge panels of opaque glass on which were etched scenes from Gershwin's life, some of his scores and portraits of Babs and Izzy's three children. Winnipeg artist Warren Carther, who executed the pieces, said it was one of his favourite commissions: "I relate well to obsessive-compulsive personalities, and Izzy's enthusiasm for Gershwin was contagious." For Asper, Gershwin represented the essential crossover between the classics and jazz, with his master work, *Porgy and Bess*, providing the junction of opera and musical comedy.

Asper's conversion from classical music to jazz, with Gershwin holding the middle ground, was a rite of passage, the trigger for his declaration of independence from his family's musty musical traditions. His father's markedly different orientation caused a rift. "He had contempt for jazz," Izzy lamented. "The war between us raged until twenty years later when I took my dad to an Oscar Peterson concert. He begrudgingly admitted that Peterson was a virtuoso, though he didn't approve of his improvisation."

Asper chose jazz because it was the music most compatible with his character and his lifestyle. The fact that jazz is invented spontaneously meshed perfectly with his way of doing business. Both were performance art. Few MBA programs would have the nerve to adopt Asper's major business deals as case histories. Like jazz, they flowed more from his gut than his brain, and thus followed no rules—except for a moderately restrained connection to the art of the impossible.

He improvised not only his music but his life—from day to day, year to year and decade to decade, as he changed his goals and professions. His complicated feuds and friendships followed few rules. Like jazz, they were as unpredictable as a hailstorm—or, as his intimates preferred to describe the process, a series of random and disruptive hailstorms. The elements of his life and career were constantly being shaken up and put together in unexpectedly creative ways. "Jazz," Asper once told me, "allows you to approach any issue on the basis that nothing is too outrageous to consider, or too ridiculous to try. You begin with a coherent proposition but admit you have no idea where it's leading. Jazz musicians do that all the time: take off on a lick and push it to the absolute limit, and so do I in business, as I attempt to make a lovely melody from seemingly irresolvable discord."

This was a tough gig, especially when he was asking for serious money from sabre-toothed Bay Street bankers who thought that jammin' had something to do with spreading sticky stuff on your morning toast.

———————

Jazz requires trade-offs. The music may be spontaneous, but it has strict limits, such as its time signatures, the size and temper of the audience and the capacity of the musicians' alcohol intake. Louis Armstrong came closer than anyone to defining the essence of jazz when he answered a jabbering New York society woman who wouldn't leave him alone until he explained to her what jazz was all about. "Lady," he said, "we play life." That was Izzy's core mantra. He played life in its many incarnations, which depended on his disposition of the moment—from dark to giddy, with not much in between. It was a ballet choreographed by the cadence of his moods, which granted not quite equal time to the tensions between cold-blooded analysis and hot-blooded passion.

He could never become one of those smug lapdogs who populate Canada's corporate scene, play it safe and avoid risking the farm. Yet it was unfair to describe him as a junkyard dog—though they're the best kind, living by their wits, beholden to no one and always sniffing out new chances while hounding their owners to distraction.

Despite the genuine and reciprocated love of family, Izzy was born a loner and died as one, always the young stranger in a world he never made, surviving on instinct, booze, cigarettes and those blaring 4/4 and 3/4 tracks in his brain. If he gave the impression that he wasn't sure what he would be doing tomorrow or the week or the month after, it was because he didn't know. Such guardians of order and habit as sheet music and management manuals were absent from house and office. These slick contrivances got you nowhere—well, nowhere interesting. Few of his associates could follow Asper's reasoning when he was off on one of his existential rants. He was jammin.' Should he write a Broadway musical, create an interstellar TV network, sell the boreal forest he owned on New Zealand's wildest shore, turn Portage into Fifth Avenue, retire to Majorca, buy Manitoba, populate Mars?—whatever.

"He was a jazz fan of the highest order," recalled Ross Porter, the Winnipegger who became the moving force in most of Izzy's jazz ventures and later, on his own, created Toronto's highly successful Jazz.FM91. "He was a very astute improviser, and to continue with the jazz analogy, he always knew where the head and the tail were—how to get into the tune and how to get out. It was the bit in between that he improvised so well. Same in business. There was some logical progression to his thoughts, but he was improvising. Like jazz, few of his business deals moved in a straight line and yet they progressed inexorably to their goal."

As a mark of respect for the jazz soloists Izzy most enjoyed, he remained true to a composition's (or business deal's) rhythmic impulses as he transformed the melodic line into exhilarating new sounds. That's what allowed the music (and his business empire) to regenerate itself. The similarity of the approaches to music and business was what kept Izzy going. "Dad also loved the music because, as he said in an interview on Cool FM, 'Jazz is never sad—you'll *never* feel angry or sad listening to it,'" his daughter, Gail, recalled. "I've tested that theory and he's right—though it *is* wistful. Blues is sad and rock can be angry."*

He was not a calm listener. Ron Polinsky, his main Winnipeg jazz buddy, recalled a Bill Evans concert they attended in New York at which the audience, driven restless by Evans's meaningful pauses and silences, started to talk. That Asper could not tolerate. "I was always concerned that he was going to end up in a fist fight with somebody by turning around and telling them to shut up," Polinsky recalled—which of course was exactly what happened. On another occasion, during a concert at Central Park's Tavern on the Green, Asper got into an argument with the leader who announced that the next number was based on "some movie from the 1950s." Asper stood up to correct him. "No, it's from the 1955 film *Pete Kelly's Blues*, and it starred Jack Webb as Kelly with Peggy Lee and Ella Fitzgerald." The band leader apologized. Izzy glowed in the dark.

"He truly had the most sophisticated taste," according to Ross Porter. "He would talk about how truth and beauty were the integral parts of the music, which comes from something that jazz pianist Bill Evans used to say. I became involved with him in a business sense when he told me that he was going to launch a jazz televi-

---

*"When he started up Cool FM, Izzy angrily complained to Tom Strike, "The play list is crap—it's gotta change." It had been constructed with repetitions, according to broadcasting formulas, which he rejected. "I don't want that. I want the sections played again, but it has to be 1,500 rotations before the song repeats itself. That's what I want. Besides, it's the wrong playlist." He then produced his own, handwritten version. When a station executive asked, "Where in hell am I going to get this stuff?" Asper shot back, "It's all in my basement. Send someone over and get it, and take it to the station and you can upload it."

sion channel. I remember saying, 'So it's a channel that plays music for grown-ups?' and he said, 'Yeah, that's it—exactly!' We stayed in touch and dealt with one another socially, and then I remember his phone call during the Toronto Jazz Festival in the fall of 2003. I was the MC at one of the concerts and was backstage when my cellphone rang. I heard the tinkling of ice against the sides of a glass, then a whisper: 'If you're having sex, tell me to fuck off.' When I reluctantly confessed that I wasn't, the martini-and-Craven-A-cured voice rasped, 'It's Izzy. We're going to do it. Can you get out to Global tomorrow for a meeting?'"

Some weeks later Porter was invited to the Aspers' Winnipeg home to cement the deal. When you walked in Izzy's front door, you went straight ahead into his little den area, where a chesterfield and a chair surrounded a large table. Izzy was seated there, kibitzing while vaguely listening to his money men debate the economics of owning a specialty jazz radio station in Winnipeg. They knew it would be a lousy investment but didn't dare rain on Izzy's parade. Finally he interrupted their prattle, leaned over and barked, "You don't understand. Just launch the fucking thing!" And that was it. The button had been pushed.

"Okay, I've got you here, you're going to sign this, but before you do I want to talk you out of it," he told Porter when he formally asked him to participate. "I want you to remember the world you come from. You're coming from the CBC, and the CBC world is very different than the world over here in terms that the stakes are high, it's cutthroat, this is about profit and sometimes art doesn't win. Do you still want the job?" Porter recalled, "And I said, 'Yes' and that was the start-up." When the station staff suggested they might increase their audience by playing "smooth jazz" (a polite term for elevator music), Izzy killed the idea with a pointed snort: "It reminds me of the soundtrack from a bad porno."

Porter recalled travelling from Winnipeg to Toronto with Asper to catch a triple-header headlined by pianists Marian McPartland

and Dave Brubeck and Canadian vibraphonist Peter Appleyard. "We went backstage with him to see Brubeck, and the enthusiasm of this man, who ran a corporation that had holdings around the world, was that of a teenage fan. He was awestruck to be with one of the architects of jazz. He felt he was in the presence of greatness. I remember how thrilled he was to have his photograph taken with Brubeck. We went to a hotel lounge later and that enthusiasm continued for hours afterward." Asper considered Brubeck the greatest of the jazz artists because he created order through which chaos shimmered. Izzy invited his quartet to Winnipeg and rented a concert hall to celebrate Canwest's twentieth anniversary, but had words with his idol when he refused to play any of his requests.

Joined as they were at the hip by their affinity not just for jazz but for the very special musicians, arrangers and composers whose artistry touched their souls, Asper felt closer to Porter than to most of his business colleagues. Porter was one of the few outside the family who caught a whiff of the profound insecurity that fuelled the man—and held him in its grip. "Outwardly and for people who didn't know him, Izzy was the ultimate overconfident tycoon. But he wasn't—not really," Porter recalled. "He was vulnerable and very unsure of himself. He had proven himself to his father and to God knows who else, but his self-confidence was a mess. For sure. There weren't many of them, but there were moments when you saw the very tender underside to him." For Izzy, jazz was joy, but it was also a crutch, a stabilizer, a sanity-preserving echo that brought him back to Planet Earth.

The most revealing clue to Asper's psyche was the poignancy of his piano playing, which was as public as his inner voice ever became—though few heard it, since he never played a concert and even his barroom interludes could be counted on one hand. Actually, on three fingers: that night at the Starlight Bar in Minneapolis when the house pianist didn't turn up; his walk-on as an itinerant pianist during the filming of Global TV's series *Traders;* and a brief interlude (not jazz—Gershwin's *Rhapsody in Blue*) tickling the ivories at a reception, shortly before he died, at Toronto's Carlu, when he announced the inaugural air date for CoolTV.*

But his best appearance was in Puerto Vallarta. "There was this empty bar, nobody was there," Babs recalled." "We were with a group of friends, one of whom was a singer. Izzy sat down and just started playing the piano in this empty bar, and his friend started singing. The next thing you know, the bar is filled up, people are shouting requests."

I could always judge Izzy's state of mind by the length and cadence of the introductions he played to whatever Gershwin tune he was teasing. Ideally, jazz musicians play for themselves, as Asper so often did, alone during those witching hours before the spreading dawn separates land from sky. His piano doodling was his personal ode to joy, an escape from the inner devils haunting him. It was both a crutch and a stabilizer, a sanity-preserving exercise that seldom failed him. His piano touch was delicate, all slides and whispers, as evocative as a Picasso charcoal drawing, with glints and ghosts of other times and other venues. His bouts at the piano were reminiscent of F. Scott Fitzgerald's description of his most evocative fictional hero, Jay Gatsby, "who possessed some heightened sensitivity to the promise of life, as if he were related to one of those intricate machines that register earthquakes ten miles away."

Izzy's son Leonard, who understands music, plays the piano with flair. His tastes, according to Anthony Wilson-Smith, writing in *Maclean's*, "run to Rush, the thinking hoser's heavy-metal band." Leonard also had some interesting theories about his father's musical style. "He used extremely complex chord combinations and tried

---

*His cameo appearance on his own network's TV show, which he imagined would be a twenty-minute filming caper, turned into a nine-hour ordeal because of all the simulated setups and alternate takes. He was not pleased that his stand-in for deciding camera angles during the rehearsals was "a big old fat guy." But when he was asked by a *Toronto Sun* reporter how he felt he had done, Izzy came through in perfect showbiz style: "My contract forbids me from discussing my performance. But let me tell you: I was terrific."

to create a symphony out of dissonance by taking notes that normally wouldn't go together and somehow melding them. He didn't just love music—he studied it. I remember countless late Saturday nights, at four in the morning, coming home not entirely sober and going into his den to say goodnight. We debated our respective musical tastes. I tried to convince him that Bruce Springsteen's lyrics rivalled those of Ira Gershwin or that Neil Peart of Rush was a revolutionary percussionist. But I would always be overwhelmed, and two hours later would emerge, Springsteen and Rush long forgotten but fully understanding the musical significance of the change of key in the song 'High Flying Adored' or the exact point when Dave Brubeck began to improvise and the precise moment he returned from a harmonic precipice to miraculously find his way back to the main theme."

Shared loneliness set the mood of Israel Asper's music. In his piano playing as in his business dealings, he chose to depend on his intuitions of the moment, which is all that any jazz musician—or entrepreneur on the make—can trust.

9

Fort Asper

"His wife, Babs, held the fort together—
she allowed Izzy to be who he was."
—Dr. Jodi Lofchy, Izzy's niece

I t was a toss-up. In serious moments, Israel Asper referred to his family foundation as his fourth child, in the sense that it had been willed a quarter of his fortune and occupied at least that much of his time. But at home in his rambling bungalow on Winnipeg's Wellington Crescent, nestled into a slight curve of the adjoining Assiniboine River, his extra child had four paws and a tail.

Two dogs dominated his days and especially his nights, because they were his constant companions during his nocturnal vigils to greet the dawn and listen to his music. They were Tuffy and Bernie the Attorney (named after the song "My Attorney Bernie," composed and sung by jazz musician Dave Frishberg). Both were Lhasa Apsos (the same breed George Gershwin favoured), and both had their idiosyncrasies. "The ones we had were not dogs—they were something else, not dogs," Babs complained. "All my life, I wanted a dog that would come, fetch and lie down—do things that dogs do. Tuffy was the Noël Coward of dogs. Every other mutt would just barge through the screen door of our cottage, but he would stand there until somebody opened it for him. It was like *Lady and the Tramp*." Tuffy couldn't be trained to do anything because canine instruction depends on being rewarded with treats and there wasn't a snack in the world that he would deign to eat. Bernie, his successor, was more plebeian but also untrainable because he was just plain dumb.

But there was another canine visitor to the Asper household, a German shepherd that stood out in any litany of the family pets. One evening when the kids were small, the doorbell rang. They couldn't see anyone out the window—except for this strange dog, patiently waiting to be let in. Izzy had gone to answer the bell first but didn't let him in. When the bell rang again it was Babs's turn. This was a good thing. Had it been her husband, some wretched soul might have concluded that the master of the house had exceeded his nightly martini ration. But this was Babs and she was stone-cold sober. When she got to the door, the damn dog was leaning on the bell. "Can you imagine a dog ringing your doorbell?" she wondered. "Our bell went off at midnight and it turned out to be this dog, ringing the bell—with his paw. We were trying to ignore it, but he just kept ringing. We let him in and he took over. He was very smart. We notified the Humane Society, and soon someone called from Saskatchewan, claiming his animal. He described it correctly and asked me to put Ringo on the phone." Babs held up the receiver to the dog's ear and the man talked to him. The dog barked at the appropriate intervals and in his excitement spotted the carpet. Babs tried to persuade the fellow to sell it to them, and the kids offered to empty their piggy banks, but the owner wouldn't budge. It must have been something the dog tattled to his master about the Aspers during their phone call. *Hark the Herald Angels Sing* . . .

Out of range of his canine compadres, Izzy lived nearly as complicated a domestic life as an office life. In both locations, he was the
main man, the king of his castle, the big enchilada, the omnipotent
mucky-muck. But at home he didn't rule the roost. This was the
domain of Izzy's wife of forty-seven years, the former Ruth Miriam
"Babs" Bernstein, who acted as kindly den mother, gutsy media-
tor, ever-present conscience, busy pacifier and instant hostess. She
accepted impossible demands with equanimity and grace, but at a
cost. "To use a metaphor," said Yale Lerner, who was a mutual friend
of both senior Aspers, "she took a sacrifice fly from age twenty to
seventy, and set back her own values to help her husband with his."
As Dr. Jodi Lofchy, Izzy's niece, put it, "Babs held the fort together—
she allowed Izzy to be who he was."*

She was described by nearly everyone as being Izzy's "anchor." It
was an inexact analogy. Anchors sit on the bottom of shallow lakes
and fast-running rivers to keep their mother ships from drifting.
Unlike Babs, they perform no activist function. Maintaining her
husband at something resembling an even keel was her next-to-full-
time preoccupation, and it was no simple assignment. Israel Asper
was one of those gladiator executives. "He could certainly induce
stress into almost any business occasion," admitted Babs. "I think
he loved it, and found the process highly creative. I may have been
a drag on him at times. He loved his family and he loved me, but
we held him back, there's no question about it. Yet without us, he
might have spun off into space. He would have if there hadn't been
something or somebody holding him down. There were lots of times
when things weren't so good. They got crazy. And I kept thinking,
'Golly, do I really want to be here?' I'm a slow learner, but I finally
decided that this was the way it was going to be. This was my life
and it was never going to slow down. This man was never going to

*On Babs's sixty-fifth birthday, Izzy secretly sent his private jet, a Hawker 800,
down to Washington, where Jack Jones (Babs's favourite singer) was performing, to
fly him and his band to Winnipeg so he could sing "Happy Birthday" to her.

change, nor should he have to. He had so much to offer, so much he wanted to do. My life kept me off balance. I kept hopping from one foot to the other. But it was all very exciting."

Babs Asper boasted a strong ego but never claimed, as so many wives-who-lunch would have, that "if it wasn't for me, he'd still be scraping chewing gum off the bottoms of the movie seats in Minnedosa." He was a high-flyer and she was firmly grounded; one couldn't do without the other. There's a relatively benign saying in feminist circles that behind every successful man, there's a surprised woman. That was true of the Aspers. Izzy never failed to astonish. His reputation for being outrageous was well earned. When I asked Babs for specific examples, she couldn't remember any. That puzzled me until I realized that the occasions of his being—or at least sounding—outrageous could not easily be isolated. He was almost always outrageous. That was the wild-side mentality that transformed the formal Israel into the hip "Izzy."

"If it wasn't for Babs making the arrangements, I'd probably have never seen my kids—or taken a holiday," he confessed. That was an exaggeration, but certainly during the middle decades of his life taking holidays ranked on Asper's set of personal priorities somewhere below being locked into a room with the heavy-metal band Metallica. He not only didn't indulge in spare-time activities—he didn't indulge in spare time. "Of course he spent time with the children," Babs was quick to point out. "But it wasn't the normal kind of time. He wasn't at the hockey games, but when it counted he was there for them and gave them a good sense of direction." The kids grew up in an incubator that allowed each of them to maintain a solid bilateral relationship with their father.*

Each offspring was a curious amalgam of his or her parents, though there was a floating consensus that Gail got Izzy's heart, David

---

*David was born in 1958, Gail in 1960, Leonard in 1964 and Leanne in 1963, but Leanne lived only six weeks.

his passion and Leonard his brain. Izzy's own assessment wasn't that different: "David—I don't want to use the word 'flamboyant,' but he's certainly theatrical, and he's fearless. Leonard is the closest to me—he is the student and reads voraciously, as I do. Gail is right in the middle—she's organized, she's systematic, she's loyal and she's caring, but I persuaded her not to become as driven as I am. She runs her kids and still goes to work. She's the only one who's balanced."

In any case, they all inherited their father's persistence, his love of repartee, his stubbornness and his tunnel vision of Israel. "In our house nothing came for free," recalled the youngest son, Leonard. "Our parents didn't give us money just because they had it. There was no reward unless you earned it—no handouts, but unconditional support." Their father paid for their education but they had to earn their own vacation travel money: Gail worked at a university library, David flipped hamburgers at Salisbury House in high school, and Leonard worked the summers in high school at Falcon Lake, and summers throughout university at Richardson Greenshields and at Lloyd Axworthy's Ministry of Transport office in Winnipeg. The year's highlights were the annual family outings to glamorous corners of the globe, including one glorious ($70,000) charter in 1991 aboard a private yacht off the Turkish coast.

The most concentrated activity in the household was Monopoly: the games, or jousts, that allowed Izzy to move well beyond its rules to give lessons in real estate. Negotiating second mortgages, amortizing construction costs over a certain number of years, full-fledged arbitration negotiations—those were some of the easier assignments. Swimming, on the other hand, was strictly optional. At the lake the family played a lot of card games, in particular war and gin rummy. Izzy insisted on living where there was access to water: the Winnipeg house had a pool; the cottage had a lake; the winter house in Palm Beach had an ocean. But the landlord got wet at each location only once a year, when Babs took a picture of the anti-aquatic Izzy self-consciously splashing himself.

His study was a combination of zoo and jungle, with animal parts strewn about, such as a zebra couch and an elephant-foot table.* "He was the only man who could get away with wearing pastel colours, no matter what the season or era," remarked his niece Jodi. "Leisure suits, velour sweatsuits, robes, safari gowns." Most of the time when he was relaxing at home he went shabby-chic informal and could have doubled for a bushwhacker villain from an old Tarzan movie. "One of my most vivid images of him as a kid was when our cartoons were playing too loud, the door would open on a Saturday morning," his daughter, Gail, remembered, "and this grizzled guy with a beard, hairy legs and a rumpled, purple multicoloured housecoat would open the door, and yell, 'KEEP IT DOWN!'" instilling the fear of God in us. He loved the family, just not too loud—no shrieking or cackling was allowed, no whining, no cracking of gum, no shuffling of cards, no slurping through an empty straw."

"The University of Izzy was a hard school," according to Fred de Koning, Izzy's friend and accountant. "His children all benefited, but I don't know if they appreciate that. Sitting at his knee, they learned a lot of things. But he was pretty to the point. I don't know if 'rough' is the right word, but with your own children you tend to be harder. I know I am. You tend to be more critical, you expect more. He was pretty demanding of his kids."

If Izzy belonged to a category of one, his eldest son, David, belonged to no category at all. A temperamental loner, behaving as if he was a pukka Mr. Universe loose among the infidels, he was described by his mother as being "broader-winged" than his siblings. Certainly he was the only Asper kid who ever did anything unexpected. Or, as he described it, "I was the trailblazer as to what my brother and sister

---

*Gail and Izzy had a "vicious row," according to Leonard, about a bison head that was in the screened porch at the cottage at Falcon Lake. Leonard was sent to buy the head, first getting a certificate from the taxidermist stating that the bison hadn't been killed for the head itself.

should not do, and if they did it—how not to get caught." He tested his daring, first aboard the dirt bike he bought with part of his bar mitzvah money; he boasted that he had collected traffic infractions even before he was old enough to officially own a vehicle. Then he challenged the Devil on his hell-bent Harley. Eternally curious and remarkably courageous, he was always the rebel—sometimes without a cause, always without a pause.

Ardent followers of rock bands classify themselves as fans, groupies, cultists or freaks. David's obsession with the Blue Bombers fit into the latter category, especially in the 2005 season, when he got into what the *Winnipeg Free Press* politely described as "a heated confrontation" with team officials after the Bombers lost a squeaker to Saskatchewan. In 2008, David bid to buy the Winnipeg team by announcing his plan to contribute $40 million to the construction of a $120-million stadium, and adding another $25 million for adjoining retail facilities.

"Without him," David said about his father, "I probably would have done nothing. He hoofed my butt into everything I ever wound up doing." David's role model, he claimed, was Pippin, the hero of the long-running Broadway musical about the hunchback son of the Holy Roman Emperor Charlemagne, the legendary king of France. But the parallels were inexact, except that Pippin fought with his father and had a hell of a time finding himself so that he could live happily ever after.

―――――――

"We lived on a nice little street, and workmen were about three doors down at the corner, repairing the road," Babs recalled. "David was fascinated with building machinery and all that kind of thing, so he would love to go and watch them. Sometimes I would pack him a lunch and he would sit with the work crew as they had theirs, and he loved it, to the extent that these guys became his and my best pals. When I went out at night sometimes, they were in some bar near the Royal Alexandra Hotel, which was in a funny part of town, and I'd

be coming out in my fancy dress and these guys would greet me—
'Hi, Mrs. Asper.' Izzy would say, 'How do you know these people?'
But David was always like that. The point is that I didn't think twice
about leaving him with them. More to the point, David was always
very easy with everyone he met. We didn't shelter our kids at all. We
encouraged them to experience everything.

"When David was maybe three, I took him to the local fire station. As I walked in, everybody said, 'Hi, David. We haven't seen you
in a while.' I realized he was getting out of my yard by himself and
almost fainted dead away. Did I know he was going over there? I did
not. He was completely fearless and handled himself very well."

For a whole combination of reasons, David's life became difficult when Izzy went into politics during his son's early teen years.
The father's political activities pushed the family into the spotlight,
publicizing their wealth and their Jewishness; David recalled being
referred to as "a dirty Jew" in the seventh grade, and teachers making nasty remarks about Izzy and the Liberals. He dropped out at
sixteen, then relented to parental pressure and was enrolled in
Brentwood College School, near Victoria, BC—far enough away to
escape being recognized as an Asper.

After David graduated with a B.A. from the University of Manitoba, Izzy took his eldest son on a North American tour to find a law
school compatible with David's temperament and vice versa. They
chose the California Western School of Law in San Diego, and after
graduating with honours and articling in New York and Manitoba,
David emerged not as the commercial legal eagle he was expected
to become, but as a criminal lawyer with a mission.

That mission turned out to be the curious case of David
Milgaard, a young drifter who had spent twenty-three years in prison
for the knife-point sex slaying of a twenty-year-old nurses' aid from
Saskatoon named Gail Miller, who was not only raped but stabbed
twenty-seven times. Milgaard, then sixteen, who happened to be in
the vicinity, was charged with the crime, found guilty and sentenced
to life imprisonment. When he was contemplating whether or not to

take the case, Asper climbed on his motorcycle and visited Milgaard in jail. He quickly became convinced of Milgaard's innocence then spent the next six years (and about $1 million in gratis legal fees) proving it. This was David's Great Izzy Moment, and the son's white-hot determination to pursue the case and win it was at least partly genetic. "I was very proud of him," Izzy said at the time. "He showed his mettle and the tenacity that a good lawyer—or successful busi-nessman—must have."*

David's relationship with his father became more complex after he grew out of their football phase. "Dad was the guy who passed on the mania I have about the Blue Bombers," David recalled. "He got me a toy Bomber helmet with the number 11 on it when I was a kid, and we played football together. He was Jack Jacobs and I was Ken Ploen. We ran pass plays in the hallway at home and Dad often overthrew me, breaking countless hanging lamps with the glo-rious sound of breaking glass. Dad and I were never able to convince my mother that it was Leonard who broke the lamps, but goodness knows we tried."

———

"It was a blizzard, a terrible November blizzard when I went into labour with David," his mother recalled. "Some of Izzy's law school friends came and dug the car out of the parking lot, and just as they finished, a snowplough came down the street and its snow trail blocked the driveway. So Izzy hailed the plough told them I was in labour and we followed it to the hospital, where nobody would talk to me. The Bombers were playing in the Grey Cup. I could have died—they were all watching television.

"David was a fun kid, hard to keep ahead of. He was always look-ing for the most mischief. I would go to bed at night thinking, okay,

---

*In a subsequent trial, Larry Fisher, a serial rapist, was convicted of the crime. Milgaard was awarded $10 million in restitution, the highest such award in the country's history. His first major purchase was a brand-new, fire-red Harley for David, his legal counsellor who never gave up.

what mischief could he possibly get into and how could I guard against it? Once I even phoned an insurance agency to see if I could get insurance on him because he could think of things to do that were just the most amazing. He was fearless. He would go anywhere and do anything. He wasn't afraid of life."

The two Aspers—father and eldest son—enjoyed an edgy relationship that pumped them both up. For David to have challenged his father from inside of what was a tightly patriarchal structure was good for both of them.

And then there is Gail, the sister. A vivacious beauty with a highly infectious manner, she swept the boards and collected solid pledges for a stunning $97 million from private sources for her late father's dream of building the Canadian Museum for Human Rights in Winnipeg. She is difficult to resist. Ideas flicker across her face like strobe lights. Her pinball eyes—feline, attentive and filled with mischief—glow with her remarkable life force. Her natural grace suggests sturdy bloodlines as she moves with a model's self-possession— but at five times the usual speed. Tenacity is her favourite trait, based on a text from U.S. president Calvin Coolidge. "Nothing in the world can take the place of persistence," he once wrote. "Talent will not; nothing is more common than unsuccessful men with talent. Genius will not; unrewarded genius is almost a proverb. Education will not; the world is full of educated derelicts. Persistence and determination alone are omnipotent."

As a youngster Gail was spirited and independent. "She was always off in a corner reading a book or listening to music—a strong, very easy child, happy and content doing her own thing," recalled Babs. "Thank God, because I could plunk her down and run off after David somewhere, because he was always doing something creative, let's put it that way. I remember one day when she was little and was listening to *The Sound of Music,* all of a sudden she burst into a song from the score. When John Kennedy was shot they were playing 'Hail to the Chief' on the TV all the time and she was always singing along. In fact, Gail sang more than she talked right from the very beginning. She's very musical and has a gorgeous voice." Gail considered a stage career and attended the Banff School of Fine Arts for a summer but didn't want to live the life. She has sung in operas, music festivals and annual amateur productions in partnership with the Manitoba Bar Association.

Like Izzy, Gail has a jukebox in her head, only this one plays Broadway musicals. "Dad lived his life in accordance with the glorious themes of those gala performances," she recalled. "There was certainly a lot of Conrad Birdie in him because he had a lot of livin' to do and he was in a constant state of impatience to savour all that life had to offer.* I'll never forget his advice to me when I was travelling alone in Europe at the age of twenty. In a long handwritten letter, he told me to try everything, to see everything and never to be afraid to take outrageous chances. True, his advice led to my near kidnapping in the red-light district of Amsterdam, but apart from that one incident I've taken that advice and will be eternally grateful that I had such a father who would take the time to give it to me."

Gail attended the University of Manitoba (to study French literature and political science), then went for a summer to the Sorbonne in Paris, followed by a law degree from her alma mater. It was there that she met her future husband, Michael James Paterson, who eventually earned a doctorate in freshwater science on a Killam fellowship at Dalhousie University and became one of that essential discipline's leading gurus. Gail followed her husband to Halifax and spent five years with two local law firms, legalizing many of the real estate deals that refurbished the ocean city's once derelict waterfront. The family was initially disappointed that she had married outside the faith, but Paterson more than made up

---

*Conrad Birdie was the lead character in *Bye Bye Birdie*, a musical based on Elvis Presley's life that played Broadway in the 1960s.

for his atheism. During his wedding speech, he brought the audience up short when he interrupted his remarks to declare, "I've decided to convert." After the appropriate dramatic pause, came the punchline: "I'm joining the Liberal Party." He turned out to be not only a mensch of the first order but was so compatible with Asper family values that he was elected the first non-Jewish president of Winnipeg's Jewish Child and Family Services.

Of all the Asper children, Gail has the most interesting take on what made Izzy run. "Dad's temperament was definitely volatile," she readily admitted. "He'd yell at you for making noise in the hallway. If you stopped making noise in the hallway, he'd quickly stop being angry. I saw him as plagued with a critical nature. And I viewed it as a plague when people were that critical, because they really could never enjoy anything fully. They were always thinking, 'Why did they do that?' or 'Why didn't they do that?' Letting it go, purging those toxins—that just wasn't in their makeup. And, of course, that was why they were so driven, and that was why they got things done. So it was like a curse." According to Gail, Izzy figured that bearing a grudge was just being practical about remembering who your real friends were, and who you could trust. Except with family. "He didn't want us to be one of those families where half the world isn't speaking to the other. So family was one area where he didn't allow fights to last.

"I love the way we were raised. Izzy indulged us all, but backtalk from the kids was not negotiable. He couldn't stand whining. (I do the same. I bark at my kids, 'You didn't lose your village in a mudslide! So let's have some perspective here!') Offspring were never allowed to skip some family function that they didn't want to attend, like a bar mitzvah. Doing work around the house, fulfilling your duties and obligations, earning your allowance in terms of doing your homework, going to school and being respectful—those duties were not negotiable. If you ever crossed the line, you knew it. If you ever had any kind of a snarky disrespectful repartee with him, he was like, 'You watch it! You just watch your mouth!' and I got into the habit of saying, 'It's a good thing you can't tell what I'm thinking.' You learned to pick your battles. You developed a thick skin."*

Gail recalled that one of the facilitators who worked with the family once told her, "I can't get over how volatile and acrimonious your discussions are." And Gail's response to this was, "That's how we were raised with this dad, and it's a kind of strategy that gets passed on. I'm not saying it's the best strategy, but it's what we were used to. We didn't find it to be particularly acrimonious or troubling but it was often a combative dialogue."

Gail Asper revels in a lively sense of the absurd. In the summer of 2007, after *Maclean's* published a feature about lawyers gone bad, advertised by the cover line "LAWYERS ARE RATS," she addressed the annual dinner of the Canadian Corporate Counsel Association—wearing a rodent's nose and a headdress carved out of cheddar cheese.

––––––––

It was easy to pick the exact date when Izzy's youngest son became his eventual heir. It all had to do with lemonade, and it happened when Leonard was four years old. He had been selling glasses of the cool drink in front of his house on a hot summer's day and proudly came home with six dollars. His father used the occasion to give him a lesson in how business really worked. "How much did it cost your mother to go to the store and what did she pay for the lemonade?" Izzy asked Leonard. "What was the cost of the ice cubes, the Dixie cups? What was the price of your little cart and the tray you used as a cash register?"—and so on. The realities of entrepreneurship must have sunk in, because Leonard readily admitted that in

––––––––

*This is in contrast to the attitude of most writers, including the author of this volume. When it comes to book reviews, it's not that we're thin-skinned; we have no skin.

adulthood he never signed a business deal without remembering the lemonade episode, even if at the time he "lost six dollars and was a puddle of tears."

The previous year he had picked flowers from the neighbour's yard and tried to sell them back to the owner, while David and Gail attempted a similar trick with crabapples. At age seven Leonard found a diamond ring in a back lane and set off to the neighbour's house to determine its owner, speculating what the reward might be. Izzy grabbed him by the scruff of his neck and said, "Kid, there should never be a reward for honesty." When Leonard was fourteen, the senior Asper urged him to read *The Revolt,* Menachem Begin's account of Israel's founding, a book powerful enough to turn young Leonard into a Zionist. "My hero growing up was Ken Dryden [the Habs' goalie], not Conrad Black, who my father recommended," Leonard recalled. "I was only eight at the time, and around the dinner table we would discuss current events and you had damn well better know what happened that day. So, I'm eight years old and trying to memorize every page of the *Globe and Mail.* We used to watch *The Brady Bunch,* and when we heard Dad coming, flip to the news. By the time I was twelve, I'd be sitting there talking to Supreme Court judges and cabinet ministers. You can't pay for that kind of education." Leonard was regularly perusing the *Wall Street Journal* and carrying around the *Canadian Securities Handbook,* although he was shy and sometimes forgot what he had rehearsed when it was his turn to speak at the dinner table. But he was also the most studious. For his higher education he picked Brandeis in Waltham, near Boston, the only non-sectarian Jewish-sponsored college in the U.S., where he graduated with honours in political science. It was his first taste of independence, and it was there that he began to gain the self-confidence that eventually drove him to aspire to the highest office in his family firm. Following his graduation, he took a law degree at the University of Toronto. "I loved contract law because in the end, it became clear that the entire world runs on the principles defined in English laws of contracts, as modified by American jurisprudence," he noted. "I was interested in constitutional law, and remain so, because I am fascinated by the inherent conflict that it has created between the Rousseau collectivist approach to rights and the more individualist approach to rights espoused by people like John Stuart Mill."

––––––––

Individuals die; family dynasties abide—so the theory went. The reality of succession in more recent times has been very different. Canada was once run by a self-perpetuating clique of moneyed clans that may have been feudal at heart but that were central to the country's evolution because most of them helped finance the economic welfare of their communities—few as passionately as Izzy did in Winnipeg. The odd patriarch may have maintained the primacy of his offspring on the basis of their seeds instead of their deeds, but in an age when global corporate conglomerates became as mean as they were lean, family-run firms were the exceptions. They seemed as quaint and out of place as the company picnics they once sponsored that featured three-legged races on summer afternoons.

During the first half of the last century, two dozen of the most powerful families that held sway over the Canadian economy lost their influence and their pride of place—not through nationalization or some other anti-capitalist device, but through the iron laws of genetics. The passage of the entrepreneurial gene or spark that had given rise to the original family empires turned out to be only rarely transferable to future generations. The notion that blood relatives, usually eldest sons, who assumed the leadership mantle could automatically be relied on to add value proved to be pure bunk. The casualty list included such once mighty family-owned giants as the Eatons, the western branch of the Siftons, the Birkses, Kofflers, Crosbies, Romans, Blackburns, Bassetts, Lundrigans, Poslunses, Creeds, Burtons, Steinbergs, Hermants, Gersteins, Jefferys, Iveys, McLeans, Woodwards, Crosses and several lesser clans. That shift was murderous in its impact. Proprietorships had guaranteed not just security but fiscal secrecy; to be one of the anointed meant never having to tell your story.* Third-generation heiresses tended to open florist shops or cutesy antique stores. The boys with brains became doctors, lawyers or saviours of polar bears; the others ended up as bank robbers, preachers or stockbrokers.

No longer. In the twenty-first century, few inheritors have been toilet-trained to take over family businesses, a fact that Israel Asper weighed heavily in choosing his successor. Judging by the general record, most heirs blow their financial wads with only the occasional genuflection to reality. Their idea of going hungry is to leave uneaten a slightly disappointing *filet de sole meunière* in a declining French restaurant. They freely spend their fathers' fortunes, all the while exhibiting resentment that their legacy has made it impossible to demonstrate their self-worth. Instead of being appreciated for the comforts it bought, their wealth is resented for all the personal problems it hasn't resolved and the magical expectations it doesn't fulfill. Izzy had read all the books about the Bacardis, Bronfmans and so many other families who lost their nerve and their clout, paralyzed by their inheritors' suspicions that even close friends and closer lovers might be there for the money. The fear of giving away the source or sum of their fortunes, of committing themselves to offers of alliances and friendships, filled their minds with smoky, ill-defined resentments. They were everybody's gravy train and nobody's intimates.

None of that applied to the Asper children. Their upbringing may not have been heaven on earth, but it was an ideal boot camp for life in the rough on the untamed pastures of global capitalism. The family's operational code was to abhor pretence and deal with one another with down-to-earth authenticity, even when it hurt. If Izzy's treatment of his kids bordered on tough love, it was because

*According to Gordon Sharwood, at one time head of the Canadian Association of Family Enterprises, only 15 percent of family companies made a successful transition to the founder's children, and fewer than 3 percent to his grandchildren.

he was running a form of dress rehearsal to determine if any of them were fit to sit in his chair.

The process of choosing Israel Asper's successor was not automatic, but neither was it dramatic, unexpected or confrontational.

It ended with the participants employing the Winnipeg equivalent of a *wai,* the Oriental manner of saluting one another with a reverential bow, hands clasped together, and with no one very excited or surprised.

Izzy was all too aware of the pitfalls of a soft-hearted offspring assuming command of the hard-earned family fortune. He had no sentimental attachment to keeping the management of Canwest within the family. "I never trained my children, or caused them to be trained, to run this company," he insisted. "I trained them to *own* the company. There's a huge difference. I would be quite content if Canwest was professionally run by disinterested parties, which is where I predict it will go eventually. You don't get friction when three owners are sitting in a room, it's only when one of them is CEO and he gets defensive about what he did last week or why dividends had to be cut because we bought Company X, and your sister or brother or your nieces and nephews are mad at you." His outside choices for the top job were Tom Strike, Jim Sward or Peter Viner.

On January 8, 1988, he told a family gathering that Canwest should be sold when he was gone and its assets should be distributed to the children's trusts. He also noted that Black Monday (October 19, 1987), when the stock markets collapsed, represented a severe setback in the firm's liquidity planning and that he hoped to develop an alternative plan over the next few months, which did not preclude the company's sale. "I love this business," he told his kids. "But I'm not tied to it, so unless you guys see any reason to continue, let's collect our marbles and go home."

Izzy had called his offspring together in his study five years earlier, indicating to them for the first time their net worth, then announced the birth of a newcomer to the party: "You just got a new brother/sister today that's called the Asper Foundation, and I want you to be on side with this, because it's going to be the glue in your relationship. You can fight all you like about the business, if you ever manage it or own it, but what will keep you together as a family is that you'll have the Asper Foundation, which will give you the opportunity to do something useful with your lives—and to make a difference."

Later, without committing himself about who should succeed him, he backed off and agreed that ownership of Canwest would be divvied up among his three children—a decision that he made only at their insistence: "I didn't encourage it," he said at the time. "In fact, I was vaguely in opposition to any of the kids coming into the business. They were all practising lawyers and they were all doing very nicely on their own. It was they who got this dynastic glaze in their eyes—which I generally discouraged. I don't believe in dynasties and I don't believe in being a ghost to your children, having to live under the constant comparison to somebody else, good or bad. It was ordained that no child would come into the business. But it happened through a series of freak, innocuous circumstances, when Gail slipped through the net. That was the end for me."

He started holding lengthy year-end briefing sessions when the family was together and spent extra time with Gail, who was fully occupied as a lawyer in Halifax but longed to be back in Winnipeg. She came aboard the Asper Express as Izzy's executive assistant and the company's general counsel in 1989, and that set off the gold rush. Her brother David had been active in the early days of CKND-TV, and set in motion much of Global's Saskatchewan operations. He then left to champion the causes of David Milgaard and other victims of the Canadian justice system. When Gail breached the corporate perimeter, her brothers soon followed, David into operations and programming, Leonard into corporate development.

Since leaving university, Leonard had purchased a theatre restaurant in Florida (it showed second-run movies during dinner),

Campus Cut-ups
Dressed in their boater hats and showbiz suits, Izzy and Ron Meyers entertain a University of Manitoba crowd at the annual student bash.

Timber Cruising
The young Izzy took only one vacation away from home, when he and Bob Kopstein spent a summer counting trees on the west coast.

Time Out
Babs and Izzy Asper relaxing in Puerto Vallarta. They left Winnipeg on at least one lengthy journey a year, mostly on jazz cruises.

Izzy & Friend
Asper admired Pierre Trudeau
as a sparring partner, but their
brands of politics were almost
opposite in both content and
presentation.

Fort Asper
A formal portrait, taken in 1973, of the family at home: Babs, Tuffy, David, Izzy,
Leonard and Gail.

Izzy's Partner
Izzy's only direct business partner was Gerry Schwartz (right), now head of the mega-successful Onex Corporation. They once fought over the sale of Monarch Life, owned by CanWest Capital Corporation, of which they were the main officers, but they later reconciled.

A TV Triumph
Global was justifiably known as "the *Love Boat* Network." *Traders* was one of Global's few Canadian hits. The show's importance lay not only in its being great entertainment but in its documenting of the runaway greed of Bay Street brokers and bankers.

Head Office Gang
(Back row) Donald Gordon, Gail Asper, Tom Strike and Jim Sward, along with (front row) Izzy Asper and Canwest director Lloyd Barber. Asper's company was run by a tight circle of competent executives who loved their jobs, aside from the insulting morning memo they inevitably received from the boss.

Significant Influence
Former New Brunswick premier Frank McKenna was a Canwest director
and acting board chairman who provided valuable psychological and
business advice.

Facing the Regulators
Appearing before the CRTC
in Montreal, Izzy dons
translation headphones
during a tense hearing into
his TV application for
Quebec City. His Quebec
licence was one of his most
valuable assets because, for
a small investment, he had
access to English-speaking
Quebecers right across
the province.

The Famous Newman
Kevin Newman (no relation to the author) has given Global News the authority and credibility to turn it into a significant information source. He has won many awards for being Canada's top TV anchor.

Messing with Conrad
Conrad Black talks to reporters while Leonard Asper looks on. In the largest media transaction in Canadian history, Izzy bought the former Southam chain from Conrad Black for $3.2 billion. That transaction placed Asper in the major leagues, both in multimedia coverage and debt assumption.

Best Political Friends
Prime Minister Jean
Chrétien poses with
Babs, Izzy, Senator
Rod Zimmer and his
wife, Deborah. Asper's
friendship with Chrétien
created tension in the
editorial department of
the *National Post*, which
triggered a revolution
among Canwest
journalists.

Honouring "The Man"
Israel Harold Asper receives
the country's most prestigious
award, the Order of Canada,
from Governor General
Roméo LeBlanc. It was
one of several medals and
doctorates that recognized
his achievements.

The New Asper
His son Leonard succeeded Izzy in 1999
and currently runs the communications
empire out of Toronto—a tough assignment.
He moved the company into specialty
channels and broadened its programming
mandates.

CanWest merges Internet units under one umbrella

TV, newspaper sites unite in canada.com

BY BARBARA SHECTER

CanWest Global Communications Corp. is merging its local newspaper and TV Web sites under the umbrella of canada.com, the company said yesterday.

When users log on to the Web

Canada.com already forms the umbrella for local sites including globaltv.com, chektv.com, tvforbc.com, and the newspaper sites of CanWest's Southam chain of daily newspapers, which the company purchased from Conrad Black's **Hollinger Inc.** last year.

"When we announced the purchase of the Hollinger assets last November, integration of the properties was the most important priority for CanWest," said Leonard

On the Web
Following Izzy's takeover of the Southam chain, the Aspers concentrated on exploiting their presence on the Internet.

Chrétien defends Asper's 'right to write'

Copps says panel will study concentration of ownership

BY ROBERT FIFE AND
JOËL-DENIS BELLAVANCE

OTTAWA • Jean Chrétien yesterday defended the right of David Asper to write a letter to newspapers owned by CanWest Global Communications criticizing their coverage of the Prime Minister's

Controversy
Prime Minister Jean Chrétien's troubled stewardship was due mainly to his former ownership of a resort in Shawinigan, Quebec. The issue brought the Aspers out in his defence, a position that was attacked by the prime minister's critics.

Black sells remaining 50% stake in Post

CANWEST TO TAKE CONTROL

'It's a robust baby we're putting into good hands'

BY BARBARA SHECTER
AND SINCLAIR STEWART

Conrad Black, chairman and publisher of the *National Post*, has sold the remaining 50% of the paper he founded in 1998 to CanWest Global Communications Corp.

The sale price was not disclosed, nths

Taking Control
With his expansion continuing outside Canada, Conrad Black decided to sell his remaining half ownership in the *National Post* to the Aspers in 2001, completing that transaction so that the Asper family fully owned the money-losing daily.

The Famous Izzy Chair
At his cottage on Falcon Lake, Izzy floated around in his chair—a martini glass in one of its arms, an ashtray in the other. It was as close as he ever got to swimming, although each of his residences had access to either a pool, a lake or an ocean.

Izzy at Play
This was the essential Israel Asper. It was only through his music that he found his soul and tested the meaning of life. A friend described him as having a jukebox in his head: It was always there, and it never stopped playing.

and hoped to expand it into a chain. Following Gail's example, he persuaded his father to let him try his corporate luck. At first it was Gail who most impressed Izzy: "She was the best of the three to run things, being the most organized and the most disciplined. But she wasn't tough enough. She wanted to do something for everybody." David all but eliminated himself by admitting that he was too emotional to lead. "I'm a shit disturber and a bit of a dreamer and probably focus too much," he told Gordon Pitts of the *Globe and Mail*. Pitts noted that "Leonard has his father's quick tongue and the love of a good fight."

Around 1990, Izzy had received a couple of expressions of interest in and offers to acquire Canwest from outside parties. He was mulling over what to do and mentioned this to Leonard when they were in Florida over Christmas of 1990. "We had a long discussion, and I said he would be crazy to sell because I had asked him what he would do with the money and he said that he would fund the Asper Foundation significantly but also distribute some to the children," Leonard recalled. "I said, thank you very much, but I would just try to start up another Canwest, so why do that, which is fraught with risk and like any business has limited chance of success, compared to taking what we have and growing it five- or ten-fold. He said, 'Fine, but I am only staying in this business for five more years, so you and David have to come in and get ready to take over, and I will train you.' At the time, David was still embroiled with Milgaard, and so we, as a family, decided he would continue to play that out and when the case finished, he would re-examine his options. So instead of going back to Cassels Brock & Blackwell, as I was scheduled to do in March once I got called to the bar, I joined Global as associate general counsel, working for Glenn O'Farrell, who was a key player in the growth of Global, single-handedly bringing CKMI online in Quebec.

"My role at Global was to work half the time for Glenn as a lawyer and the other half I spent in each of the departments of Global, including programming, sales, finance, operations, news, the transmitter group, marketing and so on. I did this for three years before moving back to Winnipeg in 1994 to become director of corporate development. Around 1993, we all agreed that David would come in as well, since his Milgaard case was wrapping up, and he started with his involvement in the Australia due diligence. Then, as part of his training, it was decided he would go run the Regina station. Right up until 1997, David and I were training in various aspects of the business, he in programming/operations after he had finished with Regina and then his UK experiences, and me in mergers and acquisitions. I spent the better part of 1994 and 1995 trying to start up Romania, then travelling through South America trying to expand our interests beyond Chile, particularly in Argentina, before launching into the Irish venture starting in 1996. I became vice-president of corporate development and brought in Greg Gilhooly, whom I had known from law school. Around 1997, as we continued to discuss succession, David indicated that he preferred operations, and managing specific businesses themselves, rather than managing a corporation, with all of the diverse activities that it required. That was why around 1997, Peter Viner started to train me to be CEO."

Asper resolved the succession dilemma in 1997 by moving up to executive chairman and appointing Peter Viner—who had joined Global in 1974, six weeks before Izzy—chief executive officer. The idea was that Viner would train Leonard, who would report to his father whenever Leonard thought he was ready. That took two years, though Izzy was still playing around with the notion of appointing Leonard and David as co-CEOs. "It's been done, there are companies that have had co-CEOs, with each respecting the autonomy of the other," mused Izzy. "But David does not love the corporate life. He likes the action, the projects. Leonard had more of the aptitude, the personality and the discipline for what is the loneliest job in the world. You're always putting fingers in dikes. You're hopping from the finance department's crisis today at ten to the communications department at eleven. That's why I said that if I had stayed CEO, there would have been no Hollinger deal. Somebody had to take that thing. Nurse it. Nurture it. Pat it. Massage it. Think it through."

David Olive, the *Toronto Star*'s ace business columnist, noted that Leonard also had "his litigious father's intolerance for dissenters, both in and outside the camp. His verbal fractiousness was evidenced by the insults he often dispensed toward critics of Canwest." Appearing before the House of Commons Lincoln Media Committee hearings in 2002, Leonard ridiculed critics of media concentration. "Canadian media are more fragmented and less concentrated than ever before," he testified. "I submit that people who believe otherwise are not looking at the facts and they also probably believe Elvis is still alive." In 2003, while announcing editorial changes at the *National Post,* he derided the paper's Toronto competitors as an "axis of snivel."

Why did Leonard win? "I think I was the only guy with my hand up," he jokes, though it was true. "I've always been very interested in business. And if I weren't in this one, I would be in business somewhere else. I would have probably done what my dad did—would have put a business plan together, raised some money, gone out and tried to do my own number. I would have either bought a business or tried to recreate another Canwest. 'Cause that's what turns me on. So once we decided to keep the company, it was really my choice. Gail had declared herself and said she wanted a sane and normal life. David and I were on the path. And I think it became apparent that what was needed in a corporate executive was different from what's needed in an operating executive. It's not just about being smart. It's not just about being motivated. It's not just about working hard. There are certain personality characteristics that I think David probably realized he didn't have. Now, he has a lot of other characteristics that are phenomenal. He's one of the best marketing brains I've ever seen. He's a phenomenal project guy. He just gets things done. But I think I have the ability to juggle a lot of things at once. Keep a lot of balls in the air and just manage. Now, I'm happier doing deals, I'll confess. And we were always a deal shop. Now that we've stopped doing deals as much and we're managing, there's no doubt I have had to evolve as a person—as a business executive. I'm not a great executive, but the family thought I was the most likely to succeed in this job and I think that was probably acknowledged consciously or unconsciously by everybody involved—that if the family wanted to stay in control on a hands-on basis, I was the person to do it. And I clearly was the person who wanted to do it. David himself ultimately said he didn't want to do it."

With Izzy's death, the young Asper became "Canada's most important media executive," according to Gordon Pitts in the *Globe*, "because unlike his rivals at Bell Globemedia, Leonard actually owns the shop."

10

The Acrobat without a Net

"Izzy was hard on people, but also very kind to them—
all at the same time. He cultivated a persona and did
things for effect, almost like an actor. He was the
William Shatner of Canada's business community."
—Tom Strike, President of Strategy and Development at Canwest

Israel Asper was an uncannily adroit corporate strategist who built his business empire on the back of 204 immutable edicts his kids called Asper Axioms, of which these were the most useful:

- Never start a war, but if you're in one, take no prisoners.
- In negotiating, never give anything without getting something in return.
- Keep your options open; don't commit until you have to.
- Whatever can happen, will happen: plan a disaster scenario.
- Never do anything unless you have an escape route.
- If you live long enough and stay in the game long enough, you eventually will go broke.

- Everything is doable, because all you need is more determination than the guys who are trying to stop you.
- Don't try to build an empire; no empire survives.
- Never do a *little* deal.
- Never forget where you came from, or what you had for breakfast.
- Be your most severe critic.
- Never forget the system is based on greed.
- Never go into a deal relying on someone who hasn't got anything on the table.

Surely sensible guidelines for aspiring Aspers. But there was another, more earthy list of Axioms:

1. Be fearless, and do not be afraid to travel in shark-infested waters. You must believe that if you fall overboard the sharks will form an honour guard and escort you to safety—out of professional courtesy, of course.
2. Be an optimist, and don't consider any challenge too great. An entrepreneur, at the age of ninety, will still be buying green bananas and celebrating when he is offered a thirty-year closed-term loan.
3. You must believe in yourself, like the devout self-made man who worships his creator.
4. Select your role models carefully. Don't emulate men who grow on trees; be the one who swings from those trees.
5. Learn how to take "yes" for an answer; and don't make the same mistake once.
6. Don't keep your nose to the grindstone, your shoulder to the wheel and your eye on the ball. It's impossible to think in that position.
7. Laugh a lot. Remember that everything is funny—especially if it's happening to your competitor.
8. If you think you're your own worst enemy, try taking in a partner.

9. Be wary of the media—they habitually collect snippets of information, separate the wheat from the chaff, then publish the chaff.

Asper once pointed out that the only way to effectively advise entrepreneurs was to fill your mouth with marbles and, as you make each point, remove one marble at a time: "Only when you've lost all your marbles will your counsel deter entrepreneurs on the make from being foolish."

Maybe, but Izzy had a secret weapon that animated his executives to much greater efforts than these sensible axioms might imply. This was the impossibly rude overnight mail he sent his senior staff members, invariably signed with the notation "IHA—dictated but not read." That sign-off was not meant to be an escape clause but merely the admission that the correspondence had been transcribed by his secretaries when they arrived to work in the morning, long after he had dictated the poison darts, sometime between 2 and 4 a.m.

Typical was this exchange with Greg Gilhooly, then the company's general counsel. "We had a situation in Australia where we were involved in some litigation, and as the company's general counsel I was responsible for retaining the legal firm on our behalf," Gilhooly recalled. "We were having a problem with our current counsel not giving us good or timely service. It got to a point where Tom Strike, who was responsible for the Australian investment at the time, came to me and said, 'We need to replace the lawyers. I want you to move the file *now.*' Well, that got my spider senses tingling because of the delicate nature of our relationships in Australia, their ongoing concerns about foreign ownership, and who knew whose interests in the shareholders group might also be represented by this delinquent law firm. We didn't want to be upsetting someone we might need. It was a complicated business. Going against Strike's direct orders, I went to Gail Asper, who had been responsible for the Australian litigation before I took the position as general counsel, and consulted her. I then went back to Tom, after having found someone to take over the file and made sure it was in place. So finally, after delaying as long as I could, Mr. Asper being away in some other part of the world and not reachable, we moved the file. I guess the senior partner of the law firm that lost it picked up the phone and gave Izzy a ring, tracked him down somewhere or sent him a note. And sure enough, when I showed up for work a day later, I've got this email and it could not have been more succinct. 'I understand you moved the file. Do that again and I will cut your nuts off. IHA—dictated but not read.'

"I was relatively new to Canwest at the time. It was a great job and I was having fun. Then all of a sudden I've got this giant of the Canadian media community threatening to chop off my testicles. I was quite seriously flummoxed at first, and then sat down and thought about it—'What did I do? What could I have done differently?' So anyway, I did all the rationalizations in my head and figured the only way to deal with this was to respond in kind. So I crafted a short email: 'Mr. Asper, I moved the file on Gail and Tom's instructions after having initially gone against his orders and not moved it immediately, and having had it confirmed in Australia. As the only single male in your management team I, unlike the rest of you, still have need for my testicles.'"

The moment Asper read it he came out of a meeting he was having with the Canadian management group, shook Gilhooly's hand and apologized. His willingness not to take a foul when someone stood up to him was as typical of the man as was the original insult.

When Gilhooly recounted his exchange to a few co-workers, one of them revealed the Da Vinci code of surviving within the Asper empire: "What you have to remember dealing with Izzy is that it's kind of like the Stanley Cup."

"What do you mean?"

"Well, it's the best out of seven. Until he has said something four times, it's not what you're supposed to do. He teases ideas." Tom Strike, who survived seventeen years of Izzy memos and maintained his stellar reputation, had his own formula: "You sort of knew when to ask for permission and when to ask for forgiveness. But you never got it completely right." Gail Asper had the most credible explanation for her father's outbursts: "People often mistook his rages for personal attacks, when they were just the way he expressed himself. His 'dictated but not read' messages were heart-stoppingly critical. To many people, they were incredibly difficult to deal with, until you got used to them. But with Dad, it didn't mean that you would be fired—though some people might be sitting there shell-shocked for a week and have to go into therapy for a month, before they realized that was just Dad's way."*

Gilhooly, who lasted at the executive heart of Canwest for a full decade, concluded that once you got into Asper's good books, he was unbelievably loyal. "The stereotypical hard-hearted, client-fisted, screw-your-partner business person—that was not him. But if you ever crossed him, he would chase you to the ends of the earth and drive you into the ground."

Even Peter Viner, the non-family member who climbed the highest in the Asper hierarchy (in fact, succeeded Izzy as Canwest's CEO), hesitated long and hard before opening his morning messages: "I would turn them over until I got the tone, then I'd say to myself, 'You know what? I don't want to get upset,' so I'd put them away for a while until I felt ready to read them. You got used to it. But once the business turned around, they put me on a pretty long leash. But he always had his lists, handwritten in cryptic fashion, maybe thirty-five items at a time. I'd tell him, 'You can't have thirty-five priorities; here are mine—there's three, and that's what I want to do

---

*Asper's last and most discreet secretary, Susan Macchia, supported that interpretation: "His midnight memos were mostly for venting. Quite a few times I would pretend that I couldn't make out some of his dictation to give him time to think about what he had said and let him decide whether or not he actually wanted it sent. There was no such thing as a normal day in his office. He would arrive with at least six letters he needed done yesterday but always said there was no rush. I knew better."

before the end of the day.'" At times Izzy would become overloaded, his burst of energy would fizzle out and he wouldn't be heard from for days or weeks at a time, only to reappear early one morning, at 3:40 a.m., with a cannonade of emails.

Richard Leipsic, Canwest's current senior vice-president and in-house legal counsel, had a down-to-earth appreciation for his boss. "Izzy had an unbelievable understanding of the law and kept pretty well current other than with the tax stuff that kept changing. I remember him asking, 'Can we still do that?' and my associate replied, 'Well, no, you never could.' Explaining a situation, he'd craft a story with such finesse that you'd be mesmerized and only later start to play it back to yourself and realize that the dots didn't get connected that way. Not in law, anyway. Not with the facts and circumstances at hand, even if a lot of people would think that he made eminent sense. My role was to make sure that it could pass muster. He would always dispense abuse. I would be saying, 'Well, Izzy, there's a couple weak links in the armoury here,' and he would be ferocious, maintaining that I wasn't being creative enough. I remember once he emailed me, 'Make sure you pass out some corporate Viagra, Leipsic!' because I had told him that we just couldn't do what he wanted. The greatest compliment he paid me—once—was when we were arguing a legal point and he wouldn't concede that I had actually been right but did admit that my advice was correct. So he said, 'I'll do as you're suggesting, but not for the reasons you're proposing.' I don't think Asper really changed a lot. He never escaped that Minnedosa mentality, which meant that he had something to prove. Money in a lot of ways was just a yardstick. It was only later that he really appreciated having it as being a passport for a lifestyle."

Harry Ethans, who was his executive assistant for a time, and who eventually became senior vice-president for corporate development, recalled Asper insisting that he was a perpetual underdog. "Many times he would say, 'You know, Harry, these guys are out to get us.' And I'd say, 'I don't think they're out to get you, Izzy. They're out to win, and as you've shown me so often, we just have to out-grind them.'" Richard Leipsic emphasized that Asper thrived on rejection, because it only made him more committed, and that his art of management came down to improvising and counterpunching.

"Izzy would really push the limits," Leipsic commented. "He certainly wasn't bashful or reserved in the terms he demanded. That was the appeal which Tom Strike, Stephen Gross and I had. We could ask for things with a straight face, knowing full well there was no way they were ever going to happen." As well as Peter Viner, Tom Strike, Richard Leipsic, Gerry Noble, Stephen Gross, Yale Lerner and Harry Ethans, Asper's corporate insiders included CFO John Maguire; PR operative Rod Zimmer; Jim Sward and Kevin Shea, both former presidents of Global Television; Doug Hoover, the programming whiz who succeeded David Mintz; Global's creative Godfather, Don Brinton, who launched the network's stations in Winnipeg, Regina, Saskatoon and Vancouver; Stan Thomas; and Jack Tomik, in later years. More recent additions include Moe Levy, executive director of the Asper Foundation. In a special category was Peter Liba, Asper's closest and longest-lasting adviser. When Liba was appointed lieutenant governor of Manitoba in 1999, Izzy interrupted a Canwest annual meeting to make the announcement, adding, "I'd like you all to applaud Peter for his years of service to the company, but more importantly to congratulate me for saving us years of severance pay."*

"Liba was just one example of Asper's capacity to have people commit their professional lives to him—it was never to the company, it was always to Izzy—because he had such a sense of connection with what he aspired to accomplish and could instill palpable enthusiasm in his troops," Leipsic recalled. "He'd be so messianic

---

*Occasionally, Asper's one-liners got him into trouble. To sweeten a Canwest stock offering, he included 6 percent of his personal holdings, and when he was asked by a *Winnipeg Free Press* reporter what he was planning to do with the money, he quipped that Babs was planning to use the proceeds to refinish her kitchen. The subsequent headline read, "WIFE TO FINISH KITCHEN WITH $75 MILLION." Mrs. Asper was not amused.

in the way he described his projects that nearly everyone was swept along—'Listen, if Izzy's doing it, I want to be part of it.' It didn't make a lot of sense objectively to put your life through that, but I never regretted it, because despite all the aggravation, I'd otherwise still be doing medium commercial work at Buchwald's. Still, you've got to pay a price. I had my laptop at home and I'd just kind of peek through the door to my study and wonder how many emails there were from Izzy. I'd look for them with trepidation. He claimed that he was a pathological deal maker—that all he needed was one out of ten." Leipsic grew to doubt it.

When he was president and CEO of the Global Television Network, Noble recalled, Izzy would go over his to-do list of future business prospects each morning. On the roster of possibilities was a TV operation that covered the few habitable huddles of Iceland's sparse inhabitants. The station had been on the market for six months and nobody had bid on it, but Izzy wouldn't take it off the list. "What are we hearing from Iceland?" he would ask, redundantly announcing, "It has a television network for sale."

"Who the hell wants to go to Reykjavik?" Noble would shoot back. "Izzy never attacked me, but whenever he called down one of his kids, I felt he was after me," Noble concluded. "We had been through a lot together, so he could treat me like one of his offspring. We were on the board of directors together at Network TEN in Australia, and I hustled Izzy out of bars and put him to bed, packed for him in the morning, wrestled him out of hotels, got him to the airport and hid him in the bathroom while he had a cigarette. We'd get off that plane from Los Angeles to Sydney after flying for fourteen hours and he'd still be on the runway when he lit up. I'd grab him by the arm and rush him into the nearest washroom and stood guard while he smoked his brains out. He was a hard man to work for because you didn't always know which way he was heading. One day it might be 'Let's conquer Spain' and the next morning, 'What the hell are you doing in Spain? Get to France.' If you made a mistake you knew it, but mostly he was just impatient—a very impatient guy."

One element of running the rapidly expanding enterprise that never tried Izzy's patience was fussing over details. On February 28, 2001, he dictated a three-page, single-spaced memo about refurbishing the top three floors of Winnipeg's tallest high-rise, which housed Canwest's headquarters, thirty-two storeys above the intersection of Portage and Main. In it, he specified what types of wood or other material should be used in each of the offices, the location of the washrooms and who should get the best views. In 1999 he purchased a dozen Group of Seven masterpieces to decorate the walls from Vancouver's Heffel Gallery, for $490,000. It was a bargain, with Tom Thomson's *Hillside in Snow* going for only $40,000 and a genuine A.J. Casson (*Approaching Thunderstorm*) for $8,000. Canwest later sold them for close to $1 million. According to Leonard, Gail and Babs were appalled by the idea, but he won the argument on the basis that whatever the banks and other corporations did, he didn't feel that it was the proper use of shareholders' money to buy expensive art, so the décor was changed to feature Winnipeg artists.

In a curious way, Izzy's office existence was the mirror image of his home life, with a cadre of remarkably loyal and effective executives taking the place of his children. The frantic pace and daily helter-skelter wasn't that different. He was constantly in a transactional mode, his brain a hyperactive switchboard, sending and receiving unconnected messages that made sense only to him.

"If you didn't know Izzy, you would think he was crazy," recalled Tom Strike, the chartered accountant who joined the company in 1986 and later moved into the pivotal positions of CFO, then COO, before being put in charge of deal structuring, negotiations and strategy. "Izzy would often have three or four things happening in his mind at once and would start talking about one thing at a meeting, then about something else without realizing that he'd switched. All of a sudden you'd find yourself in a different time zone. He was a man of considerable contradiction—this sort of spontaneous free-thinker—but if necessary he could be very analytical and exceptionally focused. He was hard on people, but also very kind to them—all at the same time. He cultivated a persona and did things for effect, almost like an actor. He was the William Shatner of Canada's business community."

Izzy existed in this sort of *Wizard of Oz* dream world in which magical things seemed possible, and if someone came in and wove him a fairy tale of profitable grandeur, he would, more often than not, bite. He picked some of his partners badly, not learning enough first about their motives and what they were really after. He always wanted to see the best in people, and too often opted for a shared control corporate structure with questionable results. In Vancouver, for example, when he took over CKVU-TV from its founding owners, the transaction became so convoluted that his four-stage acquisition manoeuvre turned into a bag of snakes. It was all too easy for each of the contending parties to hold a radically different view of the intended outcome. Izzy let the courts decide, and won.

He also rewrote the evolutionary theory that advocates survival of the fastest, with instructions such as his daily sing-song, "You're not moving fast enough, it's gotta happen, or we're gonna lose the deal. You go and get on a plane this afternoon, and settle this." Marching orders like that, if you didn't know him, would be quite debilitating. But after a while, if you had any kind of longevity (because this was not a place where most people could survive—it was chaotic, unstructured, and constantly ebbing and flowing), somehow that became the status quo and you lived with it. Despite all that, Asper garnered a blood-oath loyalty from an impressive group of capable people, founded on the respect they had for him (after they digested their post-email breakfasts). The almost hypnotic force of his in-group charisma had legs. He was one of those rare individuals who raised the quality of leadership to its most essential element: when he believed in you, you believed in yourself.

"He was always kind of over the top," Strike recalled. "And you know, it would go both ways. I remember being in a boardroom with him one night, with a few people sitting around the table—it was quite late and we were having drinks to celebrate a new television licence—when he started reorganizing the company. 'You're going to be the vice-president of this, and you're going to be the vice-president of that'—he announced this to the people around the table, like a monarch bestowing knighthoods. The next day they came into the office with heavy heads but feeling exuberant because they had been made vice-presidents. I had to unmake them, take them aside and say, 'Look-it, don't expect this to happen. What he was saying last night was that he likes you, and that you did a good job. But don't expect the latter part to happen, because it's not going to.'"

Although he was known as "Izzy" to everybody in the everyday world (even if they had never met him), official documents had to be made out in the name of Israel Harold Asper, with no abbreviations.* But he had patience for everybody. While visiting his friend Don Johnston, then head of the OECD, in Paris, Izzy spent hours advising one of Johnston's employees, a young Mennonite chef from Winnipeg ambitious to launch his own restaurant, on the best location, the ideal menu and a workable business plan. "He had a tremendous humanity about him that always struck me as being almost unique," Johnston recalled.

"The thing that people never stressed about Izzy was his background as a brilliant tax lawyer with a photographic memory for details," pointed out Matthew Fraser, who was appointed by Asper as the *National Post*'s second editor-in-chief. "He knew precisely how to lay off the costs on taxpayers. He deliberately played up the non-rational side of himself, making fun of nearly every situation. He actually was grinding down on his lawyers and accountants, doing his homework, crushing all the legal and fiscal details into a fine

---

*According to Leonard, Izzy once circulated a memo saying that he was to be called either I.H. Asper, or Israel Harold Asper, but never Israel H. Asper. David responded with a hilarious memo that insisted that he was to be referred to, from now on, as Nick or Nicholas, but never Dick Head. Leonard responded that he would prefer not to be called by his last name because he was embarrassed to be associated with either of them.

powder. People forget that he had an actuarial brain and was a genius in the way he structured his deals."

Frank McKenna, the former New Brunswick premier and Canadian ambassador to the U.S., who joined Canwest's board in 1999 and later was appointed its acting chairman, recalled his problems as a board member in bringing the firm's directors (who included the trio of Asper heirs) to something resembling order, so the board meetings could begin. "Family members were usually the protagonists, and we would just kind of put down our tools and watch them go at it hammer and tongs," McKenna recalled. "But it was always done with love and respect, and at the end of it everybody's temper would cool and we'd get on with business. Even then it could quickly turn into a furious debate, especially about politics, because David tended to be further right than the rest of the family. While Izzy was alive, he was always testing everybody's limits. His approach was the dialectical style, where he would push ideas as well as people and expect them to push back. For him that was how you found the truth. It was unlike any other board that I've been on. Izzy was the entrepreneur who started the company and that always makes for an interesting dynamic. His discourse was kind of a stream of consciousness, so that in terms of a structured debate, it was just a target that you might or you might not hit. We would always run late by hours. He would start talking about jazz or politics, which were the great loves of his life. He would regale us with stories. We would eventually wind up back on the agenda."

Izzy tackled most business problems with the thrusts of a toreador and felt virtually immune to criticism. "I absorbed blows well and rolled with the punches," he maintained. "But at times I did need emotional support. I had some very lonely, isolating periods when I needed a sanity check to answer the question, 'Is there something wrong with me?' People like Don Gordon, my dear friend who was my partner in the Minnedosa distillery; Stephen Gross, who was such a loyal executive; and Yale Lerner, our lawyer—those were some of the people who saw me through. At the end of the day, I usually got things back in balance, and realized how funny everything is. When somebody threatens your corporate life, you certainly focus on that. But then you stand back and realize that even if you get slaughtered, nothing is that serious. I could always go out and do it all over again."

———————

Asper spent his final two decades in a binge of deal-making that earned him the reputation for tweaking every deal to its last decimal point. That required the nimbleness of a circus acrobat. Being Izzy, he of course chose to perform without a safety net, but this emphatically did not mean that he flew by the seat of his pants. It was his unrelenting and interminable examination of all the elements of a deal—plus his intellectual sleight of hand—that fuelled his quest to fulfill impossible dreams. On more than one occasion, the same dynamics acted as spoilers because the arrangements he structured were too complicated for ordinary mortals.

Izzy's operational code at this climactic point in his life was best summarized in a 1998 personal memo to his son and heir, Leonard: "Keep in mind, we are heading into, at least *you* are, a whole new world and nothing is too outrageous to consider. The potential for Canwest Entertainment is limitless because it is an industry which knows no boundaries, nor the kind of limitation that regulation has imposed thus far."

He took his own advice. "Izzy would outline these incredibly complex deals, starting from a tax perspective and going into a corporate structure, brilliantly trying to help each side achieve whatever they wanted out of the transaction," recalled Leonard, who witnessed most of the bargaining. "But then the guy on the other side might just say, 'Izzy, it's too complicated for me. I don't understand this. And if I don't understand it, it means you're probably outsmarting me. So just give me the cash and I'll pay my tax and even if the deal isn't really perfect, just give me something I can understand.'"

The catalyst for this hip-hop turn in Asper's career was his discovery, on September 28, 1995, that Canwest Global had hit a market capitalization of $1 billion. Now, nothing seemed impossible. His big-game corporate hunt over the years that followed culminated in his multi-billion-dollar purchase of the Southam newspaper chain from Conrad Black—the largest media transaction in Canadian history.

Opportunities seized had turned Asper into the country's leading media mogul. Those deals negotiated but aborted would have endowed him with world-scale status. Half a dozen examples tell the story. "We were at a corporate retreat in Florida in 1997 or 1998," Leonard recalled. "Ten of us sitting around for two or three days to discuss strategy and going for it, when somebody called and told Izzy that the Eaton brothers were planning to dump their controlling interest in CTV. He was immediately on the phone, half the time with the prime minister, heads of CRTC and everybody else in authority, because of course we still owned Global—so how could we buy CTV? It was wildly complicated. We would purchase 29.9 percent because the CRTC didn't have any say at that level of ownership. There would then be a convertible debenture, options and on and on and on, and then we would have sixty days to find other partners. So Izzy had this idea to buy out his main competitor, but in the end the investment bankers who were trying to sell the Eatons' stake said, 'You know what, this is too complicated—even if we meet the letter of the law we will anger the CRTC, there'll be a huge public outcry and it's not worth it. We don't want all the grief.' But we came very close to making a deal, and nobody ever knew about that intended CTV takeover."

Another initiative was a spinoff from the Aspers' original purchase of a controlling interest in their Irish TV station. As part of it, Global ended up with about 9 percent of Ulster Television, and the Scottish Media Group signalled it would make a bid for Ulster, which wanted anybody but the Scots to take them over. "So they went around looking for a white knight, and again we were sitting in a retreat, probably a year later, when this piece of Ulster came up for sale," Leonard remembered. "Basically, these people from Ulster said, 'Why don't you come in, buy 20 percent of us, which added to your 9 percent will block the Scottish takeover.' So that was how we ended up with 29 percent. It involved a lot of money, so we sat around strategizing and then trying to buy more stock from the market. About a year later we finally opened up a dialogue with the Scottish Media Group about how we could put Irish TV in the Republic, together with Ulster in the north and the Scottish Media Group—and end up having one northern-territories broadcast group. There were synergies and opportunities. Scottish still wanted to take over Ulster, and they said, 'Why don't you join us? Roll your stock in Ulster and the Republic into Scottish and we'll issue you some shares,' so in this way we would get about a 45 percent interest in Scottish Media Group, the regional ITV franchisee in Scotland. That was right up our alley. We invited them over to Izzy's place in Palm Beach—twenty-five guys sat there negotiating a deal. We did that deal, and essentially Canwest was going to trade its assets into Scottish shares and end up with a stake that would have given us de facto control."

When the Aspers returned to England to finalize the arrangements and announce the deal, their calls to the Scottish executives, also billeted in a London hotel, stopped being returned. The announcement was due at 9:00 the next morning and the Canadians sent a draft press release over but it remained unacknowledged. Finally, at around 7:00 p.m., the Scots called a meeting. They said that they had gone back to their chairman and he had told them that the investment bankers had nixed the sale because the company was being marketed without an auction, which was against the directors' fiduciary duties—and that the board would be sued. They told the Canadians, "You can sue us on this but that's not going to do it." Amen to that.

In 1991, Larry Tisch, who owned 18 percent of CBS (and controlled its board), wanted to sell his position, which was particularly advantageous because share holdings under 20 percent required no regulatory permission. Izzy and David Asper met him in New York and discovered he wanted a billion dollars for his stake, valuing the company at $5 billion. That would have been a significant inflection point for Canwest. It came apart over $200 million. Izzy offered Tisch $800 million because he calculated that CBS was worth only $4 billion—not the $5 billion that was claimed—and was turned down.

Later, Izzy sat Leonard down in the family cottage, and told him, "We've got to get into the U.S. You cannot be a media company in this world as the borders come down without having a big position in the U.S." Their next attempt was to buy a network of stations called New World Broadcasting Inc., owned by Ron Pearlman, who had agreed to the terms. But when Izzy went to New York to finalize the deal, Rupert Murdoch appeared on the scene, topped Izzy's bid and rolled New World into his Fox network.

The most concentrated attempt to invade the American market was Izzy's otherworldly negotiation with Lowell W. "Bud" Paxson, a marketer (he co-founded the Home Shopping channel) who became a born-again Christian and organized the religious PAX TV network, consisting of seventy-three stations with transmission towers located on the fringes of most of America's urban centres. That allowed him to use his station in Bridgeport, Connecticut, for example, to access the New York market; his network reached 35 percent of the U.S. market. Izzy made a tentative deal for half of the Paxson properties, with Sony Columbia and TCI (the large cable company that later became part of John Malone's Liberty network) expected to become partners. But Sony wouldn't play because they were not in the network ownership business but only wanted to supply content. Bud invited the Aspers aboard his sixty-one-metre boat, which at the time was the biggest around, and to his $18-million mansion in Palm Beach. "One time," remembers Leonard, "Izzy and I went down to buy the stations and we had a lot of chit-chat and finally Bud said, 'I know why you're here. You're here to buy my stations. They're not for sale because they're owned by God.'

"So Izzy says, 'Would God lease them?'"

"And Paxson replies, 'I don't know. It's Thanksgiving coming up. I'll ask Him.'

"That didn't faze Izzy, who jumped in with the obvious solution: 'You could ask me, I'm right here.'

"That was the exchange. The deal finally fell apart over price."

Richard Leipsic, the Aspers' legal adviser, flew to Palm Beach to assist Izzy in making his final offer, which turned out to be far too modest. Asper's bid was returned by Paxson, with a notation scribbled across it, written with a laundry marker: "NO! NO! NO FUCKING WAY"—and that was from the head of a religious channel. "Gosh," Izzy mumbled, "do you think we didn't offer enough?" Leipsic replied, "Apparently, his answer wasn't even worthy of a pen or pencil. He must have been in the laundry room when he wrote this."

Probably Izzy's biggest potential deal was in 1994 with Bertelsmann, the giant German publishing firm which also was Europe's leading television broadcaster and had decided to sell its Vox division, a national domestic network that was losing $200 million annually. Asper had been chosen by the firm as their preferred partner, with the German principals retaining 25 percent. Izzy met with Manfred Lahnstein, a top executive, and Michael Dornemann, the firm's North American CEO at the company's world headquarters in Gütersloh. Negotiations advanced to the stage that Asper and Leonard decided to conduct detailed due diligence on the proposal.

Their next meeting was in New York to work out the final details. Dornemann, whose English was more experimental than expository, meant to say, "when we finish this deal" or "when we conclude negotiations" but inadvertently chose a very different, emotionally loaded toxic phraseology. He kept saying, "ven ve veach de final zolution"— which was particularly offensive, since Bertelsmann had, during the Second World War, exploited the rise of the Nazis to restructure itself from a mid-size educational publisher into one of Hitler's most essential propaganda arms, supplying millions of anti-Semitic texts and using Jewish slave labour. The deal breaker was the answer to Izzy's question, "What if, after two years of running Vox, we're still losing $100 million or more? We'll shut it down, right?" The answer was, "Ve vill not do dat; Ve do not klose anyting." Asper walked away, but Rupert Murdoch materialized as if he was waiting for his cue, and bought Vox on the spot, telling the Germans that if Canwest had done the due diligence, he was ready to sign. And he did.

Izzy originally tried to buy TSN, the sports channel, when Labatt owned it. After it was sold, Asper considered purchasing the brewery in order to get the TV operation as part of a consortium that would have included Gerry Schwartz, who was after the brewery. In 1995, Canwest alone bid on TSN, and then, when it became part of NetStar, Izzy went after all of NetStar again in 1998, only to be blocked by the Disney people, who had moved in and who had a connection with CTV. At one point, when Asper's investment banker realized that Izzy was going to be outbid—and she would have to forgo her commission—she told Izzy, point blank, that he was "stupid" not to pay a higher price for it. He promptly offered her a piece of the action, saying, "If you think we're so stupid, we'll pay more, but you write a cheque too." She grew very quiet, then furtively stalked out of the room.

There were other attempts, with Izzy deciding to bid in the buyout of Air Canada, providing he could move its head office to Winnipeg, only to discover that it had to remain in Montreal by statute; and a pre-emptive bid to buy Royal Trust, encouraged by its management, desperately trying to stay out of the reach of Robert Campeau. During this phase of Asper's stewardship, Canwest Global was defined almost as much by the deals Izzy didn't complete as by those he did.

II

Spiritual Homeland: King of the Diaspora

Dark recollections crowd in on us whenever we think about the
implications of defeat. Much in Jewish history is too terrible to
be believed. But nothing is too terrible to have happened.
—Former Israeli foreign minister Abba Eban

From the impressive dais of the Rothberg amphitheatre at
Hebrew University, high atop Mount Scopus in Jerusalem, Israel
Asper gazed at the Holy City, savouring its magnificence, awed by its
vestigial glory. The panorama extended into Judea and Samaria, the
Occupied Territories captured by Israel during its flash victory of
those six tumultuous days in June of 1967 that forever altered the
country's political landscape and geography.

To the east, he spotted the striking crimson hills of Jordan; to
the south, the Old City, where three singular theological impulses
had been breach-birthed into mainstream religions. Jerusalem
remained as much an epicentre of dispute as when Jesus Christ
walked its streets, preached the gospel and was crucified for it. Israel
Asper was well aware that for Jews, Christians and Muslims, nothing

was as sacred as the affirmation of faith that occurred daily within Jerusalem's prehistoric stone battlements.

If ever there was a place where God resided on Earth, it had to be here.

For twenty-five centuries the Old City of Jerusalem was the hotly contested arena of unwelcome intruders—from the Babylonians, Romans, Muslims, Crusaders and Ottoman Turks to the legendary Lawrence of Arabia's British Empire. From Izzy's personal perspective, the Jewish state's existence was the logical outcome of all that history. In the war that followed the country's bold declaration of independence in 1948, Jordan had captured the Old City and had barred Israeli access to the Temple Mount. For the next two decades, Jews were prevented from praying at the Wailing Wall, the precious relic venerated as the last remnant of King Solomon's Temple. Israel's lightning recapture of Jerusalem on June 7, 1967, restored the Jews' biblical and natural rights to the Promised Land's most sacred site. There was jubilation and dancing in the streets, from Tel Aviv to Brooklyn (and the North End of Winnipeg), the kind of exhilaration not felt since the Israelites were freed from Egyptian bondage eons before. Israeli minister of defence Moshe Dayan declared, "We have returned to Jerusalem never to part from her again."

Jewish history had imprinted itself on Asper's conscience. He identified intimately with Israel's political turmoil and spiritual imperatives, in particular the saga of Jerusalem's survival, its ramparts the haunting symbol for persecuted Jews scattered around the world. This was their City of David, the sanctuary they had never had. Asper's chief philanthropy had been the Hebrew University, and now, on June 6, 1999, he was being acknowledged for his contribution with an honorary doctorate.

With Babs, Gail, David and David's wife, Ruth, in the audience of five hundred, Izzy reflected on his spiritual quest as he climbed the steps to the dais for the ceremonial gowning. "I have stood at the top of this mountain many times," he intoned. "Each time I survey with awe the enormity of tiny Israel. For me, this place, Mount

Scopus, is the heart, the soul, the intellectual, cultural and ethical centre of gravity of the Jewish people." He vividly recounted each moment in history when the fate of his people hung in the balance: the Roman assault, the Russian pogroms, the Nazis' Holocaust and the Arab jihads. "My mind recreates all of this in horrific vivid colour every time I stand here," he went on, "but what prevents me from being overcome by grief over those demonic outrages is the miracle that we are still here. That we have, through the unshakeable unity of our people, and the studies of our scholars, teachers, scientists and thinkers, gained the capacity to ensure that when we say 'Never again,' it is not just a pious hope or some heroic slogan. It is the inevitable new reality. And those who wish us ill know it."

Despite the earnestness of his cause, Asper never lost his sense of humour about being Jewish. Addressing a fundraising audience in Toronto that had made more promises than it delivered cash, he began by recounting the unfortunate saga of two thieves who tried to rob an Israeli bank. "When they broke in," he pointedly reported, "they found $46,000 in cash and $6 million in pledges." On another occasion, dealing with the accusations that his ownership of the country's largest newspaper chain and most profitable television network constituted a Jewish conspiracy, he went back twenty-five years to recount his own version of that dubious theory: "Ken Thomson owned the largest newspaper chain, followed by Dick Malone's FP chain [which included the *Globe and Mail*], Beland Honderich's Torstar and Donald Campbell's Maclean Hunter, as well as the CBC and CTV. Everyone across this land, citizens from every corner were screaming, 'WHAT ARE WE GOING TO DO ABOUT THIS CHRISTIAN DOMINATION OF THE MEDIA?!' It is as an inspiration. We're getting there. The Conspiracy is getting there."

The aptly named Israel Asper regarded the Holy Land as the most special piece of real estate on Earth, its spirit bred into the marrow of his bones. (Hell, at times Jerusalem loomed even more important to him than Winnipeg.) He thrilled while driving among the tumbling foothills of the Gilead on the eastern border; staying at a kibbutz near the Golan Heights, still reeling from the previous night's Syrian artillery barrage; lunching on St. Peter's fish at Tiberias, on the Sea of Galilee, where King Herod had once ruled—these were some of his favoured ports of call.

His personal pilgrimages always included the shrine at Yad Vashem, not far from Jerusalem. A low, rectangular building fashioned of hewn basalt boulders, this was the national memorial to the six million Jews massacred by the Nazis. An eternal flame flickers from a jagged bronze cup, casting shadows on the mosaic floor where, in sombre letters, are inscribed the names of Hitler's death camps.

Izzy visited Yad Vashem often. It was here that he could experience most meaningfully the horrors of the Holocaust and feel the essence of Israel. Genocide on a scale consecrated in this grey and grisly place leaves visitors robbed of emotional release and moral recourse. Walking through these ghastly relics, Izzy became acutely aware of why the Israelis—and loyal legionnaires of its diaspora, like himself—felt so passionately that the survival of this postage stamp of a country was essential to human history. Jews without a homeland would quickly become displaced victims. At least six million innocents had already died for upholding their faith. It could happen again. "Dark recollections crowd in on us whenever we think about the implications of defeat," intoned Israel's former foreign minister Abba Eban. "The issue is not military occupation, but physical massacre. After all, much in Jewish history is too terrible to be believed. But nothing is too terrible to have happened."

Asper never let up. In speeches and articles, in his daily discourse and in forceful advocacy, he questioned his lifelong association with Canada's Liberal Party and denounced its leaders for their "weak-kneed policies" on Israel. Asper's diatribes against Palestinian efforts to decimate Israel reflected his core belief system. It wasn't a subject that invited civilized debate, not in the style of even-handed commentary that Canadians prefer when faced with troublesome realities. Izzy took his shots and suffered the consequences. He wouldn't—or couldn't—recognize any acceptable middle ground.

And it was this fervour that caused turmoil in his newsrooms. He didn't always get it, but he demanded that the coverage of Israel recognize that the desert republic's existence was not debatable. That was certainly a reasonable assumption, but on a personal level he often went beyond that proposition by dividing people into two categories: you were either a devout supporter of Israel or its mortal enemy. No one else need apply.

He charged that Canada's Department of Foreign Affairs was "riddled with Arabists" and had been that way since the Suez Crisis of 1956. He was exasperated by the fact that his Liberal idol, Prime Minister Jean Chrétien, could not distinguish between Palestinian terrorism and Israel's "measured" response. "Israel is entitled to conduct itself and its defence without the cluck-clucking of sanctimonious Canadian officials," he declared. "How long would the government of Canada forbear and tolerate, as it demanded of Israel, atrocities against Canadians from bases, say, in Quebec? Not a minute—just ask the members of the 1970 Trudeau Cabinet who invoked the War Measures Act."

Asper labelled Yasser Arafat and his cadre of followers as the voice, the arm and the fist of their terrorist-sponsoring state partners, Iran, Iraq, Libya, Lebanon and Syria, in their campaign to destroy Israel. "They are cut from the same cloth, belong to the same school of gangster terrorists, and Canada should treat them as such," he thundered. "We shouldn't be voting at the United Nations to condemn Israel for use of excessive force. There is no such thing as excessive force when somebody is trying to kill you."

––––––––––

Asper interpreted every anti-Israel remark, speech, rumour, article or unfavourable weather forecast as a personal insult, a poisoned arrow aimed straight at his heart and his family. Most Canadian Jews admire Israel, support its perpetual fundraising campaigns, plant commemorative trees in the country's many groves of remembrance and pay token homage to the turbulent republic as their "second home." At the same time, they are much relieved that they live in Canada, which may not entertain the fierce Jewish brand of gung-ho patriotism, but neither does it harbour aspiring suicide bombers. Though they faithfully worship at their local synagogues and observe most of the dietary laws, Canada's Jews feel little compulsion to consider themselves as God's chosen people. Instead they are content to have descended from fathers and grandfathers who escaped the Old World's persecution and pogroms by fleeing across the Atlantic to new beginnings. These forefathers may have strayed on the wrong side of the 49th parallel, mainly because they couldn't get into the States, but Canada was their home now, and their descendants recognized that—not unlike Israel—it too is a daily miracle of a country.

"Izzy stood up for Canada and for Israel when other people couldn't be found," said his friend Senator Jerry Grafstein. Another pal, Yale Lerner, made the point that Izzy was never afraid to declare his Jewishness: "I can't remember the instances, but I recall sometimes being a little worried about him. Any guy named Israel, he's obviously not Muslim."

Izzy's obsessive crusades on behalf of Israel grew to be more compelling than even his Jewishness. The struggle itself became almost as important as its outcome: a religion of its own. Reading his doomsday pronouncements, it was almost possible to imagine that he fantasized that Portage and Main might one day be threatened by forces determined to turn North America's Jews into an endangered species. Such a scenario was, of course, absurd, and Asper knew it. Yet his unrelenting attacks on the enemies of Israel, real and imagined, prompted some of his friends to speculate that at least some of that *Weltschmerz* and much of his anger were the response of a man who had faced anti-Semitism in the raw and who felt eternally under siege. As always, he was the protagonist in every drama he created—but this one was real.

While Izzy became increasingly visible as the city's most successful and most ambitious self-made lawyer and businessman, he suffered from particularly damaging forms of anti-Semitism. Sometimes it was "the silent treatment," such as not being hired for legal opinions by executives of the WASP-dominated grain trade. The banks and the great grain-trading firms seldom used Jewish legal advisers, so the clients for most of Winnipeg's Jewish firms were other Jewish businesses, local property owners or, in Asper's case, people who needed sophisticated tax advice.

It is not generally known or remembered that during the 1930s Winnipeg was the operational headquarters of the Canadian Nationalist Party, led by William Whittaker, a First World War veteran who became a professional Jew-baiter. Whittaker modelled his warlike organization on Hitler's storm troopers, dressed himself and his followers in brown shirts and riding boots, and harassed Jews wherever he could confront them. His wasn't a serious military force but neither was he playing games. His brownshirts trained at army barracks with the approval and blessing of then Winnipeg mayor Colonel Ralph Humphreys Webb. On June 5, 1934, a bloody riot developed in Market Square between Whittaker's shock troops and civilian members of the Anti-Fascist League. "Knives flashed in the fast waning sunlight, heavy clubs crashed against cap-protected skulls and huge slabs of wood were torn from the stalls of the market gardeners and used as battering rams," reported the *Winnipeg Free Press*. Some five hundred rioters were involved, and the Nazis got the worst of it.

The most telling evidence that Adolf Hitler's Berlin regarded Winnipeg as fertile ground for its anti-Semitic crusades was that the Nazi government chose to establish an official consulate there, which spread anti-Jewish hate literature. Deutsche Bund, the Nazi front for distributing this style of propaganda in Canada, also set up its headquarters in Winnipeg, as did its newspaper, *Deutsche Zeitung*. Hitler regarded German citizens, wherever they lived, as citizens of the Reich, duty bound to spread his message.

The worst kind of anti-Semitism was that voluntarily imposed by one of Winnipeg's own institutions, the Faculty of Medicine at the

University of Manitoba. It turned down Jewish students no matter how well qualified, and those who were admitted (as few as nine in some years) came in under a strict quota system. Jewish students with high marks were often rejected while WASPs with middling or even failing grades were admitted. Dean Alvin T. Mathers, who headed the faculty in the 1930s and 1940s, insisted that "certain nationalities" would never be accepted as doctors and therefore should not be admitted to medicine, and warned that the University of Manitoba "might become Jewish."

At another level, most of Canada's exclusive, members-only dining clubs across the country were anti-Semitic until the 1980s, but few more brazenly so than the Manitoba Club and the St. Charles Country Club in Winnipeg. This was particularly ironic because in no Canadian community was the local cultural life more vitally dominated by its lively Jewish community. The august gentlemen's plush rendezvous facing the historic Fort Garry Gate, the Manitoba Club symbolized the city's—and the province's—concentration of personal authority. Established only eight months after the city itself, from its founding in 1864 the club concentrated and institutionalized the province's decision-making process. It also became home of the Sanhedrin, a debating society led by John W. Dafoe, the influential editor of the *Free Press,* and its members included most of the city's intellectual elite, who huddled regularly in a corner of the club's lounge, dissecting the world, talking up free trade and spreading the gospel of Manchester Liberalism.

The only group that suffered more indignity than Winnipeg's Jews before they were admitted to membership was women. In the 1920s, the suggestion that women ought to be allowed onto the premises caused such panic that the meeting during which the suggestion was made had to be adjourned. Typical of the submissions that followed was this missive from E.H. Macklin: "I glory in the progress women have made. I rejoice in the liberty they enjoy. I would extend that freedom to embrace the granting of every privilege they might ask, every wish they might express, save one, the privilege of admission to the Manitoba Club. I appeal to you, preserve one little spot on this planet where the swish of women's skirts and the music of their voices are not heard. It is not much of a boon to ask, but it would prove a great boon to many of us who for an hour or two every now and then want to live the simple life." Half a century later, the club made the momentous decision to allow women into its billiard and snooker parlours but continued to bar them from the reading and silence rooms. But by the 1980s, the club was actually having regular ladies' nights that were barred to *men*.

Jewish entry was more complicated. In 1968, Sol Kanee, a leading Manitoba miller, long-time director of the Bank of Canada, past chairman of the Royal Winnipeg Ballet and one of the city's most civic-minded citizens, was taken to lunch at the Manitoba Club by George McIvor, then chairman of the Canadian Wheat Board. "Four days later," Kanee remembered, "McIvor called me back and said he wanted to have lunch with me again. He told me he'd been reprimanded for taking me to the club and wanted to take me again so he could thumb his nose at his fellow members. But I wouldn't go." That same year, Kanee had been approached by James Richardson (who at the time headed the Richardson financial complex) and Stewart Searle, a grain merchant who became president of Federal Industries. They proposed that Kanee, along with Albert Cohen (then president of General Distributors, which represented the Sony interests in Canada) and Mr. Justice Samuel Freedman, make an attempt to break the Manitoba Club's anti-Jewish barrier. Searle and Richardson pledged that they would resign if the trio was turned down. "I told Jim," Kanee recalled, "for me, no problem; for Albert, no problem. But that Mr. Justice Samuel Freedman, chancellor of the University of Manitoba [and later chief justice of Manitoba], should be exposed to having his application turned down—thank you very much, but the answer is, no."

The president of the St. Charles Country Club at the time was Alan Sweatman, a talented and enlightened Winnipeg lawyer, director of the Toronto-Dominion Bank and Hudson Bay Mining &

Smelting. When he tried to get Allan Waisman, a local architect, into the club, the application was rejected. Sweatman next attempted to alter the St. Charles bylaws to abolish anti-Semitism and was able to get the changes approved (on division) by the club's directors. They then had to be ratified at the annual mid-winter meeting, held at the Manitoba Club. The proposal was turned down. "I had a couple of people lined up to make the appropriate motion from the floor that evening, but when we got to the meeting, instead of the usual turnout of fifty, there were three times that many," Sweatman recalled. "It was damned obvious what was going to happen. So both my mover and my seconder backed out. I couldn't really blame them. The upshot was that the only person in the room fully in favour of the reforms was me."

Several Winnipeg families resolved the problem by becoming what was then called "ostrich Jews," changing their names and pretending they were Anglicans, or something exotic like Episcopalians or Lutherans. Winnipeg's WASP establishment tried hard, but there were a few outstanding Jews whom the country club couldn't avoid accepting, such as Mr. Justice Samuel Freedman, his son Martin, Sol Kanee and Sam Drache. But the Aspers were not among them.

The few enlightened citizens always included the magnificent Richardsons, who as the community's wealthiest and most powerful social arbiters fought the city's virulent anti-Semitism. Others practised what became known as the Vanderbilt rule, named after its inventor, Mrs. Cornelius Vanderbilt, the wife of the American railway and shipping magnate, who instructed her niece on social etiquette in 1906 and pointedly told her, "One never meets Jews." When the niece remarked on the fact that her aunt took tea each Friday afternoon with the wife of the New York financier August Belmont (whose family name in German had been Schonberg), Mrs. Vanderbilt primly replied, "Of course, one chooses *who* is a Jew."

Sometimes it worked the other way round. A prominent Jewish Winnipeg real estate operator named David Finkelstein married a wealthy *shiksa*, and when he became the second mayor of Winnipeg's suburban community of Tuxedo in 1910, he placed informal restrictive covenants against selling lots to Jews that remained in effect until 1950. (The covenants were understood rather than legal, although new homeowners had to obtain permission to build from the Tuxedo town council, and if they were Jewish, it was never granted.)

The Manitoba Club did finally admit its first Jew in 1972 (Gerry Libling, another architect) and in 1974 passed an effective non-discrimination bylaw. But Alan Sweatman, who had started the ruckus, resigned from the club anyway. "Some committee members phoned and asked me why I quit. I said, 'Look, I like playing golf with the Jews, but if you think I'm going to sit and have lunch with them, you're crazy.' I don't think they even got the joke." Asper joined the Manitoba Club in the early 1990s, and freely used it. (But his real "club" was his private table at the Velvet Glove restaurant in the hotel at Portage and Main that was originally built as the Winnipeg Inn and that has been changing its name ever since.)*

In describing the fate of the Jews during this period, Irving Abella, the scholarly co-author of the definitive *None Is Too Many*, noted, "Anti-Semitism in Canada has from the beginning never been restricted only to the cranks of society. Rather, it has always been part of the mainstream, shared to varying degrees by all elements of the nation, from the top to the bottom. Until the 1950s it had respectability. No one apologized for being anti-Jewish— and no one asked them to." The predominant notion was that the

---

*Martin Freedman, Asper's original law partner, quickly gained the reputation of being one of the city's ablest corporate counsels. A member of the venerable Aikins, MacAulay firm and former legal adviser to the Royal Commission on Corporate Concentration, he acted for part of the Sifton family during the squabble that followed Ken Thomson's bid for FP Publications. A moment of pure epiphany occurred in January 1980, expressing the transfer of power from one generation to the next, from old WASP Winnipeg to a new, unprejudiced way of doing things. Factions of the Sifton family, which still epitomizes the bedrock of Winnipeg society, had been hurling insults at one another through their lawyers and the press. Armagh Price, the last of the late Victor Sifton's children, finally had enough. Cornered by a reporter about some contradictory claims made by another lawyer, she primly announced, "Only Marty Freedman speaks for the Siftons!"

murderers of Christ would pollute Canada's puritan bloodstream, or "mongrelize" the country, as one bigot put it. Winnipeg was a test case because it had a larger proportion of Jews for its population than any other Canadian city. First to appear were the fur-trading Coblentz brothers and their families, who migrated north to the Red River from Bethlehem, Pennsylvania. Subsequent Russian and Ukrainian pogroms fed the stream, including the Asper family.

During Izzy's youth, he and his Jewish friends were subject to overt examples of anti-Semitism, such as the odd sign, "NO JEWS AND DOGS ALLOWED," or the more common and slightly less abusive admonition, "GENTILES ONLY." Victoria Beach on Lake Winnipeg was kept free of "the Unwanted." In the late 1960s, several synagogues were desecrated, swastikas were painted on Jewish stores and a Jewish cemetery was vandalized. As recently as 1995, a Winnipeg high school was spraypainted with swastikas and the message "DIE JEW!" The Aspers took every insult personally.

———————

Izzy's profound empathy for Israel was forged when he and Babs first visited the country not long after the end of the Six-Day War, in 1967. "Our first trip was very moving," remembered Babs. "I don't think either of us realized how deeply we actually cared. Izzy was fascinated by the battle stories, and the small size of the territories involved." They ventured north into the Golan Heights, the area that the Israeli army had months earlier taken from the Syrians. One day, Asper picked up a shell casing. "I think it was still live," Babs recalled, "but Izzy always did stuff like that."

A family trip followed in 1974, almost a year after the Yom Kippur War. This time the Asper clan was accompanied by their close friends Guy and Hester Kroft. They arranged to have a driver and forty-passenger bus at their disposal. For two weeks the two families traversed nearly every area of the country, from Rosh-Hanikra, the northernmost point, bordering Lebanon, to the resort of Eilat, in the southern part of the Negev. For sixteen-year-old David Asper, the trip was unforgettable. "Even though the Yom Kippur War had ended for the most part, the country felt very much like it was on a war footing," he recalled. "Security and military were everywhere, and as our bus made its way throughout the country, soldiers were hitchhiking to and from the front lines. We went to the Golan and along the way collected some grim reminders—battle-scarred helmets lying along the roadside—one of which is still at my parents' cottage at Falcon Lake. Our guide freaked out as we would leave the bus and wander off the road. The areas were still mined. We met Canadian peacekeepers in the Golan Heights and Izzy was busy trying to get them to vote Liberal in the federal election that was underway."

On another adventure, Asper decided that he and Babs should make a side trip to Beirut, Lebanon, which in those days was a cosmopolitan jewel, known as the Paris of the Middle East. They admired the city's major sites, stayed at an upscale hotel and only discovered near the end of the trip that their movements were being monitored. "One night," Babs recalled, "Izzy claps his hand over my mouth, wakes me up and shows me that there are wires coming through our wall. Izzy took pictures of them, and later showed them to the RCMP in Winnipeg. He was told they were part of a bugging device."*

As his increased wealth and expanding influence permitted, Asper emerged as a champion of Zionism, initially a movement by persecuted European Jews to create their own homeland, and later a commitment by faithful the world over to perpetuate that sanctuary's existence. Asper's arguments were not always logical, and his interpretation of Middle East history and politics was far from

---

*In the spring of 1996, when there had been a series of suicide terrorist attacks in Israel, Asper notified his children that he and Babs, as was their custom, were planning to travel to Jerusalem in June to attend the Hebrew University Board of Governors annual meeting. He invited "all directors" of the Asper Foundation to join them in Israel, but added, "This is not a command performance, so it is entirely optional. Jerusalem is a very dangerous place these days, and out of respect for the Succession Plan, I will be quite happy if some of you (or all) stay home to protect the capital pool." They did. And, in the end, so did Izzy and Babs.

flawless, but while he didn't ignore Israeli transgressions, he glossed over them because he felt there was a higher principle at stake. Since Israel's establishment in 1948, no country had been scrutinized more closely by world leaders, given as much prominent attention by the media and denounced most frequently by the United Nations. From 1955 to 1988, for example, the UN passed 429 resolutions about Israel, three-quarters of them overwhelmingly negative. In the same period, the UN didn't once criticize the Palestine Liberation Organization or any Arab state, ignoring even the actions of Syria in 1982, when its army slaughtered as many as 25,000 Sunni Muslims in the town of Hama. Far more Europeans identified with the plight of the Palestinians than with that of the Israelis. In a 2003 European Union opinion poll, nearly two-thirds of respondents regarded Israel as a greater threat to world peace than North Korea, Iran or Pakistan. Even in Canada, nearly 40 percent of Quebecers believed that the terrorist attacks of September 11, 2001, were at least partly the result of Israel's actions in the Middle East.

Throughout, Izzy remained a secular Jew, which meant that he seldom attended synagogue, yet he was inordinately proud of his tribe. Asper's Jewish identity was not steeped in the theological rituals of the temple or its swaying religious chants. "Izzy was a cultural Jew and a Zionist, but not a religious Jew," recalled Babs. "His family, curiously enough, was very orthodox, really involved in synagogue and that sort of thing. His grandfather was a shochet [a ritual slaughterer for dietary purposes] and a rabbi. His mother's faith literally carried her through some very difficult times. To attend synagogue with her on high holidays was a wholly different experience."

Growing up, Izzy had endured (and occasionally enjoyed) the lengthy Passover seders at his grandparents' home on Selkirk Avenue, where he and his cousins were expected to sing and be active participants. Though he was often the youngest in the room, Izzy usually handled the negotiations over the *afikoman*—the piece of matzah, hidden by the children, for which the adults paid a small ransom to conclude the seder. "I think that's where Izzy first learned wheeling and dealing," recalled his older cousin Aron Freedman. "He always got us the best price."

Gail Asper compared her father's religious approach to a Talmudic teaching that stated, "Study isn't the main thing; rather, it is action." From that perspective, she argued, Izzy was a very religious Jew. "He embodied the principles of Judaism more than any other Jewish person I know," she said. "He had the capacity to know that Jews were at risk—that you're never out of the woods if you're Jewish, even if you call yourself an agnostic or have converted out of Judaism. Hitler's not going to care if you claim, 'Hey, I'm not a practising Jew.' That was also why Dad had an affinity for First Nations people, and that was the reason why [as Manitoba Liberal leader] he fought so hard on the South Indian Lake project."

Mainly as the direct result of the anti-Semitism he encountered while growing up, Asper became a passionate Zionist. His convictions developed gradually. "When I was a kid in Neepawa, I was regularly beaten. We had to form phalanxes to go home from school, and I still have a bridge where I got a tooth knocked out," Izzy reminisced. When the family moved to Winnipeg in 1946, he joined the most popular Zionist youth group at the time, the left-leaning—some would say socialist—Hashomer Hatzair (Young Guardians) and participated in their summer camps and other activities. Around campfires, they debated Israel's future hopes and discussed the original heroes who, in the early 1880s, exasperated by persecution, pogroms and poverty, had arrived at the conclusion that the "Jewish Nation" required its own home in Palestine, where they "could exist as masters and not as aliens." Then, in 1948, with the searing memory of the Holocaust and the Middle East situation at its turbulent peak, the U.N. opted to partition Palestine, and the State of Israel declared its independence. As Izzy witnessed the refusal of the Arab world to accept the partition and watched the David-Goliath war that ensued, in which Israel was nearly decimated, the youthful Asper's Zionist orientation shifted sharply to the right. He became a disciple of the impassioned Vladimir Jabotinsky and of Menachem Begin, leader of the Irgun militant group that had terrorized the British, and suffered the consequences.

"The true story of Zionism hasn't been told," Asper maintained, "because the Labour Zionists got control of the educational institutions, and of the government. I utterly supported Begin from the time I was twelve or thirteen. Without him and his guerrilla revolt against the British, there would be no Israel." Begin spoke often to Asper about the tortured journey he had taken from Warsaw, where he grew up, to the day he became Israel's prime minister in 1977. The lesson Izzy drew from Begin's life and career was that defiance was often the only response to an intolerable wrong. His idol's most audacious act was the July 22, 1946, bombing of the King David Hotel in Jerusalem, in which ninety-one people died, though civilians had been warned to stay away. In one surreal moment, years later, Asper sat with Begin at the coffee shop in the King David. "I said to Menachem—we were colleagues by then—how can you sit in this bloody coffee shop 150 feet from where you blew this place up? And his response was, 'If I hadn't blown up this hotel, you and I wouldn't be sitting here having coffee.' And of course I agreed with him."

After Begin died in 1992, Asper helped raise the funds to create a museum and research centre in tribute to his late friend's achievements. Who but Izzy would dare host a dinner for forty of his closest Jewish comrades to honour a former Zionist freedom fighter—at Winnipeg's Manitoba Club? Asper didn't harvest many contributions that night, but he did deliver the best forty-five-minute oration on Zionist history ever heard within the musty confines of that cozy beehive, which for more than a century had been an exclusive sanctuary to the city's buzzing WASPs.

Even before he had real money, Asper hosted fundraising events for the Hebrew University, and in 1985 he launched the I.H. Asper Hebrew University of Jerusalem Travel Fund, which assisted Manitoba students to study at the university in Israel. By 2003, more than one hundred Winnipeg teenagers, including several non-Jews, had benefited from the program, which Asper continually topped up. "For forty years I have argued that if you want to create a Zionist and strike a blow for Jewish continuity, send people to spend time in Israel," he decreed, and he acted true to his word. But donating odd sums of money didn't satisfy Asper's determination to leave his mark on Israel. As his fortune grew during the 1990s and he found himself with surplus millions that he could tap into for philanthropic purposes, he set his eyes on something more permanent, which turned out to be the Hebrew University version of the Asper Centre for Entrepreneurship, the institution he had established at the University of Manitoba in 1999. As auspicious as the opening celebrations on June 5, 2001, turned out to be, Asper returned to Canada more concerned than ever about Israel's future. At a Toronto fundraising dinner ten days later, chaired by his former cohorts Peter Godsoe, chairman and CEO of the Bank of Nova Scotia, and Gerry Schwartz, chairman and CEO of Onex Corporation, as well as by his son David Asper, with Governor General Adrienne Clarkson in attendance, he turned the occasion into his most memorable pro-Zionist rant. The target of his remarks that night was Palestinian chairman Yasser Arafat. "I was there two weeks ago when the twenty innocent youths were mercilessly slaughtered, and dozens of young people maimed and crippled for life in Tel Aviv," he told the audience of nine hundred, "all as an expression of Yasser Arafat's unwavering, original and continuing objective of annihilating the state entirely, by any means, however ruthless, savage, barbaric and inhumane, and regardless of how long it takes." The speech was tough, unforgiving and as close as Izzy could come to declaring war on Canada's behalf. While that was precisely what could be expected from him, at Canwest's head office in Winnipeg they started to worry about security issues and about how vulnerable Izzy's home on Wellington Crescent was to a potential attack. He dismissed their concerns with a wave of his hand.

As early as 1973, during his tenure as Manitoba Liberal leader, Asper had written a twelve-page position paper entitled "The Economic War in Israel," in which several of his enduring themes emerged: the use of propaganda by its enemies to portray Israel in the worst possible light; the "double standards" employed by the media in judging Israel; the failure of the international community to come to Israel's defence; the "myth of the Palestinian refugees" whose land had been taken from them in 1948; the plight of Jewish refugees in Arab lands. These were the significant issues he studied and kept emphasizing for the rest of his life. For ammunition in this battle, he was constantly searching for what he called "bullets." "My specialty is marketing," he explained to Daniel Polisar, head of the Shalem Center in Jerusalem. "That's what I understand. You guys, you do research. I need bullets—you guys are a bullet factory. The books you guys put out and the articles, each one of them is a bullet. I need those bullets. I know how to shoot them. I know what to do with them but I can't just be making these claims about Israel without any kind of basis for it."

Nothing raised Asper's ire like the Canadian Broadcasting Corporation, which he believed was guilty of biased reporting against Israel. And he reserved his greatest fury for Neil Macdonald, the corporation's Middle East correspondent from 1998 to 2003. Tall and broad-shouldered, later the network's correspondent in Washington, Macdonald has a convincing manner when he reports a story. Macdonald was based in Jerusalem for five years, and was not shy about injecting his opinions on the Arab-Israeli conflict into his reports. His bosses back in Toronto were supportive. "To suggest that most of the world's media are involved in a conspiracy against Israel, it's just a totally extreme conception on Asper's part," declared Tony Burman, then head of CBC News. "There is something profoundly ironic about being told off about media bias by someone like Izzy Asper." This was a thinly veiled reference to the Aspers' practice of urging their papers to publish company-written editorials that expressed their owner's views, a policy that was abandoned after the fuss it caused. The controversial Canwest head-office editorial factory churned out only half a dozen group editorials and only one on Israel that the chain's newspapers were expected to publish.

"All good reporters use some form of editorializing," the CBC's Macdonald told the *Ryerson Review* in a 2005 interview. "There are people who tell you that you shouldn't judge other cultures— which I have no problem at all doing. That's what you're there for." Macdonald claimed that when he first arrived in Jerusalem, his sympathies lay with the Israelis, but after witnessing the Israeli defence forces in action, his allegiances and opinions switched. His reports featured language that the Aspers claimed was loaded to portray Israel in a poor light, and yet Macdonald was one of the first reporters in 2002 to state categorically that, contrary to published reports by European and North American journalists, there had been no massacre of innocent Palestinians by Israeli soldiers at the Jenin refugee camp on the West Bank. United Nations investigators arrived at the same conclusion several months later. Macdonald's worst offence, in Izzy's opinion, was that he followed the official CBC dictum of never using the word "terrorist" to describe suicide bombers, kidnappers or the slaughterers of civilians. In 2002, after months of dithering, the Canadian government finally decided that Hezbollah, the Party of God, was indeed a terrorist group. That hardly made a difference to Macdonald or to CBC news directors in Toronto; Hezbollah, they claimed, remained "a militant organization." "Everybody's a friggin' terrorist!" Macdonald declared. "The word has lost all meaning. It has been misused so often." Macdonald believed an apology was merited, but didn't expect one. Instead, he said, "I expect more bullying, more bombast, more ideological, anti-journalistic nonsense. I used to work for the newspapers they now own. Several of my ex-colleagues, still there, tell me they find the Aspers' approach to journalism an embarrassment. But they cannot speak publicly. Thank heavens I can."

In October 2002, at an Israel Bonds gala dinner in Montreal, Asper took the opportunity for yet another rant denouncing media bias against Israel. "I make the charge that much of the world media who are covering the Arab-Israeli conflict have abandoned the fundamental precepts of honest reporting," he argued. "They have been taken captive by their own biases, or victimized by their own ignorance. They have adopted Palestinian propaganda as the context for their stories. Thus dishonest reporting has made truth a casualty of the war, causing grievous damage to both Israel and the integrity of the journalistic profession." This time he was loaded with "bullets." In a dissection of media operations, he listed dozens of specific examples of American and Canadian journalists either deliberately distorting their reports on Israel or being victims of a Palestinian parlour game. "I have carried on a love affair with media all my adult life, and I have also been a staunch supporter of Israel," Asper concluded. "At the same time, I am an unashamed and unrelenting Canadian patriot. I am not going to stand idly back to watch any of the democratic ideals that made Canada the envy of nations be injured, sullied or disgraced."

Asper's diatribe garnered him respect among Canada's Jewish community but condemnation elsewhere. British journalist Robert Fisk, who writes for the *Independent* and had been a long-time critic of Israeli policies, labelled Asper's speeches "gutless and repulsive." "These vile slanders," he said, "are familiar to any reporter trying to do his work on the ground in the Middle East. They are made even more revolting by inaccuracies." Fisk specifically took issue with Asper's interpretation of British-Palestinian history—pointing out that, for example, the expression used in the Balfour Declaration of 1917 was "a national home for the Jewish people," rather than a "Jewish State," as Asper had suggested.

More to the point, Asper didn't give a damn. He practised what he preached. Canwest Global was "unabashedly pro-Israel," declared Murdoch Davis, who spent several years as Canwest's Winnipeg-based editor-in-chief. He wasn't kidding.

In mid-August 2001, after an Islamic suicide bomber killed fourteen people at a Jerusalem pizzeria, a Canwest editorial expressed understandable outrage and urged the Canadian government to take appropriate action. A typical editorial-board missive of that time stated, "There is no equivalency between the warring parties in Israel today, and it is wrong for Canada to continue to provide assistance, either financial or political, to Mr. Arafat's gang of murderers. They initiated this conflict, have continually escalated it and have refused to comply with virtually every peace agreement undertaken." Another editorial a few months later questioned Prime Minister Jean Chrétien's "lack of moral leadership" on Mideast issues, calling it an "international embarrassment," and castigated the Liberals for taking forever to place the military arm of Hamas on its list of terrorists. "It is long past time for this tolerance for terrorism to end. Chrétien's refusal to wholly condemn Hamas serves only to trivialize the dangers Palestinians would face under the rule of a group like Hamas or Hezbollah—a Taliban-style regime that would not only be disastrous for the Middle Eastern situation, but also devastating on a personal level to daily life in Palestine."

Journalists accused the Aspers of violating the sacred tenet of press freedom. "They do not want to see any criticism of Israel," claimed William Marsden of the Montreal *Gazette* in a CBC Radio interview. "We do not run in our newspaper op-ed pieces that express criticism of Israel and what it is doing in the Middle East. We even had an incident where a professor wrote an article for us criticizing the anti-terrorism law and elements of civil rights. Now that professor happens to be a Muslim and happens to have an Arab name. We got a call from headquarters demanding to know why we had printed this." Canwest's pro-Israel policy did lead to some nasty celebrated disputes. *National Post* columnist Patricia Pearson resigned over the issue of press freedom. In the midst of the Aspers' battle with journalists to toe the line it was reported—inaccurately, as it turned out—that editors from Victoria to Halifax were instructed not to publish columns or letters to the editor taking issue with their proprietor's position. At the same time, there was no question that the worst form of censorship in this kind of editorial climate was the self-censorship writers and editors applied to their assignments and their copy, usually by avoiding the subject entirely.*

Montreal *Gazette* TV critic Peggy Curran had a column held back and re-edited, about a Canadian documentary that was critical of the Israeli military for criticizing journalists who defended the Palestinians. "If they'll go after the TV critic, they'll go after anyone," one reporter charged. Peter Stockland, the *Gazette*'s editor, asserted that Curran's column needed "routine editing to ensure balance." Halifax *Daily News* columnist Peter March alleged he was fired for touting anti-Israeli views, while in Saskatchewan, an op-ed piece by columnist Doug Cuthand comparing the plight of Native Canadians to the Palestinians was not published. According to Leonard Asper, this was a decision made solely by the editors of the Saskatoon *StarPhoenix* and the Regina *Leader-Post*.

"There was no editorial direction given," Leonard maintained. "A lot of the noise was perception." The son followed in his father's footsteps on the issue. About a week before Izzy died, Leonard delivered a hard-hitting speech at a Winnipeg synagogue about media bias against Israel—a speech that included another shot at Neil Macdonald, suggesting that he had called Hezbollah a "national liberation movement victimized by unfair smears cast about by supporters of the Jewish state." This was not quite what Macdonald had reported. "Of course," he had written, "what this all really boils down to is the old question of what constitutes terrorism. Is Hezbollah a national liberation movement, or, as Israel and its supporters maintain, a murderous global menace? To many people in this part of the world (the Arab world), to label Hezbollah a terrorist organization is to choose sides in the defining conflict of the Middle East." Nevertheless, Leonard's speech

---

*Independently of anything Canwest management or ownership said or wanted, in 2005, Canwest News Service editors regularly altered Reuters text from "militant" to "terrorist" in a very public spat based on a definition of "terrorist" that the papers' editors themselves had formulated. Canwest won in the sense that Reuters allowed the Canadian company to continue the practice and still provided it with the material required by their contract.

was published the next day in Canwest newspapers. And the following day, Macdonald, who had more or less ignored Izzy's fron-
tal attacks, decided to retaliate against the son in an op-ed piece
in the *Globe and Mail*. "I've remained silent for the past year as
the Aspers and their editorials have relentlessly attacked me and
the CBC, but enough is enough," wrote Macdonald. "This latest
salvo is inaccurate, loathsome, and defamatory. It merits an apology." Macdonald added that he didn't expect to receive one, and
Leonard didn't disappoint him.

In the late seventies, Asper was encouraged by the Israeli government to become part of a consortium to modernize Israel's phone
system. Dangled in front of him was the prize of a cable television licence that would compete with the monopoly of the state-
run Israeli network. When Asper arrived in Israel for negotiations,
he was greeted like a visiting head of state. "We were cleared in
two minutes," remembers Leonard, then fifteen years old. "There
was no airport entry or customs check." The plan moved forward.
Editorials in Israeli newspapers extolled the idea of radically trans-
forming the outmoded phone system and bringing Israeli television into the twenty-first century. Asper flew in a cadre of expert
engineers and technicians to draw up the plans. Receptions were
held by the banks to celebrate his consortium's project. It seemed
like a done deal. On the day when the agreement with the government was to be finalized, the Labour Party cabinet minister
responsible for the negotiations kept Izzy and his group waiting
for more than an hour. Eventually the minister arrived and, with
no apologies, announced that he had "good news and bad news."
Asper's heart sank. The good news was that he was delighted to
have anyone in Israel interested in developing a new cable TV system and improving the archaic phone service; the bad news was
that the government had decided "not to proceed with the plan at
this time."

"That was the end," Asper recalled, lamenting the fact that he had wasted $1 million on a lost cause, "and the beginning of chagrin, embarrassment for my non-Jewish colleagues and pessimism of ever being able to do business in Israel, unless you wanted to manufacture souvenirs or some other innocuous endeavour." In 1993, David and Leonard, young, brash and having just signed on with Canwest full-time, worked long hours and many days assembling another consortium of investors interested in making a bid for Israel's second channel—the first commercial television network available to Israelis. The Asper siblings envisioned, as David put it at the time, "an urban, hip operation with a populist approach." The brothers found dealing with their Israeli partners more than challenging. "The Israelis are going to have to get accustomed to dealing with us on a long-distance basis. They seemed to think that someone would be in Israel a fair amount and certainly at the monthly executive committee meetings," David added in an April 6, 1993, memo. "I believe that it will be extremely important in the long term to set the ground rules of our relationship with the Israelis right off the bat. Moreover, I strongly urge that nobody speak off the cuff or dream of great things out loud. They hang on every word and believe everything we say." In the end, David's aspirations were quashed by a government decision to offer the second channel to a consortium of three unrelated broadcasting groups—with ties to Walt Disney, ABC, NBC and the BBC—in what must have been the oddest TV arrangement ever concocted, since they had to divide the channel's weekly schedule three ways. Izzy accurately called it a "Mickey Mouse" set-up.

Upon Benjamin Netanyahu's election in the spring of 1996, Asper sent the new prime minister a lengthy memo outlining a proposal for Canwest to become involved in a third national network. Yet again, nothing came of Asper's entreaties. Five more years passed before Asper was approached to take the lead in yet another consortium, for Channel 3. He was skeptical but still game. "We would be happily prepared to see our TV network become an instrument for the promotion of Israel and the Zionist cause, throughout the world, particularly the Diaspora," he wrote to one senior bureaucrat who was feeling him out. "To that end, we would commit to using a substantial portion of the station profits to ensure the production and international distribution and actual exhibition of Israel-favourable programming in news, information, public affairs, and when appropriate, through dramatic, entertainment programming. In other words, that would be our social and cultural contribution. In effect we would use our position as a PR instrument of the External Affairs department, something it badly lacks and needs. That is my underlying motive." That seemed like an offer too good to refuse, but the government managed to squash it, awarding the channel instead to three national cable companies with political connections. The litmus test of Asper's ultimate loyalty to his cause was that he never allowed the disappointment of being ostracized four times—prevented by the country's political masters from harvesting any benefits from his many philanthropies aimed at Israel—to alter his profound commitment to his second homeland.

Izzy made his final journey to Israel in the spring of 2002, leading a Jewish Federation of Winnipeg mission of solidarity during the Palestinian intifada. At the time, since there were virtually no tourists visiting the embattled country, they were greeted like long-lost cousins. On his final pilgrimage to Yad Vashem, the poignant Holocaust memorial in the hills of Jerusalem, he decided to commit $2 million to establish the I.H. Asper International Holocaust Studies Program, which would enable educators from around the globe to visit the site for training seminars and conferences. "Given where the world is, there is no place in the world I would rather be than on this ground, on this hill at the heart of Jerusalem," he declared at a ceremony marking the study program's launch. "It is the strongest symbol that I can hold that free men and women will not be terrorized, will not be dissuaded of expressing their solidarity with democratic human rights respecting people like the people of Israel."

A second event planned for the Winnipeg group was yet another Asper Foundation project: the opening of the first of three community action centres (in partnership with World Betar, the youth group associated with the right-wing Zionism of Vladimir Jabotinsky in the 1920s) designed to assist at-risk and disadvantaged youth, many of whom were Russian and Ethiopian immigrants. Here, in after-school programs, teenagers played sports or went online with the centre's state-of-the-art computers. "Izzy was a big donor," said World Betar's Danny Danon, who had first introduced Asper to the community centres on a visit to Israel a year earlier. "It is often difficult to attract big donors to this project, but not Izzy. He saw the challenge of going to the development towns. That was a brave move. It is a struggle to work with development towns, and hard to work with the Israeli bureaucracy. It is easier to give money to a university and that's the end of it. He saw the challenge and accepted it." Unfortunately, on the day of the celebration to open the first Asper Foundation youth centre in Beer Sheva, appropriately called the Winnipeg Community Action Centre, Cecilia, Asper's ninety-eight-year-old mother, died. Izzy and Babs rushed back to Canada.

By May 2003, three community enterprises, one named after Winnipeg, the others after Asper, had become fully functional. On a typical day, they are bustling with children—playing soccer, using computers, surfing the Net or just having fun.

"We're going to Winnipeg!" they shout in Beer Sheva.

"We're off to Asper," they mimic in Ofaqim.

They might not know who Israel Asper was, but in the land of Israel his spirit and his legacy live on. The man and the country became inseparable. Now, each misses the other.

12

The Canterbury Tale: Jousting with Conrad

"It all began a couple of months ago when Leonard walked by my
door and said, 'I'm going out for lunch. Can I bring you something?'
And I said, 'Yeah, would you mind getting me a couple of papers?'"
—Izzy Asper, August 2000

Marine radios are notoriously unreliable. We were in my sailboat, the *Pacific Mystic,* somewhere off the Sunshine Coast in the Georgia Strait in southern British Columbia, when I heard a familiar voice calling my name. It was one of those memorable west-coast days when the faring of the tides and the whip of the current were at one with the vessel and her crew, so that Joseph Conrad's magnificent claim that those of us who go to sea are "the grownup children of discontented earth" seemed more fact than vanity.

I couldn't quite make out what that raspy voice on the VHF radio was saying, but from hearing the signal cut out every few minutes, I knew it had to be Izzy Asper, taking time out to puff on his cigarette. "Look," he said. "I need your book about Conrad right away. I've lost my copy. Please courier me one as soon as possible. I may be doing a deal with him, and I want to know more about his character."

I wish we could have spent more time discussing his suggestion. My book—*The Establishment Man: A Portrait in Power,* originally published almost two decades earlier—might indeed have been useful, since at the time Black was only thirty-five and still a real person instead of the combative, whining metaphor he would become. He was a compelling presence then, more strategic than manipulative, less concerned with ways of making money than with making history. I fell under the spell of his command of language and his impressive feats of memory, a memory both photographic and phonographic, in that he could recite anything he had ever read and mimic almost anyone he had ever heard. His presence was impressive and what struck me most forcefully was his lust for power. He basked in its coital afterglow like a lover.

Apart from his parlour tricks, I found Black to be the most impressive newcomer in the roster of Canada's mostly comatose business Establishment, a Roman candle among the wet firecrackers then littering the landscape. His daring 1978 *coup d'état,* when in four hectic months he spun an inherited $7 million into control of Argus Corporation (Hollinger's predecessor) and its $4 billion in undervalued assets, was a bravura performance, choreographed like a well-turned-out Sadler's Wells ballet. At the same time, I noted the darker, righteous side of his nature: that no matter what he did, he somehow felt himself exempt from evil intent, assuming that any corporate behaviour that ran counter to his convenience constituted a wilful denial of his due. The regulations that hemmed in lesser beings, those not blessed by his divine right of things (be they temporal or material), were not part of his mental horizon. He regarded selling stock in his companies merely as a cheap way of accessing other people's money and showed little sense of responsibility to his shareholders. As soon as his minority partners demanded their legal rights, he dismissed them as "terrorists" and dubbed himself a "freedom fighter" for standing up to their threats.

That clash was still far off the future, but had I been able to talk longer with Izzy that day, I might have warned the Canwest CEO that despite the nearly four years of research that I had invested in my book on Conrad, he actually hated it, and thought I hadn't captured him at all. Commenting on *Establishment Man* in a letter to me dated January 13, 1983, Black complained, "What is particularly irritating is that it is not open season on me, but upon a largely fictional image that you created for me, of a chillingly ruthless and rather conceited person, obsessed with materialism, pontificating endlessly, and viewing the world through the prism of a reactionary proprietor . . ."

How could I have been so wrong?

───────────

The last time the two men met, Izzy was running his Winnipeg-based merchant bank and Conrad was just beginning to hit his loping stride of entitlement, well before becoming the English-speaking world's third-ranking media titan. He had already taught himself how to decant his frame out of mottled-leather easy chairs without bending, learned to treat servants like mobile furniture and perfected the trick of moving his limbs in a reduced rhythm that signalled his claim to be the vanguard of a social order superior to the rest of us. It was not exactly an immaculate conception, but the incarnation that elevated him into what he considered to be a position that was beyond reproach was his appointment to Westminster's upper chamber as Lord Black of Crossharbour. This fateful elevation had required him to discard his Canadian citizenship, which turned out to be the first step in his downfall.

For Izzy Asper, Black's lordship at first seemed like something out of a Gilbert and Sullivan operetta. His son Leonard evened the score by arranging to bestow on his father a title of his own: Lord of the Manor of Polington. On the eleventh of August 2002, Izzy was piped aboard the M.V. *Grace Anne,* a pleasure ship circumnavigating Lake of the Woods. At a prearranged stop, a troop of hired actors done up in costumes appropriate for the aristocratic occasion joined the Asper family aboard the vessel—and, reciting a string of *Here-ye*'s, anointed the Canadian media baron as Lord of the Manor of Polington in the Parish of Charminster in the County of Dorset.*

It is a real, if spectacularly minor, title and Asper never used it, except that one afternoon on the Lake of the Woods steamboat. It was purchased by Leonard through Daniel Sandelson, the lawyer who had been closely involved in the Aspers' UK television licence application.

Within weeks of the brief exchange on my marine radio, the first rumours of a major Hollinger transaction were being published, and three months later the biggest media deal in Canadian history was sealed. For an initial $3.5 billion Izzy Asper bought 129 newspapers and magazines from Black's communications empire, including 13 leading dailies published in nearly every important Canadian city (except, ironically, Winnipeg), along with a half interest in the *National Post,* the innovative paper that Conrad had launched to compete with the *Globe and Mail.*

---

*According to Robert Smith, chairman of the Manorial Society of Great Britain, the title dated back to the village of Polington, in the Parish of Charminster, in the county of Dorset, "situated near the confluence of the Rivers Cerne and Frome, 3 miles northwest from Dorchester and consists of 800 acres."

At the time of the Domesday Book, the record of the great survey of England completed in 1086, Polington was a village that formed part of the Manor of Charminster, for which the entry read in part, "The Bishop of Salisbury holds Charminster. Before 1066 it paid tax for 10 hides. Land for 8 ploughs. In lordship 2 ploughs; 4 slaves; 14 villagers and 12 smallholders with 6 ploughs. A mill pays 6s.; meadow, 15 acres; pasture 1 league long and 3 furlongs wide; woodland 2 furlongs long and 1 furlong wide." By 1160 the manor was in the possession of Bernard Poleyn, who either took his name from the Manor or gave it its title. Poleyn's sons and grandsons held the title for many years. The Poleyns lost it in the 14th century to the Martin family of Athelhampton. The entry traces the holders of the title into the 1700s. There were no famous Lord Polingtons—except Israel Harold Asper, of course—but Izzy didn't have to surrender his Winnipeg citizenship to claim his version of the "peerage."

Black sold most of his holdings in Canada because he needed to reduce his corporate debt and realized that the international investment community had discounted his Canadian assets. He was also convinced that newspapers as value investments were an increasingly dubious bet. More to the point, this was a time Black was moving out of such backwater colonies as his home and native land to settle with appropriate splendour in London, which he rightly considered the capital of the world. Along with his radiant bride, Barbara Amiel, he planned to dazzle and beguile the natives, as he set out into the splendiferous (a good Conrad word) upper levels of British society where status, accent and lineage were everything. Owning the *Edmonton Journal* didn't cut it.

Lord Black was ecstatic about the deal, having sold his Canadian newspaper holdings to the Aspers at the top of the market. He chose to abandon his birthright, and in October of 2001 donned the ermine robes (really dyed rabbit fur) of a British lord, though he endowed Westminster's upper chamber with his presence for only a dozen cameo appearances in the ensuing half decade.

When the purchase of Black's newspapers was consummated on August 1, 2000, Izzy was beside himself with excitement. "I feel reborn!" he exulted at the announcement ceremony. "A company has to reinvent itself, otherwise it becomes stale and moribund." Then, summoning up his customary flair for understatement, he described the *National Post* as "the most monumental media miracle of all time, an astounding first in Canadian media history." Asper pledged that he would "not lightly" interfere with the paper's successful editorial formula. "We've agreed that because Conrad Black is the founder, it's his vision which we support and endorse. For the first five years, if we disagree, he will carry the day."

The transaction more than doubled Canwest's asset base (as well as its debt load, to $4 billion) and crowned Israel Asper as the undisputed colossus of the Canadian media world. The Kid from

Minnedosa was truly a Media Mogul now, and his company, as some-body put it, "swallowed Black's biggest titles without a belch."

This was how, in a high-pressure span of only fourteen weeks, the "media deal of the century" came about—though there were, in fact, plenty of belches along the way.

The action eventually moved to exotic locations on several conti-nents. But it began with a quiet exchange of phone calls between Asper and Black in early 2000, when they were both wintering at their spreads in Palm Beach, the unofficial command post of the American business establishment. Many factors went into the mix that drove the deal to fruition. But the most essential was the prox-imity of its two principals: the fact that they both wintered in Palm Beach made the deal practical.

The gilt-edged community sits on top of a barrier reef twenty-three kilometres long and almost a kilometre across. What bonds its inhabitants is their common assumption about wealth and con-spicuous consumption. They communicate through raised eyebrows and seldom experience any conflicts of interest, since their interests so infrequently conflict. Although insider trading may have been invented among the local sand dunes, the Palm Beach fortunes regard themselves as proof to an invidiously competitive society that privilege can be spectacularly rewarded. The capricious castles in which they live are monuments to their self-indulgence. A mansion owned by the Stotesbury family actually had a forty-car garage, used to capacity with its owner's antique collection. There were private petting zoos for the kids and art collections that no museum could afford for the adults. The place swarmed with eccentrics. According to local lore, one of the Palm Beach Du Ponts imported tame igua-nas from Cuba and trained them to slither at attention, as a kind of honour guard, whenever he called them with a special whistle.

Black first visited this chi-chi world in 1969 on his way back from Cuba, where he had gone to observe the celebration of Fidel Castro's tenth anniversary in power. He hated that Communist whoop-up and gladly accepted an invitation to decompress at the Palm Beach mansion of Bud McDougald, his mentor and the Godfather of Argus Corp., which became Conrad's eventual takeover target and original grubstake. In the winter of 1978, he purchased (for $3.4 million) a relatively modest Federalist mansion at 150 Canterbury Lane, then owned by John R. Drexel III, a descendant of the Philadelphia banking family. "I've never been back to Cuba, but I have often returned here, although Palm Beach isn't everyone's cup of tea," he told me when I visited his winter digs while writing the book about him. Then he foreshadowed his future wife Barbara Amiel's legendary quip that her extravagance knew no bounds, when he said, "Some people are offended by the extreme opulence of Palm Beach. But I find it sort of entertaining. A couple of seasons ago I was standing at the corner of Worth Avenue and County Road when I heard a slight rumpus. I turned around and saw that a Silver Cloud II had been struck in the fender by a Phantom V, which had come to such an abrupt stop that a Silver Shadow had bumped into it. So you had three Rollses stuck together. It was hilarious."

After he married Amiel, Conrad's Palm Beach digs were declared inadequate and they purchased a $9.9 million mansion on Ocean Boulevard, the most prestigious part of the island, then spent another $9.9 million refurbishing it. The sliver of land on which the Black house squats was just wide enough to contain one mansion and a two-lane road. What made it unique was that the dozen palaces situated along Ocean Boulevard enjoyed two seascapes: the lengthy expanse of Lake Worth at sunset and the heaving Atlantic Ocean at sunrise. But living in such an exclusive enclave presented a problem—after all, one doesn't want to be seen scurrying across a public highway. The Blacks solved the dilemma by using a tunnel built under Ocean Boulevard, lined with glazed Italian tile, which opened up to its 300 feet of private oceanfront that included a luxury cabana. The 21,500-square-foot colonial-style Black mansion was a symphony of balconies and loggias—Italian arcades that open to the air on one side. The dwelling included a magnificent wood-panelled library plus a very special spiral staircase leading to the tower room, which commanded a Utopian view of Palm Beach. The double stairwell was carved out of onyx, a semi-precious stone that dated back to Roman times, when it was fashioned into vases and cups. The mini-palace, with nine bedrooms (decorated with vintage furniture) and seven bathrooms, was set into a lush 2.62-acre garden that featured special rose and herb areas.

Having visited this Florida-based Taj Mahal, Izzy decided it was time for him to go upscale, and confided his plans to Peter Viner, one of his most trusted executives. The Aspers had previously purchased a winter condo on Singer Island, immediately north of Palm Beach. It wasn't large enough to accommodate the family, so Izzy and Babs began searching for a house. They then found and bought that ex-Black house on Canterbury Lane, where Conrad had lived with his first wife, Shirley.*

Now, Izzy was seeking more elaborate quarters to escape Winnipeg winters. "He phoned me up and he told me he was interested in buying a house in Palm Beach," Viner recalled. "He said that he had found a couple he liked but that their owners wanted four or five million for them—and they were just rentals. Since he was worth at least a billion bucks at this stage, I said, 'Izzy, it's just one less Ferrari for the kids.'

"'I'm going to tell Babs you said that.'

"'Go ahead. Tell the kids too.'"

A month later Asper bought the 7,700-square-foot seaside palace two houses down along Canterbury Lane for $7.5 million from luxury auto dealer Roger Dean and decided to almost completely redo it. Once renovations were complete, they sold the former Black residence. The house was a show place. When Yale Lerner first saw

---

*She later changed her name to Joanna, perhaps in light of her then husband Conrad's fervent hope of receiving a British title, because Lady Joanna sounded much grander than Lady Shirley. (It turned out to be Lady Barbara.)

the mansion, he told a friend, "Izzy himself has never changed. You never knew by looking at him or his style of living that he was rich— except for that Palm Beach house. That was the first clue. I told him, that's when he became rich. Before that he was just wealthy." The Aspers added a bedroom wing but the main house still wasn't big enough, so they built a guest house in the back.

The Asper home slopes to the ocean, and you eventually get to a point where it looks as if this is it, it's all over—there is no more house. But in a bookcase on one wall, you push a button and it opens into a cavernous poolroom, set up with pictures on the wall of Izzy's buddies. Then, when you think that you really are at the endpoint of the house, you enter an office the size of a basketball court, which was where he worked, an inner sanctum where he could listen to jazz and dispatch his witching-hour emails.

The house became something of a visiting base for Canwest executives, with at least three corporate retreats having been held there, including negotiations for the massive potential deal with the Scottish Media Group, which involved twenty-five executives, invest- ment bankers and lawyers. Two corporate retreats were interrupted by a chance to by up to 30 percent of Ulster Television and the opportunity to purchase CTV.

Few Canwest staff members, however, got to visit the Asper com- pound, but an exception was a one-time drop-in by Matthew Fraser, who eventually succeeded Ken Whyte as the *National Post*'s editor- in-chief. Fraser's wife, Rebecca, who was former ambassador Allan Gotlieb's daughter, had recently died, and Izzy invited Matthew in late January 2003 to Palm Beach for a recuperative holiday. "During the day," Fraser recalled, "we would jump into his Mercedes convertible and drive around Palm Beach, with Asper pointing to such celebrity mansions as those owned by Gerry Schwartz and Heather Reisman, and the Kennedy compound that Izzy had almost bought—in fact, had made a tentative offer on. It was a frightening experience because Izzy was not an attentive driver, since he always had a cigarette in his hand, and often veered onto the sidewalks. At night we would sit up in his den, the brandy flowing liberally, as Izzy recounted dozens of tales about his business adventures and misadventures. He was in fine form." He even impersonated Issy Sharp, the man who turned the Four Seasons into a world-class brand. At one point, Asper and a friend went to the Four Seasons Hotel in Palm Beach to take in a jazz concert, only to find it was sold out. His pal, audibly enough for the maitre d' to hear, pronouncing his zeds softly, said, "Iszszy, they can't be sold out for you! Tell them who you are, and be Sharp about it." The maitre d' turned around and said, "Oh, Mr. Sharp, I didn't realize it was you—look, I can squeeze a couple of extra chairs around that table at the front"—which he did.

One visitor to his winter digs, Michael Oren, recalled: "I had no idea what to expect and I'll never forget the first glimpse of this man. He comes out wearing a pink shirt and white pants with pink stripes and white shoes, that florid face with a cigarette, and he reminded me of sort of a tropical plant in full bloom with his expansive personality. I don't think I've ever bought into somebody so quickly. He felt very, very warm, accessible and very smart—a smart, intuitive reader who understood politics and issues very well. I began to talk to him about, of all things, a film idea that I had, which was on the life of Ward Waingait, the former British General who was not Jewish but who really was the founder of the Israeli Army and the father of modern guerrilla warfare. He immediately understood the possibilities."

In the spring of 2000, Izzy was getting itchy to find a new outlet for his energies. After all, it had been an entire week since he had completed his thirty-year war to hammer together Canada's third television network. At the time, Leonard was back in Winnipeg developing Canwest's new Web strategy, which made father and son realize how inferior their existing site was compared to Canada.com, the Web outlet owned by Black and operated by his Southam newspaper group and the *National Post*. Asper and Black had had several inconclusive phone conversations to see if a merger or sale of the site might be doable, but nothing had happened.

Then, on March 20, 2000, Asper phoned Black, and boldly suggested, "Why don't we go beyond Canada.com?" He pointed out that Hollinger's Southam papers in Saskatchewan—the *Leader-Post* in Regina and the *StarPhoenix* in Saskatoon—were "hardly strategic in the scheme of things." Black agreed they should explore that and other ideas, and thus the seeds of what, for confidentiality reasons, became known as "A Canterbury Tale" were sown. The two men had last done business together twenty-two years earlier when Conrad had sold Crown Trust to Canwest, which had turned out to be a rewarding transaction for them both.

On April 25, 2000, Leonard and Izzy were in Vancouver for CRTC hearings when Hollinger announced that its stable of Canadian community newspapers was up for sale, though there was no mention of the large-city dailies. Izzy immediately called Black and arranged to meet him at Hollinger's New York office in mid-May. During the intervening weeks, a flurry of letters, faxes and emails flowed between Asper and Black, from Winnipeg to Las Vegas and London, as well as from Palm Beach to New York and Israel. Both men preferred to work late into the night, so the deal began to dribble out in what Asper referred to as his "nocturnal emissions." Black's London office had a voice-activated computer fax that he could dictate into by telephone, ordering the machine to deliver his message to any world destination. Asper recalled one notable fax addressed to him that began, "It's intermission at the opera . . ." (Conrad and Barbara were in Bayreuth, Germany, attending the annual Wagner festival when an idea hit him.)

The deal was set in motion when Izzy reported to Leonard that he had spoken to Black and that "it is now top priority for you to get every scrap of information together that is on the public record about Hollinger and/or Hollinger International, as I intend to be talking to him again soon and I want to know the dimensions of his situation." Two weeks later, on May 15, Black sent a handwritten fax to Asper, the first of several letters in Izzy's files concerning the deal. Addressing him as "Dear Izzie" (he never did learn to spell his name), Conrad laid out his proposed deal: "Essentially what is contemplated is a merger between your company and our Canadian operations with payment to us at the standard rate in the newspaper industry made up by a mixture of your shares issues at the appropriate multiple in the television industry, plus a combination of debt, assumed cash, appropriately yielding preferred shares and, if you wish, reasonably senior notes bearing a commercial rate of interest." He estimated the total price to be approximately $5 billion, "representing ten times EBITDA [shorthand for Earnings before Interest, Taxes, Depreciation and Amortization], less $19 million for his personal management fee which produced a subtotal of $4.6 billion plus $200 million for the *National Post* and $200 million for Look Communications" (an Internet company). He wanted assurances that he could appoint "an appropriate number of directors" to manage the newspaper assets, then set out numbers that made his company's projections appear highly favourable. Not aware of the Aspers' financial clout, Black was at this point proposing a partnership instead of a sale.

Izzy's answer arrived in a ten-page fax handwritten by him after midnight: "Hope you can read my scrawl—I won 'most improved writing award' on graduation from Grade VIII Neepawa Public School." The document detailed his and Leonard's reaction to the finer points of a potential deal, valuations and stock offerings, as well as what should and shouldn't be included. "It's 3:20 am—20 minutes past my bed time so I'll close," he signed off. "I agree that we are on the brink of something unique, powerful and economically extraordinary. You and I should exercise all the skills we've accumulated over a lifetime of trench warfare to manage our respective interests to make this melding happen. Besides, we'll have a lot of laughs—both internally and externally."

Black's response was friendly but guarded. Izzy messaged back, "I am heartened by your fax responding to my nocturnal emission.

Your flexibility is so encouraging that it is not necessary to comment further, as I share your confidence that the end game is so tantalizing and extraordinary, that you and I will find a way to overcome the hurdles, because we have a mutuality of mind." Here was a new Canterbury Tale being proposed: instead of an awkward and ultimately unworkable partnership, a bold takeover was suddenly in the works. "I'm a good writer," Asper recalled, "and I've written agreements all of my life. Yet this was extraordinarily complex because the tax issues were dynamite." In his reply to a fax from Tom Strike, Canwest's resident accounting wizard, who has the build of a champion wrestler and was sometimes mistaken for Izzy's bodyguard, Black chose to get tough. The Aspers were staying at the Bellagio Hotel in Vegas at the time, celebrating daughter Gail's fortieth birthday, and to maintain secrecy Black signed his missive, "Hon. Price Montague," a pseudonym that he never explained, although there was a Manitoba judge by that name before the Second World War, who rose to become a lieutenant general at Canadian military HQ in London.

Asper had made his fortune by being a brutal negotiator, seldom backing up an inch even if his life depended on it. Black was his equal. He sarcastically objected to Strike's valuations placed on Canwest assets and came close to breaking off the negotiations: "In summary you appear to be seeking to buy assets from us at 10 times EBITDA and to pay for them in part with your restricted voting shares somewhat generously valued at 16 times EBITDA, including such flamboyant Asperian flourishes as 20 times for an Australian company where you have 15% of the votes and a 42.5% minority. If we didn't have a high opinion of you and your company we wouldn't be having these discussions at all but we are no more disposed to negotiate on such a grossly uneven basis than you would be if our roles were reversed." Black scoffed at the notion that television assets were more valuable than newspapers of "the highest quality," while acknowledging that Canwest's audacious "if you don't ask, you don't get" strategy was one he often used himself.

Here, however, he warned, it simply wouldn't work. Then he added a kinder kicker: "The grandeur of the concept so inspires both of us that I propose we try to bridge the gap by some combination of less aggressive multiplication on your part, some further flexibility on ours, reducing the stock component of the consideration offered by you, and raising the multiple of our asset. In a word, you have to decide if you really want this deal, and you have to recognize that we are not going to make deals that make us look like idiots who have been fleeced out of our underclothing." After making a threat that he had plenty of other buyers clamouring in the wings, Black ended by suggesting that: "If we are unable to get an intersection of our requirements," they would have to abandon the idea of a merger and the Aspers could simply put in their bid, among others, for the assets they wanted and see who came out on top. He set a time frame on the negotiations, stating that the deal ought to live or die before they left Brussels. That was where Black and Asper were due to attend a session of the 46th Bilderberg conference, a secretive right-wing think tank founded by Prince Bernhard of the Netherlands that was due to meet at the Château du Lac, a newly renovated castle turned into a five-star hotel (with eight surrounding golf clubs) twelve kilometres south of the Belgian metropolis.

On May 22 Izzy sent a conciliatory fax from Vegas to "Hon. CMB Montague, Esquire" in London, claiming that the Canwest communication Black had received did not "convey the deal I am proposing" but was merely a corporate overview (whatever that meant). He didn't subscribe to all of Black's suggestions but agreed "with the penultimate principles." The proposed merger was fast becoming a takeover. He promised to draft a concept document for their meeting in Brussels but first had to visit Jerusalem for five days on a philanthropic errand. Then he added, "I haven't been in Vegas since the early 1980s—my, my, how things change: It's a veritable Disneyland for the Decadent."

Within the next forty-eight hours, Izzy had drafted the first version of his concept document, which he sent to his son Leonard with a note: "We had a near brush with conflagration over the weekend after Conrad received Tom Strike's 'outrageous valuation document,' which suggested we should get $32 per share for Canwest stock." He assured his son that he had smoothed things over and would be meeting Black in Brussels on June 1. ("Don't worry. We have since kissed and made up—I, his ring—he, my ass—and so we continue to be on for a possible deal.") The two titans agreed that if they couldn't hammer out a deal within two days after the end of the Bilderberg conference, they would both be free to make alternate arrangements.

The official response to Black was dispatched on May 25, attempting to calm his concerns about the valuation of the Canwest shares that Hollinger would be acquiring, now reduced to $27, while valuations of the Australian and New Zealand holdings were similarly reduced. Leonard called Black the following day, but the valuation issue remained a sticking point. Black wanted more than the offered 10 percent of Canwest stock so it would look more like a merger. Leonard told him they were flexible on that issue. Black then wished to know which newspapers Canwest especially desired because, he claimed, he was getting many offers. "The real stinger is that he has indicated the *Post* was not for sale, because it's 'his baby,'" Leonard reported to his father. "I told him that we assumed it was, at the valuation he had suggested (he then reiterated the $200 million number). I said we thought it was quite important that it be included as part of the deal and he suggested that perhaps we could accomplish this by giving us an option to buy half of it. We did not debate this further."

At this point Black appeared not to be pleased with the progress of the negotiations. He decried to Leonard what he saw as the Aspers' failure to treat the deal as a merger, accusing them of instead proposing what was really "an option to buy whatever of our Canadian assets you wish," at a decreasing price in "an attempt that would be as obvious to everyone else as it is to me to reduce my associates and me, who have been media proprietors as long as your family have, to the status in this country of employees." He objected to having to seek approval from a Liberal government "with which our state of animosity is notorious." He also again objected to the valuations placed on his companies' stock and repeated that if Canwest didn't want a merger in which "you manage what you have been managing and we manage what we have been managing," then the Aspers should make their best offer for whatever Canadian assets they wanted, adding, "I certainly don't wish to be undiplomatic but these are magnificent assets, this is a once-only opportunity, and even my long friendship and high regard for your father will not cause us to be parted from them on a commercially disadvantageous and unrealistic basis."

The deal seemed to be falling apart. Finally Conrad realized that the real sticking point was not really the stock valuations but who would control the *National Post*, which might be haemorrhaging serious money but which was the repository of the political clout that the Winnipeg entrepreneur wanted to exercise. Black suggested that the value of the *Post* remain at $200 million and that Canwest buy 50 percent. He would run it for five years, but it would be integrated so that financial returns could be maximized. The negotiations dragged on; at one point it took Izzy, who was still in Israel, two hours on the phone to locate Conrad for yet one more discussion. At this point Black was scribbling his suggested changes on a copy of the Izzy/Leonard draft, and one of them was an increase of his personal management fees to an annual $45 million. "He said they are still flexible on the management issue," Leonard reported to Izzy. "The so-called transitional period beginning upon purchase is 18 months but he said it could be one year if necessary. He still insists upon the management of the papers in the initial period but accepts oversight of a Board Committee. We agreed it needs more discussion. Black wants a true shotgun buy sell, not a put by Hollinger and a call by Canwest. Therefore he, not Canwest, could end up owning the *Post* someday. I said this was unacceptable to us. We thought we were buying control but in stages. He understood and sympathized with that expectation and desire but said it was 'one of the issues we will resolve.'"

Black pressed the younger Asper to confirm that they "were getting there." Leonard wasn't buying it. He pointed out that the quality of the deal had declined, citing the price of Canwest shares and the still unresolved *Post* arrangements. "He disputed the notion that the deal had gotten worse and of course discussion ensued," Leonard reported to his father. "I said I still thought there was a deal here but he had asked us for significant compromises and if we were going to compromise anything he would have to as well." Izzy approved his son's strategy. "I think your posture of disappointment to Conrad is the correct one in order to slow down his rapacious appetite for sweetening the deal," he faxed Leonard from Jerusalem, using his "note" format: "We should put a few new things on the table . . . suggest the *Jerusalem Post*, perhaps. Other valuation changes. We certainly get editorial control of purchased papers. On *Post*, he's in control and we can hide behind that, but I look to his early warning and giving us input. Board should be 50–50. Conrad is chair, gets casting vote, but we get policy input through board, including editorial policy. We should now surface the idea that the print company will be called 'Asper Publications,' leaving Global as our television brand. Hollinger to agree to vote for the name change. Please discuss this name issue with David and Gail before proposing it." In response, Conrad also confirmed his wish for a direct payment of the $6 million management fee into his private holding company, Ravelston.

That broke the impasse. On May 30 Leonard ecstatically faxed Izzy, "Terrific call with Conrad. I think we are there on everything except *National Post* and *Jerusalem Post* and even in those cases there is willingness to compromise. I'm very optimistic." They agreed that the operating newspaper executives would report to Black and David Radler but that they could be overruled by a newly created Operations Committee of the Canwest Board, where the majority would be Asper representatives. The relevant clause read, "The management agreement may be bought out by Canwest or cancelled by Ravelston after Dec. 31, 2000. In the former case Canwest will pay Ravelston $45 million and in the latter case the fee payable by Canwest would be $22.5 million."

Leonard replied the next day, "Dad, spoke to Conrad. He called at 1:45 a.m. London time. More hilarious antics. He tried me at the office but couldn't figure out how to get me on the directory because British telephones have no letters to guide him to enter the letters of my name. (Maybe at last a good reason to get direct lines for everyone.) He then called my home (I was at the office) and left his entire comments on the answering machine but half of them had to do with fixing typos." He did reiterate again that Asper pay Ravelston, his private holding company, an annual management fee of $6 million, and Asper agreed, providing it was subtracted from the purchase price.

The two men finally met under the auspices of the Bilderberg think-tank sessions, but they were careful not be seen together too often so that they wouldn't arouse suspicion about an impending deal. "We agreed that every night after dinner, we'd go to the bar," Izzy recalled. "And we'd schmooze with the boys for a while until they retired. Because Conrad and I are both night people, we'd then take a couple of hours to work on this new fifty-page purchase document which I'd rewritten. Except that what would happen was that we would get into intense debates with people like Bill Richardson, the U.S. secretary of energy, and then everyone would stay up late. Finally, around one in the morning, we would start negotiating. By the third night, we were both exhausted from staying up so late and still attending the early-morning conference sessions."

––––––

The main issues in dispute were the future of the *National Post* and the nature of the non-compete clauses to be included in the deal. Several years earlier, when Black had first informed Don Babick, Southam's president, about his plans to start another national newspaper, he had been told that it was a "crazy idea." (Later Babick became the *Post*'s first publisher.) Black went ahead anyway, acknowledging that it would take upwards of $150 million and five to seven years before the *Post* earned a dime of profit. He turned out to be wildly optimistic. Since its inaugural issue was published in October 1998, the paper had, by the summer of 2001, lost more than $200 million. Editorially, the *Post* became Black's personal pet project. He nurtured the paper and played a decisive role in moulding it in his own image. While its intellectual bent was decidedly conservative, its capable editor-in-chief, Ken Whyte, who had previously run *Saturday Night,* another Black publication, placed the highest priority on evocative writing about eccentric topics of the day. Instead of merely publishing the mundane details of the news, the *Post* offered Canadian readers (close to one million a day) often opinionated, but nearly always well-reasoned, conservative analyses. (The "nearly" refers to the editorial page, which was much more ideological than reasonable.) More British in style than the *Globe and Mail,* the *Post* became required reading in Ottawa. Its savage but meticulously documented attacks on the ethics of the Chrétien Liberals proved more effective than any criticisms concocted by the Official Opposition. At the same time, the paper experienced serious trouble attracting enough advertising dollars to make it commercially viable, or even sensible, to continue.

Without a Toronto-based newspaper, the Black-Asper deal wouldn't fly. Izzy needed all or part of the *Post* and was confident that with innovative management strategies, centralization of Southam and the *Post*'s financial and accounting functions, the benefits of convergence, cross-promotion with Global Television, plus the improvement and broadening of content, the paper in time could make money. Izzy and Leonard Asper didn't appear troubled by the fact that it had taken thirteen years and a $1 billion loss before the American national newspaper *USA Today* had started paying for itself—and that was on a population base ten times as large.

It took until the final night of the Bilderberg conference before Black and Izzy reached an understanding. Conrad refused to give up his interest in the *Post* but agreed to a 50–50 split with Canwest, provided that he remained in charge of the paper's editorial policies for the ensuing five years. Asper complied. "He was going back to London and I was flying back to Winnipeg," Izzy recalled. "We met in my room, finalized the details, shook hands and the deal was done."

There was a slight hiccup over the Southam website when Izzy discovered that the address canada.com (as opposed to the address www.canada.com) landed its users between the tangled limbs of a perpetual Dutch sex orgy: "If you want some fun, as well as a sobering identification with the internet problems, take someone you love, chill some martinis, put on some sexy jazz music, go to your computer, and enter the search words: www.Canada.com. Then sit back and reflect on whether or not Dutch sex orgies are what you want to present as your internet calling card. I must say I was delighted at what I assumed was your bizarre sense of humour and hubris. I am now a committed fan of Canada.com!"

The agreement also included the notorious non-compete clause Asper wanted, though no dollar amounts were mentioned in the original draft, which read, "Hollinger, Ravelston and their respective affiliates shall deliver non-competition, non-solicitation and confidentiality covenants relating to the Print News Media Business restricting Hollinger and Ravelston and any of their respective affiliates and associates from competing with the Acquired Businesses in Canada for a period of five years."

––––––––––

"We didn't pay Conrad, or any Hollinger executive," later emphasized Tom Strike, who was the senior staff negotiator on the deal. "I was part of that decision. We asked for a non-compete from every company and individual in the Hollinger chain, from Conrad Black and David Radler all the way down to the companies from whom we were buying these assets, and the reason we did that was that we knew they could compete. They had this tiered ownership structure which was like a wedding cake, with Hollinger International as the bottom layer and Conrad and David at the top, sort of standing on the cake like the bride and the groom. The two of them owned Horizon, which had newspapers in Canada. So we asked for a non-compete clause. We didn't put a price tag on the non-compete. We said that as part of this transaction, we want to make sure that for some period of time, neither you personally nor a link in this chain is going to come back and start up newspapers against the ones we just bought. It was all of them. Because they were quite capable of buying something on the periphery of Regina, and all of a sudden there is a daily newspaper in Regina. And so we wanted the non-compete to be extraordinarily comprehensive, probably more so than we would in a normal situation, because we knew that they were quite capable, in fact *were* competing at different levels, and they had all kinds of strange arrangements in that group. The day before we were actually signing the paper to buy, they came in with a number. We want to attribute this amount of money to a non-compete. I know because he asked me.

"I said that was fine if it was part of the purchase price, so it's an allocation of the purchase. We aren't paying you $80 million more for this. We are going to reduce the price of something else. In fact, when we closed the transaction in November, we paid the non-compete to Hollinger International in its entirety. How they disposed of that was something else. I don't think Hollinger International got any of that money. It all went to upstream companies. But somehow the board of Hollinger International decided that that was what should be done, rightly or wrongly. We've got clean hands. We got what we bargained for."

Black used a fax sent to him by Asper to justify his taking personally a large part of the non-compete payment that Canwest had made directly to Hollinger. But in an email to the author, Leonard was firm: "Izzy wrote a fax to Conrad to confirm that we had asked for personal non-competes, but the fax did not mention anything about a payment and we did not make any such payment. Black later used that fax, together with the argument that there was implied value, in order to justify his taking payment for same from Hollinger

International. Any statement by Black that we either paid money directly to him or suggested it is a fabrication."

———————

Harry Ethans, who had been associated with the Aspers for twenty years, was brought in to lead Canwest's due diligence team. "Hollinger had a massive data room set up in Toronto and we started examining it from stem to stern," Ethans recalled. It was clear to him that the corporate cultures of the two companies were vastly different. While Canwest's organizational structure demanded regular weekly reports and more meetings, Hollinger produced a lot less documentation, so that the kind of detail Ethans needed was often missing or difficult to find. As the due diligence was being completed, more sessions were scheduled with Don Babick and other key Southam executives. One day, Babick had arranged a meeting with Leonard Asper at 3:00 p.m. in the Hollinger offices at 10 Toronto Street but Leonard's plane was delayed. Around five o'clock, Babick received a call from reception that "Mr. Asper" was waiting for him. He went down to the main lobby area to find Izzy Asper standing there. "The first thing he did," recalled Babick, "was to apologize for his son being late and then suggested we have a chat. That was my initial official meeting with him." Finally Leonard arrived and the discussion proceeded. "It was an interesting, low-key and comfortable meeting," Babick recalled. "I still remember that Izzy wanted to smoke in the Hollinger boardroom but couldn't find an ashtray. He lit up a cigarette anyway."

The due diligence process was not without its belches. At one point Izzy complained to Tom Strike about the "board book" and its lack of financial information. "We don't even have an audited financial statement of any of the properties," he said, "and that which we have on the *National Post* is thoroughly inadequate. The bottom line is that so far, neither I nor certainly any of the board members, including Leonard, David and Gail and Peter Viner, have seen anything that answers the fundamental question: is this a good deal, in business terms? We all know the strategic generalities of convergence, control of content, etc., etc., but the rubber is hitting the road and the key questions are left unanswered." He went on to list eleven key financial issues he wanted resolved. "I am assuming that our due diligence check list has been given to Canterbury and that they are compiling the information and will provide it with sufficient time for us to go through it and clarify it prior to us being committed to write cheques for millions of dollars in standby fees, plus incurring even greater legal and accounting expense. If there is any doubt about this, we have a crisis on our hands and will not be able to proceed with this deal, which, according to my intuition (not backed by due diligence) would be a genuine shame and setback."

Black replied quickly with lengthy explanations of valuations and dealt point by point with the issues that required clarification. "The reasons our discussions in recent weeks and intermittently over nearly twenty-five years, have been so amicable and productive is that neither of us attempts any unjustified reopening of points agreed upon and I believe this latest exchange is a reaffirmation of that shared practice," he concluded.

On July 30, Leonard Asper took his three-year-old daughter Sarah to Tinkertown, a children's amusement park on the outskirts of Winnipeg. While Sarah took the wheel of the bumper car, her father was on his cellphone with Canwest lawyers smoothing over last-minute issues. "I get a call from Richard Leipsic, who was sitting in Toronto preparing a schedule of assets to be excluded from the transaction," he recalled. "There were a number of such assets, but it was discovered last Saturday night that the *Edmonton Journal* and the *Halifax Daily News*, respectively, owned tiny percentage interests in the Edmonton Oilers and Halifax Mooseheads Junior hockey team, respectively. The question was whether we wanted them. I handed the wheel over to Sarah and confirmed that we would keep the hockey team interests after confirming that we were not on the hook for cash calls." The next morning he was on the company's private jet bound for Toronto, set to make media history as he chaired the meeting that announced the landmark deal.

———————

"It all began a couple of months ago," Izzy Asper announced to a packed news conference with a wry smile, "when Leonard walked by my door and said, 'I'm going out for lunch. Can I bring you something?' And I said, 'Yeah, would you mind getting me a couple of papers?'" There were chuckles in the room, but it was all business after that. Even though it was he who had brokered most of the deal, Izzy left it to Leonard, then completing his first year as CEO, to make the official announcement and provide the details. The final sales figure was $3.2 billion, an all-time record for a Canadian media transaction. "In sum," declared the proud son, "we are tremendously optimistic about our merger agreement with Hollinger. We are now a multiple-platform media powerhouse, content rich, advertiser friendly and e-commerce ready. I don't want to seem blasé about it, but it was just another corporate event as far as I'm concerned. Because I already see us as trying to be as big as Rupert Murdoch's News Corporation, every step along the way is expected. I don't feel like we have reached the end of this yet."

For Black, who self-mockingly told the *New York Times* that he was going to be like the cartoon character Scrooge McDuck and "get into his little bulldozer every morning and plough back and forth over his gold coins," it was part of his planned withdrawal from Canada of his corporate investments and personal citizenship. Corporately, he said that it was time "to get rid of the debt, to get a little bit of a cash box to work from, to enjoy life a little more." He would never stop sparking ideological and commercial firestorms in his wake—and he was walking away with a fistful of dollars. The sale netted him and his company $2.2 billion, a 15 percent stake in the enlarged Canwest valued at $600 million and a $700 million bond from Canwest. His hefty personal take included his privately negotiated management fee, as well as most of the allocated non-compete. That ought to have been more than enough to pay off Hollinger's $2.4-billion long-term debt and still leave Black with a private fortune sizeable enough to maintain Barbara in her spend-thrift lifestyle. He agreed to remain publisher of the *Post* for five years, while he and his then partner, Radler, became members of the Canwest board, holding a 15 percent equity and 6 percent of the votes in the Winnipeg company. (By the end of November 2001, Hollinger had sold its 15 percent stake in Canwest for $271 million. Black and Radler remained on the Canwest board though Conrad never appeared at a single meeting.)

————————

Not everyone was happy. Concerns over creation of a media monopoly were voiced by the NDP as well as by the Council of Canadians and the Friends of Canadian Broadcasting. "We'd be opposed to this if Karl Marx took over all the papers," said Rob Sutherland, an NDP legislative assistant. Leonard, meanwhile, praised Canwest's bold move into newspapers as the "ultimate convergence transaction." True, the deal injected a huge debt load on the company's books, but the youthful new CEO estimated annual savings and revenue opportunities, or "synergies," of between $50 and $150 million. Responding to the critics, he said that their fears about editorial control and monopoly were misplaced: "I don't see that there is any issue of concentration because of the overwhelming number of additions to the media world in the form of television channels, radio stations and the Internet. What Canwest owns today is less a percentage of overall share than the media of the 1960s and 1970s. Each day Southam papers reach at least half the population in their cities. What we have really acquired is a quantum leap in the product we offer advertisers and a massive, creative content-generation machine."

Chris Dornan, director of Carleton University's School of Journalism, summed up the day's proceedings by pointing out that Canwest had "just bought itself the biggest news division of any broadcaster on the continent." Having negotiated the "deal of the century," Asper sat the family down and concluded with this appeal: "There are sometimes once-in-a-lifetime deals and this is one of them, with irreplaceable assets, and what it's going to mean is you're going to have to forgo other opportunities. You're going to miss out on some things, and that's just the choice we have to make. Are you guys in?" They were.

Gerry Schwartz was proud of his former partner for having followed his "carefully crafted decision by him to satisfy the things that he wanted to do. It suited Izzy's purpose to be the largest newspaper owner in Canada. That's what he wanted to be and he set about to do it. Many, many, many other people wanted to be the biggest newspaper owners in Canada and never got close. He did it." Ray Heard, Global's former head of news, saw it as a power play: "The reason people like Izzy and Rupert Murdoch own newspapers is because they want political influence. The Sulzbergers and the Grahams didn't own the *New York Times* and the *Washington Post* because they wanted to impress their accountants. People say that Izzy may have overpaid Conrad. Izzy wanted a voice. He got his voice and it was a Western Canadian voice. Who can blame him?" Harry Ethans had the most realistic read of the deal: "It was the first time that Izzy ever paid retail. We were trained to go and get the best possible deals, and I always felt that we prided ourselves on being true Winnipeggers and trying to buy wholesale. There was a little bit of a game there because Izzy had basically taken what his idea of the future value of the Canwest stock was and priced that at around $25 or $26 a share. Well, the stock hasn't come within 50 percent of that since that deal was done, and in fact dropped down to below $3 in the interim."

The most pointed criticism came from an unexpected source. Dick Thomson, the former chairman of the Toronto-Dominion Bank, who was a native Winnipegger, a former school chum of Izzy's and the banker who financed his original deals, sat him down and told him that buying the newspapers was a big mistake. "I met with him to try and convince him to sell the *National Post,* and he could have sold it to *Globe and Mail,*" Thomson recalled. "He was convinced

that it was going to be his oasis and that he could make big money
out of it. He claimed at the time that I met with him that within the
next six months he was going to make money on it, which was just
ludicrous. That was certainly a big mistake."

The question was asked behind his back by his own advisers. His
dreams had finally driven him too far, since he had allowed Conrad
Black to con him into believing that he had eager alternate bidders
for his newspaper empire and could demand a king's ransom for a
business well past its prime.

———————

Though it was not billed as such, at that dramatic press conference
on August 1, 2000, the baton was passed between the generations.
That was the day Leonard Asper came into his own. Izzy had bulled
through the fundamental strategy, but it was Leonard who completed the operational details and made the deal fly. On the day of
the press conference, he served notice that he was a different sort of
mogul than his driven father. Where Izzy, who would turn sixty-eight
ten days later, was famous for his bluntness and bluster, Leonard,
thirty-six, was poised, pleasant yet precision-minded. The son would
now be charged with the hard part: meshing Global Television with
its big-city newspaper stablemates and the intimidating realities of
the Internet—a new universe without predictable limits.

For Izzy, this would turn out to be his last major deal; it was his
ultimate corporate fantasy come true. This was the league where he
felt that he belonged, not only as an investor extending his corporate
reach—doubling it, in fact—but as a man who believed profoundly
in extolling his personal views of the world, advocating his version
of an entrepreneurial Canada and justice for the plains that were its
neglected heartland, as well as trumpeting his obsession with Israel
as his spiritual homeland to be defended beyond reasonable means.

Now Izzy assumed he would be able to exercise heavy-artillery
personal clout in all three arenas. That part of his dream would
prove to be the toughest to realize. Taken together, the Southam

publications plus the *Post* and the recently forged cross-country Global network offered Canwest control of an enormous amount of news and information—so much so that the expansion of the Asper holdings concentrated more potential influence in their hands, not only greater influence than that of any previous Canadian media empire but, at least in theory, more editorial clout than any similar communications conglomerate in any other democratic society.

For Lord Polington, a.k.a. Israel Harold Asper, the acquisition would turn out to be his most controversial act. What neither of the two titans realized as they preened and paraded their tactical nuances was that for each man this would be the final curtain call: the last great horse trade in a lifetime of hedging bets, reading (and writing) the small print and ratifying necessary evils. Within the next half decade, Israel Asper would be dead and Conrad Black, in terms of his business career, as good as dead, serving serious jail time, apparent financial ruin and the prospect of near-universal ridicule.

13

Izzy Goes to War

*Asper's sustaining dream for his media empire
was breathtaking: he wanted his television
networks and newspaper chain to be recognized
as Canada's indispensible central nervous system.*

War is a heavy metaphor, not to be used lightly. But when Israel Harold Asper, armed with an agenda cast in Canadian Shield granite, stormed the smug ramparts of Southam-nurtured editorial departments, he set off a revolution. The journalists thought of themselves as crusading reformers, taunting a Winnipeg Rottweiler who was rehearsing to be Canada's Rush Limbaugh. None of the comparisons rang true. The newshounds were no Noam Chomsky revolutionaries, threatening the established order. Rush had nothing to do with it, and Asper was no Rottweiler. On the contrary, he was the only Canadian investor willing to risk his fortune in an industry that sought to turn profits from the Dickensian technique of selling impressions made on processed wood pulp. On top of that, the audience for the daily printed word had been reduced to a shrinking and aging remnant, while most well-informed Canadians received much of their news and most of their entertainment through other media.

Izzy's purchase of Conrad Black's newspaper empire in the fall of 2000 set off a confrontation of rare intensity, made so hurtful because everyone involved had good reasons to assume they were doing the right thing—that they were merely being true to themselves, and what could be wrong with that? The journalists were defending their mandate as front-line gladiators, guarding the freedom of expression that defines their noble profession; the Aspers were exercising their legal proprietary rights over the newspapers that had cost them half their company's market value.

The mix was explosive, not unlike a cargo of nitroglycerine under a tropical sun. The contest set Canada's media world on fire, strained friendships and left a bitter aftertaste between employers and employees alike.

It soon became clear that there was no percentage in trying to make Izzy feel guilty about breaking some holy journalistic covenant of which he was blissfully unaware. His position was simple: he owned the printing press and therefore had first call on what it produced. Unlike most Jews, Izzy went through life with little, if any, sense of guilt, especially when he felt there was nothing to be guilty about. "I'm not sure that you could make Izzy feel guilty about anything," reasoned Jim Sward, who spent a decade as the head of Global TV and was well aware of his boss's foibles. "He isn't plagued with feeling guilty. If he said the most horrible thing to you in a fit of anger or frustration, ten minutes later he could laugh at it with you. He would never come back, seek you out and say, 'Oh gee, what I said about you, that was awful and I'm sorry.' He travelled through life being guilt-free; everything was competition, nothing was sin."

That didn't alter the fact that seldom had a Canadian media group so vehemently condemned its proprietor. Conrad Black, who preceded Izzy in Southam's catbird seat, had championed causes far right of Asper's, making promiscuous use of his newspapers to promote personal priorities and champion his neo-con convictions.

There was muted concern about a publisher's claiming his vain-glorious sense of entitlement in print, but criticism of Conrad remained an undertow. As soon as Izzy took over, the undertow burst into a riptide.

This was partly due to the difference in personalities between the two men. Black's passage through life was marked by his need to presume worship as he bestowed his inflated presence on the anointed—even in jail he managed to scrounge a butler of sorts and to enlist a scruffy retinue. He was catered to with such ostentatious deference in the *National Post*'s opinion pages that they read like extracts from his own self-congratulatory diary. And that was even *after* his name change—from Conrad Black to 18330–424. He set a precedent by becoming the only American jailbird allowed to publish his seminal chirps and squawks—always worth reading—in a major newspaper. Few other convicted felons within the American prison population of 2.3 million were accorded similar privilege.

In contrast, Asper was the Wyatt Earp of the Canadian Plains, a sharpshooting loner with no pretensions but with determination and energy that few could match, or would want to. Self-made to the point of caricature, Asper believed that this was the moment for him to exert the national influence that had always eluded him, to test the variables of his life and shed any residual sprinkling of insecurity that might still be haunting him. It was crunch time for the great *agent provocateur* of the second Red River Rebellion. His critics' daily attacks didn't budge his position one damn millimetre. Still, he felt, if not abandoned, very much alone, and for some reason a story he had once heard in Vegas kept him amused.

Sammy Davis Jr., of Rat Pack fame, had been invited by a local group of society lawyers to tee off at the strip's most exclusive golf club, which had neither black nor Jewish members. "What's your handicap, Sammy?" one of his hosts enquired. The diminutive black entertainer shot right back, "I'm a one-eyed black Jew. What's yours?" Izzy loved that story. He probably out-drank and out-smoked the Rat Packers, and knew and played their music, but unexpectedly found himself stuck in a strange place. Unlike his past quarrels, with part-ners and regulators, there was no law book that would lead him through any feasible settlement process in trying to pacify these rebellious journalists who thought they owned the world. *His* world.

Next to Izzy and the fourth estate, the third defining pres-ence in the rapidly escalating confrontation was David Asper, who seemed to have a prominent bull's eye painted on the back of his sports jacket, inviting hostile fire. David had taken issue with his newspaper's investigative coverage of the Shawinigan affair, which involved naughty allegations that Jean Chrétien had improperly helped a business colleague to obtain loans from a federal banking agency. This came at a time when Black was sparring with Canada's prime minister, who had tried to squash his dream of claiming a seat in the British House of Lords. In the end it turned out that Black could acquire his baronetcy only if he surrendered his Canadian citizenship. This he did with aplomb, since he dismissed those who stayed behind as a bunch of subarctic losers, and good riddance. For many Canadians, the feeling was mutual.

The initial run-in between the Aspers and journalists was the firing of Lawrence Martin, the *Post*'s distinguished national affairs colum-nist, who was and continues to be Ottawa's most lucid commentator, ostensibly over his coverage of what became known as Shawinigate, scandals involving Prime Minister Jean Chrétien. Unlike his fellow members of the Parliamentary Press Gallery, Martin had an inside edge, because he had written a definitive two-volume biography of Chrétien (*The Will to Win* and *Iron Man*). His description of the PM's mangled speech habits has never been topped: "He was born not with a silver spoon in his mouth, but rather a cement mixer."

When Black was running the *Post*, Martin's investigative Chrétien columns were front-paged; when the Aspers took over, they turned toxic. In July of 2001, just months after receiving a laudatory assess-ment from Southam editor-in-chief Murdoch Davis, Martin was dismissed, without cause or explanation. But every Ottawa insider suspected it was because of his effective analysis of the events that had led to the Shawinigate affair. The insiders were wrong. Others believed it was Lawrence Martin's overly favourable coverage of the CBC that raised Izzy's ire.

On January 5, 2001, Black, then comfortably ensconced in London, complained to Asper about his son David's concerted efforts to exert pressure on the *National Post* editorial department in defence of Chrétien and his problems. His letter was one in a vintage exchange between the two titans, letters that later found their way into court with Conrad. He was angry but not unreasonable. First, he addressed the specific difficulties that had arisen at the *Post* over publishing a letter from Françoise Ducros, the PM's press agent, in which she complained about Lawrence Martin's article on her boss. Acknowledging as "understandable" the Aspers' questions as to why the letter had not appeared when Conrad had assured them it would, he soothingly explained that Ducros had been unwilling to accede to the *Post*'s request that the letter omit two allegations which, Black said, did not relate to the paper. Hence, he felt, it was only right not to publish.

This matter dealt with, Black went on to warn that pressure by David Asper over the paper's treatment of Chrétien was at odds with their agreement, and that he would make sure that any further requests for "material alteration of the editorial content of the newspaper" would come to him—and with limited chance of success. Rounding on the prime minister for his "malicious, cowardly, ignorant, dishonest and illegal assault" upon him, Black had "shown great forbearance in encouraging as tolerant a tone in our coverage of him as I have. I have undertaken to make it difficult for reasonable third parties to criticize the fairness of the National Post's coverage of political matters. I will do that, but not more than that."

Then, on March 7, 2001, David Asper issued his own declaration of war, ignoring the Churchillian cadence usually reserved for such occasions. Don Babick, head of Southam, who knew the temper of his journalistic brood, had warned the elder Asper son about publishing his angry rant. But David was not concerned. "They said it would be a big problem," he recalled. "And I said, 'How big a problem?' They said, 'A really big problem.' And I said, 'Excellent, let's do it.'"

The day before, all Southam papers, including the *Post,* had been instructed to publish his signed op-ed piece, headed, TO CHRÉTIEN'S ACCUSERS: PUT UP OR SHUT UP. "The media's coverage of the accusations against the Prime Minister has crossed a line that delineates solid investigative reporting from adjective-driven innuendo," Asper wrote in his brief essay. "The time is now long overdue for Mr. Chrétien's accusers to 'put up or shut up' with facts and hard evidence. In Canadian law, there is a crime known as public mischief, which exists to deter and punish people from making false accusations of criminal conduct. A free press is essential to democracy provided that it acts responsibly, and in this case, the repetitive and largely unsubstantiated attacks on the Prime Minister are irresponsible. The Prime Minister is as deserving of fairness as anyone else in Canada, and it's a sad comment that our national political affairs have been hijacked by mischievous, unfair scandal-mongering as opposed to things that really count."

The response was fast and furious. Ken Whyte, the *Post*'s editor-in-chief, wrote a lengthy editorial in which he essentially challenged David, "We've put up—now why don't you shut up?" He chronicled how Chrétien had stonewalled MPs and journalists at every turn, how it appeared that he had misled the House of Commons, how the PMO had even threatened the jobs of employees in the information commissioner's office who sought to release material unflattering to the government.

At that point the Aspers owned 50 percent of the *Post,* so Whyte's rebuttal took both anger and daring, qualities he didn't parade on a daily basis. "The only observers who do not see this as serious are partisans or people unaware of the basic facts that have been on the public record for some time," he wrote. "In such circumstances, it would be a dereliction of duty and a national embarrassment if media were to ignore the story." This was particularly true since the Shawinigan coverage had helped make the *Post*'s reputation and had won a prize for its investigative reporter Andrew McIntosh. "The onus is not on newspapers to 'put up,' but on Mr. Chrétien to convince us of the propriety of his actions," Whyte concluded. "This newspaper will continue to follow the story, and it encourages all other Canadian media and all opposition politicians to do the same."

In his son's defence, Izzy assumed his whirling dervish incantation, treating David's accusers with the sense of affront he usually reserved for uppity Palestinian war lords or critics of Winnipeg culture. He even challenged Black to a duel. This was his burning reply:

March 13, 2001

Dear Conrad,

I have waited several days since the *National Post*'s outrageous handling of, and savage attack on, David Asper's opinion piece on the Chrétien/Shawinigan Hotel harangue. I had hoped that the passage of time might soften my instinctive reaction. In fact, it hasn't and my concern for a troubled relationship has heightened. The firestorm the *Post*'s staff helped unleash across all media was caused by your personal orchestration or done with your acquiescence and approval.

Given that we view this as a blatant and defiant breach of the letter of our agreement, and more saddening and provocative, the spirit of our arrangement, I consider the situation both currently and foreseeable, as in crisis.

Neither you nor I would profit from a public battle, which would give great pleasure to those who wish neither of us well, but regrettably, you have chosen to publicly throw down a gauntlet, administer a public slap in the face which has both embarrassed, humiliated and held up to ridicule and dishonour both my family and my company. You will readily understand why I won't remain silent.

Therefore, because there is only a short time before we must publicly react and risk the matter escalating beyond redemption, I suggest we meet, with or without seconds, at the earliest possible opportunity, to explore whether or not a mutually satisfactory resolution can be found.

I am sure you will understand that between now and [our next] meeting, I may take unilateral action to address the slurs and abuse that has been heaped upon us from a variety of quarters.

Sincerely,

I.H. Asper,

O.C., O.M., Q.C., Executive Chairman of the Board

In reply, Conrad emerged as the defender of the *National Post*'s editorial independence. On March 14 he wrote to Asper. In carefully measured tones, he flatly rejected as "absolutely untrue" Izzy's accusation that he had worked any sort of "personal orchestration" or "firestorm" against David. Equally unfounded was the suggestion that Black had breached the proprietors agreement between them, in letter or spirit.

The facts, he said, were quite different. Black, as well as Barbara Amiel, Ken Whyte and others, "all warned David that writing in these newspapers accusing them of injustice to Chrétien would produce great resentment amongst the journalists and would appear to anyone in the country still interested in an independent press to be servile, toadying to a rather corrupt regime in what is now more or less a one party state." The proper course to objectionable coverage would be to carefully set out exactly what was wrong or unfair and to take this for discussion with the editors of the various papers. Instead, David's piece was "unrigorous and hostile to your own employees with consequences that were foreseeable and predicted." Beyond being shown the editorial comment to be published by Ken Whyte and asking for the removal of one sentence that he felt might unintentionally offend the Aspers, Black assured Izzy that he had had no hand in the inevitable reaction to David's clumsy intervention.

Moreover, Black continued sternly, this wasn't the first time he had tried to set the Aspers on a more appropriate proprietorial path: "I have told you, David and Leonard many times that there is a way to alter the general tone of a serious newspaper, and I have offered advice, without being asked, on how to do that. I believe it is, in fact, contrary to the spirit of our arrangement and to Canwest's corporate interests for you people to tinker so recklessly with these interferences with the credibility and therefore the value of these franchises which my associates and I so swiftly built up."

While brushing aside the notion that he had anything, contractual or otherwise, to answer for, Black ended by sounding his willingness to meet with Izzy to try to mend things, but only if Asper first dropped "the more intemperate reflections" of his letter and learned not to confuse "your friends with your enemies."

In response the following day, Izzy re-entered the fray by firing a heat-seeking missile at Conrad, with what may well be the most incendiary communication since Marie Antoinette's legendary invitation to starving French peasants, deprived of their daily bread, to "let them eat cake."

> Dear Conrad,
> In no order of priority, let me deal with your assertions on the facts of our difference:

1. You say that Barbara [Amiel], Peter [Viner] et al. warned David [Asper] about the consequence of his Intervention. *Wrong.* Your observations were made *after* the fact and not as a caution in advance.

2. You resolutely deny having "orchestrated" or "acquiesced" in the *Post*'s scurrilous rebuttal, but, in conclusive repudiation of that assertion, you acknowledge that you read Whyte's vitriolic response, in advance of publication, and even edited it, for whatever reason. That's hardly consistent with

your claim of "not being party to or involved." I will not comment on the information we have that *Post* people "encouraged" the other media (non-Southam) to focus on this issue. I believe our sources.

Quite apart from the issue between us, I did not see the David Asper piece in advance of its submission, and I readily concede I would have written it quite differently. But that's not the point. This issue is, and remains, how you and the *Post* treated it.

Where I allege breach of letter and spirit of our arrangement arises as follows:

1. The Nat'l Post harangue on Chrétien/Shawinigan was excessive, unbalanced and an embarrassment to Canwest as being improper journalism—you published something like 50 accusatory opinions with *not one* exculpatory opinion.
2. We exercised our contractual right to publish a contrary piece.
3. You deliberately delayed publication of our piece to gain the time to concurrently publish a condemnation of our piece.
4. When you did publish our piece, it was relegated to the bottom of the page, while your condemnation of it, in double its length, was put on top of it. In further violation of fairness, you ran a streamer headline across the top of page 1 of the paper, drawing attention to your condemnation of our piece, which received about $1/3$ the size and prominence of your denunciation.

Conrad, read our agreement. Talk to Colson [Dan Colson, CEO of Black's *Telegraph*], and ask him if this is compliance, both in spirit and intent. I assure you we never expected that when, on the rare occasion, we exercised our right to differ with the *Post*'s editorial or opinion position, that we would be subjected to a vilification torrent as a rebuttal! That's just not a plausible interpretation of our deal.

So, bottom line, I don't withdraw any of the complaints I proffered in my letter, and if that forecloses a meeting between us, to explore *modus vivendi* options, so be it.

Given your own experience in dealing with contemptible charges, you will appreciate that I cannot remain silent. If you want the *Post* to continue this practice of withholding publication of our views until they can prepare a refutation, then we will insist that the *Post* deliver to us in advance all their opinion pieces, so that we can concurrently publish our opposing views.

There are other options. The *Globe and Mail* has offered its unlimited space to immediately comment on *National Post* opinions. Therefore, perhaps it is best that we resolve this by ignoring the *Post*'s positions, and our rights to differ, expressing ourselves through them and other media.

Of course, other options abound, including our selling out to you, or vice versa, or dividing the opinion pages equally between *Post* and Canwest commentators etc., etc.

However, be assured that we will not tolerate a torrent of refutation by *Post* writers, either personally inspired, or encouraged by you, every time we exercise our contracted right to differ.

I believe these are the options we should explore when we talk or meet. Presumably, you don't want a five-year running argument any more than I. As for the Southam papers ground rules, I expect to deal with the people there precisely as you would.

At this time, although still under reflective consideration, I intend to proclaim, nationally, Canwest's refutation of the charges and accusations levelled at us in this sorry affair.

Obviously, I may reach a different strategic plan after further consideration.

Sincerely,

Israel Harold Asper*

The lesson that Izzy Asper learned as a failed politician was that media were the essential arteries of community—and nowhere more so than in Canada, mediating and transmitting the elements that tie together or break asunder the large land's aspirations and exasperations. Asper never spelled it out in detail, but the sustaining dream for his media empire was breathtaking: he wanted his television networks and newspaper chain to be recognized as Canada's indispensible central nervous system. "I like to believe that the *National Post* will ultimately become the newspaper of record for Canada in every embassy in the world," he vowed. "It will be the authoritative voice of public opinion. Every library in the world will buy the *Post* one day."

It never happened, and of all his disappointments, that was the greatest. Izzy's purchase of Black's papers had only partly been a business decision to expand the reach of Canwest into another medium. Jim Sward had his own theory: "From about 1998, Izzy started to remove himself and Leonard became far more active," he recalled. "About a year later he named Leonard as his successor, even though he wouldn't stay out of the big stuff. He was disengaging from running the television business and handing that over. But was he disengaging from life and his other passions? No. Not for a minute. He had been terribly frustrated at Global because broadcasting did not have an electronic equivalent of an editorial page. He was always trying to come up with a way to get around this problem, demanding, 'How can we take an editorial position with

---

*The tension between the two men was dissolved in August of 2001, when Black sold the remaining half of the *National Post* to Asper. The first 50 percent, which was part of the original deal, cost Izzy $100 million; the second 50 percent went for $1.00. He paid too much both times.

this national network?' That was his major incentive for making the Southam deal. He really wanted to have a Western editorial presence and Western point of view available in Canada."

Izzy's attempt to shape public opinion by setting down strict rules of engagement for the journalists on his payroll turned out to be one of the most frustrating experiences of his career. Not to say that he didn't fight like a caged Hillary Clinton for his views, even when they didn't align with the fundamental belief system of most Canadian journalists—as perpetuated by their mutual consent rather than by any written rules or regulations.

There were as many interpretations of this unusual confrontation as there were players, but the Aspers appeared to have decided that since they owned the press, they would print only what passed their muster, and David became the front man for that heretical gospel. During a hang-'em-high speech in Oakville, Ontario, he escalated his attack, adopting a lyric from R.E.M., the first American alternate rock band to go mainstream: "It's the end of the world as they know it . . . but I feel fine," he declared, also suggesting that instead of complaining, any unhappy journalists in his employ (described by him as "riff raff engaged in pathetic politics and childish protest") should "put their money where their mouth is, and start their own papers."

John Fowles, who was among the greatest of modern British novelists, wrote that "men love war because it allows them to look serious. Because they imagine it is the one thing that stops women laughing at them." But this war was a political act, a confrontation between two polarized definitions of journalism and countervailing misunderstandings of the publishing function.

No journalist had taken the trouble to codify the complicated relationship between common scribes and capitalist publishers. The closest and wisest attempt was the analysis done for one of the Senate studies of the media by Robert Fulford, the former editor of

Saturday Night magazine, later the *Post's* impressive cultural columnist. "The press of English-speaking Canada operates according to
obscure and often conflicting principles," he wrote. "On the one
hand, the press is a creature of the modern corporation, whose central thrust is toward rationalization and profit. On the other hand,
the press inherits and attempts to maintain traditions of profes-
sionalism purchased with the blood and energy of journalists and
printers over three centuries. On the one hand, the press honours
and supports journalists of superb training and talent, men and
women who would do credit to any profession. On the other hand,
the press accommodates in its ranks, with apparent equanimity, the
worst sort of incompetence and sloppiness, to the detriment not
only of the profession but of the community as a whole. Hidden
among these contradictions, is there some bedrock of morality on
which journalism can rest, some guiding philosophy? Certainly the
best journalists believe there is, and do their work accordingly."

Fulford quoted Stuart Keate, a reporter who became publisher
of the *Victoria Times* and later the *Vancouver Sun,* on the goals that
journalists ought to set for themselves: "Any publisher, editor, or
reporter worth his salt recognizes that he has only one basic duty
to perform: to dig for the truth; to write it in language people can
understand; and to resist all impediments to its publication. That
responsibility rests on his shoulders with all the weight of 300 years
of the modern press, as we know it. The extent to which we dis-
charge it will determine our worth."

That was a highly idealistic interpretation, only tangentially relevant to a sweaty, ink-stained wretch trying to interpret his or her
illegible notes ten minutes from deadline. Most journalists are vulnerable romantics longing to align themselves with any rebel army
that has a flag and a cause, however ragged and however trivial. We
are literary taxidermists, attempting to preserve in print passions,
places and people whose interplay adds up to history in a minor key.
Fulford added, "In this world, journalists are only marginally profes-

sionals, yet they are also aware that in that margin exists not only their salvation but their reason for existence."

Having spent all but the last thirty-six months of his life in the showbiz world of television—where moral judgments turned on how amply women's décolletages could plunge in prime time—Izzy made up his own modus operandi, which did not include the tunnel mentality of journalists who dug in, as if they could exercise unilateral control over their publication's ideology and contents. The doctrine of the freedom of the press must reign supreme in any democracy. But the idea that there should be an unbridgeable gap dividing those worker bees who filled the space between the ads and those who owned the press was simply not workable.

The next and final issue in this war of words was the short-lived publication of common editorials in the Asper papers, written by Murdoch Davis, starting on December 2, 2001, and continuing at irregular intervals until they vanished. There was little in them to disturb the mind, except the obvious homogenization of editorial opinion, and that escalated into a major skirmish. It was seen as the wedge that might eventually emasculate the papers with one national TV column, one book critic, etc.

"This is not something new," Izzy wrote to his university chum Beryl Moser, who had cancelled her subscription to the Montreal *Gazette* because of the potted editorials. "It has been the practice of newspaper owners for at least a couple of centuries, except they aren't as open and transparent about it as we are. We could easily have gone through the back door or the side door and no one would have known the difference. However, we chose to be up front about it, and specifically designate that our editorials were just: the view from the rest of Canada, not on local issues, but only on national and international issues. I assure you it will add more diversity, without taking away a single thing from the quality of the newspaper. Surely you don't think that the owner of a newspaper should be denied the right to make its views known to its readers? Just watch the CBC National News and Newsworld to see their national editorials, of which nobody complains."

"My whole view on national editorials was that I didn't see how terrible they were," emphasized his son Leonard. "They were put out there as a starting point—a public debate, which was what Izzy intended. Maybe he was naive about it. He wasn't trying to say, 'This is the way it is,' he was trying to say, 'This is what I think. What do you guys think? What does the rest of the world think?'

"What we liked about newspapers was that in the Internet age at least you own your own content, you're not trying to buy it from Hollywood or rent it. The group as a whole makes close to $300 million—all profitable except the *Post*. Certainly Izzy was enamoured by the idea of the *Post* being part of it. He spent his life thinking about public policy and this was a chance to put out his ideas."

––––––––––––

The feud highlighted the faltering state of the industry. To be successful newspapers in the twenty-first century—including those that Asper had bought from Black in the summer of 2000—needed to echo and articulate the half-formed but deeply felt intuitions of their readers. The source of these perceptions was the beleaguered condition Canadians felt in the face of the tidal wave of new technology engulfing them—an audacious tsunami that obeyed only the wild winds of change. With the age of consensus ending, it proved increasingly difficult for newspapers—and other printed media— to maintain the confidence of reader-audiences of infinitely diverse views, split into ever-narrower segments. Ultimately subscribers would demand their own editions since, in its crudest form, they were already being offered nearly that luxury on the Internet.

The interval that elapsed between Izzy's acquisition of the Southam publications in 2000 and his death in 2003 was so fleeting that it was difficult to judge what type of chain-CEO he might have become once the firestorm of his primordial quarrel over the competing rights of proprietors and journalists had blown itself out.

Much of the problem stemmed from the idea that newspaper claims were originated in colonial America by Benjamin Franklin, who established editions in Boston, Philadelphia and most of the other important population centres in the thirteen colonies. In each community he took in a printer-editor as his partner to do the work while he collected most of the profit, an arrangement that allowed him to devote his time to public life and scientific inquiry. The papers had similar personalities and identical political orientations and this, ultimately, was the model the Asper family wanted to follow.

Before Conrad Black took over Southam in 1996 (promising to uphold the chain's vaunted independence, while immediately firing all its independent directors), the firm's upper management layer was populated by gentleman publishers and editors who ploughed their own ideological fields, so that there was no discernable political slant. "The Southams," George Fetherling, the Vancouver-based author who has a better appreciation of journalism's evolution than any other Canadian writer, noted, "resembled those modern Tories who keep insisting that they're really nineteenth-century English liberals. They were Sir John A.–type Conservatives and hence well inside the Canadian mainstream, though the editors were encouraged to exercise considerable freedom. After all, localness was a large part of what they were selling. Southam publications shared about as much ideological grounding as a pick-up hockey team. The Southam papers had become influential in their communities, not for any high-fluting ideologies but because they reflected local concerns and independent attitudes. The question of a newspaper's editorial excellence, or lack thereof, was the owner's ego. I don't use the term judgmentally, only descriptively. The Beaverbrook model would be the proprietor who wished his paper to exert enormous influence in political and small-c cultural terms. In his day, Lord Atholstan of the *Montreal Star* was this sort. He knew he had to make piles of money to reach that stage of influence, and did. Joe Atkinson, the guiding spirit of the *Toronto Star,* had the same sort of ego while the original Lord Thomson exhibited none. He was a small-business person who operated on an immense multinational scale. His son, known as Young Ken deep into his seventies, was concerned with the societal value of his precious *Globe,* and there his interest in newspapers ended. Asper was an essential, transitional figure in a media landscape trying to weather unprecedented, fundamental change."

———————

Most newspapers are collegial undertakings, whose success varies with their editors' intuition—their sense of audience. If there was one quality that defined Ken Whyte, the founding genius of the *National Post,* it was precisely that: he understood that newspapers seldom any longer were the first messengers of news and that the way to attract more readers was to concentrate on features and stories that were quirky but compelling because they tied directly into the real world, which was becoming progressively more bizarre. He turned the *Post* into a daily magazine that combined a slick, contemporary page design with the impressive talents of the country's most original writers: Roy MacGregor, Christie Blatchford, Robert Fulford, Paul Wells, Andrew Coyne, Mark Steyn, George Jonas, Rod McQueen, Steve Maich, Derek DeCloet, Susan Delacourt, Isabel Vincent, John Ivison, David Frum, Don Martin, Scott Feschuk and Mark Hume, not to mention the inspired observations of Shinan Govani. Whyte and his main editors, Martin Newland, Jonathan Kay, Alison Uncles and Ellen Vanstone (when she was in charge of the Avenue pages), realized that their main assignment was to command attention for the paper. They did, and attention could be sold.

The feisty crew of the *Post* operated on the principle that in the contemporary world there were no average readers, only common interests, and that any worthwhile publication should allow the community to speak to itself—through their newspaper's pages. Somehow it worked, and it all had to with Ken Whyte and his magic Ping-Pong table, where many decisions were made. He was hard to read because his answer to most questions was to say nothing and gaze into the middle distance, as if he were channelling a genie on sabbatical or William Randolph Hearst. ("I never thought he was power tripping," remarked a staff member. "For one thing, he didn't have the attention span.") Whyte assigned so many zany subjects that satire threatened to become an obsolete art form in his paper— except, of course, on the *Post*'s editorial pages. They continued to be a welcoming pasture for some of the best minds of the thirteenth or, to give them the benefit of the doubt, the seventeenth century, unspoiled by such damn-fangled novelties as compassion, pity or benevolence. Typical was the *Post* obituary for General Augusto Pinochet, the thug who had ruled Chile for twenty-five years. Apart from absconding with $27 million from the state treasury, which he hid in a hundred anonymous U.S. bank accounts, Pinochet was responsible for tens of thousands of murdered and tortured victims. The *Post* editorial ran true to form, praising his "market-oriented policies which helped Chile escape the stifling Stalinism which bedevils much of the Latin American continent to this day."

Whyte and his dedicated editorial platoon created a readership base nearly as large as the *Globe and Mail*'s within eighteen months of taking over. Ads and profits should have followed. They didn't, partly because no matter how hard the *Post* tried and how talented its editors, reporters and columnists were, it remained an enter-taining and even instructive read, instead of a *must*-read like the *Globe and Mail*. Under the intuitive leadership of publisher Phillip Crawley, editor-in-chief Ed Greenspon and their talented crew, the *Globe* responded to the unexpected competition by loosening up and becoming a much more accessible paper. The *Post* could never catch up. The advertising people, who had spent their professional lives working for Southam papers in monopoly markets, had not learned to compete. Their seasoned and inspiring leader, Jack Tomik, was unexpectedly fired, as was Doug Hoover, a protégé of Dave Mintz. Also let go was Loren Mawhinney, who gave an inspired damn about quality Canadian productions and contributed several of the best. Instigator of the purge was Rick Camilleri, recruited by

Leonard to bring order out of chaos. What Camilleri achieved was exactly the opposite.

In retrospect, Asper's problem with the Southam purchase was not only its timing—Black sold out at the very top, almost to the hour, of the business cycle—but its aftermath. To meld the rigid corporate culture of the Asper empire with the coddled approach of the Southam clan was no mean challenge. Firmly ensconced in the monopolies they controlled in nearly all of Canada's urban markets, the Southams' old boys' network had grown smug and out of touch with industry innovations. One example was the inadequacy of its Internet sites, and search engines that rarely worked. You could type in "George Bush" and the response would be "zero matches."

The reason for including the exorbitantly priced (at $100 million) *National Post* in the purchase was that Southam could not become an effective national chain—editorially or commercially—without a Toronto-based flagship publication. If the *Post* didn't already exist, Asper would have had to invent it, which would have been many times more expensive. But its losses were daunting.*

One source advocating higher expenditures for the *Post* was Hollinger's vice-president, editorial, Barbara Amiel by name. While Conrad still held 50 percent of the paper, she would attend occasional management committee meetings and, according to a fellow participant, always weighed in for more spending: "Even when Conrad was trying to impose controls on the expense accounts, Barbara was saying, 'No, no, it's the product. It's got to be fantastic. Chase the story.'"

Conrad kept insisting that the *Post* would make money next year—any year he was asked. Leonard wasn't nearly as bullish. "We've developed a three-year plan to make it profitable" was all Leonard would predict, and that was in 2004. That year he went out and visited

---

*Izzy joked that he had "offered the *National Post* to the Lebanese ambassador because if his government had to look after its losses, they wouldn't have any money for sponsoring terrorism."

50 advertisers and said, "You've got to get behind us because if we're not here, your ad rates in the *Globe* are going to double. You might as well give us the money. You're going to pay it out anyway." "When we took it over," Leonard recalled, "the *Post* was losing $63 million a year—that was in 2001. Even Conrad realized that this couldn't go on. We found a cellphone bill running at $25,000 per month—a reporter who happened to have a boyfriend in China. They had a guy up in the Arctic who was living there and he tossed $50,000 a year just to do one six-part series on northern waters. The tough part was me having to be the bad guy, walking into the *Post*'s office on August 31, 2001, to let all these people go." There were 120 people fired that day, 90 from editorial, shutting down 5 of the paper's sections. "I spent the whole time talking people off ledges," Whyte recalled. "It was by far the worst week I've had on the job. The cuts were far deeper than was anticipated. On the one hand, you want to tell people to grow up, thank their stars we're still in business. On the other hand, I can't recall a newspaper losing a quarter or more of its staff, barring shutdowns. It was a real blow." The new circumstances tested Whyte for the next year and a half. Following the departure of his mentor, Conrad Black, he had to operate under Asper-imposed budgets, yet he maintained the paper's quality and verve.

As costs multiplied and tensions about the Chrétien file mounted, a floating consensus emerged that the only way to fix the situation was to replace Whyte as editor-in-chief—though no reason or explanation was ever given. Matthew Fraser, who had been a communications professor at Ryerson University and a *Post* columnist, had come close to getting the job eighteen months earlier in September of 2000. At the end of the summer of 2001, when the Aspers took over full editorial control of the *Post* and were considering making big changes, mainly to get the editorial budget under control, Leonard invited Fraser for a drink in the bar at the top of Toronto's Park Hyatt Hotel on Bloor Street. David joined them, and they brought Matthew into the loop about the changes they were planning at the paper and asked him whether he wanted to play a role in the running of the *Post*. "I remember David being really upbeat, pumping his fist in the air," Fraser recalled. "I said that I was extremely flattered and we talked about the *Post* as a business.

Fraser continued, "David left at one point and Len and I kept talking. At the end of the evening, he said he'd get back to me by the following Tuesday. We shook hands. About a week later, I learned that Ken Whyte, the existing and founding editor, had just laid off a whole whack of the *Post*'s staff and was dropping the paper's arts and sports sections. I knew instantly that, instead of hiring me, the Aspers had decided to give Ken another chance, but only if he swallowed the bitter medicine and cut expenses. Clearly, Ken had agreed to do the dirty work. That bought him another eighteen months at the paper, but it was a miserable time for him, because he didn't have the full confidence of the Aspers, and they ended up firing him anyway."

Leonard told a friend at the time, "If I could have Ken Whyte editing anything I was involved in I would hire him in a second. When we acquired the *Post* I remember I gave a little speech and said, 'Ken Whyte's the finest editor in the land.' He really is. If he could stick to a budget he'd be on our team, if he'd ever come back. But he was just used to a different environment and I don't think he could change."

Fraser, who held a doctorate from the Institut d'Études Politiques de Paris, as a postgraduate studied at Oxford and had written widely on the new technology, was hired to succeed Ken Whyte in carefully staged phases. It was in April 2003 that concrete discussions about his appointment as editor began—and they were with Leonard, not Izzy. Only a few of the insiders knew that there were two, not one, candidates to succeed Whyte.

Actually, there were three. The first was Martin Newland, Ken's deputy editor. The Aspers talked to him for a while, but those discussions collapsed and Martin ended up being let go along with Ken. The second was Giles Gherson, who at the time was editor of the *Edmonton Journal*. Giles was the Southam candidate for the job, supported by the old boys' network inside the company, led by Gordon Fisher and Rick Camilleri, the former Sony Canada executive who had been installed by the younger Asper as his senior staff presence. A secret committee had been convened to plot Whyte's dismissal and find a successor. Camilleri chaired the group, and Gordon Fisher (later the *Post*'s publisher) was involved, as was Doug Kelly (later the paper's editor-in-chief), who was acting as an information link between the *Post* newsroom and the committee. Gherson was also a member but not as an instigator, though at that point Fisher's and Camilleri's candidate. Nearly everybody on the inside was convinced that the Southam people were finally going to retake control of the flagship paper that was resented by the Southam executives because it was allocated the most assets without returning a profit.

In late April of 2003, Leonard invited Fraser to dinner and at one point suddenly informed him that "Ken Whyte was toast" and that Martin Newland was out too. He said that the decision had been made. Fraser was stunned, and realized immediately that the meeting had a larger agenda. "Leonard asked me how I would fix the *Post*," Matthew recalled, "adding that he was impressed with my four-point plan and asked me to put it into a formal note, which I did the following morning." Later that day, Fraser got a call from Camilleri, asking to see him. He had a copy of Matthew's document, called it "very impressive" and seemed supportive, but made no mention of offering him the job. Two days later, Fraser received a phone call from Camilleri's secretary, asking him for dinner with David Asper that evening. They met discreetly at Kelsey's, a family restaurant not far from the *Post*, drank beer and ate hamburgers.

"David was pumped up again and raring to go, but still no concrete job offer," Fraser recalled. "I went home pretty sure I was going to be offered the job, but not a hundred percent certain. Near midnight, my phone rang, and it was David. 'Matthew,' he said, 'how would you like to be the next editor-in-chief of the *National Post*?' That was how the whole adventure began. On May 2, I was summoned to the Global head office in the boardroom and Leonard took me aside and we negotiated my contract literally on the back of an envelope. Len wrote it out longhand with a pen. Then he ushered me into the big boardroom. Every senior Canwest executive was either there or connected by conference call. Gordon Fisher was dumbfounded when I walked in and Camilleri announced that I was the new editor-in-chief of the *Post*. He blurted out, 'No shit!' He couldn't believe it. The former Southam people were completely flummoxed by the decision, and many were incensed. But they bit their lips, because it was the Asper decision—the word of God. But they all hated me for it, and did everything they could to make my life miserable from day one, even more so after Izzy died six months later."

Fraser later compared the ensuing events to "an out-of-body experience." "Ken Whyte and Martin Newland showed up, one after the other, and were asked to wait in some anteroom. Camilleri stepped out twice to fire each of them, and came back in to the boardroom, saying, 'Okay, I just terminated Ken Whyte.' It was like being involved in an assassination plot. And I was the newly proclaimed king. It was quite overwhelming. Within minutes it was on the radio and hundreds of phone calls started pouring in to confirm the news.*

"An hour later we drove up to the *Post*'s editorial building, where David and I addressed a group of senior editors," said Fraser. "It felt like a *coup d'état* had taken place and we were the outsiders coming in and taking over the place. David tossed his jacket on a chair, undid his cufflinks, rolled up his sleeves, clasped his hands together and announced, 'My name is David Asper and I'm the new chairman of the *National Post*, and this is Matthew Fraser, the new editor-in-chief.' The staff were stupefied and looked up at us in disbelief, astonished that this was actually taking place.

---

*Ken Whyte had offered to leave quietly, with dignity intact and a reasonable departure bonus. But Camilleri insisted that he be fired. Whyte hired Michael Levine to fight his cause and it is rumoured that he obtained a much larger settlement than he would have collected if he had been permitted to calmly resign.

"I had no prior discussion about the paper's editorial line, probably because the Aspers knew me and trusted me. I talked to David many times every day, but usually we just brainstormed. Leonard very rarely called me, so he made it clear he respected my judgments, merely wanted to pass along some complaint from someone, often a CEO of a major company complaining about a story. Izzy never attempted to interfere in how the paper was put together. But he read the *Post* thoroughly and let me know his views about something that had caught his attention. The only problem was that Izzy was very loyal to his friends, and one of them happened to be the prime minister of Canada, Jean Chrétien. I got a good deal of flak from Izzy over the way *Post* investigative reporter Andrew McIntosh was going after the PM on the Grand-Mère inn issue. Izzy also reminded me that I was 'responsible for every single syllable in the newspaper.' He was right, of course, but no editor can read every single word in the paper every day. Things slip through. But Izzy was right. The buck stopped on my desk, and if something went wrong, I had to pay the price.

"The worst episode was the *Post*'s big takeout on Conrad Black in September of 2003. I had been alerted that business writer Steve Maich had a long feature on Conrad and that it wasn't pretty. I asked to see it, and indeed it was a hatchet job by any standard. Much of it was based on quotes from his [Black's] friend and onetime business associate Hal Jackman, disparaging Black's dubious business practices, but there was very solid reporting in the piece as well. Maich was a good journalist, not known to be nasty, harbour grudges or execute vendettas. As editor-in-chief I had a problem with the story, if only because Conrad Black and his right-hand man, David Radler, were both on the Canwest board of directors at the time. There was also the potentially awkward optics of Black's former newspaper attacking him in an unbecoming manner. Nonetheless, I approved the piece for publication after inserting words like 'erudite' and 'cultivated' to describe Conrad, hoping these qualifications might take some of the sting out. I also took the precaution of telling David Asper that a piece highly critical of Conrad was in the works.

"When the article was published, the shit hit the fan, big time. It was, to our credit, the first major take on Black's questionable business practices and, in retrospect, the piece that led in time to his downfall. So, ironically, Conrad was brought down by his own newspaper, owned by a company on whose board he sat. It didn't take long for me to realize that Conrad and David Radler were calling for my head. David Asper told me that I was in deep trouble with Izzy. I honestly thought that I was going to get fired. My first reaction was to try to calm down Conrad and Radler. I couldn't find Conrad, but I got to Radler through my friend Michael Cooke, editor of the *Chicago Sun-Times*. His boss was Radler. I asked Cooke to call David and tell him that I'd offer him and Conrad a right-of-reply piece in the *Post*. Cooke called me back within an hour and said, 'I just talked to Radler and gave him your message. He said for you to 'go fuck yourself.' At that point, I knew they wanted my scalp.

"David actually handled the crisis admirably. There is a lot of talk about David's vices, because he is portrayed as a colourful Falstaffian figure, but his many virtues are often neglected. One thing about David is that he can be courageous when the going gets rough. With Conrad calling for my head, David organized a three-way conference call between himself, me and his dad. Izzy was very angry about the situation, but David defended me. I remember him saying, 'But, Dad, what if the article is right, what if it's true?' Izzy listened carefully, and finally backed down. All he said was, 'I just wish you hadn't published the damn thing.' I expressed some contrition, though held firm, and the solution we came up with was to publish an editorial defending Conrad. I later convinced David that it should appear under his byline, and it did. David took the fall in a tense situation. There was a lot of speculation later that the column, due to its rococo language, was written by Lord Tubby himself, and in any case David Asper could never write in such a baroque style. The truth is that the column was written by me but we published it under David's name. It was a resolute defence of Black's honour. And frankly, my staff at the *Post* never forgave me for it. Izzy did not live to follow the decline and fall of Conrad; only a few weeks after our controversial piece on Black was published, Izzy died. A few months later, Conrad and Radler stepped down from the Canwest board, and within a year, their downfall would begin in earnest."

The firing of Russell Mills, after an editorial calling for the resignation of Prime Minister Chrétien, was the climactic turning point of Izzy's war. Three decades a member of the *Ottawa Citizen*'s editorial department, sixteen years its publisher and president of the entire Southam group part of that time, Mills was not interchangeable with any other Ottawa journalist. It was an indication of his significance in his profession and his community that after his dismissal he was immediately awarded a fellowship by Harvard and later headed the National Capital Commission, which runs Canada's capital city.

Still, having been in a similar position, I believe that in this case the Aspers behaved as publishers must. Proprietors do have rights, and one of them is to speak through editorials, which is the tiny outcrop in all those acres of print where they can and should sound off on vital issues, such as choosing or dismissing prime ministers.

I write from experience. After spending a dozen years as an Ottawa political columnist, never having to worry about anyone's opinions except my own, in 1969 I was appointed editor-in-chief of the *Toronto Star* and unexpectedly found myself fussing over each day's editorials to make sure they reflected the paper's institutional views. Unlike columns, which magnify personal opinions, and news stories, which transmit, well, news, editorials are the institutional voice of a publication, and they deserve special treatment.

For months before my promotion, *Star* publisher Beland Honderich (the perfect stand-in for a heel-clicking U-boat captain) had interrogated me about my deeply ingrained beliefs and lightly held prejudices. There was no problem agreeing on basic principles. The comedian Dave Broadfoot once accurately labelled the *Star* as a "small-L conservative paper"—an ideological stance that the

publisher and I roughly shared. Most important, we were both economic nationalists who believed that Canadians ought to freely follow their own, not imported, policies and values. Still, I had to submit the editorial page daily to the publisher before it went to press
because it represented the institutional collective view of the paper—
the point being that before he offered me the job, Honderich made
certain that, as editor-in-chief, I would broadly support the paper's
publishing philosophy, which struck me then (and does still) as not
an unreasonable request. That didn't mean we never argued, but it
was always within the ideological matrix that had been set in place.
Which, incidentally, was the secret of Conrad Black's success as the
Post's original publisher, since editor-in-chief Ken Whyte's ideological
stance was close to his own—a position consolidated during the four
years Whyte edited Black's monthly *Saturday Night* magazine.

But Mills was unceremoniously dumped, and in an exit interview
with David Asper was offered a generous payoff to say that he had
retired instead of being fired. "I did not spend thirty years in journalism attempting to pursue the truth in order to leave on a lie," he
replied. He later settled for an undisclosed sum. In response to that
event, seventy-seven ex-Southam publishers and editors took out an
ad accusing Canwest of limiting press freedom. Other journalists—
Stephen Kimber in Halifax, Peter Worthington in Toronto, Doug
Cuthand in Regina, Michael Goldbloom in Montreal as well as several others—were terminated for similar reasons that had nothing
to do with their competence.

Even if he wanted to, Izzy Asper had no time or opportunity to staff
the fourteen major papers he had acquired with philosophically
compatible functionaries. Instead, he tried to bend editors and publishers to his very special view of the world by issuing bureaucratic
edicts, canned editorials and pink slips. His efforts were bound to
fail. By this time, Izzy had become fairly isolated, and one could
have imagined that he wasn't fully aware how profound a public rela-

tions calamity his and David's unyielding response to the revolting newshounds had caused. One of Canwest's problems, now coming to the fore, was the nature of its board of directors. Of the nine board members, six were either family members or company executives. That left only a tiny rump of independents, who had no leverage. As John Gray noted in *Canadian Business,* "Can anyone conceive of them voting to oust the person who carved the turkey on Thanksgiving?"

At this time, Izzy was thin and looking skeletal. "Enough already," he emailed a friend. "I see the future as collective bargaining over the contents of reports and columns. Grievances, wildcat strikes, arbitrations, public apologies, floggings, hangings . . . and all I wanted out of life was to buy the *Minnedosa Tribune* and practice law. I am retired, have my own agenda. So I leave the *Post* to my successors. My plate is more than full. The Museum is kids' stuff compared to what else is on my mind."

His children were highly supportive. "This issue with Russell Mills, Dad had asked for two or three priorities where, if you're endorsing the prime minister, or telling him to resign, this is something we should be discussing," Gail Asper maintained. "It's not appropriate for the editor to just decide by himself who we should or should not endorse. These are major, major issues, and that's where Dad wanted some say. But Mills wouldn't adhere to that and that's why he was fired, not because he was pro-Chrétien or anti-Chrétien.* Now the only problem was that there's a way to do this and a way not to do it, and of course the way that he did it was not necessarily the way that you want to do things. Dad kept asking himself, 'Why would I want a paper if I couldn't determine what it said?' He wasn't trying to control people and he certainly wasn't muzzling people on the Israel issues. What he wanted was the opportunity to put something in the paper that expressed his point of view, but then the argument

---

*Mills himself was adamant that his dismissal concerned the disputed editorial alone, even turning the usual tables to issue a libel notice against Leonard Asper, the *National Post* and the *Ottawa Citizen* over a report that suggested otherwise.

is that when you do that, you send this chill. It was a huge convulsion and an incredibly interesting debate on the role of the owner. In my view the journalists were arguing about crushing the free use of speech, but we always felt that the issue was interference, not from the owner but interference from the state. It's when the journalists like Juliet O'Neill are arrested for writing an article. That's when you want journalistic freedom. Take *Frank,* for example. If *Frank* magazine writers didn't write salacious, crappy stuff, they'd be fired. So clearly there isn't freedom of speech there. They are hired to do that. If a women's magazine started saying that we should all quit our jobs and stay at home and have eight children, you'd be fired. So they all do it. What bothered Izzy about the Shawinigan file was that most of the coverage smacked of Conrad Black's hatred for Chrétien because of the citizenship quarrel involving his title. So he viewed that as a personal vendetta against the prime minister for no justifiable newsworthy reason."

"I come from a more crude environment," confessed her brother Leonard. "I don't see that a journalist is any different than an employee at Wal-Mart. That's why there's this flap with the Montreal *Gazette.* If a bunch of employees at Wal-Mart are running up and down the isles at Wal-Mart declaring, 'We hate Wal-Mart, this is a terrible company and we hate its owners,' as they were doing at the *Gazette*—we just didn't see why a group of employees should be allowed to run around trashing the company and its owners. Our view of the world is that it's a family business, and we're family and you solve your problems internally. But we respected the fact, and always did, that columnists can write what they want, and if you didn't like it, you just get new columnists. Do journalists own the paper? No. They work there, they work within certain parameters, and I believe in objective reporting. I think this is a common view held among David, Izzy, Gail and I—that we were trying to get the editorial slants out of the news."

David's approach was as direct as a flaming arrow: "We own the papers. We have the right to have the papers print whatever the hell we want them to say. And if people don't like it, they can go to hell. They can leave, get another job. People knew that Conrad had a much more hands-off policy. On the other hand, in the papers he cared about, he hired people who didn't breathe without talking to him first. We inherited some of those people—for better and for worse."

There was one private confrontation between Izzy and a friend that left a lasting impression. Brenlee Werner is one of those unusually intelligent and outspoken, accomplished business-women who lend gravitas to Winnipeg society. She had attended the University of Manitoba with Izzy (they had a brief fling before he met Babs) and they remained friends. Both families have cot-tages at Falcon Lake. She visited the Asper compound one Sunday afternoon, and launched right in. "We were at a party at the lake, and it was just after he had fired all these editors and writers and was getting bad press everywhere," she recalled. "I thought he could have accomplished it in a much smarter way—that it wasn't up to his level. So when he and I found ourselves alone at the bar, I said to him, 'Listen, Izzy, what you did wasn't wrong, but the way you did it was wrong. What I would have done is to meet with each journalist who was involved and explained my position. Then they would have understood. You didn't do anything in person—you did it all as a series of edicts, and that was what got everybody's back up.'

"Izzy never smiled and didn't deliver one of his wisecracks. He told me in response, 'No, I did it just right,' then without the least bit of humour, slamming the door on other conversation, he said, 'That was exactly what I intended to do.'"

14

The Day the Music Died

Israel Asper had been a singular man
firmly in command of his worth—
and not afraid to show it.

Israel Harold Asper's funeral was a state occasion that tested the ushers' sensitivities and their politics of decorum. The most delicate-to-place attendees were the four past, current and future prime ministers of Canada, then in various states of feud: John Turner, Jean Chrétien, Paul Martin and Stephen Harper. Led to pews as widely separated as possible, they eyed one another with hooded eyes and scarcely allayed suspicion. After all, they were surrounded by Izzy's private army, encamped in the spiffy pews of the Shaarey Zedek Synagogue, come to pay the big guy a final tribute. Each of the mourners had earned pips and stripes in Izzy's service, but if it seemed to the casual observer that the late Mr. Asper had been put together from bits of these people, that impression was decidedly wrong. He had been very much his own man and now, felled by a heart attack, he was being mourned by family, friends, Winnipeg and the roving power groupies convened to sing his praises.*

So many distinguished presences slow-marched their way in and out of the crowded synagogue that the funeral took on the air of a czarist cortège in a late-nineteenth-century provincial Russian town. The corridor music, a mixture of "Hava Nagila," Gershwin preludes and a slightly uptempo version of "Autumn Leaves," broke the mood, but each selection was infused with the dark energy of its players—mostly musical buddies of the departed, keening for their late patron.

Outside, it was one of those epic Indian-summer days when the elm trees take on a russet glow, waiting for the final departure of green. In the second week of October, the initial, exploratory chills of winter usually cool Winnipeg's tempers. But not that year, not in 2003, when the temperature (thirty degrees in the shade) remained mild and pleasant. Nature had decided to honour its departing host with a display that included a burning sun to spotlight the city by day and a screaming orange harvest moon to illuminate it by night.

Inside the synagogue the funeral service, conducted by Rabbi Alan Green, had the ceremonial resonance of the passing of royalty. "Like an impressionistic painter, Izzy understood the contribution of each point of colour to a masterpiece," intoned the rabbi to the jammed congregation of two thousand. "He was one in a billion—a charismatic, creative genius who revealed the extent to which one person can positively impact an entire generation." Israel Asper had imparted to everything and everyone he touched a sense of shared excitement. He was a brazen individualist, firmly in command of his worth and not afraid to show it. That un-Canadian attitude was reflected in the temple that sad day, as the dauphins and deacons

---

*Probably the strangest sight in Winnipeg that day was that of the corporate jets stacked three layers high above the airport, impatiently waiting their turns to land and disgorge their mourners.

of Canada's political and business elite shed a tear for this son of Winnipeg (not the only "son of" he had ever been called) and shared Izzy stories.

Yes, they were crying a little, but they were laughing softly as well, because the flow of anecdotes kept the man alive, one more day. "It was almost as though he hadn't gone," Ray Heard, the father of Global News, remarked to a friend. "Few were in deep mourning because it seemed that he wasn't really dead. No one could accept that he was gone"—least of all Yale Lerner, the Winnipeg lawyer who had originally incorporated Canwest in the mid-1970s, had become Izzy's nocturnal work buddy and now sat there, half crying and half smiling, awash in memories.

Everybody had his own Izzy story, a special way to recall the friendship, but none were more outrageous than Yale's. His had been a long goodbye: "The last time I saw Izzy alive it was about a month and a half ago," he recalled. "We went to Morton's steakhouse in Toronto with Babs for dinner and weren't allowed to smoke in the restaurant but could in the bar.

"So we ate dinner with Babs, sent her back to the hotel, and when they closed the bar, we had them fill up two huge cognac glasses. There's a marble stoop about a quarter block from Morton's and we went and sat there with the cognac for three or four hours, reminiscing and kibitzing. As people came by we were begging for nickels, pennies, dimes. It was fun. I can't get over that evening. It was a lifetime. We were both plastered and were smooching in front of the hotel. We did that. There was a lot of affection . . . Izzy was my life, the last half of my life. I'm sixty-five, and thirty of those years were virtually all Izzy. He had the confidence in me and threw me into big deals, very creative stuff. I just miss him every night. I don't miss him in the daytime, but I keep the same hours we used to spend together. So now I've got nobody to play with but I'm still up till three or four every morning. When I heard he'd passed away, I had nobody to turn to. I hate to say this, but it hit me harder than when my father died. I didn't know what to do, so I went to the

Sassafraz restaurant in Yorkville. I hadn't had a gin martini in ten years, because I couldn't metabolize it anymore, but I got them to pour me a double gin martini, had a cheeseburger, and that was it. I've never had gin since and I'll never have gin—or cheeseburgers—again. It was my last goodbye."

Booze was more than a casual condiment in Izzy's life, and many of the stories the mourners told one another concerned his drinking and smoking—not that these activities were suitable fodder for funeral talk, but it was a safe bet that there were very few adults in attendance that sad day who didn't have at least one great story about Izzy's lesser habits.

Obsession was his habitual approach not just to work but to life in general. Smoking was his most visible bad habit, and he genuinely wanted to rid himself of it. One time the infomercial hucksters on TV at the time were selling a pocket-size computer that would tell you when to smoke—the trick being that it would increase the time between puffs and the user would eventually stop wanting cigarettes. Asper bought one but didn't like the idea of a computer. So he figured out the smoking intervals with a stopwatch, wrote out the schedule on a piece of paper and stuck it on a mirror or window in his office or hotel room or wherever he was. All through business meetings he would stare at the time table instead of focusing on the subject under review. Whenever it came time to smoke the next cigarette, he would stop the meeting and light up. There would be a big production about it. Eventually it became a joke and he just puffed away at ease.

"I could never figure out that a man with his kind of iron will-power couldn't just will himself to stop smoking if he really wanted to," Tom Strike, one of his most senior executives, observed. "But by the same token, he had this sort of obsessive personality."

His drinking was legendary. "I never knew Izzy any other way," confessed Yale Lerner, his chief legal adviser and fellow late-night boozer, "except that as he got older he cut back. I never saw him drunk during the daytime, and I never saw him in a situation where his drinking affected something important. He might, at night—I mean, that's where the fun in life was—he would sit back in his den at home and have so-called martinis. They were really big glasses full of gin, but they were called 'martinis' to be more polite. He was a Beefeater man, and his drinks of choice were called 'martinis' because the vermouth bottle was within ten feet. Sometimes he would switch to Bombay Sapphire because somebody told him that that was how the original martini had been poured, and he actually liked it better. His martinis were neither shaken nor stirred, just swallowed.

"Then he stopped with the martinis. I can't remember exactly when, but he started drinking wine. Somebody told him to swish Scotch in the glass first, so now we were swishing Scotch, then sipping wine, except that I noticed it was really brandy:

"'But Izzy, you only drink wine now.'

"'This *is* wine.'

"'What are you talking about? That's not wine, that's brandy.'

"'No, it's made out of grapes. It's a strong wine.'"

Izzy's health—or rather, lack of it—was his family's constant concern. "He truly believed he was immortal," lamented his wife, Babs. "The ordinary rules never applied to him. He was not going to change his life." He was a self-described "intravenous martini" guzzler, to the extent that he was once charged with impaired driving (he paid the fine). His drinking habit, combined with his chain smoking—at least three packs of Craven A's a day—reached self-destructive levels. He even smoked while sipping soup. During one lunch with John Turner, the former prime minister counted that Izzy had smoked thirteen cigarettes. When his kids took up a collection and sent him to a hypnotist who claimed to be able to cure chronic smokers, Asper solicitously attended his weekly sessions—until he returned home with a triumphant grin and proudly announced, "Well, I'm finished with the hypnotist."

"But you're still smoking," a family member objected.

"Yeah, but so is the hypnotist. I fixed him."

He swore he would quit the nasty cigarette habit cold turkey, but according to his daughter, Gail, up to the day he died he smoked his habitual three packs. Izzy energized himself with nicotine then mellowed out with Beefeater's London Gin.

His other obsession was eating, or, rather, his weight. "You could see it in everything he did, especially the times he went on exercise kicks to lose weight," Strike recalled. "His whole theory was, 'I'll lose a whole bunch of weight before I stop smoking.' He would grind himself into losing, like, one hundred pounds, walking the tread-mill for hours on end, taking his regime to incredible extremes. One time he decided that his only meaningful measure of success was whether he could fit into the suit he got married in. And he did. Another time he became determined to fit into the bathing trunks he had worn as a kid, by his sixty-fifth birthday. It was like the leg-endary magician Houdini wriggling into a handkerchief, but he did lose enough poundage to actually do it. Of course, having achieved his goal, he would then begin eating his usual cheeseburgers and the weight-loss cycle would begin all over again."

When he decided to spend winters in Palm Beach, Asper met George Cohon, a Chicago lawyer who became the Canadian head of McDonald's. The two men became fast friends, and Cohon began to worry about Asper's weight, which was ballooning out of proportion to his height. To encourage Izzy's diet regime, on March 7, 1999, George said he would contribute $2,000 to Izzy's family founda-tion—if Asper could get down to 180 pounds by September of that year. At the time he weighed in at 216 pounds. Cohon then left Palm Beach for a business trip to Toronto, vaguely asking Izzy to look after his place. He received his first report by fax on May 24, 1999:

Dear George,

I dropped by to visit your Palm Beach digs over the week-end. The demolition is going reasonably well, but I am sure you know they were delayed by the fire. Your insurance will cover the $6.3 million repair estimate. But you're not cov-ered for the stench created by the nest of skunks found in your attic. They were fried but they left behind their aroma. Not to worry, it goes away, five or six years at most. The only bad news is the Rwanda family you hired to maintain the property. Apparently they brought over all their relatives, so the group of 161 have built mud and straw huts on your property across the road. When I asked them what they were doing, assuming my Swahili is OK, their witch doctor said something about squatters' rights. Have a good summer. 14 POUNDS TO GO!

Izzy*

As his weight deadline approached, Asper became desperate: "I am still smarting over your cunning, immoral and underhanded attempt to sabotage a gentleman's bet of honour by providing me with free Big Macs and chips," he wrote Cohon. "I thought your parents came from Russia, not Romania! After a month of diet and exercise in the last two weeks of June and into July, and not shedding a single ounce, this week a big breakthrough occurred, and I knocked off two pounds. I will not give you a progress report on the weight I have achieved but with six weeks to go, unless there is a total breakdown in results, the law of averages says that I will win the bet. On September 4th, I have an appointment to have my head cut off, just to make certain. Dictated but not read—IZZY."

———

Leading to this time of last rites and high sorrow, Izzy Asper's casual bad habits came back to haunt him. The prolonged abuse of his health—the office stress, the chain smoking, his dependency on

---

*Cohon got his own back when Asper, who was out of town, sent him tickets to a George Shearing concert at the Kravis Center. After the gig, which Cohon told friends was "an all-time great night," he sent Asper this note: "Izzy, the local pops guy is running out of money on the jazz series. At the concert, most people were sound asleep. But since I was sitting in your seat, I jumped up and said, 'I'm speaking on behalf of Mr. Asper. He's got lots of money. He'll be more than glad to help.'"

alcohol and an addiction to the cholesterol-laden Salisbury House cheeseburgers—finally exacted their toll.

On the morning of October 7, 2003, Asper was in Winnipeg preparing for a trip to Vancouver, accompanied by his daughter, Gail, to raise funds for the Canadian Museum for Human Rights. He had just spent the first two nights in his brand-new, double-storey luxury condo at the foot of Wellington Crescent, fitted out with a full-scale stage and sound system to accommodate live jazz concerts. The movers and unpackers were still there in the morning, as was the interior designer, and there was so much shouting that nobody could hear anything up or down the staircase. It was chaos, but Babs, his wife of forty-seven years, recalled seeing Izzy just kind of sitting on his bed, staring into space. She thought he might be planning his Vancouver appointments and wanted to talk to him, but she was summoned downstairs to the main living room. "Some problem arose," she remembered, "and I called to him to ask where to put something. I called and called and it didn't surprise me that he didn't hear. So I went upstairs and found him lying in the closet." She rushed to help him but it was too late. Leonard, who had been at work, arrived at the condo just as a medical crew was pulling his father's body out to the ambulance. "I remember my mother being in complete denial. So I tried to pretend he was still alive but he was not. Then David showed up, looked at Mom, looked at Dad, and after I saw that he had observed the same set of facts, I told him, 'Just go with it.'"

"Izzy was very impatient in the latter years, and he didn't want to take time for things to happen," Babs later remembered. "It was almost as if he had a sense of doom, that he had to get it all done, fast, fast, fast. He wasn't relaxing. He didn't take into account his physical condition in any way, never gave an inch, because that wasn't the way he wanted to live. Gail and I kept telling him to take his time, but he said he didn't have any. He had to push things, sometimes with not positive results."

"I was having coffee with some friends at 8:30 that morning, didn't have my cellphone on," Gail recalled of that traumatic day. "I got through breakfast about nine o'clock and turned on my phone, just to check for messages, to see if there'd been any changes in the plan, because I was scheduled to meet with Dad at the airport where we would be flying to Vancouver and he would be delivering a speech to four hundred First Nations chiefs on the importance of the museum. He had been at my house the night before, and was in great shape, talking to everybody, and I had diligently packaged up leftover turkey wings and turkey legs to give to him, because those were his favourite parts. We actually had a deal on the turkey— sometimes I'd have to order extra wings because the battles would be unseemly over who got the bones. At the time when my grandma was alive, it was Grandma, Dad and me who would go for the wings, and you know there's only two wings per turkey—I would buy some extras. But anyway, we packaged everything up, and as he was running off, he said, 'I'll meet you at ten at the airport.' And then, the next thing I know, I'm checking my voice mail and hear from David that I'm supposed to get to St. Boniface General Hospital right away because Dad was down. That was all he said, so I just raced to the hospital, which, luckily, in Winnipeg, I could get to in about five minutes. But then I got to the hospital and dropped, just dropped my car right at the front door and ran in. I knew that things were not good when you've got people waiting for you at the door to usher you into a special room. David, Leonard and Mum were sitting there already, and just from the looks on their faces I knew that this could not be good. Then somebody came in and told us that he had passed away. And there was just this silence. But to be with your family, to be with all of your close family at that time, there was a great deal of comfort. And the unbelievable, indescribable pain of hearing that your father is dead was horrible to have to bear, but at least you bear it with the people who cared about him the most."

"We were just starting out on the museum odyssey at that time," Gail continued, "at the beginning of this whole journey, and we'd been having so much fun driving around the city, driving around Manitoba, going into these sales pitches. Like we were doing a road show, basically, and never knowing what he was going to say or how he was going to play it. It was just fascinating watching him and trying to talk him out of eating too much junk food on the road. After the funeral, Mum and I actually visited Sals to toast Dad and ordered the cheeseburgers."

Before she left the hospital, Gail looked down at her father one last time, and later remembered thinking, "Here he was, seventy-one, with boundless energy, and boundless resources, and boundless will. I mean, how often do you marry the desire to change the world with the creativity to be able to do it, and the money? It was an incredible package, and what a loss for the world, I kept saying to myself, 'This is an unfair loss, not just for our family, but to all the people whose lives he was going to change' . . . I had never seen a dead body before, but it wasn't like he was dead. He really looked terrific. His skin was always so soft, and he seemed really rested. So I just had a talk with him, and told him that we were going to carry on, that he could trust me—trust us—to carry out his plans. He was always worried that we weren't doing enough estate planning, and kept saying, 'I'm not going to be here forever. You guys have to get it straight. This is the way you've got to conduct yourselves.'

"I had this vision, in the room there at that moment, that this was like the time he taught me how to ride my bicycle. Because it was him, it wasn't Mom—he was the guy running along, holding the back of the bike. It was really hard to hold and hard to ride, and it was actually an aerobic achievement to have to run like that for any distance. I just have this image of him with me in Grade 1, running up and down Elm Street in his 1960s groovy-dude blue suede shoes. He didn't even have running shoes or anything. But he was running up the street, smoking, holding the back of my bike, and I will never forget talking to him. I was about five or six, and when I was half-way around the block, he'd let go. I didn't know he'd let go, turned around, and he was way at the back of the street, and he was waving, and I had been riding the bike on my own and I didn't even know it. And then of course fifty yards later I crashed into the bush, but that was good, because I was going to hit Academy Road and I didn't know how to stop. But I'll never forget the feeling of him letting go of the bike and me knowing that I could ride it.

"That's what he had been doing with us most of his life, teaching us how to ride the bike," lamented Gail. "He knew when it was time to let go and that we could ride it on our own—and that if we couldn't ride the bike at that point, we were never going to be able to ride it. That was my comfort level—knowing that he couldn't hold it anymore. And so looking at him in the hospital bed, I just made the commitment that what he had been teaching us, that we were going to remember, and going to fulfill his dreams."

———

The funeral that followed two days later was part of Izzy's legacy, as the unprecedented turnout of notables who jammed Shaarey Zedek Synagogue tried to outdo one another in paying their respects. Despite the glitz that accompanied the glowing presence of VIPs, Rabbi Green later described the event as having been *haimish* (the Yiddish word for "homey"). "It was emblematic of Israel Asper because no matter how successful he became, no matter what high circles he moved in, he remained a man of the people," he observed. Gordon Sinclair, the *Winnipeg Free Press* columnist, noted that "the self-made son of Russian Jewish immigrants—who went on to make *Forbes'* list of the wealthiest people in the world—remained as accessible and friendly as the guy next door." "Canada needs more Izzy Aspers," ex-Canwest publisher Russell Mills pointedly recalled. "The newspapers industry, however, does not."

Of all the many tributes spoken and written about him that day, one of the most apt was that of Tom Axworthy, a former Trudeau chief of staff and seminal Liberal thinker who had shared some prime times with Izzy: "Listening to him as he played his beloved Gershwin, laughing with him as he wondered why he had agreed to sponsor Canwest Global Park when he didn't even like baseball, agreeing with him when he defended the right of Israel to exist, disagreeing with him about many other political issues, Izzy loved every moment of his life. He never drew a bored breath. Family, faith and community were his values; his style was to squeeze life to the pips. A very vital force has departed Portage and Main."

Another, less florid but equally valid assessment came from a stranger, Evan Solomon, the CBC's ace broadcaster who had taped the last interview ever done with Asper (though the two had not previously met). Afterwards, when a colleague asked Solomon what Izzy was like, he replied, "To some people Israel Asper was an adversary, but he was the best kind of adversary to have—the kind of adversary who makes you better at what you do, makes you challenge your own assumptions. They don't make people like that anymore. For his fearlessness, for his boldness and his vision, Izzy will be missed all over the country."

The family's profound grief found its most poignant voices in the touching eulogies of the Asper children, Leonard, David and Gail. Leonard reminisced that when he was eighteen, his dad dropped him off at Brandeis University, where he knew no one: "As I stood there I must have looked lost, so he said to me, 'Don't worry. Your mother had you for the first eighteen years. I get you for the next eighteen.' And thus began a deep intellectual relationship that sustained me over the years.

"He taught me never to back down, and he had nerves of steel. I remember when we were at Jimmy Weston's, a jazz club in New York. Tommy Furtado was playing the piano. Five men in suits were at the next table. They were enjoying the show a little too loudly for my dad's liking. He may or may not have noticed the bulges in each of their breast pockets, but he repeatedly told them to be quiet. God forbid anybody make noise during a jazz performance. Finally they beckoned him outside and all the men got up, including Dad. He had been gone for fifteen minutes and I became very concerned. I came outside just in time to hear him threatening the lives of five men armed with Magnum pistols. Dad had lethal force too—three packs of Craven-A King Size. He won. They left.

"My dad was a regular guy. He did occasionally walk with princes, but he never lost the common touch. I remember sitting with him in a McDonald's late one night in Vancouver, years ago, wondering how many other billionaires went for a late-night cheeseburger with their son. He said, 'Len, some people just don't know how to live.'

"Dad believed passionately in individual rights and liberties, and he fought for that belief in a variety of arenas from his days as a tax columnist and author, to his days as Liberal Party leader in Manitoba, and right up to his days as a proprietor of newspapers. His drive to teach others the importance of these fundamental principles and how fragile they can be is what the Canadian Museum for Human Rights is all about.

"Dad, there is no way to put all of you into five minutes. You knew how to create, you knew how to give, you knew how to live, you knew how to nurture, you knew how to love. Thank you for what you gave to the world and to your family. We have your checklist. We know what's left to be done, and we will not let you down. Goodbye, old friend. Goodbye, Dad."

Eldest son David described life with his tough but loving father: "There was no room in his world for anything less than 100 percent effort. He always wanted to succeed, and believed that success was the probable outcome of hard work. Some say it was his curse. I say there is no finer ethic that my dad instilled in my life. I think the only thing he ever really gave up on was trying to get me to continue with piano lessons. He was right and I was wrong.

"If he hadn't dragged me to law school and kept me from quitting, in favour of becoming a shepherd in a field somewhere, I would never have experienced the depth of his love for law and human rights. I would never have had the opportunity to stand in defence of those suffering at the hand of an overbearing state; to be able to actually right an unrightable wrong; to be an unrelenting soldier in the cause of freedom.

"Our last conversation of substance over the weekend was about what's wrong with the Bombers. Of course, the lesson wasn't really about the Bombers. It was about loyalty and sticking with your team no matter what happens, win, lose or draw. It was about pride, and being proud of where you come from. And it's a life lesson that served him well and will stay with me forever. My name is David, son of Izzy and Babs, and I come from Winnipeg.

"Dad taught us about a lot of things. Humour, for example. He once tried to suggest that velour was a plant from which housecoats were made. But what overrides everything was his admonition that we cannot be spectators as the world goes by. You have all heard him on this point, and what he really hoped for was that he could create a sort of tipping point in society. He found out the hard way that change in the political world can be a slow and painful process. But in philanthropy, he believed it possible to build a Garden of Eden in the here and now.

"Dad—we heard you and will heed it well. Save me a seat at the bar."

Not long before his sudden passing, Izzy and his daughter, Gail, were discussing the Human Rights Museum when they spontaneously burst into a duet from *Man of La Mancha*. "I felt a bit weary, and he needed to remind me that sometimes you have to march into hell for a heavenly cause," she recalled. "But it also reminded me of how lucky I was to have such a renaissance man for a father. Yes—a business man, a principled politician, a tax expert, but to me a philosopher, an intellectual, a man who taught me the joy of convertibles and introduced me to the greatest music of all time, and, no, I don't mean jazz—I mean Broadway musicals.

"It wasn't always easy for him to accept this imperfect world. His thought process was the most unique I ever encountered, and I know all of us mourn the loss of that extraordinary intellect. Sure, we can all carry on his tradition of hard work and giving back to the community (and we all will), but what's been lost is irreplaceable, and our world is unequivocally diminished by his passing. In the end, we are left with so much that he has given us—not just the wonderful material wealth he showered on us (for he was outrageously generous with his friends, family and community), but his desire for excellence, for fairness, for leaving the world a better place than the way he found it. All these are wonderful things, except that nothing will change the fact that he won't be there to tell me which dress to wear for my next son's bar mitzvah; he won't be there to draw me another eight-page handwritten chart of what you should look for when you are buying a house; and he won't be there to take the trouble, as he did one night (with everything he had to do running a multi-billion-dollar company and saving the world with the Asper Foundation), to make me a tape of ten versions of 'Lost in the Stars' from *Cry, the Beloved Country* after I had mentioned to him how much I had loved that song and mentioned how grateful I was that he had taken the time to teach it to me.

"In *Man of La Mancha,* Aldonza asks Don Quixote, 'Why do you do the things you do? Why do you fight battles that are not your own?' and he responds with the words of 'The Impossible Dream.' So I guess I'll just have the memories of my father who always dreamed the impossible dream. Even though he may have seemed to be tilting at windmills, he still tried, though his arms were too weary to reach the unreachable star. That was always his quest, and his life was one long adventure in the pursuit of things that mattered, no matter how hopeless, no matter how far. What we can all believe—all us remaining Sancho Panzas and Aldonzas—is that the world will be better for this: that one man, sometimes scorned and covered with scars, can still strive with his last ounce of courage to reach the unreachable star. I love you, Dad, and I know you are watching us from heaven with an ice-cold martini, happily ensconced in the smoking section."

These moving soliloquies stole a lot of hearts that day. But it was Izzy's thirteen-year-old grandson, David's son Daniel, who brought out the handkerchiefs when he earnestly explained about his grandfather, "The reason why his heart stopped is because he put so much of it into the lives of others." Later Daniel recalled dinner a few nights before, at Gail and her husband Mike's, when the family was celebrating the end of Yom Kippur: "My final memory of him was sitting on a chair at a little coffee table having a glass of red wine and a cigarette. I waved goodbye as we were leaving. He winked at me and I waved back. That was the last time I saw him."

Police helicopters hovered overhead while the casket with the simple Star of David affixed to its lid was carried out of the temple, blessed by a stream of yellow leaves drifting down from the stately elms that surround the building, being strewn around the coffin by a sudden wisp of wind.* Police outriders were out in force that day, shepherding the funeral cavalcade (which included as many pickups as limousines) through the city's autumnal streets. When the procession drove past the main police station, Babs couldn't hold back a bittersweet smile at the cops saluting "a guy who had earned a million speeding tickets."

Izzy would have been most impressed by the ordinary Winnipeggers who had turned up spontaneously along the route of his cortège, paying silent homage to their municipal patron saint. It was no accident that the streets leading from the Shaarey Zedek Synagogue were lined by an overflow of mourners. Some leaned on walkers; others brought lawn chairs or blankets. A few jogged by and decided to stay; some cycled, or rolled their wheelchairs and parked them under the elms.

Soon the limos arrived to carry the VIPs across town to the Shaarey Zedek Cemetery in Winnipeg's North End, which was so jammed with onlookers that you couldn't see the headstones. Former premiers Frank McKenna of New Brunswick and Gerald Regan from Nova Scotia were there, as well as a clutch of former Manitoba premiers, led by the current incumbent, Gary Doer, and

---

*The pallbearers were the two sons, David and Leonard; Richard Leipsic, the Canwest legal counsel and special Izzy confidant; two relatives, Sam Brask and Neal Lofchy; Michael Paterson, Gail's husband; Moe Levy, head of the Asper Foundation; and Dr. Jack Rusen, Asper's personal physician.

Glen Murray, Winnipeg's onetime mayor ("Try," he said, "to find in Canadian history a city that has had such a generous benefactor—it doesn't exist"). What Izzy had laughingly described as "the Christian Conspiracy" that dominated the country's media was out in force: Ted Rogers, Jim Shaw, John Cassaday, Ivan Fecan, Michael MacMillan, Ken Thomson and Rob Prichard. John Harvard, a Liberal MP who became Manitoba's lieutenant governor, summed Izzy up in one sentence: "He never forgot where he came from and never compromised on where he was going." Bill Blaikie, a Winnipeg NDP member of the Commons, had some fun with his tribute: "I may be a critic of corporate concentration, but it was nice to have it concentrated in Winnipeg for a change." Diane Francis, the *National Post* business columnist, dubbed him "Canada's last Renaissance Man." On the other side of the ledger was Margaret Wente of the *Globe and Mail,* who portrayed Asper's dark side, concluding, "It was him against the world. He never got rid of the big chip on his shoulder."

"The whole city was shut down," recalled Jodi Lofchy, a distinguished Toronto psychiatrist who was Izzy's niece and admirer. "From our procession, it felt as if Israel had been a head of state. The flags were at half mast and all the people stood in front of their shops that were shut; flowers had been put out on the street, and the people standing there saluted or clenched their fists and folded them over their hearts. It was amazing. That's when you understood what he had meant to the city. To see the people standing out there with all these big bouquets of flowers they had bought and placed in front of their storefronts, as we came by. It was magical."

That evening, after Izzy was buried, the Asper family gathered at Gail's house for the shiva. "As we drove there, under the huge, blood-red moon, the sort of lunar extravaganza that Rodgers and Hammerstein had conjured up on Broadway when I was a kid, it looked too big and too Technicolor to be real," recalled Ray Heard. "Outside the house, the children were on their bikes, doing tricks or shooting hoops in the drive. Inside, the adults were remembering good times. Life went on. Aboard the Onex executive jet that flew us home, Heather Reisman read aloud from a French journalist's book about the murder of Daniel Pearl, the Wall Street foreign correspondent whose throat was slit in Karachi by local rebels, while Gerry Schwartz did incredible card tricks. Heather's words reminded us that this is a cruel world and we feared, with reason, that it will become even meaner, fears that were more than justified in the next twelve months." They were all talking about Izzy, but it was almost as though he hadn't gone. No one was in deep mourning because they couldn't accept that he was really dead.

After the shiva, which had made up for the absence of the revelry reserved for Irish wakes with the authenticity of its mourning, the family wandered over to Babs's new condo, which Izzy had so briefly occupied. Not knowing where to turn or what to say, they cried and hugged one another.

Not unexpectedly, in Izzy's room they found a stash of Craven A's, his favourite cigarettes. There ensued one of those pointless conversations, when people talk just to divert themselves from thinking about what had happened that dismal day. What do you do with a dozen cartons of cigarettes? Nobody knew. They were not really items you wanted to drop off at a hostel or old-age home. Then Gail had an idea. They all trooped down to the building's parking lot, and each family member lit a cigarette to honour the departed Izzy. "It was very symbolic," Jodi remembered. "They were his cigarettes, it was the night of the funeral and this was our way of saying goodbye. That was the only cigarette I've ever lit, but it was his, and even though I was choking to death, I smoked it, saved the butt and brought it home. We wanted to do something to mark the night, the occasion, to honour his memory in a way that he would understand."

The day Israel Asper was buried, something unprecedented happened. For Winnipeg, this was "The Day the Music Died," echoing the evocative refrain of Don McLean's "American Pie." The city would not see Izzy's like again. His boosterism had been infectious, his generosity irreplaceable. He gave Winnipeg what it needed most: grace notes from a caring citizen content to share his wealth and his loyalty with the ordinary men and women who populated his hometown.

Now that he was gone, Winnipeggers felt reduced and abandoned. They were not only lamenting the death of a unique and splendid man. They were grieving for themselves.

15

The Asper Legacy: Creating an Icon

*The prospect of raising $265 million for a museum
at the junction of two Winnipeg rivers seemed as
intimidating as climbing Mount Everest on a dinner date.*

I srael Asper had eased himself out of active corporate command
well before his deal with Conrad Black, though for public consumption he continued to bubble enthusiastically, "Even when I'm
ninety I'll still be buying green bananas and looking for a thirty-
year closed-end mortgage." In fact he had officially turned over
management of Canwest to his youngest son Leonard in 1999, naming him president and CEO while he remained an active executive
chairman. By 2003, he had stepped down from that office as well,
prompting Leonard to muse at the Canwest Chairman's Dinner that
winter, "What will this mean for me—Izzy stepping down as chairman? Nothing. I always get in the last words, 'Yes, Dad; No, Dad;
Right away, Dad!'"

With respect to the company's future, the young Asper poked
fun at an uncomfortable situation: "Obviously, Dad didn't think

we were very good deal makers. Because what he did was saddle us with so much debt [$4 billion] so we wouldn't make another deal in our lifetimes—an incredible estate plan." Leonard's dreams of exploiting media convergence as a major source of cost-cutting proved unattainable, but his push of Canwest into the frontiers of the digital Web and his Izzy-style takeover of the content-heavy, multi-channel Alliance Atlantis group corrected two of his father's neglected initiatives.

As he turned over command of the family empire to his kids, Izzy took a much keener interest in his "fourth child," the Asper Foundation, originally incorporated in 1983. That was the year he gathered his children, then in their bursting twenties and not yet in the family business, for an important meeting and told them for the first time about the Asper Foundation.

Every social and economic system requires sustaining myths to give it life and legitimacy. With all of capitalism's excesses—the disconnect between astronomical take-home pay and often falling profits; the tax shelters and padded-on or past-the-edge expense accounts—a commendable number of twenty-first-century Canadian tycoons have chosen corporate philanthropy as the equalizer for their bloated incomes. This isn't exactly a new practice, since it dates back to the Medicis of Florence, who for a time were the wealthiest family of Europe and who were so generous that they were accused of trying to buy their way into heaven. But heaven can't wait, even if the Medicis clan produced three popes who presumably pleaded their case.

Izzy was different, in that he gave money away before he had any of it in serious quantities, and in that he treated the process seriously, making donations not as a token moral gesture, either in the amounts involved or in the troubles he took to negotiate the most effective arrangements. Under his activist aegis, the Asper Foundation, in the four years before his death, distributed more than $100 million. In a private memo to Moe Levy dated February 8, 2000, Asper explained his Foundation's governing philosophy:

"You have got to get it through everybody's heads that we are not like any of the other foundations or public entities. As we are a private foundation, we do not respond to applications for donations but, rather we take our own projects, and usually lead them on the basis that it is something that should be done, but would otherwise not be done, without our leadership—such as the Holocaust, Human Rights, Jazz Series, Lyric, etc., etc. The Asper Foundation is *not* one of the public funding agencies for the Jewish community." Its original funding was injected in 1991 through new Canwest financing and the subsequent dividend flow. As Izzy explained to Conrad Black during the negotiations for the purchase of his newspaper chain, "We have so far taken little out of Canwest and therefore as part of our [estate] plan, we have planned to do a secondary stock sale to yield $200–$300 million (after tax) to fund my undisclosed 4th child, the Asper Foundation, Inc., and provide family liquidity for sibling buyouts." (The Foundation was also financed by the flow of Canwest dividends.)

Asper was generous to a fault, and that "fault," if it was one, meant that, unlike with most other philanthropists, his original gift was only the first step in the process. "People were always very surprised, because I was doing most of the legal aspect of the philanthropic deals, when I'd present them with a ten-page agreement," recalled Richard Leipsic, Canwest's senior vice-president and general counsel, who negotiated most of the donations. "Doing the universities, for example, they got very befuddled about the fact that we were willing to give money yet expected to have some commitment on the other side, some accountability, some penalties if they didn't perform. Izzy always said that it was really easy making money; the hard part was giving it away. He realized that once you give it away, you don't get it back, that the return it shows is not monetary, it's in terms of its results; and I think he always had this concern that people would view it as their own money. If somebody comes in and writes you a cheque for $1 million, you don't necessarily feel the same accountability as if you had to earn it. So he tried to impose a measure of accountability on his charitable giving. It took me a while to get converted to that notion. In the end I kind of adopted the idea that you might as well deal with your philanthropy the same way you deal with your business. You do expect people to take you seriously. The only way to do that is if you actually commit them to something."

There was a tough, unsentimental side to Asper, expressed in his personal dictum that never made it into his publicly endorsed Axioms: "You can't legislate propriety or morality or love or affection or loyalty. You can only legally cover what happens when they don't exist." There is a "code of conduct" for present and future family members: no jobs for spouses, the maintenance of a united front to outsiders, and so on. Izzy's blueprint for future generations, particularly the boundaries of his grandchildren's qualifications and ethical restraints in order to hold corporate executive offices, has been prescribed. Izzy's DNA is solidly embedded in his company's future.

Apart from his numerous and continuing donations to Israel, most of the Foundation's gifts were designed to improve Winnipeg's quality of life, focused on—but not limited to—its Jewish institutions. "Izzy infused the city with a tremendous vitality, his *own* vitality," remarked Martin Freedman, a former law partner.

That was no exaggeration. A typical day in "Asper-peg" could run as follows:

8:45 AM   You drop off the kids for school at the Asper Jewish Community Campus and go for a workout at the gym or take a sip from the water fountain donated by Gail Asper in honour of Babs Asper.

10:00 AM   You rush to the University of Manitoba for your graduate class in "Decisions and Concepts in Marketing" at the I.H. Asper School of Business.

11:30 AM   You enrol your daughter Mia in a summer program at the Curry BizCamp, sponsored by the Asper Centre for Entrepreneurship.

12:00 NOON Time for lunch with your favourite cousin, Frank, who holds the Asper Chair in the International Business and Trade Law at the University of Manitoba's Law School.

1:00 PM With your beagle, Maggie, in tow, you attend a brief volunteer meeting held in the Tuffy Asper Boardroom at the new Winnipeg Humane Society building.

1:30 PM You promised your best friend, Angie, that you would come to judge her students' current affairs videos, produced at the Canwest Global Multimedia Classroom and Studio at Red River College, where she teaches.

2:30 PM You're back for a quick stop at the Asper Jewish Community Campus to make sure your husband's relatives from Argentina, Gustavo and Claudia, make that meeting with representatives from the Asper Helping Hand organization, for an urgently needed business loan to finance the café they want to open.

2:45 PM You race downtown to enroll Alexander in classes at the Canwest Global Performing Arts program for children. You think he has potential in drama and one day will be able to apply for the Babs Asper New Play Development Fund of the Winnipeg Jewish Theatre.

3:30 PM You have two options: to watch a special daytime "Ballet in the Park" performance of *Swan Lake* at Assiniboine Park's Lyric Theatre (built and named in honour of the movie house of I.H. Asper's father, which was in Minnedosa) or to see jazz great Peter Appleyard perform as part of the Asper Foundation Jazz Series.

5:00 PM You finally get the kids and race to St. Boniface to pick up husband Roger, chief physician at the I.H. Asper Clinical Research Institute. Roger is on the verge of

a key discovery in cardiovascular research. You are so
proud!

5:30 PM You give Mia some food in the car and everyone heads
back to the Asper Jewish Community Campus so she
won't be late for her session of the Asper Human
Rights and Holocaust Program.

7:00 PM Roger and Alexander head off for a Winnipeg
Goldeyes baseball game at Canwest Global Park. They
invite you to come, but you are exhausted, since
tomorrow this routine will begin all over again . . .

That much-abbreviated timetable seems to document Asper's
ego as much as his generosity. It assumes that most Winnipeggers
are rich enough to cultivate the habit of donating civic amenities.
That isn't the case, and while Izzy was proud of what he'd done, it
was also very important to him to set a visible example for others, so
that they too would give back to their community. A prime example
was his sponsorship of the Asper Jewish Community Campus in the
mid- and late 1990s. The city's Jewish population had peaked in
1961, at 19,376, and a quarter of a century later was down to 15,000.
Its social and cultural institutions had visibly aged, notably its
schools and the downtown Young Men's Hebrew Association. These
and other Jewish institutions were now moved to one omnibus location, creating a new Jewish campus that cost more than $28 million.
Asper purchased the naming rights for $2 million, careful to put the
campus in his parents' and in-laws' names. On opening day, Asper
told the audience at a Winnipeg Symphony concert, featuring jazz
pianist Peter Nero, "We want our children to understand who we are
and where they came from. We must recognize that the campus is
the most important thing the Jewish community has ever done."

As well as these and other gifts not listed in the nominal timetable above, he operated a wide personal web, quietly supporting
worthy Winnipeggers. Most were apprentice or out-of-work jazz
musicians, but they included at least one former mayor. "I remember

the first time I ever received a letter from Izzy Asper was when I ran for the NDP in a Winnipeg federal seat," recalled Glen Murray. "I was the first gay man in Canada to adopt a foster child, was a very unlikely candidate to win the seat and was somewhat controversial as a local AIDS educator. I opened an envelope one day and there was a $500 cheque from Izzy Asper. When you're thirty-two years old and running for office and you're not exactly the kind of person who gathers support or funds, you never forget such a gesture. As I got more involved in local politics I realized that he did that for every candidate he thought was running for good reasons, whether they were left, right or centre politically, but he never made a big deal about it. For the first six years I was in municipal politics, the only time I ever saw Izzy Asper's name, when it wasn't in the paper, was on a cheque. He never phoned me, never called, never ever asked for a political favour, even when I was mayor. He just had a delightful sense of humour. I made the first donation to the Canadian Museum for Human Rights—five was my lucky number, so he came into my office to brief me about the museum, and I gave him a five-dollar bill, joking that I'd never given five dollars to a billionaire before. You could always chat with him in a very personal way. I don't think I ever met, the entire time I was in politics, anyone else who was that easygoing, who made you feel at ease, had no pretensions or airs about being in another environment."*

————————

On October 14, 1971, his first day in the Manitoba legislature as leader of the Liberal Party, Israel Asper, then not quite forty, was concerned about one issue, and one issue only: the need for a provincial bill of rights. He promptly introduced his version, parts of which became a template for similar bills in other jurisdictions. A

*To accommodate Izzy's visits, Murray, who was elected mayor partly on a stringent platform banning smoking in public places—permitted what was jokingly called the "Asper amendment": Izzy, and Izzy alone, was permitted to light up in the mayor's office.

decade earlier, Asper had actively supported John Diefenbaker's pioneering Canadian Bill of Rights, and in 1982 was one of the leading provincial activists to champion Pierre Trudeau's Canadian Charter of Rights and Freedoms. "I went to Trudeau and put the proposition to him that this was such a monumental achievement, it ought to be celebrated in some tangible way, just like the American Declaration of Independence," he recalled. "He loved the idea but his agenda was full and he just couldn't get at it."

During the lengthy interval that followed, Asper sponsored an annual travel program for Canadian students (six thousand of them—plus chaperones—from fifty cities in nine provinces) to visit Washington's Holocaust Memorial Museum, so they could bear witness to what can happen when a people lose their rights and freedoms. The program was successful but much too tiny to have any lasting impact. Obviously, some permanent institution was needed to teach not only Jewish children about the Holocaust, but all Canadians about the genocides and legal mayhem that are part of history and that can point to future threats. But where to erect such an edifice, and how to attract crowds?

Wouldn't you know, it didn't take Izzy more than fifteen seconds to come up with the solution: build it in Winnipeg, and they will come.

Ever since, most of the Asper Foundation's energies have been focused on the creation of the Canadian Museum for Human Rights, designed not only to celebrate the notions of liberty and freedom of choice but to turn the Prairie city into a tourist destination, theoretically doing for Winnipeg what the Eiffel Tower did for Paris. The Guggenheim Museum in Bilbao—the Basque city's landmark—is a better comparison. The Canadian edifice will feature a series of root-like structures at ground level that will give way to a cloud of curved, opaque glass, at the centre of which will be a hundred-metre, crystalline spire.

The practicality of the project turned on government support at all three levels, which would have to break new ground, not only in terms of the large dollar amounts required but in the format in which the public/private institution would operate. "We needed to have a sign from the federal government that they believed in Winnipeg, because Manitobans had lost hope and were leaving the province—they didn't think that anybody believed in them," Gail Asper recalled. "There's a great saying from Samuel Johnson, 'Where there is no hope, there is no endeavour.' But you give people that one spark, and they are electrified. They can leap over tall buildings if they've got that hope. One of the reasons I fought so hard to keep this thing going is that people here do need hope. I look at the original bank offices built downtown at the turn of the century, and those magnificent edifices represented people's personal belief in themselves, reflecting their self-image, and obviously they felt pretty darn good. But that was a hundred years ago. We haven't dreamt big for a very, very long time. And I learned something about architecture, which is pooh-poohed these days as a big waste of money. But architecture is one of the most phenomenal ways to express your personal inner feelings about yourself. And it's permanent. How you present yourself to the world in a physical way, whether it's through clothing or architecture, sends an important message."

The prototype that won the contract was the unusual work of New Mexican architect Antoine Predock, whose reputation encompassed his ability to focus on the spiritual interaction between individuals and buildings, creating, as one critic put it, "a strong sense of contextual appropriateness of his design with a careful interpretation of regional identity." The estimated cost was a paralyzing $265 million—compared, for example, to the new opera house built in downtown Toronto on the country's most expensive real estate, for a relatively modest $180 million.

The idea of the project won immediate and almost universal acceptance. Most Canadians quiver with happy vibes at the notion of exposing evil and promoting goodness, especially if it involves a museum instead of a battlefield. But the prospect of raising $265 million for a building at the junction of two Winnipeg rivers seemed as intimidating as climbing Mount Everest on a dinner date. It was

Gail Asper who drew the toughest assignment: to tap the private sector for $105 million. Hers was a star turn, combining her natural charm with the aggressive Asper passion for a cause inherited from her father. The big three capital pools—in Toronto, Montreal and Vancouver—were particularly difficult to tap, because by concentrating the Asper philanthropy so heavily on Winnipeg, there wasn't much reciprocity for her to draw on. Manitobans contributed $72 million, including the $20 million donated by the Asper Foundation. That she was able to come so close to her target was the real miracle of the campaign. It became a family affair, with Babs collecting a cool million or two or three in her condo tower and another $120,000 at a Calgary birthday party for Kim Koho that she attended.

In the public sector, the project would require government funding of $160 million: $100 million in federal dollars, $40 million from Manitoba and $20 million from the City of Winnipeg, plus $22 million annually as an operating budget. The actual pledging of the necessary funds involved three prime ministers (Jean Chrétien, Paul Martin and Stephen Harper), one premier (Manitoba's Gary Doer), a mayor (Winnipeg's Sam Katz) and the three animators of the Asper Foundation (Izzy, while he was still alive, Gail Asper and Moe Levy, the Foundation's executive director.)

Chrétien bought into the idea immediately, sold by the senior Asper at a meeting in the prime minister's home. He felt that from an operating perspective it would best remain in the hands of the private sector, which would control 51 percent, while the other partner—various levels of government—would hold 49 percent. The logic was that that the private sector could tell the story of human rights abuses exactly as they occurred without being whitewashed, which a government agency might be tempted to try. Chrétien immediately had Ron Duhamel, the appropriate minister at that time, commission a feasibility study, which cost $800,000, of which the Asper Foundation put up $100,000. When it was done, the PM called Izzy to report that in all his years in government he had never seen such a comprehensive business plan put together to make a case for a project. A ten-year window of support was proposed: five years prior and five years after a level of funding that would give the project—at that point not fully priced—a base level of support of $30 million. At this point a perfect storm hit the project and almost sank it. Izzy unexpectedly passed away, and with him the project's initial enthusiasm and energy dissipated. Shortly afterwards, Chrétien was pushed out of office by Paul Martin's praetorian guard, the glory-obsessed fumblers who allowed Martin to swallow himself, so that none of his good intentions went unpunished. The museum did extract a vague promise for the balance of the federal funding, but again not in any written Treasury Board format that could withstand challenge. Actually, it was worse than nothing. The only letter on the federal grant received by the Foundation set impossibly onerous conditions for the $70 million. "We would have to create either one of two things—a huge endowment of $400 million in order to spin off the $22 million in operating costs, or the Asper Foundation itself would have to pay for the bulk of the operating funds," Moe Levy complained. He spent most of five years camped outside the offices of the privy council executives, whose functionaries believed in the project but had other priorities.

"The star in all of this was Stephen Harper—I make no bones about it," says Levy. "This guy saw this project on several levels and made certain it would happen. It was March 25, 2005, when Gail and David Asper met with him, and he was all business but very friendly. He had his facts down totally in terms of what this project was all about and what the commitment was from the private sector and the other levels of government. He was prepared to look into options. He didn't say no, and for that we will always be grateful. He then turned to his deputy minister and said, 'Let's see what we can do to make this a reality.'"

It was a perfect Harper political smorgasbord. The museum would become a national asset, run by the government, which would allow the feds to contribute the $22 million a year required for operating expenses. The idea of decentralizing federal institutions, which had always been part of Harper's platform, was applied to the museum: it had been a private-sector initiative turned operational by government support, scattering the badge of federalism outside Ottawa. Harper had broken every rule in the bureaucratic book; he kept saying, "We have to do it."

And it happened.

Epilogue

Embedding Izzy's DNA

"Every Father's Day, I go to the cemetery, sit on
Dad's tombstone, and bring him a martini.
Just in case. And have a little chat. I tell ya,
if he wasn't dead, I'd kill him for leaving us."
—Gail Asper, 2008

U ntil fairly recently, the business of business was perceived to be a necessary tale, but a boring one. Even such iconic literary inventions as Scott Fitzgerald's Jay Gatsby and Arthur Miller's Willy Loman were never shown at work but treated as social symbols with day jobs. The notion that icons could be created—or destroyed—in the workplace was either inconceivable or irrelevant. But as Canadian politics became increasingly dumbified, attempts to turn Big Business into a spectator sport found widening acceptance, such that when I moved from Ottawa to Toronto in 1969, I switched from writing political tomes (about John Diefenbaker, Mike Pearson and Pierre Trudeau) to chronicling the annals of the upper levels of Canadian capitalism. I started with a historical perspective on the corporate colossus that became a nation—a quartet of volumes about the Hudson's Bay Company, reviving its proud four centuries of history making. (This was before the trading company that once owned a twelfth of the world's land surface became the plaything of American vulture capitalists, slumming in the continent's attic.) My half dozen studies of the Canadian Establishment that followed traced how economic power connects and disconnects, how it is used and abused, how this country's elite evolved from a closed club of privilege—a frigid pseudo aristocracy—to an action-oriented network that is still in the process of turning itself into a rampaging, globally focused meritocracy. Now, anything goes and everybody must earn their way into contention. There is no permanent elite. Business has become both more deadly and more fun. The losers switch jobs, sexual partners and venues. The winners act as if it's never too late to have a second childhood; their long-range planning is next Wednesday's power breakfast. They answer cellphones while making love.

Eventually, I also wrote biographies of Sam Bronfman and Conrad Black, two disparate and highly incendiary individuals who marched to their own drum corps and recognized few of the boundaries that hem in the rest of us. Sam got away with his murky beginnings in the bootlegging trade and went on to glory and remarkable philanthropy. Conrad did not, and is now serving hard time for allowing his sense of entitlement to lead him into temptation—and criminal misbehaviour. At regal receptions, he always claimed pride of place, as the most wanted celebrity in the hall; his naughty trivial pursuits earned him mention on a less desirable Most Wanted list.

The books that I scribbled over the past few decades as well as the business writings of Diane Francis, Jennifer Wells, David Olive, Rod McQueen, Steve Maich, Gordon Pitts, Fabrice Taylor, Neil Reynolds and Jason Kirby, among others, have documented the astonishing evolution of how Canadian business came to provide this subarctic capitalist society's chief totems. Though not as well known as some of his peers, Israel Harold Asper deserved high rank in this company. A lone wolf, howling at the moon, he was always ahead of the pack and created the country's largest communications empire.

Articulate, passionate and the ultimate contrarian, he packed a crowded life of what seemed like at least two hundred years into the three score and ten plus one that he was allotted. His legacy was paradoxical: anyone whose life he touched, in public or private, felt every emotion—except neutrality. His five careers were crowded with so much action that there was little occasion for relaxation or hobbies. His music—the jazz he played, collected, subsidized and listened to—was no part-time thing. The bands in his head never stopped playing. The inspirational source that fuelled his progress, from working as an usher in a small-town cinema in rural Manitoba to becoming a world-class billionaire, was rooted in the contrapuntal rhythms grooving his brain cage. If it swung, he went with it.

Occasionally, when he was deconstructing the latest outrage by some deranged competitor or misanthropic regulator, he would look down at his hands—the fingers long, slender and strong, with a pianist's stretch—and imagine he was behind his keyboard, away from whatever maddening crowd was claiming his attention.

Tom Strike, Asper's veteran chief operating officer, adept at reading his boss's mind, recalled having a defining conversation with Izzy, who was in one of his "the WASP conspiracy has struck again" moods and had spent most of a morning complaining about how he was always being mistreated, suggesting that maybe he should give it all up and get a gig playing "Moon River" in some uncharted piano bar near a railway crossing. "Izzy," replied Strike. "What you fail to realize is that people want to be *you*. You don't have to be anyone."

"He always wanted to own 10 Toronto Street, Conrad's headquarters, modelled on a London merchant bank," Strike recalled. "Izzy's idea of a suitable corporate headquarters was a fireplace in every office and a painting of some obscure British general on every

355

wall. We had a Toronto apartment for a long time, and when he had it redecorated, I came in late from Winnipeg to stay at this place. When I opened the door, I just about jumped out of my skin, because there was this guy on the wall, looking at me, and he's like, sure enough, some obscure British general dressed in gold braid and a scarlet jacket. I thought he was real, because it was about midnight and I hadn't been there since the place was redone. It was gaudy, but it was all part of what he wanted—the trappings of what he considered to represent success. He was proud of being self-made, but he wanted some sign of heritage for himself." Izzy had the Chief Heraldry Officer design a family crest, which included a lion holding a bolt of lightning in one paw and the scales of justice in the other—the shield was emblazoned with the two Stars of David.

———

Asper was far too animated—an emotional compulsive of an explosive vintage—to join any organizations that would admit him as a member, solidly in the Groucho Marx tradition. Money-minded as he was, there was a part of him they could never buy. When Ted Rogers, who alone was his equal as a visionary workaholic and whose wife, Loretta, had presented Izzy with one of her paintings, invited Asper in 1999 to a dinner sponsored by the United Nations Association of Canada, Izzy refused. His was not a "Mr. Asper regretfully declines your kind invitation" kind of reply, and had nothing to do with being busy at the dentist that day: "While I respect your willingness to support the United Nations, I am sure you will equally respect my anger and rage over the fact that the United Nations has been highjacked by the Third World, to become a political pawn of the hyperbole and rhetoric of the tin pot dictatorships of the world, who are guilty of the most ugly human repression and denigration of human rights that are the antithesis of the UN's own Declaration of Human Rights," he wrote back, all in one scathing sentence, providing a magnificent template for refusing invites.

Izzy was loved or hated—never both, that being the ideal working compromise sought by most of Canada's high and mighty. (You love the guy when you can best him, hate him when he beats you.) Izzy was tolerated, way the hell out there in Winnipeg, since his spectacular success could not be ignored and because he set the example to his less generous compadres for enlightened and truly spectacular philanthropy.

He was the object of wide and (until he went to war with his own journalists) mostly admiring profiles. Edward Greenspon, later the *Globe*'s editor-in-chief, was enthralled by the gregarious Winnipegger, whom he described as "overloaded with energy, charm and brains." Trevor Cole labelled him "a work of entrepreneurial art" and commented on his pitiless work ethic: "He will work until the dark and corrugated lids of his eyes leave slits to see through and his voice seems to rise from the centre of the earth." Gordon Pitts portrayed him in his 2002 book *Kings of Convergence* as a man of contradictions—worldly yet firmly grounded by his Manitoba roots: "He is very smart but defensive, carrying a two-by-four on his shoulder about being a Westerner and, some say, a Jewish outsider."

Canadians have always been strangers in their own land without feeling at home anywhere else. They have not merely learned to believe in muddling through but have come to rely on it. Not Izzy. Muddling through was not his style; he wrote the book on taking no prisoners, and made few moves that weren't studied and worried to near extinction. He missed some of the most significant business deals that came his way by overanalyzing them, just plain thinking too damn hard and missing the opportunity. He would probably have felt some sympathy with Philadelphia Phillies manager Danny Ozark, who came to the studied conclusion that "Half this game is ninety percent mental." Just like politics.

Asper did not swim and seldom went for walks. But one could imagine him, on the occasional stroll in the night air, across some choice acreage deep in the heart of Manitoba, voicing a comment similar to classical composer Igor Stravinsky's ode to his home-land: "The smell of the Russian earth is different, and such things are impossible to forget." Izzy felt the same way as soon as he hit Brandon. The Canadian plains have historically been a land to flee across, every whistle stop a destination. The trains, when they ran, never just left a station, they set out, steam belching and whistles blowing, moving at a pace that enhanced the landscape with its receding horizons and promise of untold future possibilities.

Izzy knew nearly everybody who counted in the Canada of his time, but he was too strong a character for anyone outside his immediate circle to understand what he was really all about—except that his grasp never quite equalled his aspirations: to own every galaxy in the universe, which he would promptly wire and sell to the highest bidders.

He was a false extrovert who pretended to enjoy the limelight but who preferred his own company. There was a horseradish sharpness about him that prevented the man from being the sum of all those people who helped make him what he became—the country's most powerful media mogul—without a muzzle. His greatest civil right was to remain true to himself, and there was no government commission yet invented that could prevent that, at least not if its chairman valued his gonads.

There was so much baggage in Izzy's upbringing that he ought to have trundled along his own airport carousel. He spent the last decade of his life trying, unsuccessfully, to lighten that load. He never made it, because much of the hysteria that characterized his daily offerings was self-created. He was his own worst enemy—and his own best friend.

He knew how to plumb the intensity of his inner life, which accounted for his not-infrequent incommunicado downtimes. ("I've been through some very lonely, isolated periods. You have to do a sanity check every so often.")

His dark side begged explanation. Why did this man who had a serious heart condition, including two multiple-bypass operations and an implanted pacemaker, continue to smoke and drink at addiction levels? This was the unanswerable question. He tried to dismiss that side of him as funky, throwaway gestures. But the balefire in his eyes told his story much better than I ever could.

But this much I know: the inner circle of Dante's Inferno is reserved for those who don't live life to the fullest. Izzy heeded that call. Nothing came easily to him. He did not pause at all the Stations of the Cross along his life's journey, only the bloody ones. But his legacy remains: he was the most generous of benefactors, and the most deadly of enemies—the media rebel who truly made a difference.

Asper's success hinged largely on winning his Thirty-Year War with Ottawa regulators, some of them prize examples of taxidermy at its best, who, in his mind, were so hidebound that they thought it daring to use an adverb. He somehow managed to cast a spell over them. Despite what he regarded as their all-too-frequent bum decisions, they still allowed him to harvest the highest dollar returns of any Canadian television network. Doug Hoover, who at one point was national vice-president of Global's programming, described the winning formula: "Canwest is the largest acquirer of U.S. network series programming in the world," he revealed. "That's our niche— we call it appointment TV. People want to have a regular pattern to their lives, and we have all the iconic hits."

It wasn't that easy, then or now. During his final drive to complete his transcontinental television facility—his holy Third Network— the CRTC dealt Asper so many karate chops that he must have felt like chopped liver, one of his favourite deli appetizers, though in the end he did lever that final link into place. He almost never visited the regulators in their Ottawa lairs. He felt more in tune with the hard-edged quick-money artists of Toronto's Bay Street, who could easily be dismissed—and who returned the compliment—or among those expressive gents with sly moustaches who dwelt among the romantic palisades of Old Montreal.

It took him several decades to feel comfortable with the notion that life comes with no guarantees, and to stop imagining he might be an exception. Shown a quote from the American poet Willa Cather—"One cannot divine nor forecast the conditions that will make happiness; one only stumbles upon them by chance, in a lucky hour, at the world's end"—he was not impressed. Gratification, according to Cather, was too long coming. He vaguely followed the counsel—if not in detail then in principle—that Machiavelli was supposed to have given his Italian prince: "Claim everything," the cynical sage advised; "concede nothing, and if defeated allege fraud." On second thought, Izzy followed its every syllable.

"A vividly ambitious man with a vaulting sense of his own potential, Asper has doggedly performed the requisites of ascendancy since he first went to work at 14 in his parents' movie theatre in Minnedosa," wrote Ted Allan, Winnipeg's sage, in *Maclean's*. "Steeped in the immigrant sensibilities of his European Jewish parents, Asper has never relaxed his assiduous attack on the vertical mosaic. When he revealed that sort of palpable self-advancement in public office, at his own peril, he would have been excused for nipping aboard the treadmill to Toronto as countless other Prairie power acolytes have done before him. He didn't—an anomalous act if ever there was one. Despite being on the road probably half his professional life, he's directed his little epiphany from Winnipeg. 'I believe Winnipeg can be a financial capital,' he says, without smiling. 'Your sense of judgment here is more discreet and less vulnerable to the hothouse pressures and street rumours.' If Izzy Asper doesn't transform Canwest into another Power Corporation, he's at least developing another Prairie genre: Hometown Boy Makes Good—at home."

Although he was viscerally a proud Canadian, that sentiment was mixed with his Winnipeg patriotism and Israeli loyalty. In fact, his dreams touched none of these bases. He revealed his youthful aspirations at what was probably the professional high point of his career: having his stock listed on the New York Stock Exchange in June of 1996. "I must admit that the proceeding had an overwhelming impact on me," he confessed. "Every kid in rural Canada grows up trudging to his hockey practice, daydreaming of scoring the winning goal, in sudden-death overtime, during a Stanley Cup final at New York's Madison Square Garden. As he ambles to his piano lesson, he daydreams about writing a great concerto, and playing it with the New York Philharmonic on the stage of Carnegie Hall. As he goes through university, studying English and drama, he dreams of writing the great Canadian play, and being at its star-studded opening night on Broadway. Or he dreams of hitting a home run, in the bottom of the ninth, with the bases loaded, in the last game of the World Series, with the tying run at first, in New York's Yankee Stadium.

"I was all of those kids, growing up in Minnedosa, Manitoba, and so, as a business man, ringing the bell to open trading and making the initial trade in Canwest Global Communications shares at the impressive ceremony which accompanies listings on the New York Stock Exchange was the equivalent of all those fantasies of my youth. I felt just like the actor in those postwar movies which open with a man on the outside window ledge of the highest building in town staring down at the dizzying traffic, and the firemen with their safety nets, and the voice-over echoing his thinking: 'How did I get here? What has brought me to this?' And the same thing happened to me; like the would-be jumper on the window ledge, I had a flashback, wondering, 'What am I doing here?'"

Modesty was not one of Izzy's dominant traits, but he was genuine in his self-assessment. "All my life I've always been my own judge. You're sorry if people don't like you, and you're also disappointed if they don't like you for the wrong reasons, but at the end of the day, you're the best judge if you are living by a code of ethics that you're satisfied with. Success is an entirely personal thing." He was a brilliant raconteur with the natural cadence of a born storyteller. That was why, in the final analysis, he was so likable. He understood human nature. Whatever other persuasions he championed, he was an entrepreneur very much on the hoof, and as such he would freely hallucinate about things that didn't exist and had yet to be done, by him, of course—the Great Spirit and the Bank of Nova Scotia's credit department willing.

With only the occasional genuflection to reality, Asper obeyed the workings of the inner gyroscopes that kept him pointed in the direction of minting profit. The preceding pages detail how he did it and the price he paid—both in dollars and in fragments of his soul. He became the sum of all his contradictions, always the young stranger in a world he never made. But he subscribed fully to the creed enunciated by César Chávez, the wonderfully articulate American fruit-packers' union organizer, who once decreed, "When we're honest with ourselves, we must admit that our lives are all that really belong to us. So it is how we use our lives which determines what kind of men we are."

Late in life, Izzy became concerned with his legacy, although he agreed with Woody Allen's view that he wanted to achieve immortality less through his work and more by never dying. "If I could compose my own tombstone," Asper told Jennifer Wells, now of the *Globe*, "I would put, 'He mattered,' or 'He didn't just take up space.'" After all the fights and years of turmoil, Asper finally has the power to write that epitaph. Even if the economics of TV fade, no one can take away its cachet, not in this lifetime. For Izzy Asper, the pieces of an impressive legacy are finally there, laid out before him. If only he can concentrate long enough to put them together."

———————

Asper spent his final restless year transferring 10,000 tunes out of his personal music library into the vaults of Cool FM, the jazz station he had founded in Winnipeg. "My life's ambition," he wrote, "is to have my computer spit out 200 or 300 more CDs with each tune programmed and hand-picked by me to provide a full year of listening to only those tunes by those artists and in the order I want them—a dream come true." But he looked unusually thin, almost skeletal, and didn't seem his usual combative or humorous self.

At about this time, as at several previous crisis points in his life, Izzy sought refuge in watching the Hollywood musical *All That Jazz*— over and over again, as if it contained some hidden, vital message.

The film was based on the suggestion by Shirley MacLaine that Bob Fosse, the legendary Broadway choreographer, direct a movie about his own death, when he was recuperating in a New York hospital after a serious heart attack. That tragic scenario found echoes in Izzy Asper's darkening mood. "To be on the wire is life. The rest is waiting" was the movie soundtrack's defining theme, spoken under its opening titles superimposed on the shot of a man falling from a high-wire trapeze. The tag line of the highly evocative melodrama, which won four Oscars, was a fairly succinct summary of Izzy's life: "All that work. All that glitter. All that pain. All that love. All that crazy rhythm . . . ALL THAT JAZZ!" The musical included memorable songs, elaborate dance sequences and spectacular production values, but its storyline was a ruthlessly autobiographical portrait of Fosse (stunningly played by Roy Scheider) as a chain-smoking genius with a triple-A-type personality who loved jazz and feared death. It wasn't Izzy's story exactly, but the film's lead character would certainly have recognized a soulmate in the Winnipeg entrepreneur: their reckless lifestyle and relentless pursuit of perfection; their dissatisfaction with personal and professional triumphs, no matter how impressive; their dedication to nocturnal smoking and drinking. Ultimately, Fosse (in the film and in real life) was felled by a massive heart attack, doing what he loved best: chain smoking, while drenched in jazz.

Over the final months of Asper's life, the tone of his emails changed. I had no idea how ill he was but knew something was very wrong from his electronic missives. Typical was his final email to me, a cry from the heart that arrived from his New York apartment: "Suddenly, sitting in my apt in NY, ready to face tomorrow's corporate onslaught, I feel lonely. Utterly alone! I'm here for a meeting on serious Jewish international concerns but being a Canadian, in a country that doesn't really count, one feels like a pygmy beside my American counterparts. But happily the music keeps playing . . . Old Izz." (That despondent sign-off was a new addition to his nocturnal emissions.)

As well as his tally of unfulfilled intentions, with which this book begins, Israel Asper left behind, as part of his will, a highly personal letter of intent dictated by him in 1969, when he thought he might die of hepatitis. Its concluding paragraphs summed up his legacy: "To my children, generally, I leave my horizons. As you come close to the age of understanding, your mother will explain them. They were carefully discerned and I think valuable in an age which seems to have lost its direction.

"Specifically to David I leave the Asper secret formula which is, 'Don't just sit there thinking about it, do it and be damned sure you do it well and quickly, giving it all you've got.'

"To Gail, I leave a little energy—the energy to get up and make things happen, the energy that changes a person who lets things happen without understanding why, into one who makes stuff happen and knows why: The difference between freedom and slavery.

"To Leonard, what can anyone say? I could tell you that there really aren't people inside the TV set or that I was always sorry when I made you cry but in thinking of you it occurs to me that not much need be said. You are the product of the influence of your brother and sister and the combination is unbeatable. You won't need much help, although your mother will not recognize it, like my mother before her. I know your strength that has carried you so proudly through almost every vicissitude life has to offer, won't fail you now.

"To Babs, as ever I leave my deep gratitude my sincere admiration, my respect and of course my undying love . . .

"To all, so much more I would like to say. But I am tired and besides, if my life has meant anything, then everything will be understood and nothing needs restating . . . IZZY."

"Life would have been a lot simpler if he'd stuck around, having dreamed up this museum thing," Gail Asper lamented. Along with Izzy's widow, Babs, who remained the indispensable, loving centre point in the family matrix, and Gail's brothers, David and Leonard, daughter Gail mourned her father's passing and saluted his legacy.

"I soothe myself, just remembering that he taught us for seventy-one years—or forty-three years, for me—and he taught us well. His examples are ingrained in our DNA. The way to conduct yourself in life, the way to get things done, knowing what was important—he just hammered all of that home. We knew what we had to do. And I don't just mean the museum; I mean in life. He did everything that a father is supposed to do with his children. And in fact, he had enough time to do it. It wasn't like he died when I was eighteen or twenty-two, and left the story. We were lucky to have had him as long as we did."

After the funeral, Gail took her kids and a large suitcase, filled with condolence cards received when her father died, to Churchill, Manitoba's deep-sea port on Hudson Bay, for a brief quiet time. "These bloody sympathy cards that I was weeping over, because they're so true," she recalled. "I mean, how pathetic is that? To be crying over Hallmark sentiments. But there's a reason for clichés, and I took enormous comfort from those wishes.

"Every Father's Day, I go to the cemetery, sit on his tombstone. I bring him a martini. Just in case. And have a little chat. I tell ya, if he wasn't dead, I'd kill him for leaving us . . ."

Spoken like a true Asper.

Acknowledgements

his book attempts to document the controversial history and impressive influence of the supremely moneyed, infinitely complex, occasionally neurotic and utterly compelling Israel Harold Asper. Little known outside his formidable foxhole in uptown Winnipeg, Izzy (as everybody called him) was an original, and that thought—that there will never be another—produced mixed feelings, not all of them suitable for filing under "nostalgia."

A hot-headed dreamer with soulful eyes and a hyper ego, he spent much of his crammed life in search of himself. This book is a chronicle of that quest. I readily admit that my portrait of the Asper dynasty's founding spirit is by no means definitive. It can't be. I spent more time with him than with any of my other biographical subjects, but only wished that I could have come to know him better, shared his joys and his devils—detours that the act of interviewing tends to stifle. "We don't really go that far into other people even when we think we do," wisely observed Martin Amis, the British novelist. "We just stand at the jaws of the cave, strike a match, and ask quickly if anybody's there."

This volume is that match.

Izzy had more incarnations than Madonna. But always, beyond any shadow of a doubt, a lawyer's lawyer, seldom in court but acutely aware of the legal limits and permissions that defined his life and fuelled his times. "I decided that practising law was the exact opposite of sex—even when it was good, it was lousy," declared Mortimer Zuckerman, the Montreal-born U.S. publishing and real estate mogul, explaining why he opted out of a legal career after graduating from Harvard Law School. Asper was exactly the opposite. He never stopped being, thinking and acting like an attorney-at-law— well, hardly ever. Lawyers know nothing about how Dave Brubeck could maintain his groove while improvising a double-time waltz in 5/4 time or play "Take the 'A' Train" in its 9/8 version. But Izzy did—and played it.

From 1985 to 1993 I published a four-volume unauthorized history of the Hudson's Bay Company that sold half a million copies and was turned into an evocative television series by the wonderful John McGreevy. My chief researcher for that weighty project was Allan Levine, who has assumed the same collaborative function in this publication, except that he also wrote the first drafts of chapters 7 and 11. He has a Ph.D. in history, spent a decade studying and writing about the Asper empire, is an author and an educator, and has been a good friend and an invaluable guide. Allan and I shared the task of interviewing the hundred-plus Asper acquaintances and critics for this book, and we are grateful to every one of them. Allan sends his personal thanks to Moe Levy, Louise Nebbs, Susie Catellier, Judi Van Mierlo, Tracy Pascal, Heather Mowatt and Faith Strecker-Nemish at the Asper Foundation; Richard Leipsic, Tom Strike, Karen Pellatt, Ashley Hendry and Karen Angus at Canwest

Global's corporate office; and Michael Woollatt, Anna Taylor, and Debra Larson at its Toronto office.

In discussing this book before publication, I was often asked whether it was a commissioned or independent work. While I received a research grant from the Asper Foundation to cover the time spent in the detailed and geographical breadth of the required research, there was from the beginning of the project a confidential agreement on one essential point: I would have complete independence on the writing of the book as well as responsibility for its contents, which meant that the Aspers could sue me if they were so inclined.

There were two overwhelming advantages to this approach. It meant that I received unexpectedly open access to the family archives (issues that might endanger Canwest's business competitiveness were not included) and that I could check the accuracy of my data with Izzy Asper's widow, Babs, and two of their children, Leonard and Gail. I am profoundly grateful for the family's unstinting and congenial assistance. David, the eldest son, refused to be part of the project.

In checking my story with the co-operating trio of family members, I insisted—and they accepted—the boundaries of that contribution, which quite simply was limited to making only suggested factual changes, not challenging issues of interpretation or judgment. They have exercised no control over the contents of this book, except to correct errors of a purely factual nature, without altering the manuscript's tone or assessments. It must have been tempting, but they never trespassed on our agreement and did not try to substitute warm legend for cold facts.

This proved to be more valuable than I realized. For example, it turned out that just after he decided to leave his original legal practice, Izzy took time off in 1970 to drop out and rethink his life. He grew a beard, listened to a lot of weird music and travelled the world wherever his itchy spirit took him. "I dropped out, quit, disappeared," he told me, with echoes of nostalgia. "I bummed around all over the place, drowned myself in jazz and booze. Was jailed in Lebanon, detained in Jordan, arrested in East Germany and really mussed up in Moscow. I did some stupid things, was quite reckless. But I loved the adventure and kind of sorted my head out."

When Babs read that romanticized version of his Bohemian period, she objected. "All of these events occurred over a period of time, not only after he left the law practice," she wrote to me. "He did grow a beard and he did drop out for a short period of time until politics grabbed him. But East Germany was in 1963 and Lebanon was in 1968. Moscow was in 1977. It may make for a good story, though as presented it's not true. But he did get arrested everywhere." I made the changes, noting the arrests.

At HarperCollins Canada I am indebted to Jim Gifford, senior editor of their non-fiction division, whose patience I tried, talent I borrowed and advice I heeded. I would also like to thank Stephanie Fysh, the copy editor for the book. My literary guardian angel, Michael Levine, continues to man the barricades, keeping me out of mischief and out of court. Brian Bethune, literary editor of *Maclean's,* fact-checked the manuscript, as he has half a dozen of my more recent books. He is a singularly talented writer and editor, and I am grateful for his time and knowledge. One example of his attention to detail: commenting on my description of Jerusalem's Wailing Wall as "the precious relic that was the last remnant of King Solomon's Temple," he pointed out, "It probably isn't, but it would be OK to say 'the precious relic VENERATED AS the last remnant of King Solomon's Temple.'" And I did. As always, no balance sheet of my debts would be complete without a tribute to Stan Kenton, whose music and cadences endowed me with the courage of the early morning.

I salute the magical epiphanies of my wonderful wife, Alvy. Her innate sense of aesthetics and depth of character are a national treasure. I am blessed. She truly is the love of my life. This volume owes its existence to many not mentioned here; only the responsibility for its imperfections is fully my own.

Peter C. Newman

aboard the cutter *Grace Note*

Bronte Harbour, Ontario, Canada

September 15, 2008

Timeline

1919
- Cecilia Zwet (mother) arrives in Winnipeg from the Ukraine with her parents, Rabbi Ben Zion and Golda Zwet.

1924
- Leon Asper arrives in Winnipeg after a delay in Belgium. Leon and Cecilia marry on August 15 in Winnipeg.

1929
- Leon Asper purchases movie theatre in Minnedosa, Manitoba, called the Lyric.

1932
- Israel Harold Asper is born August 11 in Minnedosa.

1936
- Leon Asper purchases the Roxy movie theatre in Neepawa, Manitoba.

1941
- Asper family moves to Neepawa.

1946
- Asper family relocates to Winnipeg. Leon Asper opens two theatres, the Deluxe and the Valour. Izzy attends Robert H. Smith School for Grade 9.

1947
- Attends Kelvin High School for Grade 10.

1950
- Graduates from Kelvin High School. Enrols in Arts at University of Manitoba. Member of Sigma Alpha Mu fraternity. Participates in Hillel as debater. Sports reporter and music columnist for *The Manitoban.*

1952
- Spends summer in Wadhams, BC, counting trees for the BC Forest Service.

1953
- With his partner Ron Meyers, Asper composes music and lyrics for University of Manitoba Varsity Varieties musical revue. He does so as well in 1954 and 1955.
- Receives bachelor of arts from University of Manitoba and enters University of Manitoba Law School. Articles during law school under the tutelage of Harold Buchwald at the firm of Matlin, Kushner and Buchwald.

1956
- On May 27, at the Shaarey Zedek Synagogue, Winnipeg, Izzy marries Ruth "Babs" Bernstein.

1957
- Receives Bachelor of Laws from the University of Manitoba. Is chosen class valedictorian. Buys and sells real estate with fellow law student Gordon Pollock.
- Called to the bar July 4.

1958
- Works at law firm Drache, Meltzer, Esser, & Gold.
- David is born.

1959
- Establishes Asper & Co. in the Bank of Nova Scotia building.

1960
- Joins with Martin Freedman, and law firm becomes Asper, Freedman and Company (later Buchwald Asper and Henteleff). Asper specializes in tax law and soon emerges as one of the country's most requested and most outspoken tax lawyers.
- Gail is born.

1961

• Leon Asper dies March 17.

1963

• Baby daughter Leanne Pearl born in March and dies at six weeks, from SIDS.

1964

• Receives Master of Law degree from University of Manitoba. Begins writing column "Taxes and You" for the *Winnipeg Tribune.*
• Leonard is born.

1967

• Switches tax column to FP Publications and the *Winnipeg Free Press,* then to the *Globe and Mail.* The column is soon syndicated to *Montreal Star* and other newspapers across Canada. He writes the column until 1977.
• Writes five booklets titled *An Objective View,* commenting on the Royal Commission on Taxation headed by Kenneth Carter, published by the Equitable Income Tax Foundation.

1968

• Becomes partner and secretary of Manitoba Distillery, opened in his home-town of Minnedosa. One of the partners in the business is Gerald Schwartz, a young lawyer who articled in Asper's Winnipeg law office.

1969

• Against Asper's wishes, his partners in the Manitoba Distillery decide to sell the company to Melchers of Montreal.

1970

• Writes *The Benson Iceberg: A Critical Analysis of the White Paper on Tax Reform in Canada* (Clark, Irwin 1970); the book sells 20,000 copies.
• Asper and Company merges with Buchwald, Henteleff & Zitzerman to become Buchwald, Asper, Henteleff, Zitzerman, Goodwin, Greene & Shead. Asper retires from the active practice of law.
• Elected leader of the Manitoba Liberal Party.

1971

• Clashes with Premier Ed Schreyer over the NDP government's handling of the Churchill Forest Industries (CFI) complex.

1972

• Wins seat in Manitoba Legislature in Wolseley riding by-election.

1973
- Liberals win only five seats in provincial election, including his Wolseley riding.
- Peter Liba, Asper's executive assistant, sees CRTC newspaper advertisement for applications to operate a new television station in Winnipeg.

1974
- Asper begins negotiations with Gordon McLendon, a wealthy Texas tycoon who owns KCND, a television station based across the border in Pembina, North Dakota. McLendon eventually sells for $750,000.
- Asper and partners, including Paul Morton and Seymour Epstein, obtain CRTC licence to establish their first independent television station in Winnipeg.
- Rescue of the Global Television Network in Toronto with Paul Morton, Seymour Epstein and Allan Slaight.

1975
- Resigns as leader of the Manitoba Liberal Party.
- CKND-TV signs on the air in Winnipeg.
- Appointed Queen's Counsel.

1977
- With Gerald Schwartz, establishes an investment company or merchant bank, the Canwest Capital Corporation. The company is backed by a group of prominent local and Canadian financial institutions and businessmen.
- Acquires 60 percent control of Global Television Network.

1978
- Canwest Capital acquires Na-Churs International Ltd., a chemical fertilizer company in Marion, Ohio, as well as the Monarch Life Insurance Company of Winnipeg.

1979
- Canwest Capital acquires a 54 percent interest in Crown Trust of Toronto.
- Makes financial investment in CKVU television station, Vancouver.

1980
- Canwest Capital acquires Macleod-Stedman hardware chain and 51 percent of Aristar, a U.S. financial conglomerate based in Florida.

1982
- Canwest begins to divest with sales of its interest in Crown Trust and USTV.

1983

- Against Asper's wishes, Canwest Capital sells Monarch Life.
- Suffers heart attack and has a quadruple bypass.
- Creates the Asper Foundation.

1984

- The breakup of his partnership with Gerald Schwartz. Asper keeps rights to Canwest name.
- Paul Morton and Seymour Epstein launch lawsuit for breach of contract, alleging that Izzy had agreed to sell them the network but reneged. Izzy countered there had been no enforceable agreement and that he hadn't been given an accurate valuation of the company. After a bitter struggle, the court agreed with Izzy.
- Birth of the Asper Foundation with $140 million nest egg.

1985

- Honouree of the Winnipeg chapter of the Canadian Friends of the Hebrew University of Jerusalem.
- Launches the I.H. Asper Scholarship Fund to assist students to attend the Hebrew University in Jerusalem.

1986

- Canwest is awarded a CRTC licence for new television stations in Regina and Saskatchewan. In an unprecedented move, the federal Conservative government requires the CRTC to rehear the application, and Canwest wins it again.
- Purchase of Canadian Surety, Toronto.

1987

- STV-Regina and STV-Saskatoon go on the air.
- Publicly opposes the Meech Lake constitutional accord.

1988

- Following five years of litigation, Canwest is awarded 100 percent ownership of CKVU television in Vancouver and renames it U.TV.

1989

- Wins control of the Global Television Network from Paul Morton and Seymour Epstein after a court-ordered auction.
- Named Manitoba Business Entrepreneur of the Year.

1990

- Sale of Canadian Surety and Annuity Life.

1991

- Initial public offering and listing of Canwest Global shares on the Toronto Stock Exchange.
- Investigates acquiring the financially troubled TV3 in New Zealand, the country's only privately owned station.
- Named Manitoba Business Entrepreneur of the Year for the second time.

1992

- Canwest Global purchases 20 percent stake in TV3 for less than $10 million and obtains management control. The New Zealand media dub Asper "Prince Izzy."
- Acquires 57.5 percent economic interest in Network TEN Australia, recently released from receivership. Network TEN's profits soon soar. By April 1998 the company's A$52 million initial investment in Network TEN is worth A$1.4 billion.
- The Australian Broadcast Authority begins what turns out to be a three-year investigation into whether Canwest Global is in violation of Australian broadcasting laws by controlling Network TEN.
- Publicly supports Triple-E Senate.

1993

- Purchases MITV, regional broadcaster in Halifax, Nova Scotia, and Saint John, New Brunswick.
- Awarded B'nai Brith International Award of Merit.

1994

- Acquires 50 percent interest in La Red Network, Chile.
- Acquires 25 percent interest in Talk Radio UK network.

1995

- The Australian Broadcast Authority concludes that "Canwest is not, and has not been, in a position to exercise control of [Network] TEN." Each of several investigations confirms that Canwest is in compliance with the legislation.
- David Asper leads concerted effort to secure Channel 5 licence in the United Kingdom in consortium with the Scandinavian Broadcasting System, SelecTV and Network TEN of Australia. Despite submitting the highest bid, Britain's Independent Television Commission awards the licence to a group headed by Pearson-MAI.
- Agreement reached with Télé-Métropole to purchase controlling interest in CKMI-TV, Quebec City, and extend signal throughout the province.

- Market capitalization of Canwest Global hits $1 billion, a fivefold increase from the $200 million market value at the time of the 1991 IPO.
- Acquisition of 9.7 percent of Class B shares in WIC (Western International Communications Ltd.) and first unsuccessful bid for control. This is part of Asper's grand scheme to build Canada's third national television network.
- Part of rescue effort by Winnipeg business community to oppose the relocation plan for the Winnipeg Jets NHL team. The effort fails and the team moves to Phoenix, Arizona.
- Inducted as an Officer in the Order of Canada.
- Inducted into the Canadian Association of Broadcasters Hall of Fame.

1996
- Global Television broadcasts the Canadian-produced television drama *Traders*, a one-hour series produced by Atlantis Films. Each episode costs $800,000. In one early show, Asper has a cameo role as "Izzy the lounge pianist."
- Licence awarded to establish TV4 as second private-sector television network in New Zealand.
- Canwest Global acquires interest in New Zealand chain of radio stations.
- Applications to CRTC for new television stations in Edmonton, Calgary and Victoria are turned down. CRTC does approve application for Prime TV cable network.
- Interest sold in La Red Network, Chile.
- Awarded the University of Manitoba Distinguished Entrepreneur Award by the Faculty of Management.

1997
- Interest in WIC increased, raising stake to more than 15 percent.
- Approval granted to start province-wide network in English through Global Television Network (Quebec).
- Economic interest in Network TEN Australia increased to 76 percent from 57.5 percent. Australian government orders return to 57.5 percent.
- Agreement reached with Irish consortium to lead launch of TV3 as first private-sector national television service.
- Asper inducted into Canadian Business Hall of Fame, alongside only 103 fellow laureates since Confederation.
- Donation of $1 million by the Asper Foundation creates the Asper Centre for Entrepreneurship at the University of Manitoba.
- Steps aside as chief executive officer to become executive chairman of the Canwest Global Board. Peter Viner, formerly president and CEO of Network TEN, becomes president and CEO of Canwest Global Communications. Leonard Asper is named chief operating officer.

- Canwest Canadian stations are rebranded the Global Television Network.
- Canwest Global acquires the MORE FM radio group in New Zealand.
- The Asper Jewish Community Campus is opened in the south part of Winnipeg, financed mainly by a donation of $2 million from I.H. Asper.

1998

- Sign-on of TV3, the Republic of Ireland's first private television network. Canwest Global also acquires 29.9 percent interest in Ulster Television in Northern Ireland.
- Acquires Fireworks Entertainment, an independent Canadian-based producer and international distributor of television programs and feature films.
- Receives honorary doctorate of laws and letters from the University of Manitoba.

1999

- Listed in *Forbes* magazine as one of Canada's four billionaires.
- Creation of interactive media division with the launch of globaltv.com.
- Leonard Asper assumes role of president and CEO of Canwest Global and Peter Viner becomes vice chairman.
- Opening of the Lyric theatre and music stage in Winnipeg's Assiniboine Park in honour of his family's original movie house—and the Millennium.
- Asper Centre for Entrepreneurship for the University of Manitoba's Business School is created.
- Receives honorary doctorate of philosophy from Hebrew University, Jerusalem.

2000

- Dream of third national network finally becomes reality when the CRTC approves Canwest Global's purchase of the conventional television assets of Western International Communications. The national Global Television Network is now broadcasting from Nova Scotia to Victoria, British Columbia.
- Negotiations with Conrad Black lead, after many months, to purchase by Canwest Global of Hollinger Inc.'s fourteen major Canadian daily newspapers, an additional eighteen dailies or weeklies, a number of web portals (including Canada.com), and 50 percent interest in the *National Post*. It is the largest media transaction in Canadian history.
- CRTC awards Canwest Global thirty digital specialty channel licences.

- Makes gift to the University of Manitoba Faculty of Management of $10 million and the faculty is renamed the I.H. Asper School of Business. Asper said at the time that it was the "greatest recognition he had ever received."
- Donates $10 million to the Winnipeg Foundation and the Jewish Foundation of Manitoba.
- Inducted as Founding Member of the Order of Manitoba.
- Begins work on the Canadian Museum for Human Rights.

2001
- Relaunch of the former WIC stations in Alberta and BCTV in Vancouver as Global Television outlets.
- Launch of the CH brand for television stations CHCH Hamilton, CHEK Victoria and CJNT Montreal.
- Canwest Global sells CKVU-TV in Vancouver, its interest in CFCF TV in Montreal and its 50 percent share in ROBTv. Global launches six new digital specialty channels: DejaView, Fox Sports World Canada, Lonestar, Xtreme Sports, and two channels in partnership with TVA—Mystery TV and mentv. A digital broadcast centre in Winnipeg is created to house these new channels as well as Prime TV.
- Donates $5 million to the St. Boniface Hospital Research Foundation, creating the I.H. Asper Clinical Research Institute.
- Receives the Edmond C. Bovey Award for Leadership Support of the Arts, presented annually by the Council for Business and the Arts in Canada.
- The Canadian Friends of the Hebrew University of Jerusalem hold an Israel Asper Gala Tribute Dinner at the National Trade Centre, Toronto.
- Purchase of Hollinger's 50 percent interest in the *National Post*. It is priced at $1.00

2002
- Receives honorary doctorate of laws from McMaster University.
- Steps down as executive chairman of the board and becomes chairman of the board.
- Death of Cecilia Asper at the age of ninety-eight, on April 8.

2003
- At a gala announcement at the Forks, launches the Canadian Museum for Human Rights project.
- Dies in Winnipeg, October 7.

List of Interviews

Moshe Arens, Tel-Aviv
Aubrey Asper, Winnipeg
Babs Asper, Winnipeg
Daniel Asper, Winnipeg
Gail Asper, Winnipeg
Israel Asper, Winnipeg
Leonard Asper, Toronto
Lloyd Axworthy, Winnipeg
Zita Bernstein, Winnipeg
Roy Birnboim, Toronto
Don Brinton, Vancouver
Harold Buchwald, Winnipeg
Audrey Chysyk, Winnipeg
George Cohon, Toronto
Jack Cowin, Sydney, Australia
Danny Danon, Jerusalem
Jonathan Davis, Herzliya, Israel
Michael Decter, Toronto
Fred de Koning, Winnipeg
Harry Ethans, Winnipeg
Sandy Frank, New York
Matthew Fraser, Paris
Aron Freedman, Barkai, Israel
Bob Freedman, Winnipeg

Laurence Freedman, Sydney, Australia
Martin Freedman, Winnipeg
Tony Ghee, London
Greg Gilhooly, Toronto
Peter Godsoe, Toronto
Gerald Gray, Winnipeg
Rabbi Alan Green, Winnipeg
Stephen Gross, Toronto
Aharon Harlap, Jerusalem
Ray Heard, Toronto
Tom Heintzman, Toronto
Rick Hetherington, Dublin
Harry Hurwitz, Jerusalem
Don Johnston, Montreal
Robert Kopstein, Winnipeg
Jonathan Kornbluth, Jerusalem
Justice Guy Kroft, Winnipeg
Richard Kroft, Winnipeg
Isi Leibler, Jerusalem
Richard Leipsic, Winnipeg
Yale Lerner, Toronto
Moe Levy, Winnipeg
Peter Liba, Winnipeg

Hettie Lofchy, Toronto
Jodi Lofchy, Toronto
Jack London, Winnipeg
Susan Macchia, Winnipeg
Michael MacMillan, Toronto
Menachem Magidor, Jerusalem
Laurie Mainster, Winnipeg
Dorothy Mann, San Diego
Frank McKenna, Toronto
Kip Meek, London
Dan Meridor, Tel-Aviv
Ron Meyers, Winnipeg
Cameron Millikin, Calgary
James Morris, Dublin
Glen Murray, Toronto
Benjamin Netanyahu, Jerusalem
Gerry Noble, Toronto
Michael Oren, Jerusalem
Steve Patrick, Winnipeg
Leonard Peikoff, Colorado
Greg Phillips, London
Ron Polinksy, Winnipeg
Daniel Polisar, Jerusalem
Gordon Pollock, Winnipeg
Ross Porter, Toronto

Hartley Richardson, Winnipeg
Ced Ritchie, Toronto
Daniel Sandelson, London
Edward Schreyer, Winnipeg
Gerry Schwartz, Toronto
Avner Shalev, Jerusalem
Jim Shaw, Kelowna
Kevin Shea, Toronto
Smoky Simon, Tel-Aviv
Allan Slaight, Toronto
Mira Spivak, Winnipeg
Richard Stillwater, Winnipeg
Tom Strike, Winnipeg
John Studdy, Sydney, Australia
Jim Sward, Toronto
Alan Sweatman, Winnipeg
Arni Thorsteinson, Winnipeg
John Turner, Toronto
Peter Viner, Toronto
Bill Watchorn, Winnipeg
Rick Waugh, Toronto
Brenlee Werner, Winnipeg
Emily Westlaken, Winnipeg
Rod Zimmer, Winnipeg

Index